Statistics for Social Research

This book is dedicated to
my mother
my late father
Alex, Tasos, Effi, Anne, Elli, Mimi, Costa, Anna
Erin, Ben, Luke, Sophie, Elli Rose, Jordan
Pamela, Ryan, Michelle
Timothy, Alana
Danielle, Christine, Leanne, Marie
Amanda, Lisa
Alexandra, Andrea, Christopher
Stacey, Chloe, Billie-Marie
Alexandra, Katherine, Evelyn
and the ones still to come

Statistics for Social Research

George Argyrous

School of Social Science and Policy
The University of New South Wales, Australia

First published 1997 by
MACMILLAN PRESS LTD
Houndmills, Basingstoke, Hampshire RG21 6XS
and London
Companies and representatives
throughout the world

ISBN 0–333–73023–2

A catalogue record for this book is available
from the British Library.

10   9   8   7   6   5   4   3   2   1
06   05   04   03   02   01   00   99   98   97

Printed in Hong Kong

Contents

Introduction

This book is aimed at students and professionals who do not have any existing knowledge in the field of statistics. It is not unreasonable to suggest that most people who fit that description come to statistics reluctantly, if not with hostility. It is usually regarded as 'that course we had to get through'. I suspect that a sense of dread is also shared by many instructors when confronted with the prospect of having to teach the following material.

This book will hopefully ease some of these problems. It is written by a non-statistician for non-statisticians: for students who are new to the subject, and for professionals who may use statistics occasionally in their work. It is certainly not the only book available that attempts to do this. One might in fact respond with the statement 'not another stat's book!'. However, there are important respects in which this book is different from the numerous other books in the field.

Communication of ideas   This book is written with the aim of communicating the basic ideas and procedures of statistical analysis to the student and user, rather than as a technical exposition of the fine points of statistical theory. The emphasis is on the explanation of basic concepts and especially their application to 'real-life' problems, using a more conversational tone than is often the case. Such an approach may not be as precise as others in dealing with statistical theory, but it is often the mass of technical detail that leaves readers behind, and turns potential users of statistical analysis away.

Integrated use of SPSS   This book integrates the conceptual material with the use of the main computer software package. This is the **Statistical Package for the Social Sciences (SPSS)**. The development and availability of this software has meant that for most people 'doing stats' equals using a computer. The two tasks have converged. Unfortunately, most books have not caught up with this development or adequately integrated the use of computer packages with statistical analysis. They concentrate instead on the logic and formulas involved in statistical analysis and the calculation 'by hand' of problem-solutions. At best other books have appendixes that give brief introductions and guides to computer packages, but this does not bridge the gap between the hand calculations and the use of computer software. This book builds the use of SPSS into the text. The logic and application of various statistical techniques are explained, and then the examples are reworked on

SPSS. Readers can link explicitly the traditional method of working through problems by hand and working through the same problems on SPSS. Exercises also explicitly try to integrate the hand calculations with the use and interpretation of computer output.

To help readers along, a disk with all the data necessary to generate the results in the following chapters is provided, so that all the procedures described there can be replicated. Version 6.1 of SPSS is now available for both Macintosh and Windows platforms, and operates in virtually the same way in either format. There are slight differences in the appearance of some windows, but the basic menu structure is the same for both Windows and Macintosh environments. In fact, although the data were analysed on SPSS Version 6.1, users with SPSS Version 5.0 and Version 6.0 will still find that the basic procedures detailed in this book remain the same. Users of other statistical packages can download these data files in ASCII format from the following Web address: ftp://www.arts.unsw.edu.au/Pub/

However, it is necessary to point out that this is not a complete guide to SPSS. This book simply illustrates how SPSS can be used to deal with the basic statistical techniques that most researchers commonly encounter. It does not exhaust the full range of functions and options available in SPSS. For the advanced user, nothing will replace the *User's Guide* published by SPSS Inc. But for most people engaged in social research, the following text will allow them to handle the bulk of the problems they will face.

Clear guide to choosing the appropriate procedures This book is organized around the individual procedures (or sets of procedures) needed to deal with the majority of problems people encounter in analysing quantitative data. Other texts flood the reader with procedure after procedure, which can be overwhelming. How to choose between the options? This book concentrates just on the most widely used techniques, and sorts through them by building the structure of the book around these options. Entire chapters are devoted to individual tests so that the situations in which the particular test is applied will not be confused with situations that call for other tests. Thus after working through the text, readers can turn to individual chapters as needed in order to address the particular problems they confront.

Having noted the main features of this book as compared with others in the field, it is also worth noting what this book is not. This book looks at the analysis of quantitative data, and only the analysis of quantitative data. It makes no pretence to being a comprehensive guide to social research. Issues relating to the selection of research problems, the design of research methods, and the procedures for checking the validity and reliability of results are not covered. Such a separation of statistics from more general considerations in the design of social research is a dangerous practice since it may give the impression that statistical analysis *is* social research. Yet nothing could be further from the truth. Statistical analysis is one way of processing information, and not always the best. Nor is it a way of proving anything (despite the rhetorical language it employs). At best it is evidence in an ongoing persuasive argument. The separation of statistics from the research process in general in fact may be responsible for the over-exalted status of statistics as a research tool.

Why then write a book that reinforces this separation? First, there is the simple fact that no single book can do everything. Indeed, other books exist that detail the issues involved in social research, and the place of statistical analysis in the broader research process. An example is S. Sarantakos 1993, *Social Research*, published by Macmillan. Rather than duplicating such efforts this book is meant to sit side-by-side with such texts, and provide the methods of statistical analysis when required. Second, statistical analysis is hard. It raises distinct issues and problems of its own that warrant a self-contained treatment.

Many people have helped in bringing this book to press, although none should be implicated in any remaining errors or omissions. The students and my colleagues in the School of Social Science and Policy at the University of New South Wales have provided an invaluable sounding board for many of the ideas and forms of presentation that follow. Katrina Neal, Sandra Napoli, Jason Hecht, Rogelia Pe-Pua, and Frankie Leonard read various sections and provided helpful comments and suggestions; Carol Healey, Karen Tremayne, Cathy Deane, and Simon Kozlina read the entire manuscript and rescued it from many potential errors. Phuong and Joanne at the Sydney office of SPSS tolerated my queries about the use of the software with great patience and I am especially thankful for their help.

I am indebted to the Longman Group UK Ltd, on behalf of the Literary Executor of the late Sir Ronald Fisher and Dr Frank Yates F.R.S., for permission to reproduce Tables III, IV and V from *Statistical Tables for Biological, Agricultural and Medical Research*, 6/e (1974) in Appendix Tables A2, A3 and A4; and to Professor A Hald for permission to reproduce in amended form Table 1 of *Statistical Tables and Formulas 1952* in Appendix A1.

Lastly, to the reader, I welcome any comments and criticisms, which can be passed on to me at the following address:

School of Social Science and Policy
University of New South Wales, 2052, Australia.
e-mail: g.argyrous@unsw.edu.au

Descriptive statistics

Variables and their measurement

This book is concerned with the analysis of data, which we will simply define as measurements of a variable. To gain a deeper understanding of data analysis, though, we must first define some key terms and look at the process of measurement a little more closely. The starting point is the notion of a **variable**.

> A **variable** is an attribute that has two or more divisions, characteristics, or categories.

Research questions involving variables might be: why do rates of *marijuana use* differ between age groups? What has happened to the *age at marriage* over the past one hundred years? Does a change in the *unemployment level* correspond with a change in the *crime rate*? The bulk of statistical analysis attempts to understand whether (and why) a variable takes on certain traits for some cases and different traits for other cases.

The opposite notion to a variable is a **constant**.

> A **constant** is an attribute that does not vary.

The number of cents in a New Zealand dollar is a constant: every dollar coin will always exchange for 100 cents.

However, most social science research is devoted to understanding change and/or differences in variables, and in order to answer questions such as the research questions listed above, we need to perform the task of **measurement**.

> **Measurement** is the process of determining and recording which of the possible traits of a variable an individual case exhibits or possesses.

Thus the variable 'sex' has two categories: female and male, and measurement involves deciding which of these two possible categories a given person falls into. These measurements are taken from units of analysis we term **cases**.

A **case** is an entity that displays or possesses the traits of a given variable.

Although in social research cases are often individual people, this is not always so. If I am interested in divorce rates across certain cities, the relevant cases are cities. If I am interested in retention rates for high schools in a particular district, the cases are high schools.

The extent to which we are able to take measurements of a variable from all the cases of interest will determine whether we are dealing with a **population** or a **sample**.

A **population** is the set of all cases of interest.

In everyday terms the word 'population' means the people living in a certain country at a certain date. Yet just as individual cases can be entities other than people, so too can the population be made up of elements other than individual people. For reasons we will investigate in Chapter 7, we may not be able to or not want to investigate the entire population of interest. Instead we may take measurements from only a sub-set of the population, and this sub-set is called a sample.

A **sample** is a set of cases that does not include every member of the population.

For example, an environmental protection authority may be interested in the volume of pollutants in the waterways of a region. The authority may find it too difficult or too expensive to take a pollution reading from all the rivers, streams, etc. in the region, and instead may sample only 10 such waterways.

This very brief discussion has introduced some basic definitions, many of which will only be clarified completely in subsequent chapters. Before we move on, though, to the analysis of information gathered through the process of measurement, we need to explore more deeply the issues involved in selecting and measuring variables. The first of these issues is the conceptualization and operationalization of variables.

The conceptualization and operationalization of variables

Where do variables come from? Why do we choose to study particular variables and not others? The choice of variables to investigate is affected by a number of complex factors, three of which I will emphasize here.

Theoretical framework   Theories are ways of interpreting the world and reconciling ourselves to it, and even though we may take for granted that a variable is worthy of research, it is in fact often a highly charged selection process that directs one's attention to it. We may be working within an established theoretical tradition that considers certain variables to be central to its world-view. For example, Marxists consider 'economic class' to be a variable worthy of research, whereas another theoretical perspective might consider this variable to be uninteresting. Analysing the world in terms of economic class means *not* analysing it in other ways, such as social groups. This is neither good nor bad: without a theory to order our perception of the world, research will often become a jumble of observations that do not tie together in a meaningful way. But the theoretical preconceptions upon which the choice of variables to investigate is often based should be acknowledged.

Pre-specified research agenda   Sometimes the research question and the variables to be investigated are not determined by the researchers themselves. When working in a large organization the research agenda might be pre-specified by another part of the organization. Similarly, a consultant may contract to undertake social research that has terms of reference determined in advance by the contracting body. In these situations the person or people actually doing the research might have little scope to choose the variables to be investigated and how they are to be defined, since they are doing work for someone else.

Curiosity driven research   Sometimes we might not have a clearly defined theoretical framework to operate in, nor clear directives from another person or body as to the key concepts to be investigated. Instead we want to investigate a variable purely on the basis of a hunch: a loosely conceived feeling that something useful or important might be revealed by looking at a particular variable. This can be as important a reason for undertaking research as the imperatives of social theories. Indeed, when moving into a whole new area of research, over which existing theories have not ventured, simple hunches can be very fruitful motivations.

These three motivations are obviously not mutually exclusive. For example, even if the research agenda is specified by another body, that body will almost certainly be operating within some theoretical framework. Regardless of the motivation, though, the need to undertake social inquiry will direct us to particular variables to be investigated. Usually, at this initial stage a variable has a **conceptual definition**.

> The **conceptual definition** (or nominal definition) of a variable uses literal terms to specify the qualities of a variable.

A conceptual definition is much like a dictionary definition; it provides a working definition of the variable so that we have a general sense of what it 'means'. For example, I might be interested in the variable 'income', and so I define it conceptually as 'an individual's claim over goods and services'.

But isolating a variable of interest at this *conceptual* level is only the beginning: we then need a set of rules, procedures, or *operations* that will allow us to actually 'observe' a variable in the world. What will we look for to actually identify someone's income — the extent of their claim over resources? This is the problem of operationalization.

> An **operational definition** of a variable specifies the operations used to measure a variable for individual cases.

Therefore I may begin with the conceptual definition of income, but to asses a given person's income I need to decide on the things to look for that will allow me to measure it. A statement like 'income is the sum of all cash payments, such as wages, salaries, and welfare payments, received in the previous year' provides an operational definition of income. Thus when presented with an individual I can measure his or her income by adding up all the money received through various sources over the past year.

This process of definition is a major, if not *the* major, source of disagreement in social research. Any given conceptual definition can usually be operationalized in many different ways. To illustrate the 'slippage' that can occur in moving from a conceptual to an operational definition of a variable, consider the following example. A study is interested in 'criminality' across countries. We may define criminality conceptually as non-sanctioned acts of violence against other members of society. How can a researcher identify the pattern of variation in this variable across countries? A number of operational definitions could be employed:

- counting the number of criminal arrests from public records;
- calculating the proportion of the total population that is in jail;
- asking people in different countries whether they have committed crimes;
- counting the number of executions that take place in each country in a given year;
- determining the proportion of people in each country with red hair.

Clearly, it would be very hard to justify the last operationalization as a valid one: sorting countries according to the proportion of people in each with red hair is not a useful way of comparing levels of criminality! The other operational definitions seem closer to the general concept of criminality, but each has its own problems: asking people if they have committed a crime may not be a perfect measure because people might not be truthful about such a touchy subject. Counting the number of convictions will not be perfect — this operationalization may actually be measuring a different variable from the one intended: the severity of judicial systems rather than 'criminality'. Counting the number of arrests may be affected by the number of police in a country and their enthusiasm, so this might be a better operationalization for the concept 'police vigilance' than for criminality. Using any of these operational definitions to measure the level of criminality in various countries may not perfectly mirror the result we would get if we could 'know' their criminality.

A number of factors can generate problems in arriving at an operational definition of a variable:

Complexity of the concept Some variables are not very complex: a person's sex, for example, is determined by generally accepted physical attributes.

However, social variables are rarely so straightforward. Think of socioeconomic status. There are many dimensions that make up this variable, such as the amount of property a person owns, where a person lives, his or her education, employment status, etc. Indeed each of these dimensions of socioeconomic status are conceptual variables in themselves, and raise problems of operationalization of their own. Any single operationalization that focuses on one dimension, for example, by only considering the highest level of education attained, will miss out on the other dimensions.

Availability of data   We might have an operationalization that seems to perfectly capture the underlying conceptual variable of interest. For example, we might think that number of arrests is a flawless way of 'observing' criminality. The researchers, though, may not be allowed, for privacy reasons, to review police records to compile the information. Clearly, a less than perfect operationalization will have to be employed, simply because we cannot get our hands on the 'ideal' data.

Cost and difficulty of obtaining data   Say we were able to review police records and tally up the number of arrests. The cost in doing so, though, might be prohibitive, both in terms of time and money. Similarly, we might feel that a certain measure of water pollution is ideal for assessing river degradation, but the need to employ an expert with sophisticated measuring equipment might bar this as an option, and instead a subjective judgment of water 'murkiness' might be preferred as a quick and easy measure.

Ethics   Is it right to go looking at the details of an individual's arrest record, simply to satisfy one's own research objectives? The police might permit it, and there might be plenty of time and money available, but does this justify looking at a document that was not intended to be part of a research project? The problem of ethics — knowing right from wrong — is extremely thorny, and I could not even begin to address it seriously here. It is simply raised as an issue affecting the operationalization of variables that regularly arises in social research dealing with lives of people. (For those wishing to follow up on this important issue, a good starting point is R.S. Broadhead, 1984, 'Human rights and human subjects: ethics and strategies in social science research', *Sociological Inquiry*, vol. 54, Spring, pp. 107–23.)

For these (and other) reasons a great deal of debate about the validity of social research centres around this problem of operationalization. In fact, many debates surrounding quantitative research are not actually about the techniques or results of the research but rather whether the variables have been 'correctly' defined in the first place. Unless the operational criteria used to measure a variable are sensitive to the way a variable changes between cases, they will generate misleading results.

Levels of measurement

Despite the inherent problems involved in arriving at an operational definition there are certain guiding principles in settling on one that is suitable.

> An operational definition must allow a researcher to assign each case into one, and only one, of the categories of the variable.

This statement embodies two principles of measurement. The first is the **principle of exclusiveness**, which states that no case should have more than one value for the same variable. For example, someone cannot be both 18 years of age and 64 years of age. Measurement must also follow the **principle of exhaustiveness**, which states that every case must be classified into a category. For example, a scale for measuring family status must allow for every possible type of family status that can arise.

An operational definition of a variable, which conforms to the principles of exclusiveness and exhaustiveness, will imply a certain **level of measurement**. There are four different levels at which we may undertake the process of measurement:

- nominal   • ordinal   • interval   • ratio

These levels of measurement are a fundamental distinction in statistics, since they determine much of what we can do with information gathered. In fact, when considering which of the myriad of statistical techniques to choose to analyse information, usually the first question to ask is the level at which the variable has been measured. As we shall see there are things we can do with data collected at the interval level of measurement that we cannot do with data collected at the nominal level. We speak of *levels* of measurement because *the higher the level of measurement the more information we have about a variable*.

For example, if I am interested in people's religion, each person will fall into some predetermined category, such as Catholic, Protestant, Orthodox, Muslim, etc.

> A **nominal** scale of measurement only indicates the category that a case falls into with respect to a variable.

To ensure that the scale is exhaustive nominal scales usually have a catch-all category like 'other' or 'miscellaneous' and such categories provide a quick way of identifying a nominal scale of measurement.

Another easy way to detect a nominal scale is to rearrange the order in which the categories are listed and see if the scale still makes sense. For example, either of the following orders for listing religious denomination are valid:

Christian	Muslim
Muslim	Jewish
Jewish	Hindu
Hindu	Christian
Other	Other

Obviously, the order in which the categories appear does not matter, as long as the rules of mutual exclusivity and exhaustiveness are followed. This is because there is no sense of rank or order of magnitude: one cannot say that a person in the 'Christian' category has more or less religion than someone in the 'Hindu' category. Similarly, we can assign numerical **values** to each category label as a form of shorthand (a process that will be very useful when we later have to enter data into SPSS). But these numerical values are simply category labels that have no quantitative meaning as such. Thus I may code — assign numerical values to — these categories in the following way:

1 = Muslim
2 = Jewish
3 = Hindu
4 = Christian
5 = Other

But these numbers do not 'mean' anything by themselves. They are simply used for convenience in analysing and describing data. I could just as easily have used this coding scheme to assign numerical values to each category:

1 = Jewish
2 = Christian
3 = Hindu
4 = Muslim
5 = Other

An ordinal scale of measurement also categorizes cases. Thus nominal and ordinal scales are sometimes collectively called **categorical variables**. However, an ordinal scale provides additional information.

> An **ordinal** scale, in addition to the function of classification, allows cases to be ordered by degree according to measurements of a variable.

In other words, ordinal scales enable us to **rank** cases. Ranking involves ordering cases in a quantitative sense, such as from 'lowest' to 'highest', from 'less' to 'more', or from 'weakest' to 'strongest'. Ordinal scales are particularly common when measuring attitude or satisfaction in opinion surveys. For example, if I ask students how satisfied they are with the library services, I might group responses according to the following ordinal scale:

very poor   poor   OK   good   excellent

Thus I would know that someone who rated 'excellent' exhibits more 'satisfaction with library services' than someone who rated 'good'. Put another way, someone who answered 'excellent' is ranked above someone who responded 'good'. Unlike nominal data, one response is not only different from another, it is 'better', or 'stronger', or 'bigger', or more 'intense': there is *some idea of directional change*. Here we *cannot rearrange the categories* without the scale becoming senseless. Thus, if I constructed the scale in the following way, the ranking of cases according to their level of satisfaction is lost:

very poor   *good*   *excellent*   *OK*   *poor*

As with nominal data, numerical values can be assigned to the categories as a form of shorthand, but with ordinal scales these values need to preserve the sense of ranking. Thus either of the following sets of values can be used:

1	2	3	4	5
very poor	*poor*	*OK*	*good*	*excellent*

3	18	54	102	111
very poor	*poor*	*OK*	*good*	*excellent*

Either coding system allows the categories to be identified and ordered with respect to each other, but the numbers themselves do not have any quantitative significance beyond the function of ranking. (In the following chapters we will refer to nominal/ordinal data as having a range of values. For the reasons just outlined this is, strictly speaking, incorrect. However, if we take note that for categorical variables these values are simply category labels with no quantitative significance, such terminology is not too misleading.)

Although ordinal scales permit us to rank cases in terms of a variable, they do not allow us to say *by how much* better or stronger one case is compared with another. If someone thinks the service in the library is 'excellent', and another says it is 'OK', I know that the first person possesses more of the variable 'satisfaction with library services' than the other, but there is no unit of measurement that will allow me to say *how much* more satisfaction that person has over the other. The distances or intervals between the categories are unknown.

> An **interval** scale has units measuring intervals of equal distance between values on the scale.

In other words, not only can we say that one case has more (or less) of the variable in question than another, but we can say by *how much* more (or less). Thus if today's temperature is 20°C and yesterday's was 15°C, I am able to say that it is warmer today, *and* I can also say that it is 5°C warmer. Moreover, the intervals between points on the scale are of equal value over its whole range, so that the difference in heat between 1°C and 3°C is the same as the difference in heat between 101°C and 103°C. Clearly the numerical values on an interval scale do have significance, since they indicate a measurable quantity.

A **ratio** scale of measurement has a value of zero indicating cases where no quantity of the variable is present.

Such a condition is known as a true zero point. For example, heat measured in degrees Celsius is not ratio level. There is a zero point, but 0°C does not indicate a case where no heat is present — it is cold but not that cold! Instead, 0°C indicates something else: the point at which water freezes. An example of a ratio scale is height measured in centimetres, because 0 cm literally signals a case that has no height. This feature of a ratio scale allows us to express the value of one case as a ratio of another: if we compare someone who is 180 cm with someone who is 120 cm tall, we can say that the former is 60 cm taller, *and* we can also say that he or she is 1.5 times as tall.

This distinction between interval and ratio scales of measurement is a fairly subtle one, and not important for what is to follow. We can generally perform the same statistical analyses on interval data that we can perform on ratio data. In fact, we will talk about only three levels of measurement: nominal, ordinal, and interval/ratio.

Discrete and continuous variables

One important distinction that only applies to interval/ratio data is that between **discrete** and **continuous variables**.

A **discrete variable** is measured by a unit that cannot be subdivided. It has a countable number of values.

For example, the number of children per household is discrete, since there can only be one, two, three, etc. children per household. It makes no sense to talk of 1.7 children per household, since children do not come in units of less than 1! We have to jump from one value of the variable to the next. The unit of measurement is in a sense 'built into' the definition of the variable. Other examples are the number of prisoners per jail cell, the number of welfare agencies in a district, and the number of industrial accidents in the previous year.

A **continuous variable** is measured by units that can be subdivided infinitely. It can take any value in a line interval.

Height is an example of a continuous variable, since there is no basic unit with which height can be measured. We may begin by measuring height in terms of metres. But a metre can be divided in centimetres, and centimetres into millimetres, and so on. The only limit is exactly how precise we want to be: centimetres are not as accurate as millimetres, and metres not as accurate as centimetres. Theoretically we can move continuously from one value of the variable to the next without having to jump. Practically, though, we will always have to 'round off' the measurement and treat continuous variables as if they were discrete. We do this by forming class intervals around certain points along the scale, a process we will elaborate on in later chapters. This may cause a variable such as height to appear discrete, but in fact it is continuous. Similarly with age: though we may measure age in discrete units such as years or months, the variable 'age' itself increases in a continuous way. We will simply note at this point that it is difficult to capture the truly continuous nature of a variable.

Summary

The importance of the distinction between nominal, ordinal, and interval/ratio data is the amount of information each level provides. Nominal data have the least information, ordinal data give more information because we can rank cases, and interval/ratio data capture the most information since they allow us to measure difference. The amount of information provided by each level of measurement and the tasks we are thereby allowed to perform with data collected at each level is summarized in Table 1.1.

Table 1.1 Levels of measurement

Level	Examples	Measurement procedure	Operations permitted
Nominal	Sex Race Religion Marital status	Classification into categories	Counting number of cases in each category; comparing sizes of categories
Ordinal	Social class Attitude and opinion scales	Classification plus ranking of categories with respect to each other	All above plus judgments of 'greater than' or 'less than'
Interval/ratio	Age Number of children Income	All above plus description of distances between scores in terms of equal units	All above plus other mathematical operations (addition, subtraction, multiplication, etc.)

Source: J.F. Healey, 1993, *Statistics: A Tool for Social Research*, 3rd edn, Wadsworth, Belmont, p. 14.

This chapter discussed the preliminaries that need to be taken into account before statistical information can be analysed. This was done fairly generally, since the rest of this book is concerned with the process of analysis — what do we do with data once they have been collected? Having collected data we can then proceed to analyse them, and the first step in analysis is usually to describe the data. The process of description will be discussed in the next three chapters.

Exercises

1.1 Consider the following ways of classifying respondents to a questionnaire:
  (a) Voting eligibility:
   • Registered voter
   • Unregistered but eligible to vote
   • Did not vote at the last election
  (b) Course of enrolment:
   • Physics
   • Economics
   • English
   • Sociology
   • Social sciences
  (c) Reason for joining the military:
   • Parental pressure
   • Career training
   • Conscripted
   • Seemed like a good idea at the time
   • No reason given
  Do these violate the principles of measurement? If so, which ones and how?

1.2 What is the level of measurement for each of these variables?
   • The age in years of the youngest member of each household
   • The color of a person's hair
   • The color of a karate belt
   • The price of a suburban bus fare
   • The years in which national elections were held
   • The postcode of households
   • People's attitude to smoking
   • Academic performance measured by number of marks
   • Academic performance measured as fail or pass
   • Place of birth, listed by country
   • Infant mortality rate (deaths per thousand)
   • Political party of the current Member of Parliament for your area
   • Proximity to the sea (coastal or non-coastal)
   • Proximity to the sea (kilometres from the nearest coastline)
   • Relative wealth (listed as 'Poor' through to 'Wealthy')
   • The number on the back of a football player

1.3 Find an article in a social science journal that involves statistical analysis. What are the conceptual variables used? How are they operationalized? Why are these variables chosen for analysis? Can you come up with alternative operationalizations for these same variables? Justify your alternative.

1.4 For each of the following variables describe briefly a means of measurement:
   • Racial prejudice
   • Household size
   • Height
   • Drug use
   • Voting preference

- Economic status
- Aggressiveness

For each operationalization state the level of measurement. Suggest alternative operationalizations that involve different levels of measurement.

1.5 Which of the following are discrete variables and which are continuous variables?

- The numbers on the faces of a die
- The weight of a new-born baby
- The time at sunset
- The number of cars in a parking station
- The amount of water consumed by a household per day

1.6 The following is a question from a national survey of attitudes toward unemployment:

What is your impression of the government's efforts to address the current unemployment situation? Please circle one of the following:

1 The government is doing nothing to tackle the problem

2 The government is addressing the problem, in an unsatisfactory manner

3 The government is addressing the problem, in a satisfactory manner

4 The government is doing everything it can to solve the problem

5 No opinion

What variable is this question trying to measure? Do you see any problems with the range of responses provided?

2

Basic tools of description: Tables

Tolstoy's *War and Peace* is a very long book. It would not be possible to do such a book justice in any way other than to read it from cover to cover. However, this takes a lot of time and concentration, each of which may not be readily available. If we want to simply get a gist of the story, a shorter summary is adequate. A summary reduces the thousands of words that make up the original book down to a few hundred, while (hopefully) retaining some of the essence of the story. Of course, the summary will leave out a great deal, and the way the book is summarized for one purpose will be different from the way it is summarized for another. Nevertheless, although much is lost, something is also gained when a book so large is summarized effectively.

The same holds true with social research. Most research projects will generate a wealth of information. Presenting the results of such research in their complete form may be too overwhelming for the reader so that an 'abridged version' is needed. This chapter, and the ones that immediately follow, will focus on the procedures used to provide this abridged version, which we call **descriptive statistics**.

> **Descriptive statistics** are the numerical and graphical techniques for organizing, presenting, and analysing data.

The great advantage of descriptive statistics is that they make a mass of research material easier to 'read'. By *reducing* a large set of data into a few statistics, or into some picture such as a graph or table, the results of research can be clearly and concisely summarized.

Say we conducted a survey that gathers the data for the height of two groups of 150 students. These primary data consist of two lots of 150 numbers, representing the height in centimetres of each case. I could write each of these two sets of 150 numbers down on separate pages and present them as the results of the research. It is not difficult to see that very little information is effectively communicated this way. For example, it would be very difficult to look at these pages full of numbers and decide which group was the 'tallest'.

However, we can take these sets of 150 numbers and put them through a statistical 'grinder', which produces fewer numbers — statistics — that capture the relevant information contained in the two original groups of 150 cases.

Descriptive statistics tease out some important feature of the data that is not evident if we just present the raw data. One such feature we will focus on in later chapters is the notion of average. For example, we might calculate a single figure for the 'average' height of each set of 150 people: clearly, comparing two numbers is easier than comparing two lots of 150. The measure of 'average' chosen will certainly not capture all the information contained in the primary data — no description ever does that — but hopefully it will give a general notion of what the two sets of cases 'look like' and allow some meaningful comparison to be made.

Types of descriptive statistics

We have just introduced the notion of 'average' as an important feature of a distribution of scores that we might be interested in. In more technical terms this is called a **measure of central tendency**. But there are descriptive statistics that capture other important features of a distribution. There are descriptive statistics that give an indication of the spread of cases around the average: these are called **measures of dispersion**. Chapter 4 will look in detail at how measures of central tendency and measures of dispersion are calculated, and the appropriate instances in which they can be used to describe a distribution.

There is also a variety of ways in which data can be represented visually to make the information easier to read. Chapter 3 and the rest of this chapter will look at various **charts, graphs, and tables**, and show how information can be concisely presented (and sometimes misrepresented) by such techniques.

In Chapters 19 to 22 we will also come across a more complicated set of descriptive statistics called **measures of association**. These summarize the relationship between two or more variables: the extent to which a change in the value of one variable is linked (if at all) to a change in another variable.

Table 2.1   Types of descriptive statistics

Type	Function
Measures of central tendency	Indicate the typical score of a distribution
Measures of dispersion	Indicate the spread or variety of scores in a distribution
Tables, charts, graphs	Give a visual representation of a distribution
Measures of association	Indicate the existence and strength of any relationship between two or more variables

Given the array of descriptive statistics available (see Table 2.1), how do we decide which to use in a specific research context? The considerations involved in choosing the appropriate descriptive statistics are like those involved in drawing a map. Obviously, a map on the scale of 1-to-1 is of no use (and difficult to fold). A good map will be on a different scale, and identify only those landmarks that the person wanting to cover that piece of terrain needs to know. Whether to include mountains and valleys, rivers and oceans, man-made objects or only natural parts of the environment is a decision that is specific to the task at hand. A map containing certain kinds of information may be ideal for one task but useless for another, so the amount of detail cannot be decided independently of the purpose and audience of the research.

The same considerations apply when working with descriptive statistics. Descriptive statistics are meant to simplify — to capture the essential features of the terrain — but in so doing they also leave out information contained in the original data. In this respect, descriptive statistics might hide as much as they reveal. Reducing a set of 150 numbers for each of 150 subjects' height down to one number that reflects average obviously misrepresents cases that are very different from the average. Just as a map loses some information when summarizing a piece of geography, some information is lost in describing data using a small set of descriptive statistics: it is a question of whether the information lost would help to address the research problem at hand. In other words, the choice of descriptive statistics used to summarize research data really depends on the specific context. Sometimes it might be sufficient to summarize the data in a table, at other times it might be important to also calculate some measure of average and/or dispersion.

Despite this general point, some specific factors guide the choice of descriptive statistics. For example, we will see that the level of measurement is very important. The rest of this chapter, and the ones that follow, will explore the choices in more detail, and the conditions under which they are applicable.

Percentages and proportions

According to one country's census data,[1] in 1986 there were 324 167 one-parent families, out of a total of 4 158 006 families. In 1991 there were 552 412 one-parent families out of 4 298 710. What does this tell us about the changing nature of families? On the basis of this raw data we can say that there were more single-parent families in 1991 than in 1986. Absolute numbers, though, do not tell us much about the *relative* importance of single-parent families in each year. However, if I said that such families accounted for 7.8 per cent of all family types in 1986 and 12.85 per cent in 1991, the pattern is immediately obvious: single-parent families have become a relatively larger group.

By calculating these percentages we have in effect compensated for the different total number of families present in each year. In more technical terms:

> **Percentages** are statistics that standardize the total number of cases to a base value of 100.

The formula for calculating a percentage is:

$$\% = \frac{f}{N} \times 100$$

---

[1] Australian Bureau of Statistics, 1991, *Census of Population Housing*, catalogue no.2720.0

where:

   f is the frequency or number of cases in a category
   N is the total number of cases in all categories.

We can see where the percentage figures came from in the example by putting ('substituting') the raw numbers into this formula:

$$1986: \frac{324\ 167}{4\ 158\ 006} \times 100 = 7.80\%$$

$$1991: \frac{552\ 412}{4\ 298\ 710} \times 100 = 12.85\%$$

It should be fairly clear that if I calculate the percentage of *each* family type in a given year and summed them, the total would be 100 per cent. For example, if I add the percentage of single-parent families with the percentage of non-single-parent families in 1991, the total will be 100 per cent. Thus knowing that 12.85 per cent of all families in 1991 were headed by a single parent allows me to quickly calculate the percentage of families *not* headed by a single parent:

$$100 - 12.85 = 87.15\%$$

Proportions are close cousins of percentages. A proportion does exactly the same job as a percentage, except that it uses a base of 1 rather than 100. In fact, it is calculated in exactly the same way as a percentage, except for the fact that we do not multiply by 100:

$$p = \frac{f}{N}$$

The result is that we get a number expressed as a decimal. In the example above the results expressed as proportions would be:

$$1986: \frac{324\ 167}{4\ 158\ 006} = 0.0780$$

$$1991: \frac{552\ 412}{4\ 298\ 710} = 0.1285$$

Generally, percentages are easier to work with — for some reason people are more comfortable with whole numbers than with decimals. But in later chapters we will use proportions extensively, so it is important to learn the simple relationship between proportions and the more familiar percentages.

To convert a proportion into its corresponding percentage, move the decimal point two places to the right (this is the same as multiplying by 100).

This may all seem pretty straightforward. There are some words of caution though when working with proportions and percentages, or when encountering them in other people's work. The first thing to look for when confronted with a percentage or proportion is the raw total from which they are calculated. This is because percentages and proportions are often used to conceal dramatic differences in absolute size. An increase in unemployment rates from 10 per cent to 10.5 per cent does not seem dramatic. But if this 0.5 per cent represents 35 000 people it is in socioeconomic terms a large increase. Conversely, a large change in percentage figures may be trivial when working with small numbers. The number of people attending a pro-monarchy meeting may be 150 per cent greater than the number that attended the last meeting, but if this is actually due to five people attending rather than the previous two, it is hardly a dramatic rise. Small additions to either the total or the categories that make up the total will greatly affect the percentage figure calculated.

Frequency distributions

Having learnt to summarize and describe raw data using percentages and proportions we can now proceed to the construction of **frequency distributions**.

A **frequency distribution** reports, for each value or category of a variable, the number of cases that have that value or fall into that category.

To illustrate the construction of a frequency distribution we will refer to the following data, which are the results of a hypothetical survey of 20 students in a statistics class. I am interested in three separate variables: age, sex, and attitude to statistics. Age is measured by asking students to round off their age to the nearest whole year (interval/ratio). Sex is measured by classifying cases into male or female (nominal). Finally, students' attitude to statistics is gauged by asking each whether they 'like', are 'indifferent' to, or 'hate' learning statistics (ordinal). The results are shown in Table 2.2.

The first task of a frequency distribution is to tally the number of cases that fall within each value of the variable. This is called a **raw frequency distribution**. Three separate frequency tables can be constructed for these data, one for each variable (Tables 2.3, 2.4, 2.5).

Table 2.2 Results of a survey of statistics students

Student	Sex	Attitude to statistics	Age in years
1	Male	Like	18
2	Male	Like	21
3	Female	Indifferent	20
4	Male	Hate	18
5	Female	Like	19
6	Male	Hate	18
7	Female	Hate	22
8	Male	Like	19
9	Female	Indifferent	18
10	Male	Indifferent	20
11	Male	Hate	18
12	Female	Like	19
13	Male	Like	22
14	Male	Like	19
15	Female	Hate	20
16	Female	Indifferent	18
17	Male	Hate	21
18	Female	Hate	19
19	Male	Indifferent	18
20	Male	Like	20

Table 2.3 Sex of students

Sex	Frequency (f)
Female	8
Male	12
Total (N)	20

Table 2.4 Attitude of students to statistics

Attitude	Frequency (f)
Like	8
Indifferent	5
Hate	7
Total (N)	20

Table 2.5 Age (in years) of students

Age	Frequency (f)
18	7
19	5
20	4
21	2
22	2
Total (N)	20

These tables indicate the bare minimum structure that all frequency tables must possess: a clear title explaining the variable, clearly labelled categories that are mutually exclusive, and the total number of cases. In addition, the source of data should be cited at the base of the table.

For all frequency tables some extra information can be calculated, if required. To each table, we can add a column that expresses the percentage (or proportion) of cases that fall in each category. These are called **relative frequencies** (Tables 2.6, 2.7, 2.8).

Table 2.6   Sex of students

Sex	Frequency	Percentage (%)
Female	8	$\frac{8}{20} \times 100 = 40$
Male	12	$\frac{12}{20} \times 100 = 60$
Total	20	100

Table 2.7   Attitude of students to statistics

Attitude	Frequency	Percentage (%)
Like	0 8	$\frac{8}{20} \times 100 = 40$
Indifferent	5	$\frac{5}{20} \times 100 = 25$
Hate	7	$\frac{7}{20} \times 100 = 35$
Total	20	100

Table 2.8   Age (in years) of students

Age	Frequency	Percentage (%)
18	7	35
19	5	25
20	4	20
21	2	10
22	2	10
Total	20	100

Tables 2.6 and 2.7 show the calculations involved in producing the relative frequencies. Of course, when actually reporting results these calculations are not included, as in Table 2.8. Notice also that the column of percentages must add up to 100 per cent, since all cases must fall into one classification or another.[1]

With ordinal and interval/ratio data one further extension to the basic frequency table can be made. This is the addition of columns providing information on **cumulative frequencies** and **cumulative percentages**. Since ordinal and interval/ratio data are on a scale that gives some sense of increase or decrease, it is sometimes interesting to know the number, and percentage, of cases that fall above or below a certain point on the scale. A cumulative frequency distribution shows the number of cases in each category up to and including that category. (See Tables 2.9 and 2.10.)

Table 2.9 Attitude of students to statistics

Preference	Frequency	Cumulative frequency	Percentage (%)	Cumulative percentage (%)
Like	8	8	40	$\frac{8}{20} \times 100 = 40$
Indifferent	5	8 + 5 = 13	25	$\frac{8+5}{20} \times 100 = 65$
Hate	7	8 + 5 + 7 = 20	35	$\frac{8+5+7}{20} \times 100 = 100$
Total	20		100	

Table 2.10 Age (in years) of students

Age	Frequency	Cumulative frequency	Percentage (%)	Cumulative percentage (%)
18	7	7	35	35
19	5	12	25	60
20	4	16	20	80
21	2	18	10	90
22	2	20	10	100
Total	20		100	

Thus, if I was interested in how many students in the group did not hate statistics I look at the sum of cases in the first two rows of Table 2.9. The cumulative frequency at this point in the table is 13, which is 65% of all cases.

[1] Sometimes tables do not follow this rule strictly when numbers have been 'rounded off'. For example, exact percentages may have decimal places such as 22.3%, 38.4%, 39.3%. This may affect the readability of the table, and so the figures are rounded to the nearest whole number: 22%, 38%, 39%. These rounded numbers only add up to 99%. Where this occurs a footnote should be added to the table stating 'May not sum to 100 due to rounding', or words to that effect.

Similarly if I am interested in how many students are over 19 years of age, I can see that because 60% are 19 or below there must be 40% above this age.

Class intervals

One additional point needs to be made about working with interval/ratio data, as we have been with the age distribution of students. With interval/ratio data we often use **class intervals** to construct a frequency distribution.

A **class interval** is a range of values on a distribution that are grouped together for presentation and analysis.

Class intervals are an inherent issue when working with a continuous variable. For example, the variable 'age' is continuous, in the sense that we can, if we choose, measure it in infinitely more precise units. Theoretically we can measure this variable so that there is a smooth progression from one point on the scale to the next. Practically, though, we have to measure this variable in some whole unit, such as years or months or days, and this causes the scale to 'jump' from one value to the next. For example, students' ages have been rounded to the nearest whole year, so that the value for 18 actually represents students whose ages fall within the interval 17.5–18.5 years. Those who are given a value of 19 actually have ages that can range from 18.5 to 19.5, and so on. Thus one student might be 19 years and 3 months of age whereas another is 18 years and 10 months, but because we are rounding to the nearest whole year, these two students are classified as 19 years of age.

In other words, around each value for age (18, 19, 20, etc.) there is a range of values that the chosen unit of measurement (whole years) is not refined enough to detect. The use of these class intervals causes us to cluster cases together into distinct groups. Hence we sometimes describe such a distribution as **grouped data**.

Class intervals can also be used when working with discrete variables, especially where the variable has many possible values. For example, the number of telephones per 100 households is a discrete variable. There is no sense in which we can subdivide the unit of measurement — number of telephones — into more refined units. It is silly to talk of 12.5 telephones per hundred households, or 54.3 telephones, or anything other than a whole number. Nevertheless, if I surveyed 80 countries there might be 80 different values for the number of telephones per 100 households. A frequency table will therefore have as many rows as there are cases, which is very awkward to work with. Instead I might collapse these values down into five or six ranges that retain a sense of the spread of values across countries, but in a more manageable form.

In either the case of continuous or the case of discrete variables, the point of using class intervals is to collapse data into a few easy-to-work-with categories. Measuring age in whole years gives in the example above a 'workable' number of values to organize the data into. Working with a more refined unit such as months may yield too much information that will clutter up the results with unnecessary detail. Working with less refined measurements, such as 5 year intervals, will not provide enough detail to isolate the differences between students that I am interested in. The difference is that with continuous variables we *have to* work with class intervals, since the truly continuous nature of the variable can never be captured by a particular scale of measurement. With discrete variables, on the other hand, we only use class intervals if the range of values is so large that it makes presentation and analysis awkward.

There are some general rules that apply to the construction of class intervals. The first relates to the choice of **stated class limits**. These are the upper and lower bounds of an interval that determine its width. Generally, class intervals should have the same width. The actual width of class intervals depends on the particular situation, especially the amount of information required. The wider the class intervals the easier it is to 'read' a distribution, but less information is communicated. For example, if we are surveying the age of a wider cross-section of the population rather than just an undergraduate statistics class, the choice of intervals will be different from that used above. A frequency table for such a distribution of ages will be very long if we have a separate row in the table for every possible age, measured in years. To simplify the data I might group it into 5 year intervals, so that all 0–4 year olds are in one group, 5–9 year olds in another, 10–14 in another, and so on.

Table 2.11   Population by age group, 1991

Age	Persons	Percentage (%)
0–4	1 262 783	7.5
5–9	1 256 059	7.5
10–14	1 245 657	7.4
15–19	1 314 229	7.8
20–24	1 343 396	8.0
25–29	1 335 574	7.9
30–34	1 386 903	8.2
35–39	1 292 505	7.7
40–44	1 261 676	7.5
45–49	1 000 949	5.9
50–54	820 618	4.9
55–59	704 582	4.2
60–64	715 223	4.2
65–69	651 746	3.9
70–74	501 234	3.0
75–79	376 723	2.2
80–84	225 323	1.3
85–89	106 681	0.6
Over 89	45 449	0.3
Total	16 847 310	100

Source: Australian Bureau of Statistics, catalogue no. 2720.0.

All that is required is that the class intervals be mutually exclusive.

Thus in choosing 5 year class intervals to group the ages of this population the stated class limits of each interval are 0–4, 5–9, 10–14, and so on.

Notice that the upper stated limit of each interval does not 'touch' the lower stated limit of the next interval: there appears to be a gap between 4 and 5, 9 and 10, 14 and 15, and so on. Won't some cases fall down this gap and not be included in any interval? This will not happen because I have chosen to measure age in terms of years. *Provided that the unit with which the variable is measured is the same as that used to construct the class intervals*, all cases will fall into one class or another. Someone is either in the 0–4 group or the 5–9 group. A person cannot fall in between because of the units in which age is measured: no one can have an age of 4.6 years, simply because we have not measured age at that level of precision. If age is measured in a more precise unit, such as months, the class intervals will have to be expressed in months as well.

With continuous variables, we also have **real stated limits** for each class interval. These real limits take into account the fact that although there appears to be a gap between each interval, the variable is actually continuous. To obtain the real limits of each interval we follow this procedure:

1 Identify the limits of each interval stated in the distribution.
2 Divide the unit of measurement in half.
3 Add half a unit to the upper limit of the interval.
4 Subtract half a unit from the lower limit of the interval.

Thus to find the real class limits for the 65–69 class interval in the preceding table:

1 the stated limits are 65 and 69;
2 the unit of measurement is 1 year, so half of this is 6 months;
3 adding 6 months to 69 produces 69 years and 6 months;
4 subtracting 6 months from 65 produces 64 years and 6 months.

Thus the real limits for the 65–69 interval are 64.5 years and 69.5 years.

Another concept that will be used in later chapters when working with class intervals is the **mid-point** (*m*) of the interval. This is simply the sum of the lower and upper limits divided by 2:

$$\text{mid point} = \frac{\text{upper limit} + \text{lower limit}}{2}$$

For example, the mid-point for the class interval 65–69 is:

$$
\begin{aligned}
m &= \frac{65 + 69}{2} \\
&= 67
\end{aligned}
$$

Thus the stated limits, real limits, and class mid-points for a selection of class intervals in the table for the age distribution in Table 2.11 will be as shown in Table 2.12.

Table 2.12   Limits and mid-points

Stated limits	Real limits	Mid-point
65–69	64.5–69.5	67
70–74	69.5–74.5	72
75–79	74.5–79.5	77
80–84	79.5–84.5	82
85–89	84.5–89.5	87

Exercises

2.1 How does a proportion differ from a percentage?

2.2 Why will a proportion always be smaller than its equivalent percentage value?

2.3 Convert the following proportions into percentages:
- 0.01
- 0.13
- 1.24
- 0.0045

2.4 Convert the following percentages into proportions:
- 12%
- 13.4%
- 167%
- 3.5%

2.5 If a friend told you her age was 22 years, what would be the true limits of her age? If she told you her age was 22 and 4 months, what would be the true limits?

2.6 The following data have been collected as part of a psychological study, regarding the time, in minutes, taken for subjects to complete a certain task:

12	3	45	26	23	56	45	8	35	37	25
42	32	58	8	7	19	16	56	21	34	36
10	38	12	48	38	37	3	42	27	39	17
31	56	28	40	8	27	37				

Using class intervals 1–9, 10–19, 20–29, and so on, organize these data into a frequency table, displaying both raw and cumulative frequencies and percentages. What are the mid-points of these class intervals?

2.7 The following data were collected from a Bureau of Statistics publication, *Survey of attendance at selected cultural venues, June 1991:*

Attendance at public libraries, 1990–91 ('000)

State	Attendees
A	1409
B	1142
C	713
D	423
E	497
F	130
G	90
H	38
Total	4442

Attendance at popular music concerts, 1990–91 ('000)

State	Attendees
A	1166
B	870
C	604
D	280
E	332
F	99
G	32
H	74
Total	3456.4

For each of these tables add columns and calculate the relative frequencies for each state. Why is it inappropriate to calculate cumulative frequencies on these distributions?

2.8 From a recent newspaper or magazine find examples of the use of the techniques outlined in this chapter. Do these examples follow the rules of description outlined here?

3

Graphs

The previous chapter looked at ways of summarizing data by producing frequency tables. However, often the most striking way of summarizing information is with a graph. A graph provides a quick visual sense of the main features of the data. The particular graphs that can be constructed in any given context are determined largely by the level of measurement (Table 3.1).

Table 3.1   Type of graph according to level of measurement

Level of measurement	Graph
Nominal and ordinal	Pie graph
	Bar graph
Interval/ratio	Pie graph
	Histogram
	Polygon

In this chapter, to illustrate the procedures and principles involved in constructing a graph, we will use the hypothetical data for the class of statistics students that we introduced in Chapter 2.

Table 3.2   Sex of students

Sex	Frequency
Female	8
Male	12
Total	20

Table 3.3   Attitude to statistics of students

Attitude	Frequency
Like	8
Indifferent	5
Hate	7
Total	20

Table 3.4   Age in years of students

Age	Frequency
18	7
19	5
20	4
21	2
22	2
Total	20

Some general principles

The same general rules that apply to the construction of tables also apply to graphs:

- A graph should be a self-contained bundle of information. A reader should not have to search through the text in order to understand a graph (if one does have to search the text this may be a sign that the graph is concealing information rather than illuminating it).
- A graph should have an appropriate title.
- The categories or values of the variable should be clearly identified.
- The units of measurement should be noted for interval/ratio data.
- The total number of cases should be indicated.
- The source of the data should be indicated where appropriate.

Pie graphs

A pie graph can be constructed for all levels of measurement.

> A **pie graph** presents the distribution of cases in the form of a circle. The relative size of each slice of the circle is equal to the proportion of cases within each category.

A pie graph has been drawn for the distribution of statistics students by sex (Figure 3.1). We can see that female respondents represent 8 out of 20 students, so the slice representing the frequency of female respondents is $8/20^{ths}$ of the circle (40%).

Pie graphs (also called pie charts) can be constructed using either the raw scores or the percentage frequencies (as in Figure 3.1): in either case the actual pie will look exactly the same. However, when percentages are used, the total number of cases from which the percentages are derived should be indicated.

Pie graphs emphasize the relative importance of a particular value to the *total*. They are therefore mainly used to highlight distributions where cases are concentrated in only one or two values. For example, Figure 3.2 illustrates the distribution of students by age, and clearly reflects the large proportion of the total that are 18 years of age.

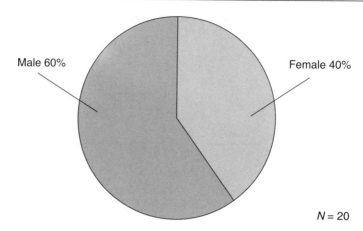

Figure 3.1   A pie graph showing the distribution of statistics students by sex.

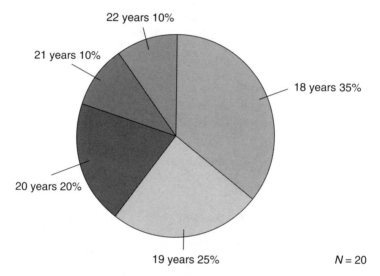

Figure 3.2   A pie graph showing the distribution of students by age.

Pie graphs begin to look a bit clumsy when there are too many values of the variable (about six or more is a good rule of thumb). If we look at the pie graph for the age distribution of students, we can see that if there were any more slices to the pie the chart would begin to look a little cluttered.

Bar graphs

When there are many values for a variable, a pie graph can look clumsy and lose its illustrative power. In such a situation a bar graph (often called a bar chart) might be preferred. Bar graphs emphasize the frequency of cases in each category *relative to each other*, rather than (as with pie graphs) relative to the total number of cases.

A bar graph has two sides or axes:

- Along the horizontal base of the graph are the values of the variable. This axis of the bar graph is called the **abscissa**.
- Along the left vertical side of the graph are the frequencies, expressed either as the raw count or as percentages of the total number of cases. This vertical axis is known as the **ordinate**.

> A **bar graph** presents the frequency of each category as a rectangle rising vertically above each category label, with the height of the bar proportional to the frequency of the respective category.

Using this logic we get the simple bar graphs for the distribution of students according to sex and attitude to statistics, as shown in Figures 3.3 and 3.4.

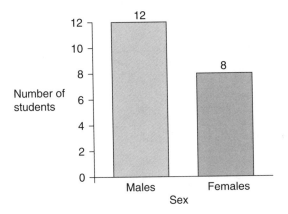

Figure 3.3   A bar graph illustrating the distribution of statistics students by sex.

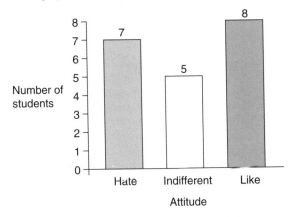

Figure 3.4   Distribution of students by attitude to statistics.

One advantage of bar graphs is that a number of distributions can be layered on top of each other into a single chart, provided the scale of measurement is the same. This is called a **component bar graph** or **stacked bar graph** and is especially helpful in comparing distributions over time. Each bar is divided into layers, with the area of each layer proportional to the frequency of the category it represents. For example, the class instructor may want to compare the distribution of his current group of students in terms of attitude to statistics with those for the previous 2 years (Table 3.5).

Table 3.5   Students' attitude to statistics, 1993–95

Attitude	1993	1994	1995
Like	3	6	8
Indifferent	9	6	5
Hate	15	11	7
Total	27	23	20

Translating this into a stacked bar graph we get a valuable comparison as shown in Figure 3.5.

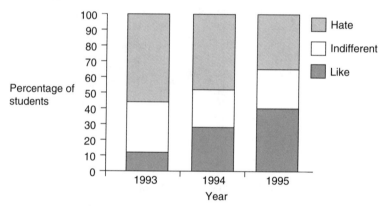

Figure 3.5   Distribution of students by attitude to statistics, 1993–95.

We can immediately see that, relatively speaking, students are becoming more positive about studying statistics (in this hypothetical class at least). Notice that we are using percentages in this graph to standardize the distributions, since the totals for each year vary. Stacked bar graphs have the same limitations as pie graphs, especially when there are too many values stacked on top of each other. The previous graph contained only three values stacked on top of each other to form each bar, but when there are more than five, and some of the layers are very small, the extra detail hinders the comparison across years that we want to make, rather than illuminating it.

An alternative is to sit the bars for each category side-by-side along the horizontal. For example, I may have another class of 20 students who responded to the same questionnaire. (See Figure 3.6.)

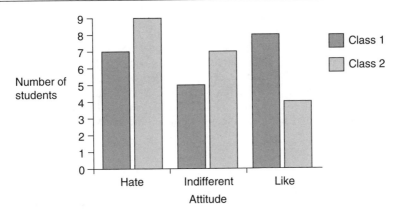

Figure 3.6 Distribution of two different sets of students by attitude to statistics.

I can quickly compare the two classes and see that the second class does not warm to statistics as much as the first!

Histograms

Bar graphs constructed for nominal and ordinal data always have gaps between each of the bars. This indicates that the scales of measurement are not continuous: there is no gradation between male and female, for example. Variables measured at the interval/ratio level, on the other hand, are often continuous. A person's age, for example, is continuous, in the sense that it progressively increases. Even though we have chosen discrete values for age to organize the data, as we discussed in Chapter 2 there are actually continuous intervals around these values called class intervals. As a result, the bars on a histogram, unlike a bar graph, are 'pushed together' so they touch. The class mid-points are displayed along the horizontal, and a rectangle whose width is set by the real class limits is erected over each point. The area of each rectangle is proportional to the frequency of the class in the overall distribution.

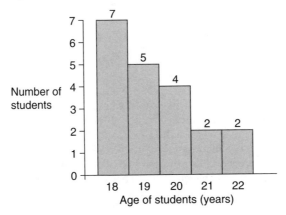

Figure 3.7 A histogram showing age distribution.

Using the example of the age distribution of students we can construct the histogram shown in Figure 3.7.

We can see that the area for the rectangle over 18 years of age, as a proportion of the total area under the histogram, is equal to the proportion of all cases having this age. The histogram indicates that we are using class intervals, and the real class limits for these intervals are 17.5–18.5 years, 18.5–19.5 years, 19.5–20.5 years, 20.5–21.5 years, and 21.5–22.5 years, with the stated ages of 18, 19, 20, 21, and 22 acting as the mid-points of the intervals.

Frequency polygons

When working with continuous interval/ratio data, we can represent the distribution in a slightly different way from that of a histogram. If we place a dot on the top and centre of each bar in a histogram, and connect the dots, we produce a **frequency polygon**. (See Figure 3.8.)

A **frequency polygon** is a continuous line formed by plotting the mid-points of each class interval against the class frequency.

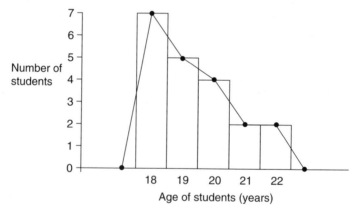

Figure 3.8 A frequency polygon.

Notice that the polygon begins and ends on a frequency of zero. To explain why we 'close' the polygon in this way we can think of this distribution as having seven values for age rather than five by including the class intervals for those students whose age to the nearest whole year is 17 and 23. Since there are no such students in this group the dot at the mid-point of these intervals (16.5–17.5, and 22.5–23.5) is on the abscissa, indicating a frequency of zero.

There are certain common shapes to polygons that appear in social research. For example, Figure 3.9 illustrates the bell-shaped (symmetric) curve, the J-shaped curve, and the U-shaped curve. The bell-shaped curve is one we will explore in much greater length in later chapters.

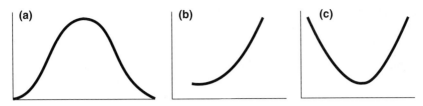

Figure 3.9   Three polygon shapes: a bell-shaped curve (**a**); a J-shaped curve (**b**); a U-shaped curve (**c**).

One aspect of frequency polygons (and histograms) that will be of utmost importance in later chapters needs to be pointed out, even though its relevance may not be immediately obvious. A polygon is constructed in such a way that the area under the curve between any two points on the horizontal, as a proportion of the total area, is equal to the proportion of cases in the distribution that have that range of values. Thus the shaded area in Figure 3.10, as a proportion of the total area under the curve, is equal to the proportion of cases that are aged 21 or above. This is 4/20, which is 0.2 of all cases.

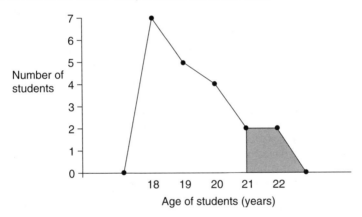

Age of students (years)

Figure 3.10   The area under the curve between any two points on the horizontal is equal to the proportion of cases in the distribution that have that range of values.

Another way of looking at this is to say that the **probability** of randomly selecting a student aged 21 years or more from this group is equal to the proportion of the total area under the curve that is shaded. This probability is 0.2, or a one-in-five chance of selecting a student in this age group.

Common problems and misuses of graphs

Unfortunately graphs lend themselves to considerable misuse. Practically every day in a newspaper we can find one (if not all) of the following 'tricks', which can give a misleading impression of the data. (For those wishing to look at this issue further the starting point is Darrell Huff's cheap, readable, and entertaining classic, *How to Lie with Statistics*, W.W. Norton & Co, New York, various printings.)

Relative size of axes The same data can give different graphical 'pictures' depending on the relative sizes of the two axes. By stretching either the abscissa or the ordinate the graph can be 'flattened' or 'peaked' depending on the impression that we might desire to convey. Consider for example the data represented in Figure 3.11.

This provides two alternate ways of presenting the same data. The data are for a hypothetical example of the percentage of respondents who gave a certain answer to a survey item over a number of years. Graph (**a**) has the ordinate (the vertical) 'compressed' relative to graph (**b**); similarly graph (**b**) has the abscissa (the horizontal) relatively more 'compressed'. The effect is to make the data seem much smoother in graph (a) — the rise and fall in responses is not so dramatic. In graph (b) on the other hand, there is a very sharp rise and then fall, making the change appear dramatic. Yet the two pictures describe the same data!

In order to avoid such distortions the convention in research is to construct graphs, wherever possible, such that the vertical axis is around two-thirds to three-quarters the length of the horizontal.

Truncation of the ordinate A similar effect to the one just described can be achieved by cutting out a section of the ordinate. Consider the data on the relative pay of women to men in a given country between 1950 and 1975, shown in Figure 3.12.

Graph (**a**) is complete in the sense that the vertical axis goes from 0 through to 100 per cent. The vertical axis in graph (**b**) though has been truncated: a large section of the scale between 0 per cent and 50 per cent has been removed and replaced by a squiggly line to indicate the truncation. The effect is obvious: the improvement in women's relative pay after 1965 seems very dramatic, as opposed to the slight increase reflected in graph (**a**).

Selection of the start and end points of the abscissa This is especially relevant with data that describe a pattern of change over time. Varying the date at which to begin the data series and to end it can give different impressions. For example, we may begin in a year in which the results were unusually low, thereby giving the impression of increase over subsequent years, and vice versa if we choose to begin with a year in which results 'peaked'. Consider, for example, the time series of data over a 15 year period shown in Figure 3.13.

The overall picture is of a moderate rise over the 15 years with a downturn in the middle. If the horizontal axes ended in 1988, though, the impression would be that things were on the decline. If 1988 is used as the starting point, on the other hand, the impression is of steady increase.

(a)

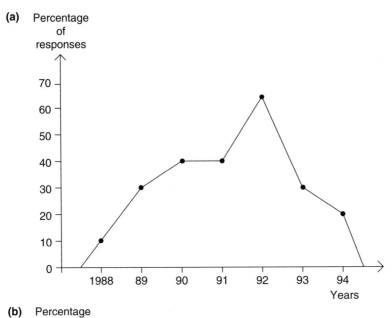

(b)

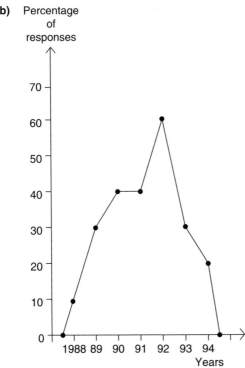

Figure 3.11   Two ways of presenting data.

(a)   Percentage

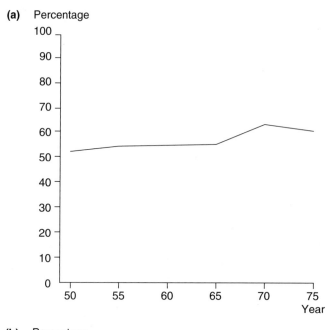

(b)   Percentage

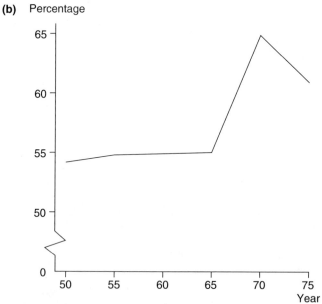

Figure 3.12   Women's income as a percentage of men's income, 1950–75 presented in two different ways.

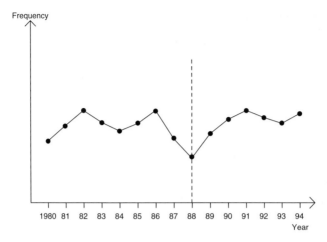

Figure 3.13

Exercises

3.1 Explain the difference between a bar graph and a histogram.

3.2 Survey your own statistics class in terms of the variables age, sex, and attitude to statistics. Use the graphing techniques outlined in this chapter to describe your results. Use the appropriate graphing techniques to compare your results with those in this chapter.

3.3 In Exercise 2.6 the following data were used to construct a frequency table (time, in minutes, taken for subjects to complete a certain task):

12	3	45	26	23	56	45	8	35	37	25
42	32	58	8	7	19	16	56	21	34	36
10	38	12	48	38	37	3	42	27	39	17
31	56	28	40	8	27	37				

Using the class intervals from your answer to 2.6 select an appropriate graphing technique to illustrate the distribution. Justify your choice against the other available options.

3.4 Consider the following list of prices, in whole dollars, for 20 used cars:

8600	9200	8200	11 300	10 600
7980	11 100	12 900	10 750	9200
13 630	9400	11 800	10 200	12 240
11 670	10 000	11 250	12 750	12 990

From these data:

(a) Construct a raw frequency table using class intervals 7000–8499, 8500–9999, 10 000–11 499, 11 500–12 999, 13 000–14 499.

(b) Construct a histogram using these class intervals.

(c) Construct a frequency polygon using these class intervals.

3.5 Construct a pie graph to describe the following data:

Migrants in local area, place of origin

Place	Number
Asia	900
Africa	1200
Europe	2100
South America	1500
Other	300
Total	6000

What feature of this distribution does your pie graph mainly illustrate?

3.6 From a recent newspaper or magazine find examples of the use of graphs. Do these examples follow the rules outlined in this chapter?

Measures of central tendency and measures of dispersion

The previous two chapters looked at ways of describing data in tabular and graphical form. These forms of describing data give some sense of the overall distribution of cases. However, we sometimes want to capture something a little more specific about the data: what does the 'typical' or 'average' case look like? Similarly, we might ask how much variety or similarity there is among the cases. For example, we might know that the average score in an exam is 65, and that all the scores lie between a minimum of 24 and a maximum of 87. The first of these numbers (65) — which represents the 'average' or 'typical' score — is called a **measure of central tendency**. The second set — which indicates the spread of cases across the values of the variable — is called a **measure of dispersion**.

Measures of central tendency

Measures of central tendency indicate the typical or average value of a distribution.

There are three common measures of central tendency or average: mode, median, and mean. Choice of the appropriate measure of central tendency depends on the level at which a variable is measured (Table 4.1).

Table 4.1   Measures of central tendency

Measure	Level of measurement
Mode	Interval/ratio, ordinal, nominal
Median	Interval/ratio, ordinal
Mean	Interval/ratio

To see how each of these measures of central tendency is calculated we will use the tables from Chapter 2 containing the hypothetical results shown in Tables 4.2, 4.3 and 4.4.

Table 4.2 Sex of students

Sex	Frequency
Female	8
Male	12
Total	20

Table 4.3 Attitude to statistcs

Attitude	Frequency
Like	8
Indifferent	5
Hate	7
Total	20

Table 4.4 Age in years

Age	Frequency
18	7
19	5
20	4
21	2
22	2
Total	20

The mode

We will start with the nominal level of measurement and the distribution of cases between male and female. At this level, the only measure of central tendency that is appropriate is the **mode** (M_o).

> The **mode** is the value or category of a distribution with the highest number of cases.

The mode is the only measure of central tendency that can be calculated for nominal data, and even with ordinal and interval/ratio data its great advantage over other choices is that it is calculated very easily. A simple inspection of a raw frequency table is enough to determine the modal value or category.

For example, the category for sex of students that has the highest frequency is male, with 12 responses (see Table 4.2); that is, the mode (M_o) = Male.

Although it is exceptionally easy to determine the mode, occasionally people make the mistake of specifying the *frequency* that occurs the most as the mode. That is, sometimes 12 might be reported as the mode for Table 4.2 since this is the highest frequency. This is incorrect — the important point to remember is that the *value* or *category* of the variable is the mode, not the number of times it appears in the distribution.

One thing to note is that, unlike the other measures of central tendency, there can be more than one mode for the same distribution. For example, assume we have the distribution for age shown in Table 4.5.

Table 4.5   Age in years

Age	Frequency
18	7
19	5
20	4
21	2
22	7
Total	25

We can see that two categories have the highest frequency: 18 years and 22 years. Such a distribution is bimodal.

The median
We can also calculate the modal response for attitude to statistics, which is measured at the ordinal level. More students responded that they 'liked statistics' than any other particular response. But for ordinal (and interval/ratio) data we can also calculate the **median** (M_d) score. If all the cases are ranked from lowest to highest, the median is the value of the case in the middle of the distribution.

> For an odd number of cases, the **median** is the middle score for a rank-ordered set of cases.
>
> For an even number of cases, the **median** is the average of the two middle scores for a rank-ordered set of cases.

Thus if I lined up the 20 students in the survey, starting with the 7 that hate statistics at one end, then the 5 that are indifferent, and then the 8 that like statistics, we can see that the mid point of the distribution (between the 10th and 11th students in line) is in the indifferent group (Figure 4.1).

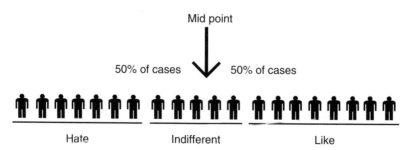

Mid point

50% of cases   50% of cases

Hate   Indifferent   Like

Figure 4.1

Table 4.6   Attitude to statistics

Attitude	Frequency
Like	8
Indifferent	5
Hate	7
Total	20

Mode: Like
Median: Indifferent

Interval/ratio data can also be rank-ordered so that a median can be calculated. For the age distribution of students the median will be as shown in Figure 4.2.

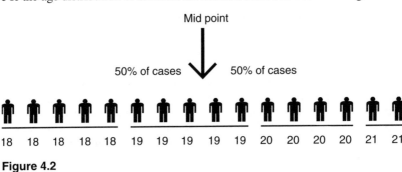

Figure 4.2

With an even number of cases, as we have here, the median is the average of the two middle scores. Here both middle scores are 19, so the median will be 19:

$$\text{Median} = \frac{19 + 19}{2}$$

$$= 19 \text{ years}$$

However, if the 10th student was 19 years of age, and the 11th was 20 years of age, the median would be:

$$\text{Median} = \frac{19 + 20}{2}$$

$$= 19.5 \text{ years}$$

If a cumulative frequency table has been generated, an easier way to calculate the median is to identify the value at which the cumulative frequency passes 50 per cent (Table 4.7).

Table 4.7   Age of respondents

Age	Frequency	Cumulative percentage (%)
18	7	35
19	5	60
20	4	80
21	2	90
22	2	100
Total	20	

Example
Find the median score for the following data: 93, 25, 87, 3, 56, 64, 12.
First we rank-order these from lowest to highest:

Score:	3	12	25	56	64	87	93
Rank:	1	2	3	4	5	6	7

Since there are 7 cases (an odd number) the median value will be the 4th in line, which is 56.
If the same data set included one additional value of 98 the rank-ordering would be:

Score:	3	12	25	56	64	87	93	98
Rank:	1	2	3	4	5	6	7	8

We now have 8 cases (an even number). The median will therefore be the average of the 4th and 5th values:

$$\text{Median} = \frac{56 + 64}{2} = 60$$

The mean

With interval/ratio data the (arithmetic) **mean** can also be calculated. This is the notion of average that is most commonly used, and involves a simple calculation.

> The **arithmetic mean** is the sum of all the scores in a distribution divided by the total number of cases.

When calculating the mean for an entire population we use the symbol μ (pronounced 'mu'). When calculating the mean of a sample, we use the symbol $\overline{X}$ (pronounced 'X-bar'). In either case, the equation for the mean will be:

$$\mu = \frac{\Sigma X_i}{N}$$

$$\bar{X} = \frac{\Sigma X_i}{N}$$

where:

N is all cases from which a measurement is taken.

The Greek letter, Σ (pronounced sigma), means 'the sum of' (or 'add up'), and X_i is each individual score. So we would 'read' these equations in the following way: 'the mean equals the sum of all scores divided by the number of cases'. Thus if I had the following distribution of sample scores:

$$12, \quad 15, \quad 19, \quad 21$$

the mean will be:

$$\bar{X} = \frac{\Sigma X_i}{N} = \frac{12 + 15 + 19 + 21}{4} = 16.75$$

With the hypothetical sample of statistics student we do not have the age for each student listed individually. Instead we have a frequency distribution of data grouped in years. In this case we use the following formula to calculate the mean:

$$\bar{X} = \frac{\Sigma f X_i}{N}$$

This formula instructs us to multiply each value in the distribution by the frequency (f) with which it occurs; sum these products; and divide by the number of cases. Here we have seven students aged 18, five aged 19, four aged 20, two aged 21, and another two aged 22. The mean is:

$$\bar{X} = \frac{(18 \times 7) + (19 \times 5) + (20 \times 4) + (21 \times 2) + (22 \times 2)}{20}$$

$$\bar{X} = 19.35 \text{ years}$$

Sometimes frequency tables only specify the class intervals in which data fall, rather than the specific values and the frequency with which each value occurs. For example, we may have the distribution of scores shown in Table 4.8.

Table 4.8

Scores	Frequency
1–5	7
6–10	10
11–15	6
Total	23

With grouped data presented in terms of class limits, we multiply the frequency by the class mid-point (m):

$$\overline{X} = \frac{\Sigma fm}{N}$$

Thus for data in the example the mid-points and the mid-points multiplied by the frequency of each class are as given in Table 4.9.

Table 4.9   Calculations for the mean for grouped data

Scores	Mid-point (m)	Frequency (f)	fm
1–5	3	7	21
6–10	8	10	80
11–15	13	6	78
Total		N = 23	Σfm = 179

Substituting this information into the formula we get (rounding to one decimal point):

$$\overline{X} = \frac{\Sigma fm}{N}$$

$$= \frac{179}{23}$$

$$= 7.8$$

Choosing a measure of central tendency

We have seen that it is possible to calculate all the measures of central tendency on a variable measured at the interval/ratio level, such as age in years (Table 4.10).

Table 4.10   Age in years

Age	Frequency
18	7
19	5
20	4
21	2
22	2
Total	20

Mode: 18
Median: 19
Mean: 19.3

It is clear from Table 4.10 that measures of central tendency will not always give the same answer, even when calculated on the same raw data. This is because each measure defines 'typical' in a slightly different way. In fact, unless the distribution is perfectly **symmetrical**, that is if the distribution is **skewed**, there will always be some difference in the various measures of central tendency. We can see examples of symmetrical and skewed distributions in Figure 4.3.

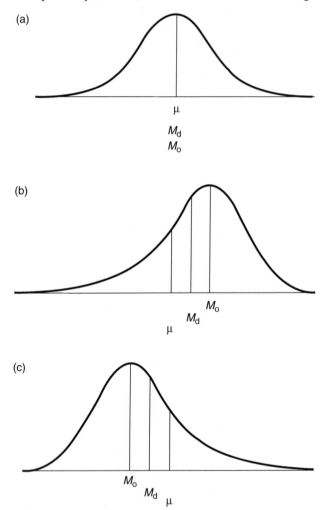

Figure 4.3 Relationship among the mean μ, median M_d, and mode M_o for a bell-shaped curve (symmetrical) (**a**); a distribution skewed to the left (**b**); and a distribution skewed to the right (**c**).

The symmetrical curve has a nice bell-shape, and the measures of central tendency are equal, but with skewed distributions the measures diverge. Notice also that in describing the direction to which a distribution is skewed we refer to the side of the curve that has the long tail, and not the side with the 'hump'.

Generally, when a distribution is heavily skewed, the mean is a misleading notion of 'average'. The reason is that the mean uses every case in the distribution and is therefore influenced by extreme scores (called outliers). For example, we may have the following exam scores:

$$X_1 = 60$$
$$X_2 = 64$$
$$X_3 = 66$$
$$X_4 = 70$$
$$X_5 = 71$$

The mean for this distribution is:

$$\overline{X} = \frac{\Sigma X_i}{N}$$

$$\overline{X} = \frac{60 + 64 + 66 + 70 + 71}{5}$$

$$\overline{X} = 66.2$$

Consider the effect on the mean if the scores vary only slightly so that the fifth score is 90 instead of 71:

$$X_1 = 60$$
$$X_2 = 64$$
$$X_3 = 66$$
$$X_4 = 70$$
$$X_5 = 90$$

Even though only one score has changed, the value of the mean has changed dramatically:

$$\overline{X} = \frac{\Sigma X_i}{N}$$

$$\overline{X} = \frac{60 + 64 + 66 + 70 + 90}{5}$$

$$\overline{X} = 70$$

The 'average' student suddenly looks a lot smarter, because of this one change. However, the median for both distributions is 66: this is the score that the student in the middle of the distribution received. Since the median depends solely on the value of this one score at the mid point, it is not 'pulled' in one direction or another by scores at the extreme ends of the range, and is therefore best used for skewed distributions.

Measures of dispersion

We have seen that there are various ways by which the average of a distribution can be conceptualized and calculated. But how average is average? Consider the two distributions of cases according to annual income shown in Table 4.11.

Table 4.11   Annual incomes

Group A ($)	Group B ($)
$X_1 = 5000$	$X_1 = 20000$
$X_2 = 6500$	$X_1 = 28500$
$X_3 = 8000$	$X_3 = 35000$
$X_4 = 55000$	$X_4 = 36000$
$X_5 = 85000$	$X_5 = 40000$

The mean income for each of these groups is:

$$\overline{X}_A = \frac{5000 + 6500 + 8000 + 55\,000 + 85\,000}{5} = \$31\,900$$

$$\overline{X}_B = \frac{20\,000 + 28\,500 + 35\,000 + 36\,000 + 40\,000}{5} = \$31\,900$$

These distributions have the same mean, yet it is clear that there is also a major difference between the two. Although the mean is the same, the spread or **dispersion** of scores is very different.

Measures of dispersion are descriptive statistics that indicate the spread or variety of scores in a distribution.

The range

The simplest measure of dispersion is the **range**.

The **range** is the difference between the smallest score and the largest score in a distribution.

This is a quickly and easily calculated measure of dispersion, because it involves a straightforward subtraction of one score from another. Thus for the two distributions of income the ranges will be:

$$R_A = 85\,000 - 5000 = \$80\,000$$
$$R_B = 40\,000 - 20\,000 = \$20\,000$$

We can immediately see that even though the two distributions have the same mean, there is considerable difference in the spread of scores around this average. Group A has much more variation.

The advantage of the range as a measure of dispersion is that it is very easily calculated, since it is simply the subtraction of one number from another. However, this advantage is also its major limitation: it only uses the extreme scores, and therefore changes with the values of the two extreme scores. Consider the distribution of income for group B, which falls within the range of $20 000 to $40 000. If we add a sixth person to this group, whose annual income is $150 000, the range is suddenly stretched out by this one score. It is now $130 000. To compensate for the effect of such outliers, a slight variation on the range, called the **interquartile range** can be generated.

The interquartile range

The interquartile range (IQR) overcomes the problems that can arise with the simple range by ignoring the extreme outliers of a distribution.

> The **interquartile range** is the difference between the upper limits of the first quartile and third quartile. In other words, it is the range for the middle 50 per cent of rank-ordered cases.

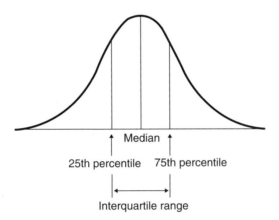

Figure 4.4   The interquartile range

To see how the IQR is calculated we will use the age data from the 20 statistics students. There are 20 students, so each quartile will consist of $^{20}/_4 =$ 5 students. The first quartile ends with a student 18 years of age. The third quartile ends with a student (the 15th student) who is 20 years of age (Figure 4.5).

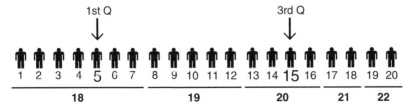

Figure 4.5

The interquartile range is:

$$IQR = 20 - 18 = 2 \text{ years}$$

This figure will not change dramatically if we add one or two people who are much older or much younger to either end of the distribution.

Deciles

A similar indication of the spread of scores, but one that uses even more information, is the calculation of **deciles**. The set of cases is rank-ordered, and 'split' into 10 groups of equal size. This is commonly used to analyse data on the distribution of income. For example, we could order all families in a certain population in terms of income, from the poorest to the richest, and then split them into 10 equally sized groups. The first decile comprises the 10 per cent of families that are poorest, the second decile comprises the next 10 per cent of families, right through to the tenth decile, which comprises the richest 10 per cent of families. By looking at the proportion of total income held by each decile, we can get a sense of income distribution and the nature of changes that have occurred (Table 4.12).

Table 4.12   Distribution of gross income, by decile 1981 and 1989

Decile	Share of gross income 1981	Share of gross income 1989
Lowest	1.9	1.7
Second	3.0	2.8
Third	4.3	3.9
Fourth	5.6	5.2
Fifth	7.5	6.8
Sixth	9.2	8.6
Seventh	11.1	10.7
Eighth	13.6	13.4
Ninth	17.1	17.3
Highest	26.8	29.4

It is clear that the distribution of gross income has become less egalitarian over these years (according to this measure), with all deciles losing some of their 1981 share, except for the 20 per cent of the richest families, who increased their share of the 'pie'.

The standard deviation

Many readers will have had the experience of dining out with a large group of people, where one or two people proceed to order expensive meals and lots of drinks, and when the bill arrives they suggest dividing it up evenly to make the calculation of everyone's share easier! Everyone at the dinner table will be fairly aware of the difference between the value of their own dinner and the cost of the 'average' meal so that they can gauge whether paying the average will put them ahead or behind. In this situation everyone is aware of the difference between average and spread, and how the mean may be a misleading representation of a distribution when taken just on its own.

In a similar manner the standard deviation tries to capture the average distance that each score is from the average. The standard deviation assesses spread by employing in its calculation the difference between each score and the mean. When calculating the standard deviation for a *sample*, we use the symbol *s*, and the formula:[1]

$$s = \sqrt{\frac{\Sigma(X_i - \overline{X})^2}{N - 1}}$$

When calculating the standard deviation for a *population* we use the Greek symbol σ, and the formula:

$$\sigma = \sqrt{\frac{\Sigma(X_i - \mu)^2}{N}}$$

If we look closely at each of these formulas[2] we can see how they capture this idea that the standard deviation is the average distance that each score is from the average. The numerator is simply the difference between each score and the mean, and the denominator adjusts those differences by the number of observations. The formulas are slightly more complicated, since the differences are squared and the square root of the whole lot taken (for reasons that are not necessary to the present discussion), but the basic idea is still evident.

To focus on the notion of standard deviation more sharply, consider again the distribution of ages in the class of 20 statistics students. We have already calculated the mean to be 19.3 years. All the scores deviate from the mean to a greater or lesser degree, either above or below it. This is illustrated in Figure 4.6. The age of each student is plotted on a graph, with the line for the mean age running down the middle. The distance from the mean to each student's age is then drawn in. Students 7 and 13 are relatively a long way above the mean, while students 5, 8, 12, 14, and 18 are only slightly below the mean. What is the average of these distances?

Unfortunately, we cannot simply add all the positive deviations (scores above the mean) with all the negative deviations (scores below the mean), since by definition, this will sum to zero. This is why the equation for the standard deviation squares the differences: it thereby turns all the deviations into positive numbers, so that the larger the differences, the greater the value of the standard deviation.

---

[1] Another closely related measure of dispersion that will occasionally crop up in later discussion is the variance. This is simply the square of the standard deviation (s^2).

[2] The reason why 1 is subtracted from the sample size in the formula for a sample is due to a technical point that we will explore in later chapters. For the moment we just note this difference in the formulas for a sample and a population.

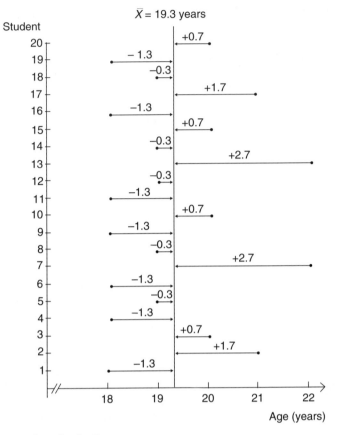

Figure 4.6   Age distribution

Let us actually calculate the standard deviation for this distribution. We can use the equation above, but we have only introduced it because it captures the idea of the average distance from the mean. In actually calculating the standard deviation we work with a slightly different equation that is easier to compute, but will always give us the same answer as the equation above:

$$s = \sqrt{\frac{\Sigma X_i^2 - \frac{(\Sigma X_i)^2}{N}}{N-1}}$$

The term ΣX_i^2 reads 'the sum of all the squared scores', while the term $(\Sigma X_i)^2$ reads 'sum of all the scores squared'. For the first term we square all the scores and then add them all, while the second term reverses the procedure: we add up the scores and then square the total.

Table 4.13 goes through each of these steps.

Table 4.13   Calculations for the standard deviation of the age of students

Student	Age in years X_i	X_i^2
1	18	324
2	21	441
3	20	400
4	18	324
5	19	361
6	18	324
7	22	484
8	19	361
9	18	324
10	20	400
11	18	324
12	19	361
13	22	484
14	19	361
15	20	400
16	18	324
17	21	441
18	19	361
19	18	324
20	20	400
	$(\Sigma X_i) = 387$	$\Sigma X_i^2 = 7523$

Substituting these numbers into the equation, we get:

$$s = \sqrt{\frac{\Sigma X_i^2 - \frac{(\Sigma X_i)^2}{N}}{N-1}}$$

$$= \sqrt{\frac{7523 - \frac{(387)^2}{20}}{20-1}}$$

$$= \sqrt{\frac{7523 - 7488.45}{19}}$$

$$= 1.348 \text{ years}$$

There is no absolute way of saying whether 1.348 years is a large or small dispersion of scores around the mean. Moreover, the standard deviation for one set of observations cannot be compared with that for another in order to decide which distribution is the more disperse. For example, two distributions may have standard deviations of 1.3 years, but if the means of each are 5 years and 50 years respectively, it is clear that this standard deviation represents relatively more variation for the distribution with the smaller mean. To account for this, to provide a standardized measure of dispersion, we can calculate the **coefficient of relative variation**, which expresses the standard deviation as a percentage of the mean:

$$CRV = \frac{s}{\overline{X}} \times 100$$

In Table 4.13 we listed each student's age separately. However, we often group data in a frequency table, since listing each individual score in a distribution separately can be an inefficient way of presenting information. With grouped data organized in a frequency table we use the following formula to compute the standard deviation:

$$s = \sqrt{\frac{\Sigma f X_i^2 - \frac{(\Sigma f X_i)^2}{N}}{N-1}}$$

where:
   f is the frequency of each value in the distribution.

In other words, we multiply each value by the frequency with which it appears in a distribution. Thus if we were working with the grouped data for age, rather than with a complete list of all ages, the computations would be as shown in Table 4.14.

Table 4.14   Age (in years) of statistics students

Age X_i	Frequency f	X_i^2	fX_i^2	fX_i
18	7	$18 \times 18 = 324$	$7 \times 324 = 2268$	$7 \times 18 = 126$
19	5	$19 \times 19 = 361$	$5 \times 361 = 1805$	$5 \times 19 = 95$
20	4	400	1600	80
21	2	441	882	42
22	2	484	968	44
			$\Sigma fX_i^2 = 7523$	$(\Sigma fX_i) = 387$

$$s = \sqrt{\frac{\Sigma f X_i^2 - \frac{(\Sigma f X_i)^2}{N}}{N-1}}$$

$$= \sqrt{\frac{7523 - \frac{(387)^2}{20}}{20 - 1}}$$

$$= \sqrt{\frac{34.55}{19}}$$

$$= 1.348 \text{ years}$$

We get the same answer as when we listed each case separately.

Summary

We have worked through a number of ways of summarizing data and displaying a distribution. Many formulas and rules have been encountered and the options may seem a little overwhelming. Fortunately, computers have made life easy for us, and all the measures we have introduced can be generated with the click of a button. However, life should not get too easy. There is a level of understanding that is obtained by working through the hand calculations, especially an understanding of the limits to many of the techniques we have introduced.

Exercises

4.1 Can we calculate the mean on ordinal data? Why or why not?

4.2 What are the advantages and disadvantages of the range as a measure of dispersion?

4.3 Calculate the mean and median, and the range and standard deviation for each of the following distributions:

(a) 5,   9,   13,   15,   26,   72
(b) 121,   134,   145,   212,   289,   306,   367,   380,   453
(c) 1.2,   1.4,   1.9,   2.0,   2.4,   3.5,   3.9,   4.3,   5.2

4.4 A student switched from one class to another. His 'friends' suggested that such a move raised the average IQ of each class. What does this comment suggest about the relationship of this student's IQ to the average in each class.

4.5 Consider the following data set:

43, 22, 56, 39, 59, 73, 60, 75, 80, 11, 36, 66, 45, 57, 20, 36, 68, 87, 50, 68, 9.

(a) Rank-order these values and determine the median.
(b) Calculate the mean.
(c) By comparing the value for the mean and the median, determine whether the distribution is symmetric, skewed to the left, or skewed to the right.
(d) If a score of 194 is added to this data set, how will it affect the median and the mean? Explain the changes to the previous calculation for these measures.

4.6 Consider the following data regarding the annual income (in $'000) for people employed in a particular agency:

12	40	22	30	18	36	45	19	22	22	37	35
72	28	36	29	42	56	52	35	16	23	37	26
22	29	35	73	62							

(a) Calculate the mean, median, and mode for these data.
(b) Calculate the range, interquartile range, and standard deviation for these data.

4.7 In Exercise 2.6 the following data (time, in minutes, taken for subjects to complete a certain task) were used to construct a frequency table using class intervals:

12	3	45	26	23	56	45	8	35	37	25
42	32	58	8	7	19	16	56	21	34	36
10	38	12	48	38	37	3	42	27	39	17
31	56	28	40	8	27	37				

Calculate the mean and median, using both the raw data and the grouped data. Are these values different from your calculations for the ungrouped data? Explain.

4.8 Consider the following data sets:

Degree of enrolment

Value labels	Value	Frequency
Social Science	1	32
Arts	2	45
Economics	3	21
Law	4	13
Other	5	8

Time spent studying for an exam

Value labels	Value	Frequency
1 hour	1	12
2 hours	2	25
3 hours	3	27
4 hours	4	30
5 hours	5	26

Satisfaction with employment

Value labels	Value	Frequency
Very dissatisfied	1	12
Not satisfied	2	25
Satisfied	3	92
Very satisfied	4	38

For each of the data sets:
(a) Indicate the level of measurement.
(b) Calculate all possible measures of central tendency. Explain any differences between the measures and discuss which is most appropriate.

4.9 Consider the following data from a survey of employees of a factory:

School years completed

Years	Number of employees
1–4	127
5–8	500
9–12	784
13–16	59
17–20	8

(a) Calculate the mean, median, and mode of this distribution.
(b) If they differ, explain why.
(c) Which measure of central tendency is the most appropriate description of the data?

5

Descriptive statistics on SPSS

The previous chapters raised some of the conceptual issues involved in defining and measuring variables, and then describing the results using graphs, tables, and summary statistics. To illustrate the issues involved, we made use of the data from a hypothetical survey of 20 statistics students.

Table 5.1   Results of a survey of statistics students

Student	Sex	Attitude to statistics	Age
1	Male	Like	18
2	Male	Like	21
3	Female	Indifferent	20
4	Male	Hate	18
5	Female	Like	19
6	Male	Hate	18
7	Female	Hate	22
8	Male	Like	19
9	Female	Indifferent	18
10	Male	Indifferent	20
11	Male	Hate	18
12	Female	Like	19
13	Male	Like	22
14	Male	Like	19
15	Female	Hate	20
16	Female	Indifferent	18
17	Male	Hate	21
18	Female	Hate	19
19	Male	Indifferent	18
20	Male	Like	20

We can use SPSS to record this information (and we will be referring back and forth to this table throughout). When first running SPSS a window will appear with **untitled data** at the top (see Figure SPSS.A).

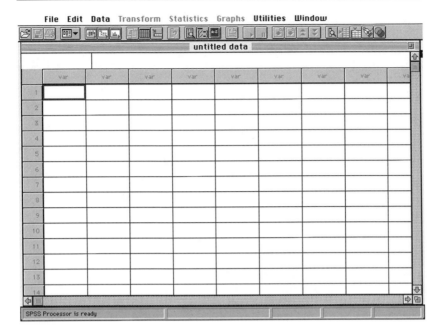

Figure SPSS.A

This is the 'data page' on which all the information will be entered. Think of it as a blank table, like Table 5.1 before any information was typed into it. At the top of the page is a menu of options.

File   Edit   Data   Transform   Statistics   Graphs   Utilities   Window

Figure SPSS.B

We enter and analyse data by selecting options from this menu. Usually selecting an option from the menu will bring up on the screen a small rectangular area, which we call a dialogue box or window, from which more specialized options are available, depending on the type of procedure we want to undertake. By the end of this chapter (hopefully) this way of hunting through the SPSS menu for the appropriate commands will be very familiar. In fact, it is very similar to many other software applications that readers have encountered, such as word processing and spreadsheet software.

The data window is made up of a series of columns and rows, which form little rectangles called *cells*. As with Table 5.1 above, each column will contain the information for each one of the variables, and each row will contain the information for each case. The first row of cells (the ones at the top of each column) are shaded and contain a faint **var**. This row of shaded cells will act like the first row of Table 5.1, which contains the names of the variables whose information is stored in each column. Similarly, the first column is shaded and contains faint numbers from 1 on. This is analogous to the first column in Table 5.1, which contains the numbers (1–20) that have been assigned to each student. These are sometimes called *case numbers.*

You should also observe that the unshaded cell at the top left of the page has a heavy border, which indicates that it is the **active cell** (Figure SPSS.C).

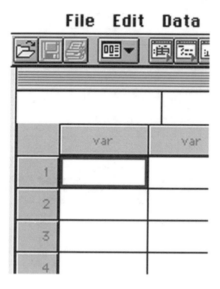

Figure SPSS.C

The active cell is the cell in which any information will be entered if I start typing. Any cell can be made active by simply pointing the cursor to it and clicking the mouse.

The process of data entry involves three basic steps, which we will work through individually. The first step involves attaching a variable label to the top of each column in which data will be stored; the second involves specifying the meaning of the values that will be entered in the cells; and the third is the actual data entry process.

Assigning variable labels: The Define Variable command

The first step in setting up an SPSS data file is to define the variables to be analysed using the **Define Variable** command. Table 5.2 shows the steps involved in preparing SPSS to receive data on the variable 'sex'.

Next we proceed to define the variable 'attitude to statistics' (See Table 5.3). This variable will occupy the second unshaded column so we need to make one of the cells in this column active by clicking on it. Setting up this column involves a slight complication, however, because of the length of the variable name. *SPSS will only allow variable names*

Table 5.2   Define Variable command on SPSS

SPSS command/action	Comment
1 Make any one of the cells in the first column active, and from the menu click on **Data**. When the pull-down menu appears select **Define Variable . . .** or double-click on the shaded cell with the faint **var** at the top of the first column	Try both methods to see that the result will be the same: a window headed **Define Variable** appears in front of the data page
2 In the area next to **Variable Name:** highlight over **VAR00001** and type **sex**	**VAR00001** is the name that SPSS will give the variable in column 1 unless we tell it otherwise
3 Click on **OK**	The **Define Variable** window will disappear, and **sex** will appear in the shaded cell at the top of column 1 instead of the faint **var** that was originally there

to have eight characters or less. So we need to think of some abbreviation for 'attitude to statistics'. We will use **attitude**. A problem might arise, however, if we relied solely on abbreviated variable names, especially when working with lots of variables. If we generated results and the output contained information about a variable called **attitude**, we may have forgotten by that point what that abbreviation really stands for. 'Attitude to what?' we might be left asking. Similarly, I might remember what **attitude** really refers to, but others looking at the results will be left scratching their heads. To guard against this, SPSS allows us to enter the 'long' variable name, called the **variable label**, if we have used an abbreviation as the title of a column. The long name will not appear on the data page, but will be printed with any results generated, so that in any output we will see that the brief variable name **attitude** is really a shorthand way of writing 'attitude to statistics'. (See Table 5.3.)

Now repeat the same procedure for age. With interval/ratio data it is helpful to use the **Variable Label** command to specify the units of measurement (for reasons we will detail shortly). Thus, although **age** is already brief, it will prove helpful to type **age in years** under the **Variable Label** command.

Defining values: The Value Labels command

Having defined the variables we are interested in, we can now proceed to define the range of scores or categories that each variable can take. The categories for each of the variables are initially described in words, called **value labels**. Thus sex has two value labels: female and male. To

Table 5.3   Define Variable command on SPSS, with variable labels

SPSS command/action	Comment
1 Bring up the **Define Variable** window either by pulling down the **Data** menu, or by double-clicking on the shaded cell at the top of the column	
2 Highlight over **VAR00001** and type in **attitude**	The abbreviation we choose to use for a variable that has a long name is arbitrary. We could type in **attstats**, instead of **attitude**; in fact we could type in **dog, house**, or any other word of eight characters or less. Ideally though, if we have to type in an abbreviated variable name, we should choose an abbreviation that gives some indication of the real variable we are interested in
3 Click on **Labels . . .**	This will bring up another window titled **Define Labels:** The cursor will be flashing next to **Variable Label:**
4 Type in **Attitude to Statistics**	
5 Click on **Continue**	
6 Click on **OK**	

perform statistical analysis, and to make data entry quicker, it is best to link each value label to a specific number or **value**.

Thus we assign a number to each value label, and enter these numbers into the data file. For example, with the variable 'sex' we could arbitrarily code female responses as 1, and male responses as 2. Instead of typing in male or female for each case, we type in the number assigned to each of these labels — a much faster procedure.

With a nominal scale such as 'sex' the actual numerical code given to each value label is arbitrary: we can just as easily reverse the order and assign 1 to male and 2 to female. In fact, we could assign 3 to female and 7 to male, or any other combination of values. But generally, the simpler the coding scheme the better. (See Table 5.4.)

With an ordinal scale, such as that used to measure 'attitude to statistics', we also assign a value to each value label. However, we have less discretion as to the choice of numbers to use, since these numbers need to preserve the ranking that ordinal scales are meant to reflect, with higher numbers indicating an increase in the quantity or intensity or strength of the variable. For example, we can assign 1 to 'hate', 2 to 'indifferent', and 3 to 'like'.

In this way, for nominal and ordinal data, each point on the scale is described twice: once using words and again using numbers. However,

Table 5.4   The Value Labels command on SPSS

SPSS command/action	Comment
1 Double-click on the shaded cell with **sex** contained in it	This will bring up the **Define Variable:** window
2 Click on **Labels . . .**	This will bring up the **Define Labels:** window
3 In the box next to **Value:** type **1**	
4 In the box next to **Value Label:** type **female**	You will notice that as soon as you start typing, **Add** suddenly darkens, whereas it was previously faint
5 Click on **Add**	This will paste the information into the adjacent area so that **1='female'**. The cursor will automatically jump back to the box next to **Value:**
6 Type **2**	
7 In the box next to **Value Label:** type **male**	Click on **Add**. This value and value label will now be added to the list, so that **2='male'**.
8 Click on **Continue**	
9 Click on **OK**	

we need to raise a word of caution when assigning values to the labels on an ordinal or nominal scale. Using numbers can give the impression that the variable is measured at the interval/ratio level when in fact it is only ordinal or nominal. For example, someone who scored 3 (Like) does not like statistics three times as much as someone who scored 1 (Hate). The numbers only indicate the group or category each case falls into, and with ordinal scales also give a sense of rank. These numbers do not actually quantify the variable in the strict sense of measuring the amount of the variable present.

With interval/ratio data this dual system of coding — one in words, one in numbers — is unnecessary because the values do quantify the variable. When defining the variable label for age we specified the unit of measurement: *'Age in Years'*, so that we know the quantity these numbers refer to. Thus the number assigned to any given case will indicate the number of units; for example, '19' indicates 19 years, '20' indicates 20 years, and so on. We do not need to then provide value labels for each of these numerical codes, since their meaning is self-evident.

The coding scheme for these three variables can be summarized as in Table 5.5.

In fact we can ask SPSS to provide this same information regarding variable definitions by selecting from the menu **Utilities/File Info** (see Figure SPSS.D).

Table 5.5 Coding scheme

Variable	Variable label	Value	Value label
Sex	(unnecessary since the variable name is short)	1 2	Female Male
Attitude	Attitude to statistics	1 2 3	Hate Indifferent Like
Age	Age in years	18–22	(unnecessary since the information is already in numerical format)

Figure SPSS.D

This will generate the following information in the output window, which can be printed off for reference during the analysis:

```
List of variables on the working file

Name                                                          Position

SEX                                                               1
          Print Format: F8
          Write Format: F8

          Value     Label

            1      female
            2      male

ATTITUDE  attitude to statistics                                  2
          Print Format: F8
          Write Format: F8
```

```
Value    Label

    1    hate
    2    indifferent
    3    like

AGE      Age in Years                                    3
         Print Format: F8
         Write Format: F8
```

The numbers under Position on the right-edge of the page indicate the column in which the variable appears.

Data entry

Once the variables and values have been defined, the data from the survey can be entered. We will begin with the information on the sex of each student. (See Table 5.6.)

Table 5.6 Data entry on SPSS

SPSS command/action	Comment
1 Click on the cell next to the shaded cell **1** and below the shaded cell **sex**	This will be the active cell, which is where any information typed will be pasted
2 Type **2**	This indicates that student 1 is male, according to the coding scheme specified in the **Value Labels** command
3 Press **return**	The label **male** should appear in the first cell, and the cell for student 2 will now be active
4 Type **2**	This indicates that student 2 is also male
5 Press **return**	The label **male** should appear in the second cell, and the cell for student 3 will now be active
6 Continue this procedure until the first 20 rows of this column contain either **male** or **female**	

Think how time consuming this data entry process would have been if we had to type male or female into each cell, rather than just 1 or 2: this should indicate the advantage of using the value labels command when setting up the data file.

To enter the data for **attitude** we need to make the first cell in the second unshaded column active by pointing the cursor to it and clicking. The student who has been assigned to be case 1 'likes' statistics. According to our coding scheme we therefore enter **3** into this cell by typing this number and pressing the **return** key. Student 2 also 'likes' statistics, so we repeat the procedure, and so on down to student 20.

Finally we make the first cell in the third unshaded column active and begin typing in each student's age.

If at any point we make a mistake, or we need to change the information in any particular cell, we simply make that cell active and type in the new information. On hitting the **return** key the new value will replace the old.

If all these procedures are followed the data page will look very much like Table 5.1 at the start of this chapter (see SPSS.E).

	sex	attitude	age	var	var	var	var	var	va
1	male	like	18						
2	male	like	21						
3	female	indiffere	20						
4	male	hate	18						
5	female	like	19						
6	male	hate	18						
7	female	hate	22						
8	male	like	19						
9	female	indiffere	18						
10	male	indiffere	20						
11	male	hate	18						
12	female	like	19						
13	male	like	22						
14	male	like	19						

Figure SPSS.E

We can alternately ask SPSS to display the values rather than the value labels on the data page by selecting **Utilities** from the menu and scrolling down to ✔**Value Labels** (Figure SPSS.F).

This will transform the data page so that it has only values appearing (Figure SPSS.G).

To bring back the value labels we simply repeat the procedure.

	sex	attitude	age	var	var	
1	male	like	18			
2	male	like	21			
3	female	indiffere	20			
4	male	hate	18			
5	female	like	19			
6	male	hate	18			
7	female	hate	22			

File Edit Data Transform Statistics Graphs Utilities Window

Utilities menu:
- Command Index...
- Fonts...
- Variables...
- File Info
- Output Page Titles...
- Define Sets...
- Use Sets...
- ✓ Grid Lines
- ✓ Value Labels
- ✓ Auto New Case
- Designate Window

Figure SPSS.F

File Edit Data Transform Statistics Graphs Utilities Window

untitled data

	sex	attitude	age	var	var	var	var	var	va
1	2	3	18						
2	2	3	21						
3	1	2	20						
4	2	1	18						
5	1	3	19						
6	2	1	18						
7	1	1	22						
8	2	3	19						
9	1	2	18						
10	2	2	20						
11	2	1	18						
12	1	3	19						
13	2	3	22						
14	2	3	19						

SPSS Processor is ready

Figure SPSS.G

Saving a data file

The last action we need to take in setting up the data window is to save the file (Table 5.7).

Table 5.7   Save As command on SPSS

SPSS command/action	Comment
1 From the menu select **File**	
2 From the pull-down menu select **Save As...**	
3 Type a file name	The limits on the length of the file name will depend on whether SPSS is running on a Macintosh or Windows environment
4 Specify a location on the hard disk or floppy disk to store the information	The exact procedure for doing this will vary depending on whether SPSS is running on a Macintosh or Microsoft Windows
5 Click on **Save**	

In fact, you should not wait until the end of your data entry session to save the file. Mishaps can happen, often at the worst time. Losing many data, after spending a considerable amount of time entering them, can be very demoralizing. We should get into the habit of saving work every 15 or so minutes. After using the **File/Save As...** command, a file can be quickly re-saved since we don't need to re-specify the file name or the location where it is stored, once this has been done the first time. To re-save a file we use the **File/Save Data** command instead of **File/Save As...** (Figure SPSS.H).

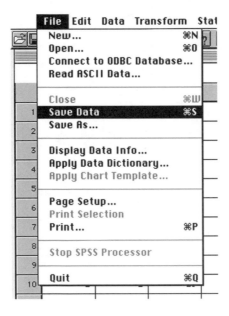

Figure SPSS.H

Opening a data file

Opening a data file that we have created in previous work sessions is much like saving the file. From the menu we select **File/Open...** and then select the appropriate directory and the file (Figure SPSS.I).

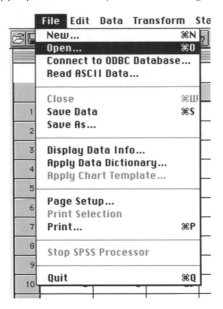

Figure SPSS.I

For example, the files that will be used in later chapters are all located on the floppy disks that came with this book. They can be selected by highlighting the appropriate file, or typing its name, once the floppy disk has been selected as the location where the files reside.

Frequency tables using SPSS

Now that we have entered the data with all the appropriate labels, we can generate frequency tables similar to those in Chapter 2. (See Table 5.8.)

The set of instructions shown in Table 5.8 will generate the minimum information available under the **Frequencies...** command: a table with raw, relative and cumulative frequencies (basically a computer-generated version of the tables in Chapter 2):

Table 5.8   The Frequencies command on SPSS

SPSS command/action	*Comment*
1 From the menu select **Statistics/Summarize... / Frequencies...**	This will bring up a dialogue box headed **Frequencies**. This will contain an area with a list of the variables for which data have been entered
2 Select the variable(s) to generate a frequency table by clicking on their name(s)	
3 Click on ➤	This will paste the selected variable(s) into the area below **Variable(s):**, which is the list of variables for which a frequency table will be generated. A number of frequency tables can be generated simultaneously by pasting more than one variable into the **Variable(s):** box. Here we want all three variables, so we will paste all of them
4 Click on **OK**	

```
AGE       Age in Years


                                         Valid    Cum
Value Label            Value  Frequency  Percent  Percent  Percent

                        18        7       35.0     35.0     35.0
                        19        5       25.0     25.0     60.0
                        20        4       20.0     20.0     80.0
                        21        2       10.0     10.0     90.0
                        22        2       10.0     10.0    100.0
                              -------    -------  -------
                       Total     20      100.0    100.0

Valid cases      20    Missing cases      0
```

ATTITUDE Attitude to Statistics

Value Label	Value	Frequency	Percent	Valid Percent	Cum Percent
hate	1	7	35.0	35.0	35.0
indifferent	2	5	25.0	25.0	60.0
like	3	8	40.0	40.0	100.0
	Total	20	100.0	100.0	

Valid cases   20   Missing cases   0

- -

SEX

Value Label	Value	Frequency	Percent	Valid Percent	Cum Percent
female	1	8	40.0	40.0	40.0
male	2	12	60.0	60.0	100.0
	Total	20	100.0	100.0	

Valid cases   20   Missing cases   0

We can immediately compare these tables with the ones we generated 'by hand' in Chapter 2 to confirm that all the figures are the same. The usefulness of the **value labels** that we specified should now be obvious. If we had not specified that **1=female** and **2=male**, for example, then the last table would not have these value labels printed along the left. Thus we might be left scratching our heads or hunting back through our notes to remember which category the value 1 represented and which category 2 represented. Here we have all the information printed with the output.

Valid cases and missing values

Each frequency table includes a column of numbers headed **Valid Percent**, which in this case is identical to the **Percent** column. At the bottom of each table a row is included, which specifies:

Valid cases   20   Missing cases   0

This information is generated because sometimes the data include cases for which a variable has not been adequately measured. These are called *missing cases*, and the number of valid cases is equal to the total number of cases minus the number missing:

Valid cases = total cases – missing cases

For example, suppose that in filling out the questionnaire, 2 of the 20 statistics students forgot to fill in the question regarding their sex, and it is not feasible to go back to the class and find out who they are and complete the information. Suppose that these 2 students are actually males, but the researcher cannot know this from the returned questionnaires. As far as the researcher is concerned, there are 2 missing cases out of the total of 20, leaving 18 usable responses (valid cases): 8 females and now only 10 males. The frequency table for this variable, *using only the valid cases*, would then be as shown in Table 5.9.

Table 5.9 Sex of students

Sex	Frequency (valid cases)	Valid percentage
Female	8	$\frac{8}{18} \times 100 = 44.4$
Male	10	$\frac{10}{18} \times 100 = 55.6$
Total	18	100%

To do this in SPSS, the 2 missing cases need to be coded with a missing value. A missing value is a number that indicates to SPSS that the response is not 'usable' and should not be included in the analysis. In selecting a number to be the missing value, therefore, we need to be careful to select a value that the variable cannot possibly take. In this example, we can choose 9 to be the missing value, since it is impossible for the variable in question to take on this value. Obviously if we were measuring the age of primary school children, 9 would not be an appropriate choice for the missing value; 99 might be better because it is highly unlikely that such a score could actually represent a real case. (See Table 5.10.)

Table 5.10 Missing Values command using SPSS

SPSS command/action	Comment
1 Double-click on the shaded cell **sex**	This will bring up the **Define Variables** window
2 Click on **Missing Values...**	This will bring up the **Missing Values** window. Next to **No missing values** there is a small circle with a black dot. This indicates that the default setting is for no missing values to be specified
3 Click on the small circle next to **Discrete missing values**	The circle to the left of **Discrete missing values** will now contain the black dot, and the cursor will be flashing in the adjacent rectangle
4 Type **9**	
5 Click on **Continue**	
6 Click on **OK**	

If 9 is now typed into the cells for these two males, rather than 2, the **Frequencies...** command for **sex** will produce the following output:

```
SEX        sex


                                             Valid      Cum
Value Label             Value  Frequency  Percent  Percent  Percent

Female                    1         8      40.0     44.4     44.4
Male                      2        10      50.0     55.6    100.0
                          9         2      10.0   Missing
                                   -------  -------  -------
                        Total      20     100.0    100.0

Valid cases      18    Missing cases     2
```
- -

The last row in this table indicates that 2 cases had a value of 9 and this is the missing value. The **Valid Percent** and **Cum Percent** are now calculated on the basis of the remaining 18 valid responses as we did in Table 5.9.

Measures of central tendency using SPSS

The measures of central tendency that were calculated in Chapter 3 for these data can also be generated on SPSS as part of the **Frequencies...** command.[1] We will begin by generating the relevant measure of central tendency for **sex**. Since this is measured at the nominal level the appropriate measure is the mode. (See Table 5.11.)

Notice that we could have clicked on the other options for central tendency along with mode. These would then also be printed in the output. The computer does not discriminate between levels of measurement and will calculate anything we ask for, but we know that the mean and median of a nominal variable make no sense. It is up to us, that is, to choose only the appropriate measure so that the output is not cluttered with unnecessary statistics.

The result that appears on the output window, at the bottom of the familiar frequency table, is:

Mode 2.000

We know that **2** is the value label for males, indicating that male is the modal response for this variable.

---

[1]It is possible to calculate measures of central tendency and dispersion through the **Statistics/Summarize/Descriptives** command: in fact this would seem the appropriate way to go about it. Unfortunately (for some strange reason), this option only allows the mean to be calculated as a measure of central tendency. Similarly, the interquartile range is not available to measure dispersion. And given that it is usually best to calculate descriptive statistics with frequency tables, generally the **Statistics/Summarize/Frequencies** command is the preferred way of generating descriptive statistics.

Table 5.11   Measures of central tendency using SPSS

SPSS command/action	Comment
1 Select **Statistics/Summarize... / Frequencies...** from the menu	This will bring up the **Frequencies** window
2 Select the variable(s) to be analysed (in this case **sex**)	The selected variables will be highlighted
3 Click ➤	This will paste the highlighted variable(s) into the area headed **Variable(s):**
4 Click on **Statistics**	This will bring up a new window headed **Frequencies: Statistics**. One of the areas in this window will be headed **Central Tendency**
5 Click on the square to the left of **Mode**	This will paste × in the square next to **Mode**
6 Click on **Continue**	
7 Click on **OK**	

We perform the same procedure for the other two variables. The only variation is that we click on **Median**, in addition to **Mode**, for **attitude**, and also **Mean** for **age**. The line at the bottom of each table will be expanded to include the values for these measures. For **attitude** this will be:

Median   2.000   Mode   3.000

For **age** this will be:

Mean   19.350   Median   19.000   Mode   18.000

Compare these results with the tables in Chapter 2 to confirm that SPSS has given us the same results as those generated by hand.

Measures of dispersion using SPSS

You may have noticed that the **Statistics** window also provides a list of measures of dispersion to choose from together with the list of measures of central tendency. That is, both sets of measures are generated using the same procedures under the **Statistics/Summarize/Frequencies...** command. Measures of dispersion can be calculated in addition or alternatively to measures of average simply by clicking the appropriate selections under the **Statistics** button. For example, with **age** we select **Std. deviation** and **Range** in the **Dispersion** list, and **Quartiles** in the list headed **Percentiles Values**. The results will be:

AGE

Std dev	1.348	Range	4.000		
Percentile	Value	Percentile	Value	Percentile	Value
25.00	18.000	50.00	19.000	75.00	20.000
Valid cases	20	Missing cases	0		

The standard deviation is 1.348 years, indicating that there is not too much variation in age within this group. The range is 4, as we calculated in Chapter 4.

The interquartile range (IQR) is not actually calculated, but we have all the information to do it ourselves. The first (25%) quartile has an upper value of 18. The third (75%) quartile has an upper limit of 20. The difference of 2 years is the IQR.

Summary

It may help to stop and reflect on these procedures for generating descriptive statistics. It should be evident that SPSS provides a number of choices as to the way information is entered and the way results are obtained from this information. We have taken each of these sets of choices in turn, but usually, once a level of proficiency is gained, these various options are taken together. For example, we normally do not generate a frequency table for a variable, and then go back to generate the appropriate measure of central tendency, and then go back again to generate the appropriate measure of dispersion. We normally ask SPSS to do all of this simultaneously. For example, with the variable **attitude** we would ask for a frequency table, a calculation of mode and median, and a range, all by clicking on the appropriate options. We would thereby get a result that contained all this information at once:

Value Label		Value	Frequency	Percent	Valid Percent	Cum Percent
hate		1	7	35.0	35.0	35.0
indifferent		2	5	25.0	25.0	60.0
like		3	8	40.0	40.0	100.0
			-------	-------	-------	
		Total	20	100.0	100.0	
Median	2.000	Mode	3.000	Range		2.000
Valid cases	20	Missing cases	0			

At a glance, we would very quickly have all the summary information for this variable in front of us.

Exercises

5.1 In Exercise 4.2 the mean, median, range, and standard deviation were calculated for the following data:

    (a) 5,   9,   13,   15,   26,   72

    (b) 121,   134,   145,   212,   289,   306,   367,   380,   453

    (c) 1.2,   1.4,   1.9,   2.0,   2.4,   3.5,   3.9,   4.3,   5.2

    Enter these data into SPSS and generate these statistics to check your hand-calculations.

5.2 In Exercise 4.6 the following data (Time, in minutes, taken for subjects to complete a certain task) were used:

12	3	45	26	23	56	45	8	35	37	25	42	32	58
8	7	19	16	56	21	34	36	19	38	12	48	38	37
3	42	27	39	17	31	56	28	40	8	27	3		

    Enter these data into SPSS and check your calculations for that exercise.

5.3 A research project has collected information from 10 people on the following variables:

Television watched per night (minutes)	Main channel watched	Satisfaction with quality of programs
170	Commercial	Very satisfied
140	Public/government	Satisfied
280	Public/government	Satisfied
65	Commercial	Very satisfied
180	Commercial	Not satisfied
60	Commercial	Not satisfied
150	Public/government	Satisfied
160	Commercial	Not satisfied
200	Public/government	Satisfied
120	Commercial	Not satisfied

Prepare an SPSS data file for these data, creating variables and variable labels, values and value labels. Generate all the relevant summary information to describe each of these variables and interpret the results.

The normal curve

Chapter 3 looked at the options available for displaying a distribution of results in the form of a graph. A researcher will encounter many distributions when collecting data on different variables, each of which will probably have a unique shape when graphed.

This chapter will detail the properties of one particular distribution, called the normal curve. The term 'normal' is not meant to signify 'usual' or 'common'. In fact, it might seem like a very artificial construct that is anything but normal. Although it is a distribution rarely encountered in the 'real world', it is of the utmost importance as a *theoretical* distribution that is the basis for much that will follow in later chapters. So although the reasons for studying this particular distribution, among the multitude on which we can focus, may not be apparent just at this point, hopefully they will become evident later.

The normal distribution

This chapter will try to 'circle in' on the nature of the normal distribution. We will begin with a very simple and approximate definition, gradually expanding on this definition as we become more familiar with it.[1]

> The **normal curve** is a smooth, unimodal curve, that is perfectly symmetrical. It has 68.26 per cent of the area under the curve within one standard deviation of the mean.

We might be interested in people's height. If height is normally distributed, 68 per cent of cases will fall within 1 standard deviation of the mean, regardless of the particular values for the standard deviation and mean. For example, we may have three sample distributions describing the height of three different sets of 100 people (Table 6.1).

---

[1] A mathematical definition of the normal curve can be found in M.G. Bulmer, 1967, *Principles of Statistics*, Dover, New York, p. 109.

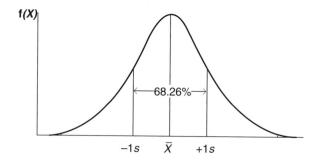

Figure 6.1 Area under the theoretical normal curve

Table 6.1 Average height and spread of students

Group	Mean height (cm)	Standard deviation (cm)
1	168	5
2	174	4
3	180	2

Each distribution has a mean and standard deviation different from the others, but if they are all normal they will conform to the rule that 68 per cent of cases will fall within 1 standard deviation of the mean: 68 people in group 1 will have a height between 163 cm and 173 cm; 68 people in group 2 will have height ranging from 170 cm to 178 cm; and for group 3 the range is 178 cm to 182 cm (Figure 6.2).

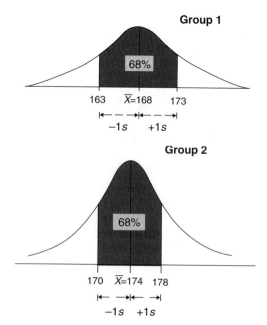

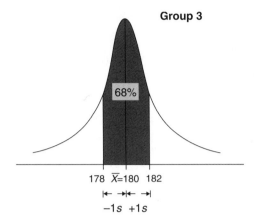

Figure 6.2   Three normal distributions with different means and standard deviations

This process of measuring the spread of cases in terms of the number of standard deviations from the mean is called **standardizing a distribution,** and produces the **standard normal distribution**. This distribution will have a mean of zero (obviously, by definition, the mean is zero standard deviation units from the mean, and one standard deviation is one standard deviation unit away from zero) (Figure 6.3).

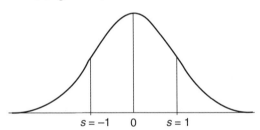

Figure 6.3   The standard normal distribution

This standardization procedure allows us to measure all normal distributions in terms of a common unit — standard deviation units — regardless of the units in which the variable is initially measured. It is analogous to expressing the price of various goods from different countries in terms of a common currency. We may have a whole list of prices some of which are expressed in US dollars, some in British pounds, others in Swiss francs. But if we convert all the prices into a single currency a comparison can be made. Similarly, a distribution may be expressed in terms of centimetres, or crime rates, or births per thousand. But expressing these various distributions according to standard deviation units gives a common scale of measurement.

We noted that the normal curve is symmetrical. Since it is a symmetrical distribution the same percentage of cases falls within a certain range *above* the mean as falls within the same range *below* the mean. In other words, if 68 per cent of all cases fall within 1 standard deviation unit *either side* of the mean, half of this (34.13%) will fall *above* the mean, and the other half (34.13%) *below* the mean. For group 3 in Table 6.1, this will imply that 34 people will be between 178 cm and 180 cm tall, and another 34 will be between 180 cm and 182 cm tall.

The other thing to notice about the spread of cases under a normal curve in Figure 6.4 is that the percentage of cases falling further than 1 standard deviation from the mean is equal to the total number of cases (100%) minus the percentage that fall within the range (68.26%):

$$100 - 68.26 = 31.74\%$$

Again we can divide this region in two so that 15.87 per cent of cases have height above 1 standard deviation from the mean (i.e. for group 3 this will be greater than 182 cm), and another 15.87 per cent of cases are at the other end of the curve.

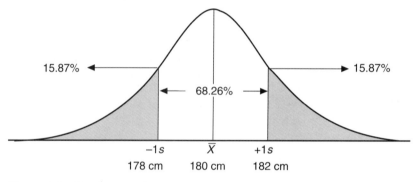

Figure 6.4 Distribution of height for group 3

Thus if someone from this group informs me that she is 185 cm tall I will also know that she is in the tallest 16 per cent of that group.

We can now expand the definition of the normal curve a little, and define the percentage of the total area under the normal curve within 2 standard deviation units from the mean, and within 3 standard deviation units (Figure 6.5).

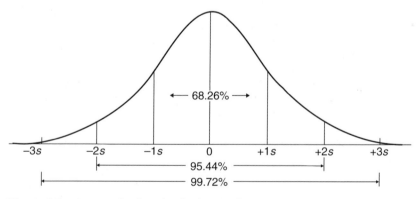

Figure 6.5 Area under the standard normal curve

- Between ±1 standard deviation from the mean lies 68.26 per cent of the area under the curve.
- Between ±2 standard deviations from the mean lies 95.44 per cent of the area under the curve.
- Between ±3 standard deviations from the mean lies 99.72 per cent of the area under the curve.

This information can be presented in a simple table (Table 6.2).

Table 6.2   Areas under the standard normal curve

Standard deviation units	Area under curve between *points*	Area under curve beyond *both points* (two tails)	Area under curve beyond *one point* (one tail)
±1	0.6826	0.3174	0.1587
±2	0.9544	0.0456	0.0228
±3	0.9972	0.0028	0.0014

There are a two aspects to Table 6.2 worth noticing:

- Instead of expressing the area under the curve as a percentage, it is expressed as a proportion. Thus 68.26 per cent is converted to 0.6826, and so on.
- The values in the first two columns will always sum to 1 (e.g. 0.6826 + 0.3174 = 1). This is simply because the two areas must equal the total area under the curve, which is 100 per cent.

The normal curve is a very specifically defined frequency polygon: a type of graph we introduced in Chapter 3. This allows us to interpret the proportions in the table as **probabilities**. A probability in this context is simply the chance that any given case will have a certain value, or fall within a certain range of values. In other words, the probability that any given case from a normal distribution will have a value within 1 standard deviation from the mean is 0.6826. This way of interpreting the area under the normal curve as a probability will be especially useful in the following chapters on inference.

z-scores

Instead of using the expression 'number of standard deviations from the mean' we will instead speak of *z*-scores. A *z*-score of +1 indicates 1 standard deviation unit above the mean. A *z*-score of –1.5 indicates $1\frac{1}{2}$ standard deviations below the mean.

For a normally distributed sample, we can work out the z-score for any actual value using the formula:

$$z = \frac{X_i - \overline{X}}{s}$$

where:

X_i = the actual value measured in original units
$\overline{X}$ = the mean of the sample
s = the standard deviation of the sample.

For a normal population the formula is:

$$z = \frac{X_i - \mu}{\sigma}$$

where:

μ = the mean of the population
σ = the standard deviation of the population.

For example, consider the 100 people in group 2 above, with a mean height of 174 cm and standard deviation of 4 cm. If a member of this group told me he was 182 cm tall, I can put this information into the formula and calculate the *z*-score associated with this height:

$$z = \frac{X_i - \overline{X}}{s}$$

$$= \frac{182 - 174}{4}$$

$$= \frac{8}{4}$$

$$= 2$$

This immediately tells me that 182 cm is 2 standard deviations above the average. By referring to the last column in Table 6.2, we conclude that the percentage of the sample with a height of 182 cm or more is 2.28 per cent.

In fact, statisticians have worked out the area under the curve between the mean and every point along the horizontal axis of the normal curve. This information is summarized in a table called the 'area under the standard normal curve', which appears in the back of every statistics textbook (including this one). In fact, because we are going to work with it frequently throughout this chapter, and to familiarize ourselves with it, it is reproduced below (Table 6.3)

Why bother defining the normal curve in such minute detail? Why have statisticians gone to such lengths as to actually work out and have printed a table that indicates the number of cases that fall within defined regions of a normal distribution? After all, there are an infinite number of possible frequency distributions we could come across — the distribution of families according to total income will be different from the distribution of cities according to crime rates, and neither will be remotely like a normal distribution. Why don't we construct tables that define the areas under these curves?

There are two reasons why studying a normal distribution is very important.

- There are some empirical distributions (i.e. in the 'real world') that are *fairly close to being normally distributed*, so the table will be a handy descriptive tool for these distributions. This is similar to the way in which we frequently apply the equation for the area of the circle to shapes that are not exactly a circle. We frequently use the notion of a circle in everyday life, but if we define it precisely it is clear that it is in fact a rare shape. A circle is defined as a region where every point along the circumference is equidistant from the centre; that is, the radius is constant. A figure defined in this way has an area of πr^2, but there are enough shapes in ordinary life that are close enough to a circle such that using this formula to estimate their areas is not unreasonable. Just as with figures that are 'close enough' to being a circle, there are instances when it is not unrealistic to assume that a distribution is 'close enough' to being normal, even though, strictly speaking, it isn't. In other words, just as we never encounter perfect circles, yet still use the formula for the area of a circle in everyday life, we can construct precise descriptive statements about any empirical distribution that (we think) is **approximately** normal. Sometimes near enough is good enough. Many *physical* characteristics of people, for example, are normally distributed. This is why we used the example of height — if we took a random sample of people and measured their height we would actually find that about 68 per cent of our sample falls within 1 standard deviation of the mean. What the mean and the standard deviation will be, in terms of natural units, cannot be predicted. The average may turn out to be 165 cm, or 172 cm, or 176 cm, and the standard deviation may be 6, or 9 or 12.5 cm. But whatever these values turn out to be, we will find that the distribution of cases will be approximately normal.
- Most importantly, though, the normal curve forms the basis of inferential statistics, which will be covered in Part 2. The convenience of having the table for the area under the normal curve will then be most apparent.

Table 6.3   Area under the standard normal curve

z (standard deviation units)	Area under curve between points	Area under curve beyond both points	Area under curve beyond one point
±0.1	0.080	0.920	0.460
±0.2	0.159	0.841	0.4205
±0.3	0.236	0.764	0.382
±0.4	0.311	0.689	0.3445
±0.5	0.383	0.617	0.3085
±0.6	0.451	0.549	0.2745
±0.7	0.516	0.484	0.242
±0.8	0.576	0.424	0.212
±0.9	0.632	0.368	0.184
±1	0.683	0.317	0.1585
±1.1	0.729	0.271	0.1355
±1.2	0.770	0.230	0.115
±1.3	0.806	0.194	0.097
±1.4	0.838	0.162	0.081
±1.5	0.866	0.134	0.067
±1.6	0.890	0.110	0.055
±1.645	0.900	0.100	0.050
±1.7	0.911	0.089	0.0445
±1.8	0.928	0.072	0.036
±1.9	0.943	0.057	0.029
±1.96	0.950	0.050	0.025
±2	0.954	0.046	0.023
±2.1	0.964	0.036	0.018
±2.2	0.972	0.028	0.014
±2.3	0.979	0.021	0.0105
±2.33	0.98	0.02	0.01
±2.4	0.984	0.016	0.008
±2.5	0.988	0.012	0.006
±2.6	0.991	0.009	0.0045
±2.7	0.993	0.007	0.0035
±2.8	0.995	0.005	0.0025
±2.9	0.996	0.004	0.002
±3	0.997	0.003	0.0015
±3.1	0.998	0.002	0.0001
±3.2	0.9986	0.0014	0.0007
±3.3	0.9990	0.0010	0.0005
±3.4	0.9993	0.0007	0.0003
±3.5	0.9995	0.0005	0.00025
±3.6	0.9997	0.0003	0.00015
±3.7	0.9998	0.0002	0.0001
±3.8	0.99986	0.00014	0.00007
±3.9	0.99990	0.00010	0.00005
±4	>0.99990	<0.00010	<0.00005

Using normal curves to describe a distribution

The rest of this chapter will work through a series of examples. The objective is to familiarize ourselves with the use of the normal curve as a descriptive tool. In the process we will also familiarize ourselves with the procedures for looking up values in the area under the standard normal curve table, which will be useful for later chapters.

As already mentioned, one of the variables that actually has a normal distribution in the 'real world' is height. Assume that we measure the height of 100 students and obtain the following results:

$$N = 100$$

$$\overline{X} = 180 \text{ cm}$$

$$s = 10 \text{ cm}$$

Knowing that this group of students is normally distributed according to height allows us to answer various questions about this variable.

The area between the mean and a point on the distribution

For example, I might want to know how many students are between the mean (180 cm) and 185 cm in height. The first thing to do is convert 185 into a z-score:

$$z = \frac{X_i - \overline{X}}{s}$$

$$z = \frac{185 - 180}{10} = \frac{5}{10} = 0.5$$

The next step is to refer to the table for the area under the standard normal curve and find the area between this point and the mean. A condensed version of the table is presented in Table 6.4 to show its use. For a z-score of 0.5 we get the result shown below.

Table 6.4 Area under the standard normal curve

z	Area under curve between *points*	Area under curve beyond *points*	Area under curve beyond *one point*
±0.1	0.080	0.920	0.460
±0.2	0.159	0.841	0.4205
±0.3	0.236	0.764	0.382
±0.4	0.311	0.689	0.3445
±0.5	**0.383**	0.617	0.3085
±0.6	0.451	0.549	0.2745
±0.7	0.516	0.484	0.242
±0.8	0.576	0.424	0.212
±0.9	0.632	0.368	0.184
±1	0.683	0.317	0.1585
. . .	. . .	. . .	
±4	>0.9999	<0.0001	<0.00005

In other words, 0.383 of all cases will have a height within 5 cm above or below the mean. Since we are interested in only those z-scores that are 0.5 z-scores *above* the mean, we divide this in half:

$$\text{proportion of cases between } 180 \text{ cm and } 185 \text{ cm} = \frac{0.383}{2} = 0.1915$$

Thus, in this group, I can say that just over 0.19 (19%) of people are between 180 cm and 185 cm in height (remember that a proportion can be transformed into a percentage by moving the decimal point two places to the right). (See Figure 6.6.)

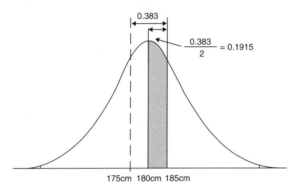

Figure 6.6

The area beyond a point on the distribution

A very similar logic applies to finding the percentage of cases that fall beyond a certain point on the distribution. For example, I might be interested in the percentage of people in this group whose height is above 185 cm (Figure 6.7).

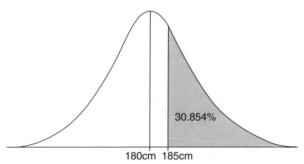

Figure 6.7

From the previous exercise we know the z-score associated with 185 cm is:

$$z = \frac{X_i - \overline{X}}{s}$$

$$z = \frac{185 - 180}{10} = \frac{5}{10} = 0.5$$

This time, when referring to Table 6.5 we refer to the column for the area *beyond* the point defined by a *z*-score of 1.5. In other words we are only interested in the area under **one tail** of the distribution.

Table 6.5   Area under the standard normal curve

z	Area under curve between *points*	Area under curve beyond *points*	Area under curve beyond *one point*
±0.1	0.080	0.920	0.460
±0.2	0.159	0.841	0.4205
±0.3	0.236	0.764	0.382
±0.4	0.311	0.689	0.3445
±0.5	0.383	0.617	**0.3085**
±0.6	0.451	0.549	0.2745
±0.7	0.516	0.484	0.242
±0.8	0.576	0.424	0.212
±0.9	0.632	0.368	0.184
±1	0.683	0.317	0.1585
. . .	. . .	. . .	
±4	>0.9999	<0.0001	<0.00005

This indicates that 0.3085 (30.85%) of this group have a height *above* 185 cm.

If we look at the answers to these two problems we can see that the probabilities sum to 50 per cent. This is because the two areas that we have defined together make up exactly half the curve (Table 6.6, Figure 6.8).

Table 6.6

Range of height	Percentage of cases (%)
Between 180 cm and 185 cm	19
Above 18 cm	31
Total	50

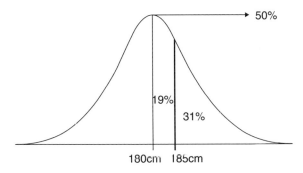

Figure 6.8

The area between two points on a normal distribution

Another question in which we might be interested is the percentage of cases that fall within a range not bounded on one side by the mean. For example, we might be interested in the proportion of cases that fall between 170 cm and 175 cm in height (Figure 6.9).

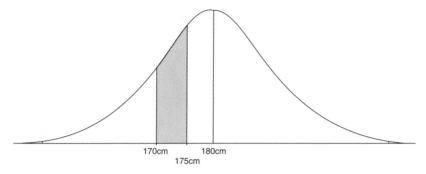

Figure 6.9

The solution to this puzzle is apparent by looking at Figure 6.10.

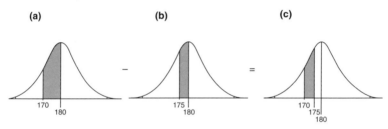

Figure 6.10

The area between 170 and 175 is what is left if we subtract the area between 175 and the mean from the total area between 170 and the mean. In other words we need to calculate two proportions, that bounded by the mean and 170 cm and that bounded by the mean and 175 cm (Figure 6.11).

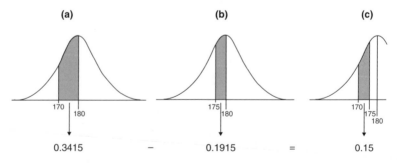

Figure 6.11

The result is 0.15, or 15 per cent, of cases have a height between 170 cm and 175 cm.

Calculating values from z-scores

In the above examples we wanted to identify the percentage of cases that have a certain range of height. However, the problem we want to address might be slightly different. We might already have a predefined proportion of cases we are interested in, and want to derive the height range within which this percentage falls. For example, we might be interested in the range of heights that will identify the middle 50 per cent of cases. Another way of posing this problem is to ask which scores mark the upper and lower bounds of the interquartile range.

We begin by looking at the table for the area under the standard normal curve to find the z-scores that will mark off the 0.5 region. We look down the column for the area under the curve between points and find the cell that has a probability of 0.5 (or the closest to it).

Table 6.7   Area under the standard normal curve

z	Area under curve between *points*	Area under curve beyond *points*	Area under curve beyond *one point*
±0 1	0.080	0.920	0.460
±0.2	0.159	0.841	0.4205
±0.3	0.236	0.764	0.382
±0.4	0.311	0.689	0.3445
±0.5	0.383	0.617	0.3085
±0.6	0.451	0.549	0.2745
±0.7	0.516	0.484	0.242
±0.8	0.576	0.424	0.212
±0.9	0.632	0.368	0.184
±1	0.683	0.317	0.1585
. . .	. . .	. . .	
±4	>0.9999	<0.0001	<0.00005

The closest value to 0.5 is 0.516, which is associated with z-scores of +0.7 and –0.7 (Figure 6.12).

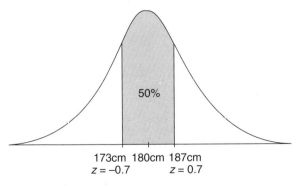

173cm 180cm 187cm
z = –0.7   z = 0.7

Figure 6.12

To convert these z-scores into the actual units (centimetres) in which we are measuring the variable, we rearrange the basic formula slightly:

$$z = \frac{X_i - \overline{X}}{s} \rightarrow X_i = \overline{X} + z\,(s)$$

If we put the two z-scores that define the region into this equation we obtain:

$$X_i = \overline{X} + z(s)$$
$$X_i = 180 + 0.7(10)$$
$$X_i = 180 + 7$$
$$X_i = 187$$

$$X_i = 180 - 0.7(10)$$
$$X_i = 180 - 7$$
$$X_i = 173$$

Therefore the 'middle' 50 per cent of students have a height between 173 cm and 187cm. This also means that 25 per cent of students are below 173 cm and 25 per cent of students are above 187 cm.

Normal curves on SPSS

We will now work with another example, and then use SPSS to confirm the results we obtain from the hand calculations. Assume that we have been able to survey 400 people within a small community and measure their ages to the nearest whole year. The results of this survey are displayed in Figure 6.13.

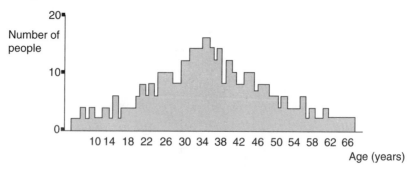

Figure 6.13   Age distribution of the community

The mean for this distribution is 35.5 years and the standard deviation is 13.33 years.

Looking at the histogram in Figure 6.13, we can see that the distribution 'sort of' has the bell-shaped, symmetric features of the normal curve. In more technical terms, we say that it is **approximately** normal. A normal curve is a smooth continuous distribution — there are no 'jumps' from 18 to 19, 19 to 20, and so on. We, on the other hand, are using a histogram with data arranged into class intervals with a width of 1 year. The actual ages are really class mid-points for the intervals 1.5–2.5, 2.5–3.5, 3.5–4.5, and so on. Since histograms will always have jagged edges brought about by the use of discrete units of measurement, they will never perfectly fit the smoothly rising and falling normal curve.[1]

Having looked at the distribution and judged it to be approximately normal, we can use z-scores to analyse it. For example, we might be interested in the proportion of people who are not eligible to vote because of their age. This means finding the proportion of people who are 17 years of age or less. The first step is to determine how many z-scores 17 lies from the mean of 35.5 years. Since we are working with a population distribution the appropriate formula is:

$$z = \frac{X_i - \mu}{\sigma}$$

$$= \frac{17 - 35.5}{13.33}$$

$$= -1.4$$

Since we are only interested in the area in one tail of the distribution, we refer to the column for the area under the curve beyond one point when referring to Table 6.8 for the standard normal curve.

Only 0.081, or 8.1 per cent, of the curve lies beyond a z-score of –1.4 (Figure 6.14).

---

[1] There are a number of statistical measures for assessing the extent to which a distribution is normal, one of which we will explore in Chapter 12. A more detailed examination of these measures is beyond the scope of this book. Here we will rely simply on 'eye-ball' examination of the histogram to decide whether the distribution is approximately normal.

Table 6.8   Area under the standard normal curve

z	Area under curve between *points*	Area under curve beyond *points*	Area under curve beyond *one point*
±0.1	0.080	0.920	0.460
±0.2	0.159	0.841	0.4205
±0.3	0.236	0.764	0.382
±0.4	0.311	0.689	0.3445
±0.5	0.383	0.617	0.3085
±0.6	0.451	0.549	0.2745
±0.7	0.516	0.484	0.242
±0.8	0.576	0.424	0.212
±0.9	0.632	0.368	0.184
±1	0.683	0.317	0.1585
±1.1	0.729	0.271	0.1355
±1.2	0.770	0.230	0.115
±1.3	0.806	0.194	0.097
±1.4	0.838	0.162	**0.081**
±1.5	0.866	0.134	0.067
±1.6	0.890	0.110	0.055
±1.645	0.900	0.100	0.050
±1.7	0.911	0.089	0.0445
±1.8	0.928	0.072	0.036
±1.9	0.943	0.057	0.028715
±1.96	0.950	0.050	0.025
±2	0.954	0.046	0.023
. . .	. . .	. . .	
±4	>0.9999	<0.0001	<0.00005

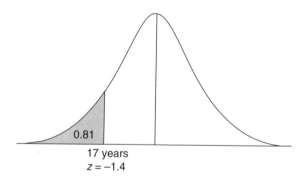

0.81

17 years
z = −1.4

Figure 6.14

name 6.sav   We can use SPSS to assess the extent to which the spread of scores can be described by a normal distribution. To do this we simply extend the procedure we learnt in the previous chapter for generating a frequency table. In the process of generating a frequency distribution we can ask SPSS to also generate a histogram, and to 'fit' a normal curve onto this histogram. By looking at the results we can see the extent to which the distribution of data approximates a normal distribution. The data for this example have been entered on SPSS. To generate a frequency table, with a histogram and a normal curve centred on the mean super-imposed on the histogram, we use the procedure shown in Table 6.9.

Table 6.9   Generating a histogram with a normal curve on SPSS

SPSS command/action	Comments
1 From the menu select **Statistics/Summarize... / Frequencies...**	This will bring up a dialogue box headed **Frequencies**. This will contain an area with a list of the variables for which data have been entered
2 Select the variable to generate a frequency table for by clicking on **age**	
3 Click on ➤	This will paste the selected variable(s) into the area below **Variable(s):**, which is the list of variables for which a frequency table will be generated
4 Click on **Charts...**	This will bring up the **Frequencies: Charts** dialogue box
5 In the square entitled **Chart Type** click on the circle next to **Histogram(s)**	A ● will appear in the circle to indicate that a histogram will be generated with the output
6 Click on the small square next to **With normal curve**	A × will appear in the small square to indicate that a normal curve will be 'fitted' to the histogram
7 Click on **Continue**	
8 Click on **OK**	

These procedures will generate the following output:

Value Label	Value	Frequency	Percent	Valid Percent	Cum Percent
	2	2	.5	.5	.5
	6	2	.5	.5	1.0
	7	4	1.0	1.0	2.0
	8	2	.5	.5	2.5
	9	4	1.0	1.0	3.5
	10	2	.5	.5	4.0
	11	2	.5	.5	4.5

13	4	1.0	1.0	5.5
14	2	.5	.5	6.0
15	6	1.5	1.5	7.5
16	2	.5	.5	8.0
17	4	1.0	1.0	9.0
18	4	1.0	1.0	10.0
19	4	1.0	1.0	11.0
20	6	1.5	1.5	12.5
21	8	2.0	2.0	14.5
22	6	1.5	1.5	16.0
23	8	2.0	2.0	18.0
24	6	1.5	1.5	19.5
25	10	2.5	2.5	22.0
26	10	2.5	2.5	24.5
27	10	2.5	2.5	27.0
28	8	2.0	2.0	29.0
29	8	2.0	2.0	31.0
30	12	3.0	3.0	34.0
31	12	3.0	3.0	37.0
32	14	3.5	3.5	40.5
33	14	3.5	3.5	44.0
34	14	3.5	3.5	47.5
35	16	4.0	4.0	51.5
36	14	3.5	3.5	55.0
37	12	3.0	3.0	58.0
38	14	3.5	3.5	61.5
39	8	2.0	2.0	63.5
40	12	3.0	3.0	66.5
41	10	2.5	2.5	69.0
42	8	2.0	2.0	71.0
43	8	2.0	2.0	73.0
44	10	2.5	2.5	75.5
45	10	2.5	2.5	78.0
46	6	1.5	1.5	79.5
47	8	2.0	2.0	81.5
48	8	2.0	2.0	83.5
49	6	1.5	1.5	85.0
50	6	1.5	1.5	86.5
51	4	1.0	1.0	87.5
52	6	1.5	1.5	89.0
53	4	1.0	1.0	90.0
54	4	1.0	1.0	91.0
55	4	1.0	1.0	92.0
56	6	1.5	1.5	93.5
57	2	.5	.5	94.0
58	4	1.0	1.0	95.0
59	2	.5	.5	95.5
60	2	.5	.5	96.0
61	4	1.0	1.0	97.0
62	2	.5	.5	97.5
63	2	.5	.5	98.0
64	2	.5	.5	98.5
66	2	.5	.5	99.0
67	2	.5	.5	99.5
69	2	.5	.5	100.0
Total	400	100.0	100.0	

Hi-Res Chart   # 4:Histogram of age of respondent

Valid cases   400   Missing cases   0

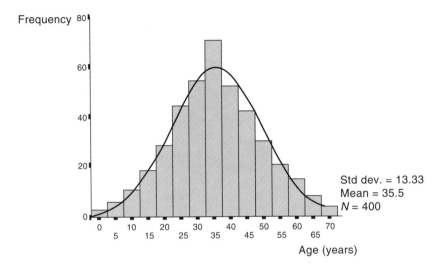

Looking firstly at the histogram with the normal curve superimposed on it, we can see that even though the original data comprise age measured in years, SPSS will group cases together into more manageable class intervals. Here the class intervals are 5 year periods, with the mid-points for each class interval being 0, 5, 10, 15, and so on. We can also see that our earlier conclusion that the distribution of these 400 ages is close to normal is reasonable. There are some bars in which the normal curve does not pass exactly through the mid-point. For example, the bar for the middle group in the distribution, with a mid-point of 35 years, has more people in it than would be the case if the distribution was perfectly normal. Despite this variation, the distribution appears to the eye to be approximately normal.

We can confirm this by looking at the proportion of cases that fall within certain ranges around the mean. For a normal curve we know that 68 per cent of cases will fall within 1 standard deviation, or 1 z-score, from the mean. The interval that defines 1 standard deviation around the mean is:

$$\mu \pm \sigma = 35.5 \pm 13.33$$

$$= 22.17, 48.83$$

If we go back to the frequency table and add the percentage of cases that have ages between 22 and 49 (inclusive) the sum will be 70.5 per cent, which is consistent with a normal approximation.

Similarly, to find the number of cases with an age of 17 years or less, we look at the cumulative percentage at this age. From the SPSS output we see that at age 17, the cumulative frequency is 9 per cent of cases. This is very close to the figure of 8 per cent we obtained in the calculation above, using the normal curve to approximate this distribution.

This little exercise indicates that when a distribution is approximately normal, the calculation of z-scores can be a quick way of determining the proportion of cases within any range of values that may interest us. Of course, because any distribution is only *approximately* normal, the proportions obtained by using z-scores will not exactly equal the actual proportion of cases within the range of values we are interested in.

Exercises

6.1 From the table for the area under the standard normal curve find the probability that a normally distributed variable will have a z-score:
  (a) above 1.3
  (b) below 1.3
  (c) between 0.5 and 3.4
  (d) between –2.3 and 2
  (e) greater than 2.3 and less than –1.4
  (f) less than –1.6 and greater than 1.6
  (g) less than –1.96 and greater than 1.96.
  For each of these regions draw a sketch of the normal curve with the appropriate area shaded in.

6.2 If a set of cases is normally distributed, using the table for the area under the standard normal curve, find the z-score(s) that defines the following proportions of cases:
  (a) the middle 0.683 of cases
  (b) the 0.018 cases with the highest scores
  (c) the 0.05 cases with the lowest scores
  (d) the 0.134 cases which together form the extremes of the distribution.
  For each of these regions draw a sketch of the normal curve with the appropriate area shaded in.

6.3 If X_i is a variable with a normal distribution, a mean of 60, and a standard deviation of 10, how many standard deviations from the mean are the following values for X_i?
  (a) 60
  (b) 52
  (c) 85
  (d) 43
  (e) 73

6.4 A (hypothetical) study has discovered that the income of families headed by a single mother is normally distributed, with an average annual income of $17 500, and standard deviation of $3000. If the poverty line is considered to be $15 000, how many families headed by a single mother will be living in poverty? Sketch the normal curve to illustrate your answer.

6.5 If the mean life of a certain brand of light bulb is 510 hours and the standard deviation is 30 hours, what percentage of bulbs lasts no more than 462 hours? (Assume a normal distribution.)

6.6 The average selling price of a new car is $19 800 and the standard deviation is $2300. What proportion will sell for less than $16 000? Within what limits will the middle 95 per cent fall? (Assume a normal distribution.)

6.7 The reaction time of a motorist is such that when travelling at 60 km/h his average breaking distance is 40 m with a standard deviation of 5 m. If the motorist is travelling at 60 km/h and suddenly sees a dog crossing his path 47 m away, what is the probability he will hit it? How far away will the dog have to be to have a 95 per cent chance of not being hit? (Assume a normal distribution.)

6.8 In the example used in this chapter for the distribution of the ages of 400 community residents, calculate, using z-scores, the proportion of cases that are of working age, that is, between 18 and 65 years old. Calculate the range of ages that determine the middle 50 per cent of cases. Confirm your calculations by referring to the frequency table generated by SPSS for this distribution.

6.9 Based on past results, a charity organization expects that donations for the forthcoming year can be modelled using a normal curve. It expects to receive donations of $1.5 million in the following year, with a standard deviation of $200 000. Its target is $1.7 million in donations. What is the expected probability of meeting this target? If the charity considers $1.2 million to be the minimum amount it requires to cover costs and meet the basic needs of the poor in its area, what is the expected probability that it will receive enough to meet this minimum?

6.10 A local energy-generating program is proposed using wind generation. This form of energy generation is only viable if wind speed in a certain area is over 15 km/h for at least 25 per cent of the time. The average wind speed is 12 km/h with a standard deviation of 6 km/h. Is there sufficient evidence to suggest that the project will be viable?

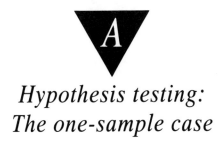

Part

2

Inferential statistics

A

Hypothesis testing:
The one-sample case

7

Sampling distributions

So far, we have looked at ways of summarizing information; we collect measurements from a set of cases and then reduce these hundreds (sometimes thousands) of numbers into one or two descriptive statistics such as the mean and standard deviation. We have seen how such descriptive statistics provide a useful summary of the overall picture, saving us the trouble of having to wade through each and every case from which we take a measurement.

If the set of cases from which we take a measurement included all the possible cases of interest — the population — the empirical research process would end with the calculation of these descriptive measures. An investigation that includes every member of the population is a **census** and the descriptive measures for a population are **parameters**.

> A **parameter** is a numerical value that describes some feature of a population.

When using mathematical notation, parameters are denoted with Greek symbols, such as μ for the population mean, and σ for the population standard deviation.

Sometimes we do actually have information about the whole population of interest, such as when a government agency conducts a census of people and can tell us the age distribution of the entire population at a certain date. Other times we don't have information about the population — it is out there but we just can't get our hands on it. Therefore, in social research we often work with a smaller sub-set, or **sample**, of the population, and the descriptive measures used to summarize a sample are **statistics**. These sample statistics are denoted, in mathematical notation, with Roman letters: $\overline{X}$ for the sample mean, and s for the sample standard deviation.

The distribution of a sample and the distribution of a population are *empirical distributions* in the sense that they exist in the 'real world'. There are several reasons, though, why we may draw a sample from a population, rather than conduct a complete census:

- Samples are usually cheaper and quicker.
- It is sometimes impossible to locate all the members of a population, either

because a complete list of the population is unavailable, or some of its members are difficult to get to or unwilling to participate in the study.
- Sampling sometimes destroys the unit of analysis so that a census would destroy the population. For example, a factory might be interested in a quality control check of the batteries it produces. Testing that the products have sufficient battery life may involve running the units down until they are flat — a process that will cause bankruptcy if it is applied to all the batteries that the firm produced.
- Sometimes sampling is more accurate. If there is reason to believe that the survey process generates errors, then a full-scale census may amplify these errors. For example, assembling the research team required to undertake a census may lead to inexperienced survey staff being used to collect data, whereas a smaller team might be better trained and more experienced.

For whatever reason sampling is undertaken, a central problem arises. Are the descriptive statistics we get from a *sample* the same as the corresponding parameters we would get if a complete and accurate census was undertaken? In other words, are the statistics obtained from the sample in some sense 'representative' of the population from which the sample is drawn? Even though we may do everything in our power to draw a 'representative' sample from a population, the operation of **random variation** may cause the sample to be 'off'. On what basis then can we make a valid generalization from the sample to the population?

For example, we might sample a group of 120 people from a certain area and ask each their age in years. Here the variable of interest (age) is measured at the interval/ratio level. We can describe the information contained in the data in three ways:

- **Calculate a measure of central tendency**   With interval/ratio data that is not heavily skewed this is the mean ($\overline{X}$).
- **Calculate a measure of dispersion**   In this example the appropriate measure is the standard deviation (s).
- **Draw a graph**   With a continuous interval/ratio variable such as age we would draw a frequency polygon.

This information might be interesting in itself, but usually we compile information about a sample because we have another issue to address: what is the average age of *all* people in this area? If the average age for this sample is 36 years, can I generalize from this to the whole population? This is where the operation of random variation may cause us to feel uneasy about making such generalizations from the sample statistics. How can we be sure that our sample did not happen by chance to include a few disproportionately old or disproportionately young people, in relation to the population?

We address this problem by using **inferential statistics**.

Inferential statistics are the numerical techniques used for making conclusions about a population, based on the information obtained from a random sample drawn from that population.

To undertake statistical inference we generate three separate sets of numbers:

- **Raw data**   These are the measurements taken from each case for a variable (e.g. the age of each person, measured in years). This will often be a very large set of numbers, depending on the actual sample size.
- **Descriptive statistics** (e.g. mean, standard deviation, frequency distribution) These summarize the raw data obtained *from the sample only*. These are also known as sample statistics.
- **Inferential statistics**   These help us to make a decision about the characteristics of the population.

Although the detailed steps involved in making inferences vary from situation to situation, we use the same general procedure of calculating these three sets of numbers. This procedure is illustrated in Figure 7.1.

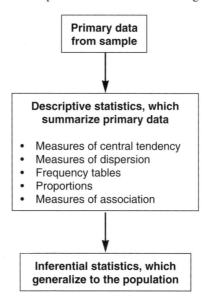

Figure 7.1

Random samples

The first condition that must apply if we are to use inferential statistics is that the sample must be **randomly selected** from the population.

> **Random selection** is a sampling method where each member of the population has the same chance of being selected in the sample.

A telephone survey of the population is not perfectly random. Only people in a household with a telephone at the time of the survey have a chance of being sampled. This excludes the homeless and households without a phone. Similarly, it gives households with more than one telephone number a greater chance of being included. In fact, very few surveys will be perfectly random in terms of the strict definition. The important consideration is whether the deviation from random selection is likely to systematically over-represent or under-represent cases of interest such that the results will have a **bias**. A biased sample favors the selection of some members of the population over others.

Sometimes there are good reasons to deviate from simple random selection by using **stratified random sampling**. A stratified random sample is used when working with a population that has easily discernible strata. Each stratum is a segment of the population that we suspect is uniform in terms of the variable we want to measure. We firstly predetermine the proportion of the total sample that will come from each stratum. We then randomly select cases from *within* each stratum. For example, we might feel that men are similar to each other in terms of a particular variable and that women are also similar to each other in terms of this variable, but there is a difference between men and women. Thus we might stratify a sample so that 50 per cent of the sample are women and 50 per cent men. Having divided the sample into two segments we then randomly select the required number of women and the required number of men.

Random sampling is often called **probability sampling**, for reasons that will soon become obvious. But there are a whole range of non-probability (non-random) sampling techniques, such as **snow-ball sampling**. Snow-ball sampling involves selecting cases on the basis of information provided by previously studied cases. Such a sampling method is particularly useful when conducting research on close-knit populations that are difficult to get to, or whose exact size and composition cannot be known in advance. There is no inherent reason why probability sampling should be considered 'better' than non-probability sampling. Each method is appropriate for different research questions, and sometimes our research question will be better addressed by choosing a non-probability sampling method. One of the implications of using a non-probability sampling method, though, is that we cannot use the inferential statistics we are about to learn. This is not necessarily a bad thing, and other ways of interpreting information are as valid as statistical inference, and sometimes more so.

Unfortunately, the professional and academic worlds do not always see it this way. Research seems to acquire a 'scientific' look when dressed in terms of inferential statistics, and often research is forced into this framework just to suit the fashion. Inferential statistics are sometimes calculated even on samples that are not randomly selected. In other instances, the research project is structured in such a way as to make inferential statistics applicable, even though other methods may have been more insightful. This is a problem with the practice of research that raises broader issues than can be dealt with here. All we will do now is issue a word of caution: the choice of research methods should never be undertaken on the basis of the technique to be used for analysing data — it should be chosen on the basis of best addressing the research problem at hand, and if that happens to involve the kind of statistical analyses we will be learning below, then we will know how to deal with it. If not, then the project is not lost — it simply means other avenues should be pursued.

The sampling distribution of a sample statistic

Inferential statistics only apply to random samples, because the central tool used to make inferences is based on the assumption of random sampling. This tool is the **sampling distribution of a sample statistic**. Before defining the sampling distribution, we will illustrate the idea behind its construction through a very simple experiment. Assume that we have a board that consists of rows of nails that are evenly spaced and protrude from the board (Figure 7.2).

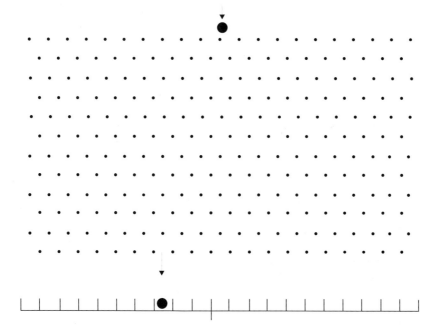

Figure 7.2

A ball is dropped directly above the middle nail in the top row and allowed to find its way down to the bottom. The path the ball takes will depend on a whole host of factors — but eventually the ball will bounce around and emerge somewhere at the bottom. The point at which any *individual* ball will fall is a random event.

However, if I dropped 100 identical balls from the same position and let each find its way down the rows of nails to pile up at the bottom, we might get a distribution that looks like Figure 7.3.

Most balls will bounce around, but since they are dropped from the same point plenty of balls will pile up in the centre. But not all the balls will travel this path. Some will just happen to bounce to the left of each nail more often than they bounce to the right, and therefore emerge over to one side, and some will happen to keep bouncing to the right more often and come out on the other side. In fact the occasional odd ball will land way out to the left

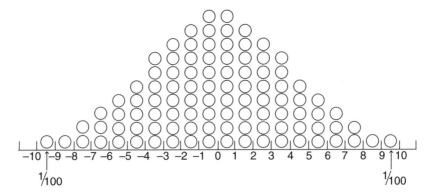

Figure 7.3

(position –9) or way out to the right (position 9). But we can see that the chances of a ball landing way out to the left, if allowed to fall freely, is only 1-in-100. In other words, although the location of any individual ball is random, the shape of the overall distribution of repeated drops is not random — it has a definite shape.

What has all this got to do with social statistics and inference? To see how the same logic applies in the social world rather than just with balls and nails, let's go back to the example in Chapter 6 where people from a small community were surveyed and their age in years recorded. The parameters for this population of 400 were:

$$\mu = 35.5 \text{ years}$$

$$\sigma = 13.33 \text{ years}$$

Let us assume, however, that we do not survey all 400 members of this community. Instead we carry out the following experiment. We randomly select 120 people and ask only these 120 their respective ages. We then put these people back into the community of 400 and randomly select another 120 residents (which may include members of the first sample). We proceed to draw a third sample of 120 residents. We keep doing this over and over again — taking a random sample of 120 community members and calculating the average age for each *sample*.

This should sound a little like the experiment of dropping 100 balls down the board and seeing where they land, except instead of balls we are taking samples and seeing where the sample means 'fall'. I have actually performed this hypothetical experiment (not with real people but using SPSS, as will be illustrated below), and the results of these 20 repeated random samples are displayed in Table 7.1, in the order in which they were generated, rounding to the nearest decimal point.

Table 7.1 Distribution of 20 sample means (N = 120)

Sample number	Sample mean
1	35.1
2	35.9
3	35
4	34.8
5	38
6	34.2
7	35.7
8	35.3
9	35.8
10	35
11	34.4
12	33.6
13	36.3
14	35.6
15	36.45
16	33.8
17	37.1
18	36.6
19	36.1
20	35.8

These results are plotted in a graph (Figure 7.4).

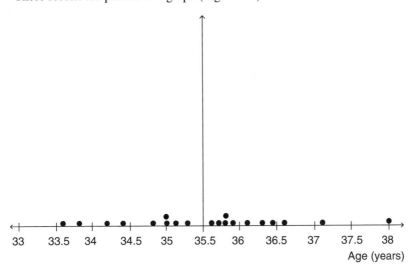

Figure 7.4

We can see that most of the results are clustered around the population value of 35.5 years, with a few scores a bit further out and one 'extreme' score of 38 years. This is obviously a sample that just happened by chance to select a few relatively older members of the community. Even so it is interesting to note that despite the fact that the individual ages of the 400 people in the community range from 2 years to 69 years of age, the means of the *samples* have a very narrow range of values. Nearly half of the 20 samples I took produced mean ages within half a year of the 'true' population average. This gives us some sense of the value and reliability of random samples.

Let us push this hypothetical example a little further, and imagine that we theoretically take an infinite number of random samples of equal size from this population and observe the distribution of the sample means. The pattern we have already observed with just 20 random samples will be reinforced. Most of the samples will cluster around the population mean, with the occasional sample result falling relatively further to one side or the other of the distribution. Such a distribution is a **sampling distribution**.

> A **sampling distribution** is the theoretical probability distribution of an infinite number of sample outcomes for a statistic, using random samples of equal size.

It is a *theoretical distribution* in that it is a construct derived on the basis of a logical exercise — the result that would follow *if* we could take an infinite number of random samples of equal size.

Here we are dealing with the **sampling distribution of sample means** since it is the distribution of all the possible *means* obtained from repeated samples. This sampling distribution of sample means will have three very important properties:

- **The mean of the sampling distribution is the same as that for the population** In other words, the average of the averages ($\mu_{\bar{X}}$) will be the same as the population mean. This is written formally in the following way:

$$\mu_{\bar{X}} = \mu$$

- The standard deviation of the sampling distribution, known as the **standard error** ($\sigma_{\bar{X}}$), will also be related to, but not the same as, that for the population. This is because the standard error is affected by sample size. If we are only taking samples of five people, and one of the people in this small sample happened to be 60 years of age, the average for this sample will be greatly affected by this one score, so that samples of size $N = 5$ will produce a very wide dispersion of results. But if sample size is 200 the effect of this one large score will be diluted by a greater number of cases that are closer to the true mean. So the repeated samples will be clustered closer to the population value. This is captured by the following formula for the standard error:

$$\sigma_{\bar{X}} = \frac{\sigma}{\sqrt{N}}$$

- **The sampling distribution will be normally distributed**

These features of the sampling distribution of sample means are illustrated in Figure 7.5.

(a)   Population

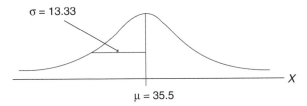

$\sigma = 13.33$

$\mu = 35.5$

(b)   Sampling distribution, $N = 20$

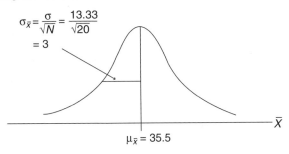

$$\sigma_{\bar{x}} = \frac{\sigma}{\sqrt{N}} = \frac{13.33}{\sqrt{20}}$$
$$= 3$$

$\mu_{\bar{x}} = 35.5$

(c)   Sampling distribution, $N = 100$

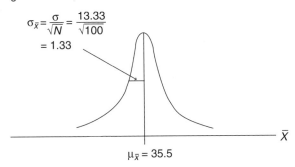

$$\sigma_{\bar{x}} = \frac{\sigma}{\sqrt{N}} = \frac{13.33}{\sqrt{100}}$$
$$= 1.33$$

$\mu_{\bar{x}} = 35.5$

Figure 7.5

Figure 7.5 (**a**) displays the distribution of all 400 people which is the population of the community. Figure 7.5 (**b**) is the sampling distribution of sample means for samples of size $N = 20$. In other words, it is the distribution of means we would get if we could repeatedly sample 20 people from this community. Figure 7.5 (**c**) is the sampling distribution of sample means for samples of size $N = 100$. We can see that both sampling distributions will be centred on the population mean of 35.5 years. Both will also be normally distributed. However, the standard error for each sampling distribution will vary. With repeated samples of size $N = 20$ there is a greater spread of means, with a standard error of 3 years, whereas with the larger samples the sample results are clustered more tightly around the mean. Both sampling distributions are normal, in that 68 per cent of all cases fall within 1 standard deviation from the mean. But for the sampling distribution where $N = 20$ this range will be between 32.5 years and 38.5 years:

$$35.5 \pm 3 = 32.5, 38.5 \text{ years}$$

Whereas for the second sampling distribution this range will be much narrower, having a lower limit of 34.17 years and an upper limit of 36.83 years:

$$35.5 \pm 1.33 = 34.17, 36.83 \text{ years}$$

The central limit theorem

We have thus far looked at the properties of a sampling distribution derived from a population that is normally distributed. In particular, the sampling distribution will also be normal. However, there are few populations in the social world that are even approximately normal. What if the ages of the 400 people in our small community are distributed in the way shown in Figure 7.6.

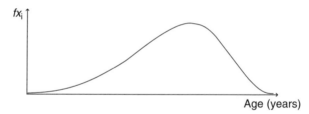

Figure 7.6 Age distribution of the community

The distribution is skewed to the left, indicating that there are relatively more older people than younger people in this community. It would seem that repeated random samples from this distribution would produce a skewed sampling distribution as well. However, this is not so. According to one of the key principles in statistics, the **central limit theorem** states that under certain conditions the sampling distribution will be normal, even though the population distribution from which the samples are drawn is not normal. (A proof of this theorem can be found in J.E. Freund, 1962, *Mathematical Statistics*, Prentice-Hall, Englewood Cliffs.)

The **central limit theorem** states that if an infinite number of random samples of equal size is selected from a population, the sampling distribution of the sample mean will approach a normal distribution as the sample size approaches infinity.

The population may be non-normal, yet repeated sampling will (theoretically) generate a normal sampling distribution. In fact, the sample size does not have to be as large as suggested in the formal statement of the theorem: once the sample size is greater than 100, the sampling distribution of sample means will be *approximately* normal.

Generating random samples using SPSS

We can generate repeated random samples on SPSS to see the spread of sample means. In fact this is how I got the results presented in Table 7.1. This is a fairly repetitive procedure, since we need to generate a large number of random sample means. There are two steps repeated in sequence over and over. The first is to select a random sample, and the second is to calculate the mean for the sample.

Selecting a random sample

Filename 7.sav   Using the data that have been entered on the ages of the 400 residents of our hypothetical community, the first step is to ask SPSS to randomly select a certain number of cases, which in this instance will be 120 (Table 7.2).

Table 7.2   Repeated random sampling on SPSS

SPSS command/action	Comments
1 From the menu select **Data/Select Cases...**	This will bring up the **Select Cases** dialogue box. The default setting is for SPSS to use all cases, indicated by the ● in the small circle next to **All cases**
2 Select **Random sample of cases** by clicking on the small circle next to this option	A ● will appear in the small circle next to **Random sample of cases** and the text below it will darken
3 Click on the **sample** button	This will bring up the **Select Cases: Random Sample** dialogue box. This gives us the option of selecting a certain percentage of cases, or a certain number of cases. Here we want a certain number of cases (120)
4 Click on the small circle next to **Exactly**	The cursor will jump into the box next to **Exactly**
5 Type 120	
6 Type 400 in the box next to **from the first**	
7 Click on **Continue**	
8 Click on **OK**	

Calculating the sample mean

The next step is to ask SPSS to calculate the mean for this sample using the **Statistics/Summarize/Frequencies...** command we learnt in Chapter 4. It might be helpful to select only the mean in this option, so that we do not get a frequency table and other descriptive statistics for each repeated sample, since this will generate more output than is necessary for our purpose here.

If you refer to the data window you will see that SPSS has placed a slash through most of the numbers in the shaded column on the left of the page. These cases are the ones that are not included in the calcualtion of the mean — the ones that have not been randomly selected. Similarly, you will notice that SPSS has created a new 'variable', which it calls **filter_$**. We do not actually use the filter ourselves, even though it will appear in variable lists. SPSS uses this variable to choose some cases in the sample and ignore others, by assigning a value of 1 to cases without a slash through their case number and 0 to those that have been 'slashed'.

Repeating the sampling procedure

Running these two commands in sequence will generate a mean for the randomly selected sample of 120 cases. To draw another random sample all that is required is that we select the **Data/Select Cases...** command and then click *directly* on **OK**. It is not necessary to again tell SPSS to randomly select 120 cases — it will automatically repeat the previous set of instructions and choose a new sample of 120. Similarly, by selecting **Statistics/Summarize/Frequencies...** and then clicking on **OK** a mean will be calculated without having to reselect all the options within this command. I have done this 20 times and the results are printed below.

AGE   Age of Respondent

Mean   35.76

Valid cases   120   Missing cases   0

AGE   Age of Respondent

Mean   34.983

Valid cases   120   Missing cases   0

AGE   Age of Respondent

Mean   34.367

Valid cases   120   Missing cases   0

AGE   Age of Respondent

Mean   33.608

Valid cases   120   Missing cases   0

AGE   Age of Respondent

Mean   36.317

Valid cases   120   Missing cases   0

AGE   Age of Respondent

Mean   35.625

Valid cases   120   Missing cases   0

AGE   Age of Respondent

Mean   36.450

Valid cases   120   Missing cases   0

AGE   Age of Respondent

Mean   35.092

Valid cases   120   Missing cases   0

AGE   Age of Respondent

Mean   35.883

Valid cases   120   Missing cases   0

AGE   Age of Respondent

Mean   35.025

Valid cases   120   Missing cases   0

AGE   Age of Respondent

Mean   34.800

Valid cases   120   Missing cases   0

AGE   Age of Respondent

Mean   38.000

Valid cases   120   Missing cases   0

AGE   Age of Respondent

Mean   34.242

Valid cases   120   Missing cases   0

AGE   Age of Respondent

Mean   35.700

Valid cases   120   Missing cases   0

AGE   Age of Respondent

Mean   35.308

Valid cases   120   Missing cases   0

AGE   Age of Respondent

Mean   33.817

Valid cases   120   Missing cases   0

AGE   Age of Respondent

Mean   37.142

Valid cases   120   Missing cases   0

AGE   Age of Respondent

Mean   36.600

Valid cases   120   Missing cases   0

AGE   Age of Respondent

Mean   36.142

Valid cases   120   Missing cases   0

AGE   Age of Respondent

Mean   35.780

Valid cases   120   Missing cases   0

Your own set of 20 results will differ from this, since we are working with random samples. These results do not constitute a true sampling distribution, since there are only 20 random samples, whereas a sampling distribution is theoretically the distribution of an *infinite* number of random samples. Despite this the general pattern is clear:

• Most of the sample results are very close to the population value of 35.5 years. There is some variation around this, but most sample results are clustered around the population parameter.
• The mean of these 20 means is 35.5 years.

- One sample mean is 38 years, which is relatively a great distance from the population parameter of 35.5. There is always a possibility that an individual sample may produce an 'odd' result, but repeated samples will tend to be 'true' to the population value.

Summary

We have spent a great deal of time in this chapter dealing with abstract theoretical concepts. In particular we have played around with a thought experiment: what if we could take an infinite number of samples of equal size from a certain population, and calculate the mean for each of these samples? At some point the critical reader will have thought 'but who gets to take an infinite number of samples?' Usually a social researcher only gets to take one sample from a population and has to determine what the population looks like from that one sample. What use is the sampling distribution then? In the next chapters we will see that it is the foundation stone on which inferences can be made from a single random sample to a population.

Exercises

7.1 What is the difference between a parameter and a statistic?

7.2 What is the difference between descriptive statistics and inferential statistics?

7.3 What is random variation? How does it affect our ability to make a generalization from a sample to a population?

7.4 If the mean of a normal population is 40, what will the mean of the sampling distribution be with $N = 30$; with $N = 120$?

7.5 What is meant by the standard error? Will it be equal to, greater than, or less than, the standard deviation for the population? Why?

7.6 Sketch the sampling distribution of samples means when $N = 30$ and when $N = 200$. In what way are these two distributions different, and in what way are they similar?

7.7 A teacher wants to evaluate a course by surveying registered students. She writes the letters in the alphabet on separate pieces of paper and selects the one with G written on it out of a hat. She therefore selects all students in class whose last name begins with G. In what ways, if any, is this sampling method non-random.

7.8 A library wants to assess the condition of the books in its possession. It randomly selects Thursday, and examines the condition of all books returned to the library on the following Thursday. In what ways, if any, is this sampling method non-random.

7.9 Describe a research project that might use the process of stratified random sampling.

7.10 Why is the central limit theorem so important to social research?

7.11 Using the data for the age distribution of the community of 400 people, draw another 20 random samples, this time using sample sizes of 30. How does the spread of results differ from that in the text, where sample size was 120?

Estimation and confidence intervals

In Chapter 7 we looked at the properties of a sampling distribution of sample means. This sampling distribution has three very important properties:

- The mean of the sampling distribution is equal to the population mean:

$$\mu_{\overline{X}} = \mu$$

Although the mean of any individual sample may differ from that of the population from which it is drawn, *repeated* random sample means will cluster around the 'true' population value. In other words, although results will vary from sample to sample, *on average* the sample means will be equal to that of the population. This property of a sample mean makes it an **unbiased estimator** of the population value.

> A sample statistic is **unbiased** if its sampling distribution has a mean equal to a population parameter.

- The second important property of the sampling distribution is that the spread of sample results around the population value is affected by the sample size. In fact, the standard deviation of the sampling distribution, called the standard error, is defined by the following equation:

$$\sigma_{\overline{X}} = \frac{\sigma}{\sqrt{N}}$$

As sample size increases the standard error of the sampling distribution gets smaller, so that sample results are more tightly clustered around the population value. In other words, large samples provide more **efficient** estimators of the population values.

> **Efficiency** is the degree to which sample results are clustered around a population parameter.

- The sampling distribution of sample means is normal.

These three properties of the sampling distribution of sample means allow us to refer to the table for the area under the standard normal curve in order to gauge the probability that any given sample mean will be within a certain range of values around the population mean. For example, we know that 95 per cent of repeated samples will have a mean within 1.96 standard errors of the population mean (Figure 8.1).

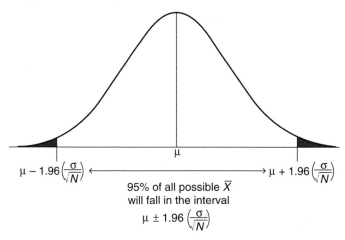

$$\mu - 1.96\left(\frac{\sigma}{\sqrt{N}}\right) \longleftarrow \qquad \longrightarrow \mu + 1.96\left(\frac{\sigma}{\sqrt{N}}\right)$$

95% of all possible $\overline{X}$
will fall in the interval

$$\mu \pm 1.96\left(\frac{\sigma}{\sqrt{N}}\right)$$

Figure 8.1   Sampling distribution of $\overline{X}$

This allows us to specify a range or **interval** of scores within which 95 per cent of all possible sample means will fall, defined by the formula:

$$\mu \pm 1.96\left(\frac{\sigma}{\sqrt{N}}\right)$$

Estimation

In Figure 8.1 we posed the problem in a certain way. We have a population parameter, and estimate the range of values that 95 per cent of all random samples drawn from that population will take. However, in research the problem usually poses itself in a different way. We have a single sample result, and we need to estimate the population value from the sample (Figure 8.2).

For example, in the previous chapter we randomly selected a series of samples of size $N = 120$ from a population of 400 residents of a hypothetical community. The average age for this population was 35.5 years, but we saw that the averages for each of these samples were not equal to the population value, but most of them clustered around the population value. But what if we did not know that the mean age of the population was 35.5 years, and all

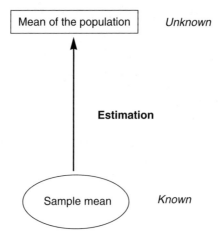

Figure 8.2

we had to work with was *one* of these samples of 120 residents? Let us assume that this one-and-only sample is the one that produced an average age of 36.3 years and our task is to estimate the population parameter (which for the moment we are pretending we do not know) from this one sample result.

In estimating the population parameter we start with an assumption. We assume that the sample actually falls within a certain region of the sampling distribution. We assume that the sample mean is not one of those few, very unlikely and extreme results that are very different from the population value. For example, we might feel comfortable with the assumption that this one sample of 120 residents is one of the 95 per cent of all *possible* samples that will fall within ±1.96 standard errors from the population mean.

Remember that this is only an assumption: we may have actually drawn one of those freakish samples that has a mean very different from the population parameter. We can never know if this is the case, but given the very low probability of this being the case (less than 5-in-100), the assumption seems reasonable. In other words we can be confident that this assumption is correct. In fact, we call this assumed probability the **confidence level**; in this instance we choose a 95 per cent confidence level.

Given this assumption — that the sample result is within the range that 95 per cent of all possible sample results will fall — we can make an **estimate** of the population value. We know that the sampling distribution will have a standard deviation, called the standard error, of:

$$\sigma_{\overline{X}} = \frac{\sigma}{\sqrt{N}}$$

Here, though, we do not know the standard deviation for the population, σ, so we use the sample standard deviation instead, which for this sample is equal to 13.3 years. For reasons we will come to in later chapters, when assuming that the population standard deviation is equal to the sample standard deviation we also have to subtract 1 from the sample size in the denominator of the equation:

$$\sigma_{\overline{X}} = \frac{s}{\sqrt{N-1}}$$

$$= \frac{13.3}{\sqrt{120-1}}$$

$$= 1.2 \text{ years}$$

Given this value for the standard error the furthest the population parameter can be *below* the sample value such that the sample value remains within the 95 per cent region is –1.96 standard errors. This is called the **lower limit** of the estimate. It sets the maximum distance that the population value will be below the sample (Figure 8.3).

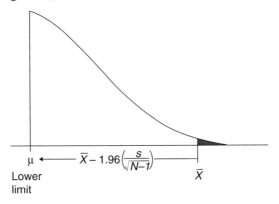

Figure 8.3

$$\text{lower limit} = \overline{X} - z\left(\frac{s}{\sqrt{N-1}}\right)$$

Using similar reasoning, the furthest the population parameter can be *above* the sample value so that the sample value is within the 95 per cent region is +1.96 standard errors. This is called the **upper limit** (Figure 8.4).

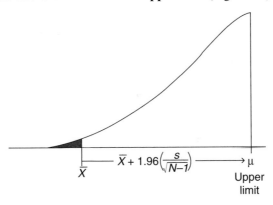

Figure 8.4

$$\text{upper limit} = \overline{X} + z\left(\frac{s}{\sqrt{N-1}}\right)$$

Putting these two pieces of logic together allows us to define a range of values, called a **confidence interval**, within which we estimate lies the population parameter.

> A **confidence interval** is the range of values that, it is estimated, includes a population parameter, at a specific level of confidence.

The steps involved in determining the lower limit and the upper limit of a confidence interval (*ci*) (Figure 8.5) can be combined in the following equation:

$$ci = \overline{X} \pm z\left(\frac{s}{\sqrt{N-1}}\right)$$

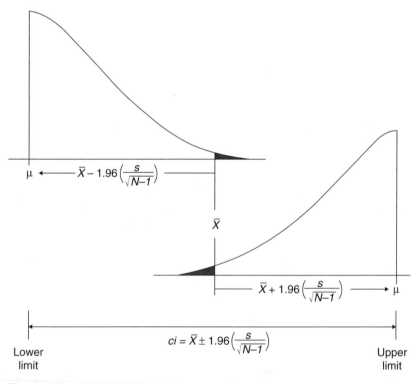

Figure 8.5

This equation simply states that we add and subtract from the sample result a distance defined by the maximum number of z-scores we assume the sample result can be from the population parameter. We have been working with a z-score of 1.96, because we assumed that the sample was one of the 95 per cent of all possible samples that fall closest to the population mean. In the example of the age of our residents, the lower and upper limits are:

$$\text{lower limit} = \overline{X} - z \left(\frac{s}{\sqrt{N-1}} \right)$$

$$= 36.3 - 1.96 \left(\frac{13.3}{\sqrt{120-1}} \right)$$

$$= 36.3 - 1.96(1.2)$$

$$= 33.95$$

$$\text{upper limit} = \overline{X} + z \left(\frac{s}{\sqrt{N-1}} \right)$$

$$= 36.3 + 1.96 \left(\frac{13.3}{\sqrt{120-1}} \right)$$

$$= 36.3 + 1.96(1.2)$$

$$= 38.65$$

We write such an estimate in the following way: 36.3 [33.95, 38.65].

Another way of illustrating this result is shown in Figure 8.6.

We have constructed a confidence *interval* because in estimating the average age of the population from a single sample we need to allow for the effects of sampling variation. Looking at the estimate we have constructed from this sample, we can see that it includes the actual population average of 35.5 years, which we pretended we did not know. The confidence interval is accurate in that the range of values between 33.95 and 38.65 years includes this real average. Normally we do not know whether the estimate is accurate, but the confidence level indicates the probability of being accurate.

In fact I have constructed a confidence interval around all the 20 random samples drawn from this hypothetical population in Chapter 7. The sample averages have been graphed and the confidence intervals around them drawn in Figure 8.7.

Looking at Figure 8.7 we can see the potential problem with making an estimate using sample results. If the one sample we drew happened to be the one that produced an average of 38 years, our estimate would be inaccurate. The assumption that this is one of the 95 per cent of samples that will fall

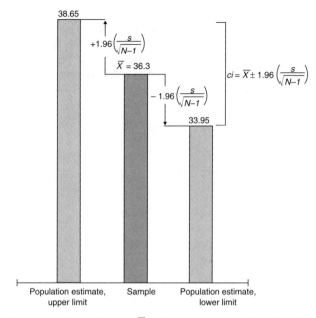

Figure 8.6 Population estimate, $\bar{X} = 35.5$ years, $\alpha = 0.05$, $N = 120$

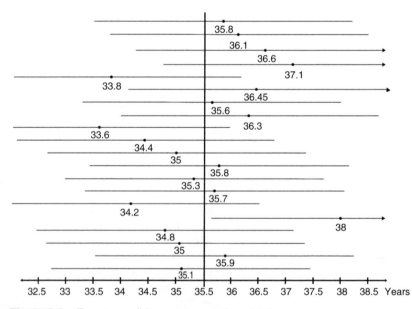

Figure 8.7 Twenty confidence intervals ($\alpha = 0.05$)

within 1.96 standard errors from the population value is invalid: it is one of those 5-in-100 samples that fall a relatively long distance from the mean. Therefore the interval constructed on the basis of a 95 per cent confidence level will not take in the parameter of 35.5 years. We can never know whether this is the case — whether the one sample we do undertake just happens to be 'freakish'. However, we can see from Figure 8.7 that such an event is highly unlikely. In fact, 19 out of the 20 intervals do include the true population value of 35.5 years, which is in accord with the confidence level of 95 per cent.

Another way to think of this is that with a confidence level of 95 per cent we are prepared to be wrong only 5 times in every 100 samples (i.e. 1-in-20). This is the risk we take of not including the population parameter in our interval estimate, given that we have to make an estimate based on a sample that is affected by random variation. This probability of error is known as the **alpha level** (α), which is simply 1 minus the confidence level (expressed as a proportion). Thus the 95 per cent (0.95) confidence level is the same as an alpha level of $\alpha = 0.05$. A 90 per cent confidence level is the same as an alpha level of $\alpha = 0.10$, or a risk of being wrong 1-time-in-10.

Changing the confidence level

In this discussion, we chose a confidence level of 95 per cent. This is why we multiplied the standard error by a z-score of 1.96, since this defines the region under the sampling distribution that includes 95 per cent of repeated sample results. This is the commonly used confidence level, but we can choose either larger or smaller levels, depending on how accurate we want to be. The larger the confidence level the more likely that the interval derived from it will include the population mean. If we choose a 99 per cent confidence interval, for example, then we are assuming that a given sample mean is one of the 99-in-100 that falls **2.58** standard errors either side of the true mean:

$$ci = \overline{X} \pm 2.58 \left(\frac{s}{\sqrt{N-1}} \right)$$

However, making the starting assumption safer by choosing a larger confidence level comes at a cost. In order for us to argue that the sample is one of the 99 per cent that fall within a certain region around the true value, that region has to be widened. Rather than multiplying the standard error by $z = 1.96$, we multiply by $z = 2.58$. It is like firing an arrow at a target. Making an assumption that an arrow is likely to fall within 1 m of the bullseye is safer than making the assumption that it will fall within 10 cm of the bullseye, but it has come at the cost of some accuracy. Making the target 'bigger' by widening the confidence interval means we are more likely to 'hit it' (i.e. make sure that the interval includes the population value), but we are no longer as precise in our marksmanship.

To see the effect of choosing different confidence levels we will work through the following example. A random sample of 200 carpenters is taken and each person asked his or her annual income in whole dollars. These 200 carpenters have an average income of $35 000, with a standard deviation of $5000.

$$\overline{X} = \$35\,000$$

$$s = \$500$$

$$N = 200$$

What is our estimate for the average annual income of all carpenters? If we choose a 95 per cent confidence interval the range (rounded to the nearest whole dollar) is:

$$ci = \overline{X} \pm z\left(\frac{s}{\sqrt{N-1}}\right)$$

$$ci = 35\,000 \pm 1.96\left(\frac{5000}{\sqrt{120-1}}\right)$$

$$ci = 35\,000 \pm 695$$

The upper and lower limits will be:

lower limit: $35\,000 - 695 = \$34\,305$

and

upper limit: $35\,000 + 695 = \$35\,695$

We therefore estimate that the average income of all carpenters, with a 95 per cent level of confidence, will lie within the following range:

$$\$34\,305 \le \mu \le \$35\,695$$

The interval width is:

interval width $= 35\,695 - 34\,305 = \$1390$

With a 99 per cent confidence interval, the z-score we use in the calculation is 2.58. The calculation will thereby be:

$$ci = \overline{X} \pm z\left(\frac{s}{\sqrt{N-1}}\right)$$

$$= 35\,000 \pm 2.58 \left(\frac{5000}{\sqrt{200-1}} \right)$$

$$= 35\,000 \pm 915$$

$$= 35\,000\ [34\,085,\ 35\,915]$$

To be more confident that the interval will actually contain the true population value, it has become much wider; it now ranges from $34 085 to $35 915.

If, on the other hand, I want to be more precise in my estimate I will choose a 90 per cent confidence level, but this will be at the higher risk of being wrong. The confidence interval for this level will be, with $z = 1.645$:

$$ci = 35\,000 \pm 1.645 \left(\frac{5000}{\sqrt{200-1}} \right)$$

$$= 35\,000 \pm 585$$

$$= 35\,000\ [34\,415,\ 35\,585]$$

The effect of these changes to the confidence level on our estimates is summarized in Table 8.1.

Table 8.1 The effect of confidence levels on interval width ($N = 200$)

Confidence level (%)	z-score	Confidence interval	Interval width
90	1.645	$35 000±585	$1170
95	1.96	$35 000±695	$1390
99	2.58	$35 000±915	$1830

We can see this illustrated in Figure 8.8.

Using a smaller confidence level reduces the interval width in which we estimate the population value lies. However, because this interval width is smaller the chances of being wrong (which is equal to the alpha level) have also increased. Having a narrower range of values increases the chance that it will not include the mean of the population. Making the bullseye on a target smaller allows us to say that we are better archers if we hit it, but it also increases the chances of not hitting it. On the other hand, choosing a confidence level of 99 per cent widens the interval estimate so that it is more likely to include the population value, but it may as a result make the estimate meaningless. Knowing that the mean annual income of carpenters can be anywhere between $34 085 and $35 915 may actually be saying nothing of practical importance.

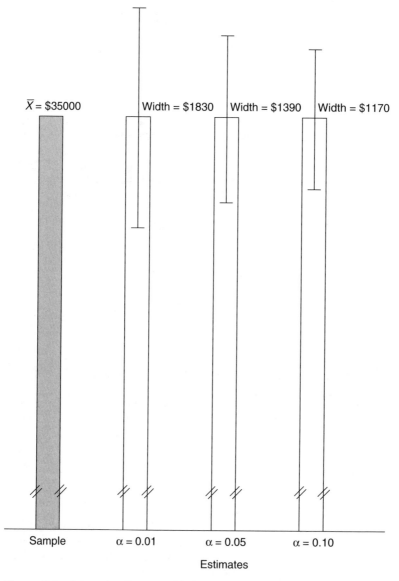

Figure 8.8 Interval estimates with three different confidence levels ($N = 200$)

Changing the sample size

Apart from the alpha level, the other factor that will determine the width of the confidence interval is the sample size. If we stick with a confidence level of 95 per cent, and only vary the sample size, we will see that the width gets smaller (we increase our accuracy) as sample size increases (Table 8.2, Figure 8.9).

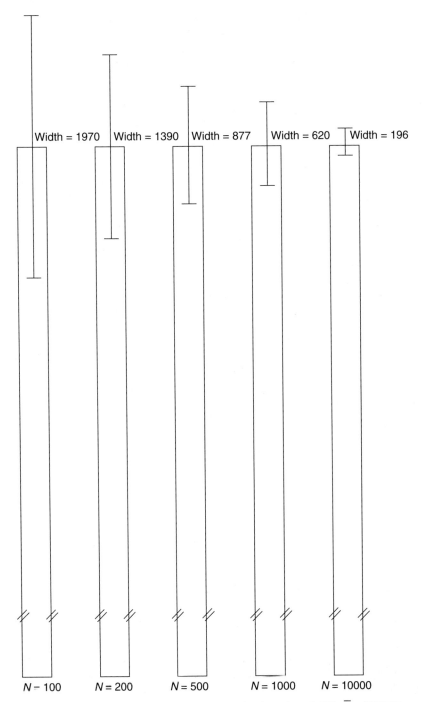

Figure 8.9   Interval estimates for five sample sizes ($\alpha = 0.05$), $\bar{X} = \$35000$

Table 8.2   The effect of sample size on interval width ($\alpha = 0.05$)

Sample size	Interval width
100	$1970
200	$1390
500	$877
1000	$620
10000	$196

One thing to notice about the effect of sample size is that enlarging the sample has its greatest effect on the interval width with small samples. Increasing the sample size from 100 to 200 reduces the interval width by $580, which is more than the reduction in interval width when sample size is expanded from 1000 to 10 000 ($424). This is why many social surveys and public opinion polls, even when generalizing to a population of millions, will have sample sizes of only 1200–1400. Samples of this size narrow the confidence interval to a relatively small width, and to increase sample size any further would increase research costs without obtaining much greater accuracy.

Example 1
We want to estimate the mean age of all children in preschool. A random sample of 140 preschool children has a mean of 3.75 years and a standard deviation of 0.8 years. What do we estimate the average age of all preschool children to be?

$$\overline{X} = 3.75$$

$$s = 0.8$$

$$N = 140$$

$$\text{at } \alpha = 0.05 \; z = 1.96$$

$$ci = \overline{X} \pm z \left(\frac{s}{\sqrt{N-1}} \right)$$

$$ci = 3.75 \pm 1.96 \left(\frac{0.8}{\sqrt{140-1}} \right)$$

$$ci = 3.75 \pm 0.13$$

We therefore expect the average age of all preschool children to be between 3.62 years and 3.88 years of age. We would write this estimate as 3.75 years [3.62, 3.88].

Example 2

A random sample of 300 people watches, on average, 150 minutes of television nightly, with a standard deviation of 50 minutes. What can we estimate the population average to be?

If we choose a confidence level of 95 per cent the lower limit will be:

$$\text{lower limit} = \overline{X} - z\left(\frac{s}{\sqrt{N-1}}\right)$$

$$= 150 - 1.96\left(\frac{50}{\sqrt{300-1}}\right)$$

$$= 150 - 5.7$$

$$= 144.3 \text{ minutes}$$

The upper limit will be:

$$\text{upper limit} = \overline{X} + z\left(\frac{s}{\sqrt{N-1}}\right)$$

$$= 150 + 1.96\left(\frac{50}{\sqrt{300-1}}\right)$$

$$= 150 + 5.7$$

$$= 155.7 \text{ minutes}$$

Thus the estimated average amount of TV watched nightly, with a 95 per cent confidence level, is 150 minutes [144.3, 155.7].

Choosing the sample size

In designing a research project a number of factors enter into the decision-making. Sampling can be a very expensive procedure, if we account for training, travel, and time that may be involved in conducting a large survey. Thus we want to ensure that we have a sufficiently large sample that will give us the accuracy we seek, but not larger than is necessary. We can use the logic of estimation to determine the 'right' size sample we need, given the level of accuracy we are after. For example, we might already have in mind a certain interval width; in the example we used above for the income of carpenters, we might want to estimate within $1000 the average annual income of this group of people. Thus the interval width is pre-specified by the research problem, and now we work 'backwards' to determine the appropriate sample size that will yield a confidence interval of this size. Without going through the proof, we can derive the formula for selecting the appropriate sample size from the formula we used above:

$$N = \frac{z^2 \times \sigma^2}{\left(\frac{\text{width}}{2}\right)^2}$$

Here we have pre-specified the width we want: $1000. If we choose a 95 per cent confidence level, $z = 1.96$.

The last remaining bit of information needed to derive the sample size is the standard deviation for the population, and this is what limits the use of this technique. Since it is a procedure for designing a research project, rather than a procedure for analysing data that we already gathered, we obviously cannot use the sample standard deviation as a substitute for σ. The sample hasn't been taken yet! Thus this procedure is restricted to situations where the population standard deviation is known. Let's assume for the sake of exposition that the population standard deviation is known to be $5000. We can substitute the relevant information into the equation and determine the appropriate sample size:

$$N = \frac{z^2 \times \sigma^2}{\left(\frac{\text{width}}{2}\right)^2}$$

$$= \frac{1.96^2 \times 5000^2}{\left(\frac{1000}{2}\right)^2}$$

$$= 384$$

We need a sample size of at least 384 if we are to derive a confidence interval with a width no greater than $1000.

To illustrate the procedure again, let us now assume that we want to be much more accurate: we want our estimate to be no wider than $500, at a 95 per cent level of confidence. For some reason we need to be much closer to the mark. What size sample should we be prepared to take?

$$N = \frac{z^2 \times \sigma^2}{\left(\frac{\text{width}}{2}\right)^2}$$

$$= \frac{1.96^2 \times 5000^2}{\left(\frac{500}{2}\right)^2}$$

$$= 1586$$

We can see the same idea as that discussed above: to be more accurate in our estimate we need to take a much larger sample, since larger samples have a smaller standard error around the true population parameter. To narrow the estimate of carpenters' annual income to a smaller band of $500 we have to use a sample of 1586.

Exercises

8.1 What is meant by interval estimation?

8.2 Explain what is meant by a confidence level. How do changes in the confidence level affect the width of the interval estimate?

8.3 How does sample size affect the confidence interval?

8.4 How does the standard deviation of the population affect the width of a confidence interval?

8.5 For the examples in the text construct interval estimates for 90 per cent and 99 per cent confidence levels.

8.6 A survey is conducted to measure the length of time, in months, taken for university graduates to gain their first job. Assuming that this is a normally distributed variable, derive the interval estimates for the following sets of graduates, using a 95 per cent confidence level:

Degree	Sample size	Mean	Standard deviation
Economics	45	6	2.5
Sociology	35	4	2
History	40	4.5	3
Statistics	60	3	1.5

8.7 To gauge the effect of enterprise bargaining agreements, union officials select a sample of 120 workers from randomly selected enterprises across an industry. The average wage rise in the previous year for these 120 workers was $1018, with a standard deviation of $614. Estimate the increase for all workers within this industry (use both 95 per cent and 99 per cent confidence levels).

8.8 A hospital checks the records of 340 randomly selected patients from the previous year. The average length of stay in the hospital for these patients was 4.3 days, with a standard deviation of 3.1 days. What would be the estimated average length of stay of all patients in the previous year (at a 99 per cent confidence level). How would this compare with the average length of stay for all patients in another hospital of 4 days? What could the hospital do to improve the accuracy of the estimate?

8.9 A study of 120 divorced couples who had been married in the same year found an average length of marriage of 8.5 years, with a standard deviation of 1.2 years. What is the estimate for the average length of marriage for all divorced couples, using a confidence level of 95 per cent.

9

Introduction to hypothesis testing: The *z*-test for a single mean

Hypothesis testing: The general idea

The previous chapter analysed the process of estimating an unknown population parameter from a sample result. The general problem addressed in that chapter can be illustrated as shown in Figure 9.1.

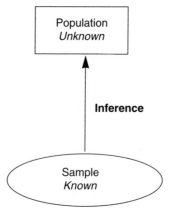

Figure 9.1

In estimation, that is, we try to find what the value of the population parameter is. However, in social research we are often confronted with a slightly different problem; one that we will see involves the process of **hypothesis testing**. We often make an inference from a sample statistic to a population parameter so that we can compare the parameter with a specific value. That is, in hypothesis testing we asses whether or not the population parameter has a specific value, rather than just try to determine the range of values that will include the parameter.

There are two situations where we might want to investigate whether a population parameter takes on a specific value. The first is where a particular value is chosen for practical or theoretical reasons. For example, a company may decide that anything more than a 5 per cent reject rate for its product is unacceptable. It therefore instructs its quality control department to sample 300 randomly selected products and determine whether the reject rate is 5 per cent or more. Thus the company is not simply interested in finding whatever the value of the population parameter happens to be; it wants to know whether this population parameter is specifically 5 per cent or more.

The other situation in which we will have a specified 'test' value is where we want to compare the population under investigation with another population whose parameter value is *known*. For example, we want to compare two populations in terms of their respective average heights: *all* statistics students and *all* other university students. We know the average height of all students. However, we only have a sample of statistics students, so we have to make an inference (which is basically a fancy word for an educated guess) whether the height of all statistics students is equal to the known value for all other students.

In both instances we are only making one inference, so they are called a one-sample problem. This one-sample problem, for the example of the height of students, is illustrated in Figure 9.2.

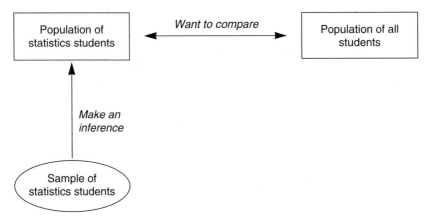

Figure 9.2

We decide whether a population parameter takes a specific value through the process of hypothesis testing. But before turning to a detailed description of hypothesis testing procedures, we will pose this problem in a slightly different way: as a problem of betting on a two-horse race.

Assume you are at a racetrack and about to place a bet on an upcoming race that only has two horses running. From the form guide you know that one of these horses will win 1 race in every 100 — will you put your money on it? Probably not. If the odds of this horse winning are 1 in 20 races, will you bet on it? Maybe. Essentially, inferential statistics involves the same mental exercise — two 'runners' are lined up against each other, and the odds of one of these runners 'winning' are calculated. We then decide which one we will bet on.

The reason we have to gamble is that, as we have seen, information from a random sample is not always an accurate reflection of the population from which the sample is drawn. To see this we will elaborate the example of the height of statistics students. From the Student Records Office it is learnt that all students at a university have an average height of 170 cm with a standard deviation of 30 cm around the mean.

We also obtain a list of statistics students and from this list we randomly sample 150 and measure their height:

$$\overline{X} = 162 \text{ cm}$$

It is clear that there is a difference between the *sample* of statistics students and the population of all students, but does this reflect a difference between the *population* of statistics students and other students?

There are two possible explanations for this difference:

- Statistics students *are the same as* all other university students, but our sample just happened to select, by chance, a lot of short people. We will call this explanation of our sample result the 'null hypothesis of no difference'. Mathematically we will write this as:

$$\mu = 170 \text{ cm}$$

In other words, if we could survey *all* statistics students we will find that their average height (μ) is the same as that for all other students (170 cm), but random variation caused the sample of 150 to be a little unusual (Figure 9.3).

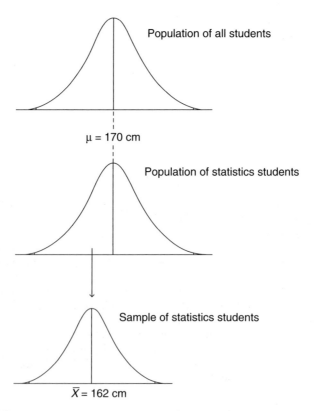

Figure 9.3

- All statistics students *are not like* all university students in terms of their average height. For one reason or another, statistics students are systematically different from all other students. Our sample reflects this difference (Figure 9.4).

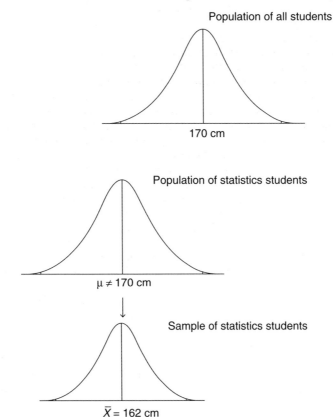

Figure 9.4

We will call this the 'alternative hypothesis'. Symbolically, we write:

$$\mu \neq 170 \text{ cm}$$

These two hypotheses are mutually exclusive: if one is right the other is wrong. Statistics students are on the whole different or they are not. This is like the two-horse race where only one can win. If I now said that the chances that the null hypothesis of no difference being correct is 100-to-1, will you bet on it? What about if the odds were 10-to-1? Inferential statistics provide us with these odds.

The whole hypothesis testing procedure proceeds on the *assumption* that the null hypothesis of no difference is correct. This may at first seem strange, since usually we undertake research in the hope of discovering a difference. Why then assume no difference? It is because we think this assumption is incorrect that we make it. The logical exercise involved in hypothesis testing is to show that the assumption of no difference is 'inconsistent' with our research findings, thereby leading us to argue that this is an unjustified assumption. We try to prove that there is a difference by *disproving* its opposite — the assumption of no difference. This may seem like the long way to go about reaching a conclusion, but if we work through enough examples in the following chapters we will see that we are *testing an assumption* by seeing whether our research data are 'plausibly' consistent with it.

To expand on this logic a little further let us go back to the example of the height of statistics students. Assume that statistics students are on average the same height as everybody else (i.e. 170 cm). We are, in other words, *assuming* that the null hypothesis of no difference is true. The sample of 150 statistics students, however, produced an average height of 162 cm. Is this sample result inconsistent with the assumption that the population average is 170 cm? What is the probability of getting a sample with average height of 162 cm or less from a population with the hypothesized value of 170 cm?

This is where the sampling distribution of sample means enters the picture. Remember that the sampling distribution is the distribution of means for repeated random samples of equal size. We can therefore refer to the sampling distribution, whose properties we know in detail, to determine the probability of getting a sample mean of 162 cm, *if* the population value is 170 cm. This will give us the odds to allow us to place our bet on either the null hypothesis or alternative hypothesis. Deriving these probabilities is a fairly straightforward procedure, which we are now familiar with: convert the sample statistic — the mean height in centimetres — into a z-score and look up the associated probability from the table for the area under the standard normal curve:

$$\text{Sample result} \rightarrow \text{calculate } z \rightarrow \text{look up probability}$$

So the first step is to calculate the z-score that is associated with our sample result. When calculating z-scores for this case we use the following formula:

$$z = \frac{\overline{X} - \mu}{\sigma_{\overline{X}}} = \frac{\overline{X} - \mu}{\sigma / \sqrt{N}}$$

For the sample of 150 statistics students whose average height is 162 cm, the z-score is:

$$z_{\text{sample}} = \frac{\overline{X} - \mu}{\sigma / \sqrt{N}}$$

$$= \frac{162 - 170}{30 / \sqrt{150}}$$

$$= \frac{-8}{2.45}$$

$$= -3.3$$

The next step is to look up the table for the area under the standard normal curve (Table 9.1) and determine the probability of getting a z-score of -3.3 or more.

Table 9.1   Area under the standard normal curve

z	Area under curve between *points*	Area under curve beyond *points*	Area under curve beyond *one point*
±0.1	0.080	0.920	0.460
±0.2	0.159	0.841	0.4205
±0.3	0.236	0.764	0.382
±0.4	0.311	0.689	0.3445
±0.5	0.383	0.617	0.3085
±0.6	0.451	0.549	0.2745
±0.7	0.516	0.484	0.242
±0.8	0.576	0.424	0.212
±0.9	0.632	0.368	0.184
±1	0.683	0.317	0.1585
±1.1	0.729	0.271	0.1355
±1.2	0.770	0.230	0.115
±1.3	0.806	0.194	0.097
±1.4	0.838	0.162	0.081
±1.5	0.866	0.134	0.067
±1.6	0.890	0.110	0.055
±1.645	0.900	0.100	0.050
±1.7	0.911	0.089	0.0445
±1.8	0.928	0.072	0.036
±1.9	0.943	0.057	0.029
±1.96	0.950	0.050	0.025
±2	0.954	0.046	0.023
±3.1	0.998	0.002	0.0001
±3.2	0.9986	0.0014	0.0007
±3.3	0.9990	0.0010	0.0005
±3.4	0.9993	0.0007	0.0003
±3.5	0.9995	0.0005	0.00025
±3.6	0.9997	0.0003	0.00015
±3.7	0.9998	0.0002	0.0001
±3.8	0.99986	0.00014	0.00007
±3.9	0.99990	0.00010	0.00005
±4	>0.99990	<0.00010	<0.00005

The area under the curve beyond this z-score is 0.0005, which is equivalent to the probability of drawing, from a population with an average height of 170 cm, a sample with an average height of 162 cm or less; that is, only 5-in-10 000 samples.

We are left with a choice. Either:

- we can still hold that the assumption of no difference is correct, and dismiss the sample result as one of those fluke 5-in-10 000 events, or

- we can say that the assumption of no difference is wrong — the sample statistic is not a 'freak', but instead reflects that the underlying population does not have an average height of 170 cm.

It might be a safer bet, therefore, to reject the assumption that the sample came from a population with an average height of 170 cm. It is clear that the difference between our sample result and the population value we compare it with is so great it is most unlikely that it came about by random variation. It reflects that we are sampling from a population with an average height less than 170 cm.

To illustrate this procedure again, let's suppose that the sample of 150 statistics students yielded the result:

$$\overline{X} = 172 \text{ cm}$$

To find out how many random samples will produce an average of 172 cm or more, *if* the null hypothesis is true, we need to convert the sample result into a *z*-score:

$$z_{sample} = \frac{\overline{X} - \mu}{\sigma / \sqrt{N}}$$

$$= \frac{172 - 170}{30 / \sqrt{150}}$$

$$= \frac{2}{2.45}$$

$$= 0.8$$

In other words, 172 cm is only 0.8 standard deviations from the population mean. The table for the area under the standard normal curve indicates that the probability of obtaining this *z*-score is 0.212 (see Table 9.2).

Since 21-in-100 samples drawn from a population with an average height of 170 cm will have an average height of 172 cm or more, we can say that the difference between the sample we have taken and the population came about by chance. We assumed (hypothesized) that the population had an average height of 170 cm. The sample, though, produced an average of 172 cm. Despite the difference the result is not inconsistent with the assumption. It seems safe to assume, that is, that all statistics students have an average height equal to all other students, and the 2 cm difference observed here is due to random variation.

Hypothesis testing in detail

The material to be presented in later chapters is simply variation on this theme. The variation is due to the different amount of information that we

Table 9.2   Area under the standard normal curve

z	Area under curve between *points*	Area under curve beyond *points*	Area under curve beyond *one point*
±0.1	0.080	0.920	0.460
±0.2	0.159	0.841	0.4205
±0.3	0.236	0.764	0.382
±0.4	0.311	0.689	0.3445
±0.5	0.383	0.617	0.3085
±0.6	0.451	0.549	0.2745
±0.7	0.516	0.484	0.242
±0.8	0.576	0.424	0.212
±0.9	0.632	0.368	0.184
±1	0.683	0.317	0.1585
±4	>0.9999	<0.0001	<0.00005

encounter in doing research. These differences, however, do not change the basic method of approach. In fact, we can approach just about any problem of inference using the following five-step procedure:

Step 1:   State the null and alternative hypotheses.
Step 2:   Choose the test of significance.
Step 3:   Establish the critical score(s) and critical region.
Step 4:   Calculate the sample score(s).
Step 5:   Make a decision.

We will go through each of these steps in more detail before turning to a couple of examples that illustrate this procedure.

Step 1: State the null and alternative hypotheses

An **hypothesis** is a well defined statement or claim about the characteristics of a population.

There must be three elements to a well-stated hypothesis:

- It must be clearly capable of being accepted or rejected.
- It must be amenable to quantification.
- It must state the population(s) for which an inference is made.

For example:
'Men from Sydney are on average taller than men from Melbourne.'

'People who smoke cigarettes suffer from higher rates of lung cancer than people who do not smoke.'

'Students from private schools have higher drop-out rates at university than students from public schools.'

As we did above, we normally state hypotheses in two opposite, mutually exclusive ways:

- **The null hypothesis of no difference (H_0)** This is a statement that the population parameter under investigation will equal a specified value. In other words, we hypothesize that the population value will not be different from some predefined value. In our previous examples the null hypothesis was that the average height of statistics students equalled 170 cm.

  An abbreviated way of writing the null is in mathematical shorthand, depending on the feature of the population we are making an hypothesis about. If we are making an hypothesis about the population mean, for example, the general form of the null hypothesis is,

  $$H_0: \mu = X$$

  where X is the prespecified 'test' value.
- **The alternative hypothesis (H_a)** This is a statement that the population parameter does not equal the pre-specified value; that *there is a difference*:

  $$H_a: \mu \neq X$$

The alternative hypothesis can actually take another, more precise, form. Instead of arguing that there is a difference, we might also suspect that the difference will have a *direction*. For example, we might suspect that statistics students are not only likely to have a different average height, but we also suspect that they might be systematically *shorter* than the rest of the student body, or, we may say that statistics students are likely to be on average *taller* than the rest of the student population:

$$\mu < X \ \text{ or } \ \mu > X$$

Step 2: Choose the test of significance

There are many tests available to help us decide between the null and alternative hypotheses. All of these tests require random samples (or at least reasonably random samples), but they vary according to the information available to the researcher. In this chapter we have introduced the most basic test, called the one-sample z-test of a mean. Often these tests of significance are given a shorthand name based on the statistician who first devised them, such as the Wilcoxon test. Generally, the important factors that determine the choice of a test are:

- the level of measurement;
- the sample size;
- the number of samples from which inferences are being made;
- the amount of information we have about the population(s);
- whether we have independent or dependent samples.

Tables 9.3 to 9.6 provide a quick guide for selecting the appropriate test of significance, based on these factors. These do not exhaust all the possible hypothesis tests available; they present only those that will be covered in this and following chapters.

Table 9.3   Tests of significance: The one-sample case

Level of measurement	Test of significance
Nominal/ordinal	• *z*-test for a proportion (binomial distributions) • Chi-square goodness-of-fit test • Runs test for randomness
Interval/ratio	• *z*-test for a mean (population standard deviation is known) • *t*-test for a mean (population standard deviation is unknown)

Table 9.4   Tests of significance: The two independent samples case

Level of measurement	Test of significance
Nominal	• Chi-square test for independence (can also use a *z*-test for proportions with binomial distributions)
Ordinal	• Wilcoxon rank-sum test (equivalent to Mann–Whitney test)
Interval/ratio	• *t*-test for the equality in means

Table 9.5   Tests of significance: More than two independent samples

Level of measurement	Test of significance
Nominal	• Chi-square test for independence
Ordinal	• Kruskal–Wallis test
Interval/ratio	• Analysis of variance *F*-test for the equality of means

Table 9.6   Tests of significance: Two dependent samples

Level of measurement	Test of significance
Nominal	• McNemar test for binomial distributions
Ordinal	• Wilcoxon signed-ranks test
Interval/ratio	• *t*-test for the mean difference

When using these tables to select a test, it should be remembered that any test that can be applied to a specific level of measurement can also be applied to higher levels of measurement. Thus a test listed in the tables for nominal data can also be applied to ordinal and interval/ratio data. Similarly, ordinal tests can be applied to interval/ratio data. Looking at the situations under which the various tests are applicable will be the subject of the rest of the chapters on inference. The chapters are basically organized around these individual tests, so that the conditions under which each is applicable will be clearly delineated.

This chapter will cover the use of a single sample z-test for a mean. The conditions that allow this test to be used are:

- the level of measurement is interval/ratio;
- the population is normally distributed along the variable; and/or
- the sample size is large ($N \geq 100$).

Either of these last two conditions, according to the central limit theorem, will guarantee that the sampling distribution of sample means is normal.

Step 3: Establish the critical score(s) and critical region
This step can be broken down into three parts:

Choosing the level of significance
In the examples we used to analyse the height of statistics students, the decision whether to reject or not to reject the null hypothesis was easy. In the first instance, with a sample mean of 162 cm the probability of the null hypothesis being true was very small; in the second instance with a sample mean of 172 cm the probability was very large. But what if the sample result falls somewhere in between? At what point does the probability get small enough for us to say that the assumption of no difference is no longer valid? Determining this cut-off point is called choosing the **level of significance**, or the **alpha** (α) level. We indicate a 0.05 level of significance as:

$$\alpha = 0.05$$

To understand the issues involved in selecting a level of significance we have to distinguish between a **type I error** (alpha error) and a **type II error** (beta error).

A **type I error** occurs when the null hypothesis of no difference is rejected, even though in fact there is no difference. In assessing whether statistics students on average had the same height as all students, on the basis of a sample average of 162 cm, we rejected the null hypothesis of no difference. The chances of getting such a sample from a population where the average is 170 cm is less than 5-in-10 000. However, we may have actually conducted one of those fluke 5-in-10 000 samples. There may be no difference between all statistics students and all university students, but the sample just happened to randomly pick up a few especially short people. There is always a chance of such an event — that is why we speak in terms of probabilities. It is a question of the chances we are prepared to take of making this error.

A **type II error** occurs when we fail to reject the null hypothesis when in fact it is false. For example, where the sample of statistics students produced an average height of 172 cm, we concluded that there was no difference between all statistics students and other university students. The difference between the sample statistic and the hypothesized parameter value is so small that it can be attributed to random variation. However, it may in reality be that there is a difference, but our sample just happened to select some unrepresentative statistics students.

The relationship between these two possible error types is summarised in Table 9.7.

Table 9.7

		Truth about the population	
		H_0 true	H_a true
Decision based	Reject H_0	Type I error	Correct decision
on sample	Do not reject H_0	Correct decision	Type II error

It is clear that these two error types are the converse of each other so that **minimizing the chance of one occurring increases the chance of the other occurring**. It is a question of which mistake we most want to avoid, and this depends on the research question. If we are testing a new drug that may have harmful side effects we want to be sure that it actually works. In other words, we don't want to make a type I error (conclude that the drug does make a difference when it doesn't) because the consequences could be devastating. The difference in the rate of improvement observed between a test group taking the drug and a control group that is not will have to be very large before we can say that such an improvement is not due to chance (say 1-in-1000). What we would be doing here is selecting a significance level of 0.001 before accepting the alternative hypothesis that the drug really does make a difference.

We can see the effect of choosing different levels of significance in Figure 9.5.

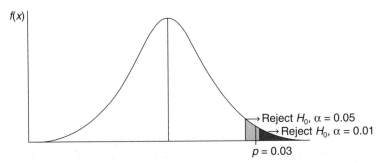

Figure 9.5   Rejection regions for $\alpha = 0.05$ and $\alpha = 0.01$ (one-tail test)

A sample result has a probability of occurring of 0.03, if the null hypothesis of no difference is true. It is clear that the level of significance we choose will determine whether we reject or do not reject this assumption of no difference. If we choose $\alpha = 0.01$ then the difference between the sample and the population value can be attributed to random variation: do not reject the null. But if we choose $\alpha = 0.05$, then the *same* difference between the sample and the hypothesized parameter value will lead us to reject the null.

One-tail or two-tail test?

To calculate the critical score(s) we also decide whether to use a **one-tail** or **two-tail test**. Here we look at the alternative hypothesis as stated in step 1 to see whether we are just concerned about the difference between the hypothesized parameter value and the sample score (by how much), or whether we are concerned about the direction of difference as well (by how much *greater or less than*).

In our example, for instance, there may be theoretical reasons to suspect that statistics students are systematically *shorter* than the rest of the university population: they spend too much time in dark libraries and computer labs, so their growth is stunted. Therefore a one-tail test is conducted because we are interested in whether the sample result falls far enough to the left of the population mean.

But say we had no *a priori* reason to believe this to be the case: students studying statistics could be either systematically shorter *or* taller. In this case the critical region is split in two — one at each end of the sampling distribution.

If we have specified a direction of difference in the alternative hypothesis so that we need to use a one-tail test, we should be careful that we refer to the appropriate tail of the sampling distribution. If the alternative hypothesis holds that the population value will be *less than* the specified value, the critical region will be in the left tail; if it holds that the population value will be *greater than* the specified value, the right tail is the relevant one (Table 9.8).

Table 9.8

Alternative hypothesis	Tail of the sampling distribution
$H_a: \mu \neq X$	Both
$H_a: \mu < X$	Left
$H_a: \mu > X$	Right

Calculate the critical score(s)

Once we have chosen a level of significance, and decided on a one-tail or two-tail test, we derive the critical score(s) (sometimes called the **test statistic**) that delineates the **critical region**.

> The **critical region** is the range of scores that will cause the null hypothesis to be rejected. The critical region is also called the **region of rejection**.

To determine these critical scores we refer to the table for the area under the standard normal curve:

$$\alpha \to z_{critical}$$

With a two-tail test we refer to the column for the area under the curve beyond both points and read off both the positive and negative values for the z-score; with a one-tail test we refer to the column for the area under the curve beyond one point and read off either the positive *or* the negative value for the z-score, depending on the appropriate tail. For example, the z-score that marks off the critical region, with a level of significance of $\alpha = 0.05$ on a two-tail test, is ± 1.96 (see Table 9.9).

Table 9.9   Area under the standard normal curve

z	Area under curve between *points*	Area under curve beyond *points*	Area under curve beyond *one point*
±0.1	0.080	0.920	0.460
±0.2	0.159	0.841	0.4205
±0.3	0.236	0.764	0.382
±0.4	0.311	0.689	0.3445
±0.5	0.383	0.617	0.3085
±0.6	0.451	0.549	0.2745
±0.7	0.516	0.484	0.242
±0.8	0.576	0.424	0.212
±0.9	0.632	0.368	0.184
±1	0.683	0.317	0.1585
±1.1	0.729	0.271	0.1355
±1.2	0.770	0.230	0.115
±1.3	0.806	0.194	0.097
±1.4	0.838	0.162	0.081
±1.5	0.866	0.134	0.067
±1.6	0.890	0.110	0.055
±1.645	0.900	0.100	0.050
±1.7	0.911	0.089	0.0445
±1.8	0.928	0.072	0.036
±1.9	0.943	0.057	0.028715
±1.96	0.950	0.050	0.025
±2	0.954	0.046	0.023
. . .	. . .	. . .	. . .
±4	>0.9999	<0.0001	<0.00005

Thus a probability of 0.05 is divided into two regions of equal size, one at either tail of the distribution. Beyond a *z*-score of +1.96 is 0.025, or 2.5 per cent, of the area under the curve, and beyond a *z*-score of −1.96 lies another 0.025 of the area under the curve (Figure 9.6).

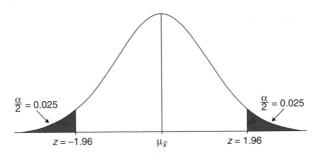

Figure 9.6   Critical regions for two-tail test, $\alpha = 0.05$

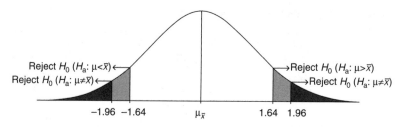

Figure 9.7   Critical regions for one-tail and two-tail test, $\alpha = 0.05$

The difference between a one-sided and two-sided test is illustrated in Figure 9.7.

On a one-tail test, with an alpha level of 0.05, the critical region under the sampling distribution begins either at -1.645 or $+1.645$ but not both, depending on the direction of difference expressed in the alternative hypothesis. On a two- tail test this region has to be split in two because we are interested in a sample result *either* shorter or taller than the population value. This pushes the critical z-score outward to ± 1.96.

Certain alpha levels are conventionally chosen in most research contexts, and the associated z-scores for these conventional levels of significance become familiar through regular use. If you work often enough with inferential statistics the following information will eventually be memorized. This is especially so for an alpha level of 0.05, which is by far the most common significance level used in social research (see Table 9.10).

Table 9.10   Common critical scores

	$z_{critical}$	
α	Two-tail test	One-tail test
0.01	$+$ and $-$ 2.58	$+$ or $-$ 2.33
0.05	$+$ and $-$ 1.96	$+$ or $-$ 1.645
0.10	$+$ and $-$ 1.645	$+$ or $-$ 1.28

Step 4: Calculate the sample score

Now that we have our critical scores we take the relevant measurements from the sample, and calculate the mean ($\overline{X}$). We calculate z_{sample} using the formula:

$$z_{sample} = \frac{\overline{X} - \mu}{\sigma_{\overline{x}}} = \frac{\overline{X} - \mu}{\sigma / \sqrt{N}}$$

From the table for the area under the standard normal curve we then determine the probability of obtaining a particular sample z-score if the null hypothesis is true. This is called the significance of the sample statistic, commonly called the 'p-value'.

Step 5: Make a decision — comparing sample and critical scores

Now that we have calculated everything we need to calculate we can decide either to reject or not to reject the null hypothesis. Notice that the conclusion is always stated in terms of the null hypothesis: reject or fail to reject.

When making a decision we make either one of two comparisons:

- compare z_{sample} and $z_{critical}$

or

- compare the p-value with the alpha level.

Since any given z-score is uniquely related to a particular probability, and vice-versa, we will get the same answer regardless of the comparison we choose to make.

A summary of the hypothesis testing procedure is given in Table 9.11.

Table 9.11   Summary of hypothesis testing procedure

Critical scores step 3	Sample scores step 4	Decision making step 5
	$\overline{X}_{sample}$ $\downarrow$	
$z_{critical}$	$z_{sample} = \dfrac{\overline{X} - \mu}{\sigma_{\overline{x}}}$	if z_{sample} is further from 0 than $z_{critical}$ reject null hypothesis
$\uparrow$ Table for area under normal curve $\uparrow$	$\downarrow$ Table for area under normal curve $\downarrow$	
α	p	if $p < \alpha$ reject null hypothesis

It may be helpful at the decision-making stage to actually sketch a normal curve and plot the critical and sample values (as we have been doing above). This provides a quick visual indication as to whether the null should be rejected, if the sample score falls in the region of rejection.

A common confusion often arises right at this point of decision-making. In observing the so-called 'p-value' of the sample score, students are often dismayed if it proves to be very close to zero. We are used to thinking that small numbers indicate that 'nothing is there' and therefore the difference we suspected or hoped to find has not eventuated. Actually, the opposite is true. Usually we do want to find a low p-value (lower than the alpha level), since this indicates that the null hypothesis of no difference should be rejected. A very high p-value, on the other hand, indicates that the null hypothesis of no difference should not be rejected.

When reporting the results of an hypothesis test, even if we are confident with the decision made about the null hypothesis, sufficient information should be provided so that the reader can make his or her own judgment. In particular, the exact probability associated with the sample z-score (and the z-score itself) should be reported, not just whether it is above or below the chosen alpha level. This allows readers to decide whether they feel the probability is sufficiently small for it to warrant rejecting the null. It leaves the decision making up to the readers, rather than just with the person conducting the test: the readers can compare the probability to the alpha level *they* think is warranted in the context rather than simply being told that a result 'is significant at the 0.05 level', or words to that effect. If the preceding statement is all that is reported, the sample probability could have been 0.049 or 0.00001 — there is no way of knowing without doing the calculations. This may be frustrating to a reader who feels that an alpha level of 0.01 is warranted in the circumstances rather than the stated alpha of 0.05. Stating the actual probability of the sample z-score, in other words, gives readers maximum information, so that they can arrive at their own conclusions about whether to reject or not to reject the null hypothesis, given *their* preparedness to make a type I or type II error.

What do inference tests 'prove'?

After having performed all the calculations and conducted all the tests, and having either rejected or failed to reject the null hypothesis of no difference, what have we actually 'proven'? Firstly, and most importantly, we have not *proven* anything! Remember that we are working with probabilities only, and we are simply deciding which hypothesis *probably* explains a sample result. Samples do not always exactly mirror the populations from which they are drawn, so making an inference from a sample to a population always involves a risk of error.

Given this probabilistic nature of inference testing, we need to explore the meaning of the test a little further. Although we begin with the presumption that the null hypothesis is true, and then proceed to test this assumption, researchers are usually interested in rejecting the null. Normally we make comparisons because we believe a difference exists, so that a decision to reject the null is usually the desired outcome. In most instances a low 'p-value' is the desired result since this will allow the null to be rejected. In other words, we are using the logic of proof by contradiction: we want to find support for the alternative hypothesis, by showing that there is no support for its opposite, the null hypothesis.

Does this mean that if we fail to reject the null, the difference we are searching for does not exist? Not necessarily: failing to reject the null hypothesis of no difference simply means *there is not sufficient evidence* to think that the null hypothesis is wrong. This does not necessarily mean that it is right, though. Simply, there is not enough 'evidence' to support the alternative hypothesis. There might actually be a difference 'out there', but on the basis of the sample results, such a difference has not been detected. This is a bit like the presumption of innocence in criminal law. A defendant is presumed not guilty unless the evidence is strong enough to justify a verdict of guilty. However, just because someone has been found not guilty on the strength of the available evidence does not mean that that person is in fact innocent: all it means is that, given that either verdict is possible, we do not choose 'guilty' unless stronger evidence comes to light. Similarly, with a verdict of 'no difference': not rejecting the null hypothesis does not mean the alternative is wrong. It simply states that with the information available, the null can explain the sample result without stretching our notion of reasonable probability.

Therefore, failing to find a significant difference should not be seen as conclusive. If we have good theoretical grounds for suspecting that a difference does really exist, even though a test suggests that it doesn't, this can be the basis of future research. Maybe the variable has not been operationalized effectively, or the level of measurement does not provide sufficient information, or the sample was not appropriately chosen or was not large enough. In the context of social research, inference tests do not prove anything; they are usually evidence in an ongoing discussion or debate that rarely reaches a decisive conclusion.

The significance of statistical significance

A further word of caution needs to be made about the decisions made through hypothesis testing. When we reject the null we say that we have found a 'statistically significant difference'. So what? What have we learned about the world, and should we do anything about it? These questions are not ones that hypothesis testing as such can answer. A **statistical** difference is simply a difference between two numbers. A student who scores 60 in an exam is statistically different from a student who scores 61, or 66, or 90. Similarly, there may be a statistically significant difference between a sample of students that averages 60 in final exams and another with an average of 61, or 66, or 90. A statistically significant difference simply tells us that two numbers are not the same. Whether such a difference is of any practical or theoretical importance — whether it is significant in any other sense — is really something we as researchers or policy-makers have to decide for ourselves.

To give this a concrete application assume that I, as a statistics teacher, want to know whether I should have the university spend more money on computer workshops and hire extra instructors to help students with their statistics classes. The university argues that it will only do this if there is a 'significant' difference between grades in statistics and grades in other courses that these students undertake at university. I collect a sample of students and find that their average statistics mark is 55, and compare that with the overall university average of 62, and find this to be statistically significant at an alpha level of 0.05. Have I won my argument with the university? Not necessarily. I might consider the difference in average marks to justify the extra expenditure because I think that statistics is very important to a well-rounded education. But the university has every right to say that given all the other possible ways it can spend its money, a difference of 7 marks is something it can live with. The university, in other words, may have no argument with me over the statistical difference; that is, accepting that the difference really is there in the population and not just due to sampling variation. However, it may strongly disagree that this is of practical significance in the sense that it should prompt the university to try to close the gap.

This illustrates an all-too-often neglected point. It is not uncommon for researchers to simply, and blandly, state that a result is significant at the 0.05 or 0.01 level, without further comment, as if this is all that needs to be said. In fact this should just be the entry point to the more creative and interesting (but usually more difficult) research problem: what does this tell us about the world and what we can do about it?

A two-tail *z*-test for a single mean

Suppose that the university is interested in the academic ability of foreign students in a particular program. In this program, the university knows that the average mark for all students is 62 with a standard deviation of 15. From a random sample of foreign students ($N = 150$) the average score is calculated as 60.5. We can summarize this information in the following shorthand:

$$N = 150$$

$$\mu = 62$$

$$\sigma = 15$$

$$\overline{X} = 60.5$$

Are foreign students different?

Step 1: State the hypotheses
- H_0: There is no difference in the average grades of foreign students and the average grades of all other students.

$$H_0: \mu = 62$$

- H_a: There is a difference between the average grades of foreign students and the average grades of all other students.

$$H_a: \mu \neq 62$$

Step 2: Choose the test of significance
Two factors are important:

- The variable (academic performance) is measured at the interval/ratio level (final marks).

- The sample is large ($N > 100$). Therefore, according to the central limit theorem, the sampling distribution of sample means will be normal, even though the actual population of students might not be normally distributed in terms of grades.

These two factors allow us to conduct a z-test for a single mean.

Step 3: Establish the critical score(s) and critical region
Following convention we will choose the 0.05 level of significance:

$$\alpha = 0.05$$

The alternative hypothesis states that the average mark for foreign students is not equal to that for all students:

$$H_a: \mu \neq 62$$

Note that it does not specify whether the average mark of foreign students will be *higher* or *lower* than that of the rest. Since we do not have any reason to suspect that foreign students on average will perform any better or worse than all other students — we are simply interested in whether they perform differently — a two-tail test is appropriate. From the table for the area under the standard normal curve, we know that the critical scores for a two-tail test, with $\alpha = 0.05$, will be:

$$z_{critical} = \pm 1.96$$

Step 4: Calculate the sample scores
From the information derived from the sample we know that the sampling distribution will have a mean:

$$\mu_{\bar{x}} = \mu = 62$$

and a standard error of:

$$\sigma_{\bar{x}} = \frac{\sigma}{\sqrt{N}} = \frac{15}{\sqrt{150}} = 1.22$$

From this we can calculate the sample z-score we will use to compare with the critical z-score:

$$z_{sample} = \frac{\bar{X} - \mu}{\sigma_{\bar{x}}}$$

$$= \frac{60.5 - 62}{1.22}$$

$$= -1.2$$

From Table 9.12, for a z-score of ± 1.2, the probability is 0.23.

Table 9.12   Area under the standard normal curve

z	Area under curve between *points*	Area under curve beyond both *points*	Area under curve beyond *one point*
±0.1	0.080	0.920	0.460
±0.2	0.159	0.841	0.4205
±0.3	0.236	0.764	0.382
±0.4	0.311	0.689	0.3445
±0.5	0.383	0.617	0.3085
±0.6	0.451	0.549	0.2745
±0.7	0.516	0.484	0.242
±0.8	0.576	0.424	0.212
±0.9	0.632	0.368	0.184
±1	0.683	0.317	0.1585
±1.1	0.729	0.271	0.1355
±1.2	0.770	0.230	0.115
±1.3	0.806	0.194	0.097
±1.4	0.838	0.162	0.081
±1.5	0.866	0.134	0.067
±1.6	0.890	0.110	0.055
±1.645	0.900	0.100	0.050
±1.7	0.911	0.089	0.0445
±1.8	0.928	0.072	0.036
±1.9	0.943	0.057	0.028715
±1.96	0.950	0.050	0.025
±2	0.954	0.046	0.023
. . .	. . .	. . .	. . .
±4	>0.99990	<0.00010	<0.00005

Step 5: Make a decision

We can immediately see that, by comparing the sample result with the critical score, it appears that the grades of foreign students are not sufficiently different from the test value for us to reject the null hypothesis of no difference (Figure 9.8).

The one-and-a-half mark difference between the sample of foreign students and all other students can simply be the result of random variation when sampling, in a situation where there is no underlying difference between *all* foreign students and the rest of the student population. We can see that z_{critical} of -1.96 is much further from the population mean than the z_{sample} of -1.2.

We can also make a decision by comparing the probabilities associated with these sample and critical values. The alpha we have chosen is 0.05, but our sample probability is 0.23. In other words, even if there is no difference between foreign students and all other students in terms of final grades, 23 samples in every hundred will have an average grade of 1.5 marks or further from 62.

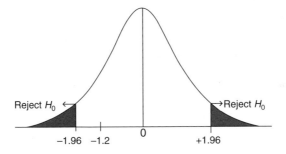

Figure 9.8

The procedure just outlined can be summarized as in Table 9.13.

Table 9.13   Summary of hypothesis testing

Critical scores step 3	Sample scores step 4	Decision making step 5
	$\overline{X}_{sample}$ ↓	
$z_{critical} = -1.96$	$z_{sample} = \dfrac{\overline{X} - \mu}{\sigma_{\overline{x}}} = -1.2$	if z_{sample} is closer to μ than $z_{critical}$ therefore do not reject H_0
↑ Table for area under normal curve ↑	↓ Table for area under normal curve ↓	
$\alpha = 0.05$	$p = 0.23$	$p > \alpha$ therefore do not reject H_0

A one-tail z-test for a single mean

A group of workers in a factory suspect that working conditions are unsafe and have caused them to suffer a high rate of respiratory illness. They are gathering evidence for their claim, which has been dismissed by management. The management claims that there is no way of knowing for certain what caused the higher rate of illness, and therefore the particular working conditions in the factory had nothing to do with the rate of illness.

The workers remain unconvinced so they call in a social researcher who randomly selects 100 workers and asks them how many hours work they had lost the previous year as a result of respiratory illness. The average number of hours lost was 15 hours per worker. From information available from official sources, the researcher also knows that for all factory workers in the country, the average number of hours lost due to respiratory illness that year was 12 hours, with a standard deviation of 7.5 hours around this mean. In shorthand notation, this information can be summarized as follows:

$$N = 100$$
$$\overline{X} = 15$$
$$\mu = 12$$
$$\sigma = 7.5$$

Which is the most likely explanation: the workers' claim that due to working conditions in the factory, they systematically have a higher incidence of respiratory disease; or the claim of management that any difference between the rate of respiratory illness in the factory and that for the whole population is due to random variation from sampling? Obviously there is some difference between the sample of factory workers and the rest of the population but is this difference big enough to suggest that it is more than just random chance?

These claims can be formally tested.

Step 1: State the hypotheses
- H_0: There is no difference between the rate of respiratory illness suffered by workers in this factory and the rate suffered by all factory workers.

$$H_0\colon \mu = 12$$

- H_a: There is a difference between the rate of respiratory illness suffered by workers in this factory and the rate suffered by all factory workers, and we expect that workers in this factory to have a higher rate of illness.

$$H_a\colon \mu > 12$$

Notice that the alternative hypothesis does not just specify a difference, but also a direction of difference. This will be important in determining whether to use a one-tail or two-tail test.

Step 2: Choose the test of significance
- Level of measurement is interval/ratio (number of hours lost).
- It is a large sample ($N = 100$).

Since these conditions hold we conduct a z-test for a single mean.

Step 3: Establish the critical score(s) and critical region
Since management requires a lot of convincing, the workers want to show that the high rate of respiratory illness in the factory is extremely unlikely to

be the result of sample selection. Therefore they set the level of significance at $\alpha = 0.01$. Since the alternative hypothesis does not just specify a difference, but also a direction of difference, we will use a one-tail test. From the table for the area under the normal curve this means that:

$$z_{\text{critical}} = 2.33$$

The direction of difference specified in the alternative hypothesis is that the average will be *greater* than 12, so the relevant tail is to the right of the distribution (Figure 9.9).

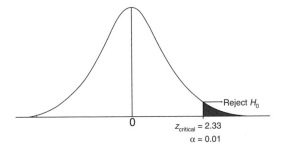

Figure 9.9

Step 4: Calculate the sample scores

The sampling distribution of sample means will be normal with the following values:

$$\mu = \mu_{\bar{x}} = 12$$

$$\sigma_{\bar{x}} = \frac{\sigma}{\sqrt{N}} = \frac{7.5}{\sqrt{100}} = 0.75$$

These sample results give a z-score of:

$$z_{\text{sample}} = \frac{\overline{X} - \mu}{\sigma_{\bar{x}}} = \frac{15 - 12}{0.75} = 4$$

From the table for the area under the normal curve, we find that if the null hypothesis is true, the chance of getting such a sample result is less than 1-in-10 000. That is:

$$p_{\text{sample}} < 0.0001$$

Step 5: Make a decision

If we compare the sample and critical values we see that our sample result falls in the critical region of rejection. That is, because our sample result is *further from the mean* than our critical score, we reject the null hypothesis: the workers do have a legitimate claim (Figure 9.10).

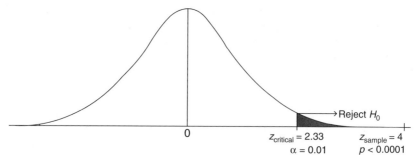

Figure 9.10

Summary

We have just worked through the steps involved in the most basic of hypothesis testing procedures: the z-test of a single mean. However, in practice this test is very rarely employed because it requires a great deal of information about the population. We begin with it, though, because it provides the clearest exposition of the process of hypothesis testing. Having learnt this basic procedure we are now able to deal with more complicated situations that are more likely to arise in 'real life'. The following chapters detail the tests to be used in these situations.

Exercises

9.1 Under what conditions will the sampling distribution of sample means be normal in shape?

9.2 What is meant by type I and type II errors? How are they related?

9.3 How does the choice of significance level affect the critical region?

9.4 Specify some research questions that will involve one-tail tests. Which tail on the sampling distribution will hold the critical region in each situation?

9.5 Complete the following table:

Probability	Test	z-score
0.230		±1.2
0.100	Two-tail	
0.018		±2.1
	Two-tail	±2.3
	One-tail	±3.4

9.6 Sketch the critical region for the following critical scores:
$z > 1.645$
$z < -1.645$
$z > 1.96$ or $z < -1.96$

What is the probability of a type I error associated with each of these critical regions?

9.7 For each of the following sets of results, calculate z_{sample}

(a)

$\mu = 2.4$

$\sigma = 0.7$

$\overline{X} = 2.3$

$N = 180$

(b)

$\mu = 18$

$\sigma = 1.1$

$\overline{X} = 16.7$

$N = 100$

9.8 A particular judge has acquired a reputation as the 'hanging judge' because he is perceived as imposing harsher penalties for the same sentence. A random sample of 40 cases is taken from trials before this judge that resulted in a guilty verdict for a certain crime. The average jail sentence he imposed for this sample is 27 months. For all crimes of this type the average prison sentence is 24 months, with a standard deviation of 11 months (assume a normal distribution). Is this judge's reputation justified? (Pay close attention to the form of the alternative hypothesis.)

10

The *t*-test for a single mean

The previous chapters introduced the logic of statistical inference. The examples used to illustrate the hypothesis testing procedure provided us with a great deal of information to make an inference, in particular, the mean and standard deviation of the population are known. With this information we are able to draw up the sampling distribution. But what if all of this information is not available? Specifically, what if the standard deviation of this population is not known?

The student's *t*-distribution

When we don't know the standard deviation of the population (and provided we can assume that the population is normally distributed) a slight change is required to the basic procedure outlined in the previous chapter. In step 3 of the hypothesis testing procedure we can no longer use the *z*-distribution to derive the critical scores. This is because the sampling distribution of sample means will no longer be normal. Instead, the sampling distribution we refer to is the Student's *t*-distribution, and we conduct a *t*-test. (It is called the Student's *t*-distribution after the person who first defined its properties. As an employee of the Guinness brewing company, he was not permitted to publish under his own name. He therefore chose the 'the Student' as his alias.) A *t*-distribution looks a lot like a *z*-distribution in that it is a smooth, unimodal, symmetrical curve. The difference is that the *t*-distribution is 'flatter' than a *z*-distribution. Exactly how much flatter depends on the sample size (Figure 10.1).

> As sample size increases the *t*-distribution will converge on the normal distribution, and will be the same as the normal distribution when sample size is greater than 120.

The *t*-distribution, where sample size is 30, has much 'fatter tails'; these tails become thinner for a sample size of 90; and eventually are identical to the normal curve when sample size becomes very large.

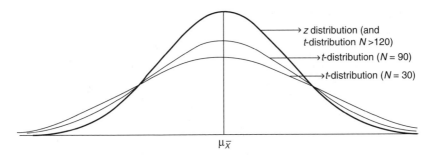

Figure 10.1   The distribution of *t* for sample sizes $N = 30$, $N = 90$, and $N > 120$

Table 10.1, which provides the area under the *t*-distribution, is very much like the one for the *z*-distribution, but with two main differences:

- The column on the left is not expressed in terms of sample size, but in terms of **degrees of freedom** (*df*).
- Across the top is a select set of probabilities (areas under the *t*-distribution), and down the columns are the actual *t*-scores for those critical values and degrees of fredom.

When we look at the last line of Table 10.1 for the *t*-distribution, which has the infinity symbol, ∞, the scores should be familiar. For example, on a two-tail test at an alpha of 0.05 the *t*-score is 1.96. This is exactly the same value for *z* at this level of significance. In other words, when sample size is greater than 120, the *t*-distribution and the *z*-distribution are identical, so that the areas under the respective curves for any given scores are also identical. For this reason, all the examples that follow will refer to *t*-scores, even where a *z*-test could have been conducted instead, since we will get the same answer either way. As Table 10.2 indicates, since *t*-scores are correct in both large and small sample cases, whereas *z*-scores are correct *only* in the large sample case, we (and SPSS) will always use *t*-scores when the population standard deviation is unknown, regardless of the sample size.

An important, but often neglected, assumption behind the use of *t*-tests needs to be pointed out before moving on. With small samples, the sampling distribution of sample means will have a *t*-distribution only where the population is normally distributed. This assumption is **robust** in that the sampling distribution will still approximate a *t*-distribution even where the population is moderately non-normal. Even so, we should be cautious about conducting a *t*-test simply because we have interval/ratio data, without thinking about the validity of this assumption first. Chapter 12 provides a way of assessing this assumption based on the sample data, and if there is reason to believe that this assumption does not hold, a whole range of **non-parametric** tests are available. These will be investigated in later chapters.

Table 10.1 Distribution of *t*

Degrees of freedom (df)	Level of significance for one-tail test (α)				
	0.10	0.05	0.025	0.01	0.005
	Level of significance for two-tail test (α)				
	0.20	0.10	0.05	0.02	0.01
1	3.078	6.314	12.706	31.821	63.657
2	1.886	2.920	4.303	6.965	9.925
3	1.638	2.353	3.182	4.541	5.841
4	1.533	2.132	2.776	3.747	4.604
5	1.476	2.015	2.571	3.365	4.032
6	1.440	1.943	2.447	3.143	3.707
7	1.415	1.895	2.365	2.998	3.499
8	1.397	1.860	2.306	2.896	3.355
9	1.383	1.833	2.262	2.821	3.250
10	1.372	1.812	2.228	2.764	3.169
11	1.363	1.796	2.201	2.718	3.106
12	1.356	1.782	2.179	2.681	3.055
13	1.350	1.771	2.160	2.650	3.012
14	1.345	1.761	2.145	2.624	2.977
15	1.341	1.753	2.131	2.602	2.947
16	1.34	1.746	2.120	2.583	2.921
17	1.333	1.740	2.110	2.567	2.898
18	1.330	1.734	2.101	2.552	2.878
19	1.328	1.729	2.093	2.539	2.861
20	1.325	1.725	2.086	2.528	2.845
21	1.323	1.721	2.080	2.518	2.831
22	1.321	1.717	2.074	2.508	2.819
23	1.319	1.714	2.069	2.500	2.807
24	1.318	1.711	2.064	2.492	2.797
25	1.316	1.708	2.060	2.485	2.787
26	1.315	1.706	2.056	2.479	2.779
27	1.314	1.703	2.052	2.473	2.771
28	1.313	1.701	2.048	2.467	2.763
29	1.311	1.699	2.045	2.462	2.756
30	1.310	1.697	2.042	2.457	2.750
40	1.303	1.684	2.021	2.423	2.704
60	1.296	1.671	2.000	2.390	2.660
120	1.289	1.658	1.980	2.358	2.617
∞	1.282	1.645	1.960	2.326	2.576

Table 10.2   When to use *t*-scores and *z*-scores

	$N \leq 120$	$N > 120$
t-scores	✔	✔
z-scores	✕	✔

Degrees of freedom

The table for the distribution of *t* is not expressed in terms of sample size but in terms of degrees of freedom. The concept of degrees of freedom can be illustrated with a simple example. If there are five students and their final exam grades *must* have an average of 10, a restriction has been placed on the range of possible scores these students can get. For example, the first four marks could come out as follows:

$$X_1 = 12$$

$$X_2 = 7$$

$$X_3 = 15$$

$$X_4 = 11$$

$$X_5 = ?$$

Four scores are free to vary; to take on any value. But once I have recorded these first four marks, the fifth mark *must* be 5 for the total to produce an average of 10. We have lost one degree of freedom because we have imposed a certain result on the data. Instead of N degrees of freedom, here we have $N - 1$. In this example, we have four degrees of freedom.

A similar correction applies when working with *t*-tests. The *t*-test is based on the assumption that the population standard deviation (which is unknown) is equal to the sample standard deviation (which is known). The imposition of this assumption on the data means we lose one degree of freedom.

The practical effect of substituting the sample standard deviation in calculating critical scores, rather than the population parameter, is that we do not use the total sample size to calculate the critical values. Instead we use the sample size minus the number of restrictions imposed on the data. For the one sample *t*-test this will be the sample size minus one ($df = N - 1$), where the restriction is the assumption that the sample standard deviation is equl to the population value.

The number of degrees of freedom affects the value of both the critical *t*-score and sample *t*-score. With the critical score, the larger the sample size (and therefore degrees of freedom) the more likely that any difference between the sample mean and the test value will prove to be significant. For example, with a sample of 150 ($df = 149$) the value of t_{critical} will be ±1.96. For a sample of only 30 ($df = 29$) the critical region will be marked by *t*-scores of ±2.04 (Figure 10.2).

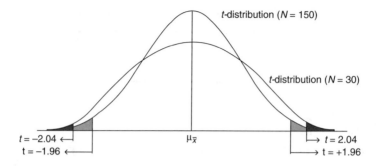

Figure 10.2   Critical regions for sample sizes of 150 and 30 (α = 0.05, two-tail)

Since the *t*-distribution is 'flatter' with smaller samples, the critical score lies further out compared with the *t*-distribution for the larger sample.

When calculating the sample *t*-score we also take into account the number of degrees of freedom. The standard error for the sampling distribution is:

$$\sigma_{\bar{x}} = \frac{s}{\sqrt{N-1}}$$

The value of t_{sample} will therefore be:

$$t_{\text{sample}} = \frac{\overline{X} - \mu}{s / \sqrt{N-1}}$$

Apart from these minor adjustments to the determination of critical and sample scores, the basic hypothesis testing procedure remains the same.

Example 1

A large chain of fast food outlets has recently featured in its advertising a claim that it is a 'good employer'. One way of assessing this claim is to see whether it discriminates against women in job promotions. We know from national employment figures that for all similar establishments there are on average 2.5 women in management positions for establishments of that size. The standard deviation for the population, though, has not been calculated. We survey 31 of the outlets involved in the advertising campaign and find that they, on average, employ 1.9 women in management positions, with a standard deviation of 1. In shorthand we summarize this information as follows:

$$N = 31$$

$$\mu = 2.5$$

$$\sigma = unknown$$

$$\overline{X} = 1.9$$

$$s = 1$$

Step 1: State the null and alternative hypotheses

H_0: There is no difference in the average number of women employed as managers between the food chain and other stores:

$$H_0: \mu = 2.5$$

H_a: There is a difference in the average number of women employed as managers between the food chain and other stores:

$$H_a: \mu \neq 2.5$$

Step 2: Choose the test of significance

We have the following information:

- the data are interval/ratio (number of women in management);
- the population variance is unknown.

Therefore, we will use a one sample *t*-test for a mean, with degrees of freedom of 30:

$$df = N - 1 = 30$$

Step 3: Establish the critical score(s) and critical region

We will use $\alpha = 0.05$. Since there is no reason to suspect that this food chain will be either a better or worse employer of women, we will use a two-tail test. From the table for the distribution of *t*, with degrees of freedom of 30, the critical value at this level of significance is 2.042 (Table 10.3).

Table 10.3   Distribution of *t*

Degrees of freedom (df)	Level of significance for one-tail test				
	0.10	0.05	0.025	0.01	0.005
	Level of significance for two-tail test				
	0.20	0.10	0.05	0.02	0.01
1	3.078	6.314	12.706	31.821	63.657
2	1.886	2.920	4.303	6.965	9.925
. . .	. . .	. . .	. . .	. . .	. . .
21	1.323	1.721	2.080	2.518	2.831
22	1.321	1.717	2.074	2.508	2.819
23	1.319	1.714	2.069	2.500	2.807
24	1.318	1.711	2.064	2.492	2.797
25	1.316	1.708	2.060	2.485	2.787
26	1.315	1.706	2.056	2.479	2.779
27	1.314	1.703	2.052	2.473	2.771
28	1.313	1.701	2.048	2.467	2.763
29	1.311	1.699	2.045	2.462	2.756
30	1.310	1.697	**2.042**	2.457	2.750
∞	1.282	1.645	1.960	2.326	2.576

$$t_{critical} = \pm 2.042$$

Step 4: Calculate the sample score(s)
Using the formula for converting the sample value into a *t*-score, we get:

$$t_{sample} = \frac{\overline{X} - \mu}{s / \sqrt{N-1}}$$

$$= \frac{1.9 - 2.5}{1 / \sqrt{31-1}}$$

$$= -3.3$$

From Table 10.4 we can see that at 30 degrees of freedom t_{sample} falls beyond the largest reported value of 2.750, which has a probability of 0.01.

Table 10.4   Distribution of *t*

Degrees of freedom (df)	Level of significance for one-tail test				
	0.10	0.05	0.025	0.01	0.005
	Level of significance for two-tail test				
	0.20	0.10	0.05	0.02	0.01
1	3.078	6.314	12.706	31.821	63.657
2	1.886	2.920	4.303	6.965	9.925
. . .	. . .	. . .	. . .	. . .	. . .
21	1.323	1.721	2.080	2.518	2.831
22	1.321	1.717	2.074	2.508	2.819
23	1.319	1.714	2.069	2.500	2.807
24	1.318	1.711	2.064	2.492	2.797
25	1.316	1.708	2.060	2.485	2.787
26	1.315	1.706	2.056	2.479	2.779
27	1.314	1.703	2.052	2.473	2.771
28	1.313	1.701	2.048	2.467	2.763
29	1.311	1.699	2.045	2.462	2.756
30	1.310	1.697	2.042	**2.457**	**2.750**
∞	1.282	1.645	1.960	2.326	2.576

This means that t_{sample} has a probability of occurring of less than 0.01, on a two-tail test.

Step 5: Make a decision
It is clear that the sample value of *t* is much further away from the mean than the critical score (Figure 10.3).

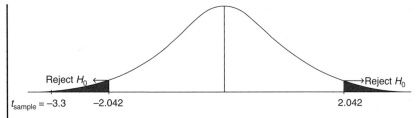

Figure 10.3

This leads us to reject the null hypothesis. The food chain is not living up to its claims!

Example 2
In response to the embarrassment it suffered from its claims of being a good employer, the fast food chain switches its advertising strategy, emphasising that it offers 'value for money'. One way of assessing this is to compare its prices with those of other stores selling similar products. From a sample of 24 stores in the chain, we calculate the average price of a 'basket' of goods to be $11.50, with a standard deviation of $2. The national average for a similar basket of goods is $12. Can the chain argue that this proves it provides cheaper goods?

$$N = 24$$
$$\mu = 12$$
$$\sigma = unknown$$
$$\overline{X} = 11.50$$
$$s = 2$$

Step 1: State the null and alternative hypotheses
H_0: There is no difference in the cost of goods between the food chain and other stores:

$$H_0: \mu = 12$$

H_a: The cost of goods is lower in the food chain than other stores:

$$H_a: \mu < 12$$

Step 2: Choose the test of significance
• It is a random sample.
• Data are interval/ratio (cost of goods in dollars).
• The population variance is unknown.

Therefore, we will use a *t*-test for a single mean, with degrees of freedom of 23:

$$df = N - 1 = 23$$

Step 3: Establish the critical region and critical scores(s)
We will use the 0.05 level of significance. Since we are interested in
whether the food store is significantly *cheaper* than the other comparable
stores, we will use a one-tail test. From the table for the distribution of *t*,
with degrees of freedom of 23, the critical value at this level of significance
is −1.714 (Table 10.5).

Table 10.5   Distribution of *t*

Degrees of freedom (df)	Level of significance for one-tail test				
	0.10	0.05	0.025	0.01	0.005
	Level of significance for two-tail test				
	0.20	0.10	0.05	0.02	0.01
1	3.078	6.314	12.706	31.821	63.657
2	1.886	2.920	4.303	6.965	9.925
. . .	. . .	. . .	. . .	. . .	. . .
21	1.323	1.721	2.080	2.518	2.831
22	1.321	1.717	2.074	2.508	2.819
23	1.319	1.714	2.069	2.500	2.807
24	1.318	1.711	2.064	2.492	2.797
25	1.316	1.708	2.060	2.485	2.787
. . .	. . .	. . .	. . .	. . .	. . .
∞	1.282	1.645	1.960	2.326	2.576

$$t_{\text{critical}} = -1.714$$

Note the negative sign in front of the critical score. This signifies that in
determining whether to reject the assumption of no difference we are only
interested in a sample result that falls far enough *below* the hypothesized
value.

Step 4: Calculate the sample scores
The formula for deriving the sample *t*-score is:

$$t_{\text{sample}} = \frac{\overline{X} - \mu}{s \Big/ \sqrt{N-1}}$$

$$= \frac{11.5 - 12}{2 \Big/ \sqrt{24-1}}$$

$$= -1.2$$

Step 5: Make a decision
It is clear that t_{sample} is closer to the mean than our critical value, as illustrated in Figure 10.4.

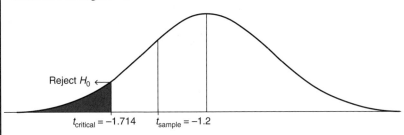

Reject H_0 ←

$t_{\text{critical}} = -1.714$ $t_{\text{sample}} = -1.2$

Figure 10.4   *t*-test with $\alpha = 0.05$, one-tail, $df = 23$

We therefore do not reject the null. Despite the fact that the sample average was lower than the population parameter, we cannot reject the possibility that this is just due to random variation when sampling, and that all the stores in the chain on average do not differ from the national average.

The one sample *t*-test using SPSS

Filename 10.sav   We will now work through another example, and then generate the same results using SPSS. According to A.C. Nielsen, a market research company, children in the United Kingdom between the ages of 5 and 12 years watch on average 196 minutes of television per day. For the sake of exposition we will assume that this is the 'true' value for the population of British children in this age bracket. A survey is conducted by randomly selecting 20 Australian children within this age group to see if Australian children are significantly different from their British counterparts. The descriptive statistics that summarize the results of this survey are:

$$\overline{X} = 165.85 \text{ minutes}$$

$$s = 29.29 \text{ minutes}$$

$$N = 20$$

The null hypothesis is that Australian children watch on average the same amount of television each night as their British counterparts:

$$H_0: \mu = 196$$

Substituting this information into the equation for *t*, we get a sample *t*-score of:

$$t_{sample} = \frac{\overline{X} - \mu}{s \Big/ \sqrt{N-1}}$$

$$= \frac{165.85 - 196}{29.29 \Big/ \sqrt{20 - 1}}$$

$$= \frac{-30.15}{6.7}$$

$$= -4.5$$

From the table for the *t*-distribution, at 19 degrees of freedom, we find that this has a probability of occurring by chance from a population with a mean of 196 of less than 0.005, or less than 5-in-1000 times. In other words, the sample result is so different from the test value that it cannot be attributed to random variation. The sample must come from a population with a mean different from 196 minutes.

If the same data for the 20 Australian children are entered into SPSS, with the variable coded as **tvtime**, the procedure for generating a one-sample *t*-test is as shown in Table 10.6.

Table 10.6   The one-sample *t*-test command using SPSS

SPSS command/action	Comments
1 From the menu select **Statistics/Compare Means/ One-Sample T Test...**	This will bring up a window headed **One-Sample T Test**
2 Select **tvtime** from the list of variables	
3 Click on ➤	This will paste **tvtime** into the box headed **Test Variable(s):**
4 In the small square next to **Test Value:** type **196**	This is the hypothesized value against which the sample mean will be compared
5 Click on **OK**	

The output from this set of commands will be:

One Sample t-tests

Variable	Number of Cases	Mean	SD	SE of Mean
TVTIME TV Watched per Nig	20	165.8500	29.290	6.550

Test Value = 196

Mean Difference	95% CI Lower	Upper			t-value	df	2-Tail Sig
-30.15	-43.858	-16.442			-4.60	19	.000

The first table provides all the descriptive statistics: the number of cases (20), the mean for the sample (165.85), and the standard deviation for the sample (29.29). The last figure for the first table, **SE of Mean**, is the standard error. This is the value in the denominator for the equation for *t*. The slight difference between our value for the standard error (6.7) and SPSS's value of 6.55 is due to rounding in the hand calculations.

The second table in the output contains the results of the inference test. The difference between the test value of 196 and the sample mean is –30.15. This is the numerator of the equation for *t*. The *t*-value is –4.6, as we have already calculated (with a slight difference due to rounding in the hand calculation), which at 19 degrees of freedom (**df**) has a two-tail significance of less than 0.0005 (SPSS has rounded this off to three decimal points). This is the probability of obtaining a sample with a mean of 165.85 or less from a population that watches on average 196 minutes of TV a day, that is, less than 5-in-10 000 samples of 20 children. Clearly this assumption that the population mean is 196 minutes should be rejected: Australian children watch significantly less TV on average than children in the United Kingdom.

Another way of reaching the same conclusion is to look at the confidence interval constructed around the sample mean. At a 95 per cent confidence level the interval for the *difference* between the sample and the test value ranges from a lower limit of –43.858 to an upper limit of –16.442. In other words the *difference* between the average amount of TV watched by the two sets of children lies somewhere between this range, at a 95 per cent confidence level. Since this range *does not* include the value of zero, which would indicate no difference, we can reject the hypothesis of no difference.

Exercises

10.1 What assumption about the distribution of the population underlies the *t*-test?

10.2 From the table for the distribution of *t*, fill in the following table:

t-score	Probability	Test	df
2.015		One-tail	5
	0.02	Two-tail	10
1.708	0.05	One-tail	
	0.05	Two-tail	65
	0.10	One-tail	228

10.3 Conduct a *t*-test, with $\alpha = 0.05$, on each of the following sets of data:

$\overline{X}$	s	H_0	H_a	N
62.4	14.1	$\mu = 68$	$\mu \neq 68$	61
62.4	14.1	$\mu = 68$	$\mu < 68$	61
2.3	1.8	$\mu = 3.1$	$\mu \neq 3.1$	25
2.3	1.8	$\mu = 3.1$	$\mu \neq 3.1$	190
102	45	$\mu = 98$	$\mu \neq 98$	210
102	45	$\mu = 90$	$\mu \neq 90$	210

10.4 An exercise at the end of Chapter 8 asked you to estimate the 95 per cent and 99 per cent confidence intervals for the following example: to gauge the effect of enterprise bargaining agreements, union officials sampled a total of 120 workers from randomly selected enterprises across an industry. The average wage rise in the previous year for these 120 workers was $1018, with a standard deviation of $614. The union was worried that its workers had not reached its bargaining aim of securing a wage rise of $1150. Conduct a two-tail *t*-test with alpha of 0.05 and 0.01 to assess whether this objective has been met. Does this conform to your estimates based on the confidence intervals?

10.5 The following data are ages at death for a sample of people who were all born in the same year:
34, 60, 72, 55, 68, 12, 48, 69, 78, 42, 60, 81, 72, 58, 70, 54, 85, 68, 74, 59, 67, 76, 55, 87, 70
Calculate the mean age at death and standard deviation for this sample. What is the probability of randomly obtaining this sample from a population with an average life expectancy of 70 years? Replace the **?** in the following SPSS output with the appropriate statistics from your calculations:

One Sample t-tests

Variable	Number of Cases	Mean	SD	SE of Mean
AGE Age in Years	25	?	?	3.326

Test Value = ?

Mean Difference	95% CI Lower	Upper		t-value	df	2-Tail Sig
−7.04	−13.904	−.176		?	?	.045

Is the estimate of the 95 per cent confidence interval consistent with your results? Enter this data into SPSS and check your answers.

10.6 A health worker wanted to gauge the effect of hip fractures on people's ability to walk. On average, people walk at a rate of 1 m/sec. Walking speed for 43 individuals who had suffered a hip fracture 6 months previously averaged 0.44 m/sec, with a standard deviation of 0.28 m/sec. What should the health worker conclude?

10.7 A.C. Nielsen has provided the following figures for the average number of minutes of TV watched by children in some selected countries:

Average number of minutes of TV watched by children, selected countries

Australia	Canada	United Kingdom	Singapore
159	140	196	212

In the text we compared the hypothetical results of a survey of 20 Australian children, which had an average viewing time of 165.85 minutes and standard deviation of 29.29 minutes, with the 'population' value for the United Kingdom. Compare this sample with the population values for Canada and Singapore, as well as the population value for Australia, and test whether there is a significant difference.

The *z*-test for a single proportion

The previous chapters looked at *z*-tests and *t*-tests for a single **mean**. However, social research is not always interested in investigating the mean of a distribution. We might be interested in other aspects of the population under investigation. For example, we might not be interested in the average height of people studying statistics, but rather the **proportion** of people above or below a certain height. Although this question is slightly different from one that investigates the mean of a distribution, the procedures for making an inference are basically the same. We will still conduct a *z*-test, but this time based on a sample proportion rather than a sample mean.

Making inferences about a proportion also extends the use of *z*-tests to nominal and ordinal data. A *z*-test (and *t*-test) for a mean is by definition restricted to situations where the variable of interest is measured at the interval/ratio level, such as height in centimetres or cost in dollars. When we are working with nominal or ordinal data a mean cannot be calculated, but we can still test whether a certain proportion of cases falls into one category of the variable or another. Since a proportion can be calculated for any level of measurement the *z*-test of proportions can be applied widely, often after collapsing values of the variable into two discrete categories.

Binomial variables

It is not uncommon in social research to encounter variables that have only two values or categories. Sex is an obvious example: someone is either male or female. Sex is an example of a **binomial** (or **dichotomous**) **variable**.

> A **binomial variable** has only two possible values or categories.

Some variables are intrinsically dichotomous. A classic example is a coin toss. A coin toss has only two possible outcomes: either heads or tails. Similarly, questions in opinion polls that allow only Yes/No responses are dichotomous.

However, even where a variable does not initially have only two values, it can be transformed into one that does. In fact, practically any variable can be turned into a binomial by collapsing categories:

- A nominal distribution that does not intrinsically have only two values can be collapsed into a binomial by simply specifying the number of cases that fall into a certain category (or combination of categories) *or not*. For example, a nominal distribution of cases according to religious denomination might begin with five classifications for religion: Catholic, Protestant, Jewish, Orthodox, and Muslim. These can be collapsed into a binomial distribution in one of two ways: either by referring to the proportion of cases that fall into one of the existing categories (or not), such as Catholic and Non-Catholic, or by creating two entirely new categories by combining the existing ones, such as Christian and Non-Christian (see Figure 11.1).

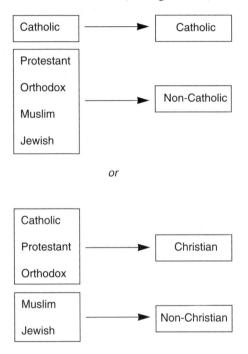

Figure 11.1

- Ordinal or interval/ratio scales can be collapsed into a binomial distribution by simply specifying the number of cases that fall above (or below) a particular value on the scale. Thus a list of exam scores can be collapsed into a binomial by selecting 50 per cent as the dividing line and organizing the scores into 'Pass' and 'Fail'. Similarly, rather than calculate average age for a set of cases, one might be interested in the proportion of cases that are above or below 20 years of age.

After having defined the relevant proportion of cases that we are interested in, we can then proceed to conduct an inference test on this proportion. To do this we have to know the properties of the sampling distribution of sample proportions.

The sampling distribution of sample proportions

In the previous chapters we had a sample average and we were interested in making an inference from this sample average to the average for the population. To make this inference we needed to know the properties of the sampling distribution of the sample means. This knowledge allows us to assess the probability of obtaining the sample average, if the assumption of no difference is true. When working with a binomial variable, however, the descriptive statistic calculated from the sample is no longer the mean. Instead it is the **proportion** of cases that fall within one of the two possible categories of the variable. Having calculated the sample proportion we then need to make an inference about the proportion for the population as a whole. Thus we need to explore the properties of the sampling distribution of sample proportions: the distribution of sample proportions that will arise from repeated random samples of equal size.

For example, we might know that 50 per cent of all students at a (hypothetical) university are male and 50 per cent are female. Despite this, if we take a random sample of 100 university students we will not necessarily get 50 males and 50 females. Random variation will cause some samples to include slightly more females, while other samples will include slightly more males. But most of these repeated proportions will have a proportion of each sex either equal or close to 0.5. In other words, while there is some variation in the distribution of repeated sample proportions, these sample proportions will cluster around the 'true' population value of 0.5.

If we take an infinite number of random samples of equal size from a population, and calculate the proportion of cases in each that have a certain value for a binomial variable, the sampling distribution of these sample proportions will have the following properties:

- The sampling distribution is approximately normal with a median proportion equal to the population value. It is only approximately normal because a binomial is a discrete variable, whereas the normal curve is continuous. However, the larger the sample size the more closely the distribution approximates the normal.
- The standard error of the sampling distribution will be:

$$\sigma_p = \sqrt{\frac{P_u(1 - P_u)}{N}}$$

where:
P_u is the population proportion.

This is a very useful result, as we discovered in previous chapters. Knowing the distribution of *all possible* sample proportions allows us to calculate the probability of getting any given sample result from a population with an hypothesized parameter value. For example, if a *sample* is drawn that is 60 per cent female, we can calculate the odds that this was the result of sampling error when drawing from a *population* that has an hypothesized proportion of 50 per cent females.

The z-test for a single proportion

In practical terms the steps involved in an hypothesis test for a proportion are exactly the same as when conducting an hypothesis test of single sample mean. The only variation is the formula used to calculate z_{sample}:

$$z_{sample} = \frac{(P_s - 0.005) - P_u}{\sqrt{\dfrac{P_u(1 - P_u)}{N}}} \quad \text{where } P_s > P_u$$

or

$$z_{sample} = \frac{(P_s + 0.005) - P_u}{\sqrt{\dfrac{P_u(1 - P_u)}{N}}} \quad \text{where } P_s < P_u$$

where:

P_s is the sample proportion
P_u is the population proportion.

The addition or subtraction of 0.005 (0.5%) to or from the sample proportion is made because, strictly speaking, a binomial distribution is not exactly normal and the addition or subtraction of 0.005 (called a continuity correction) gives us a good approximation. (With samples larger than 30 this approximation will be fairly accurate, but with less than 30 the approximation is not accurate and an exact binomial probability test should be used. Many statistics books print tables for the binomial distribution for various sample sizes, and these can be used instead of the z-approximation. SPSS automatically calculates an exact binomial probability in the small sample case.)

Example

A researcher is concerned that her local area is harder hit by recession than the rest of the country. She knows that the national unemployment rate is 0.11. She randomly asks 120 local people who are in the labor market if they are unemployed. The sample produces a result of 18 people unemployed, or 0.15 of the sample:

$$N = 120$$

$$P_s = \frac{18}{120} = 0.15$$

Does this indicate that this local area is harder hit by recession?

Step 1: State the null and alternative hypotheses

H_0: There is no difference between local area and national unemployment rates:

$$H_0: P_u = 0.11$$

H_a: The local area has a higher unemployment rate than the rest of the nation:

$$H_a: P_u > 0.11$$

Step 2: Choose the test of significance
We have the following information:

- the variable has a binomial distribution;
- the sample size is greater than 30.

Therefore we will use a single-sample z-test for a proportion.

Step 3: Establish the critical score(s) and region
The researcher chooses a 0.05 level of significance (α = 0.05) and, since she suspects that the local region is harder hit by recession, she will use a one-tail test. Since the direction of difference specified in the alternative hypothesis is that the unemployment rate is *higher* than the national average, the relevant tail is to the right of the sampling distribution. From the table for the area under the standard normal curve, the critical value of z will be +1.645 (see Figure 11.2).

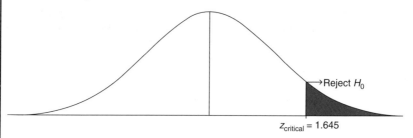

→Reject H_0

$z_{critical} = 1.645$

Figure 11.2 z-test of a proportion, one-tail test, α = 0.05

Step 4: Calculate the sample score

$$z_{sample} = \frac{(P_s - 0.005) - P_u}{\sqrt{\dfrac{P_u(1 - P_u)}{N}}}$$

$$z_{sample} = \frac{(0.15 - 0.005) - 0.11}{\sqrt{\dfrac{0.11(1 - 0.11)}{120}}}$$

$$= 1.23$$

Note: In the formula we use the proportions, and not the percentage values. In other words, we use 0.11 as the test proportion and not 11 per cent.

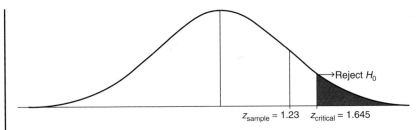

Figure 11.3   z-test of a proportion, one-tail test, $\alpha = 0.05$

This sample score is clearly closer to zero than the critical value (Figure 11.3).

Step 5: Make a decision
The sample value of $z = 1.23$ is not greater than the critical value of 1.645. The difference is not big enough to suggest that the local area systematically suffers from higher than average unemployment rates. We cannot reject, at this level of significance, the null hypothesis.

The z-test for a single proportion using SPSS

Filename 11.sav   In order to work through this test on SPSS, the data for the previous example has been entered into a data file. The variable has been called **empstats**, which has the variable label **Employment Status**, and has been coded in the **Value Labels** command so that **1=unemployed** and **2=employed**. SPSS calls the test of proportion a binomial test, and the commands needed to carry out this test are as shown in Table 11.1.

Table 11.1   Binomial test on SPSS

SPSS command/action	Comments
1 From the menu select **Statistics/Nonparametric Tests/Binomial...**	This will bring up a window headed **Binomial Test**
2 Click on the variable name, **empstats**	
3 Click on ➤	This will paste **empstats** into the **Test Variable List:**
4 In the square next to **Test Proportion** type 0.11 over 0.50	The default setting is .50, which means that SPSS will compare the sample proportion with 0.5 unless we specify an alternative, as in this case where we specify 0.11 as the test proportion
5 Click on **OK**	

The output from this analysis will be:

`- - - - - Binomial Test`

`EMPSTATS  Employment Status`

```
Cases
                Test Prop. =   .1100
  18  = 1       Obs. Prop. =   .1500
 102  = 2
 ---            Z Approximation

120 Total       1-Tailed P =   .1048
```

This result confirms the calculations above: the one-tail probability of 0.1048 indicates that *if* the null were true at least 1-in-10 samples would have an unemployment rate of 0.15 or more, even though the population from which the sample was drawn only had an unemployment rate of 0.11. This is not too unlikely: the assumption that the null is true cannot be rejected.

SPSS always produces a one-tail test when a test proportion is specified. If the alternative hypothesis requires a two-tail test, then we simply double the one-tail probability. If one tail of the sampling distribution, at this z-score, contains 0.1048 of the area under the curve, two tails will contain 0.2096 (20.96%) of the area under the normal curve.

Example

A survey of 300 eligible voters investigates the proportion of people who plan to vote for one of the two major parties at the next election. At the previous election this proportion was 0.85. The sample proportion of people is 0.72. Can we say that there is a greater level of dissatisfaction with the major parties? Since we are dealing with a situation where $P_s < P_u$ we use the following formula to calculate the test statistic:

$$z_{sample} = \frac{(P_s + 0.005) - P_u}{\sqrt{\dfrac{P_u(1 - P_u)}{N}}}$$

$$= \frac{(0.72 + 0.005) - 0.85}{\sqrt{\dfrac{0.85(1 - 0.85)}{300}}}$$

$$= -6.1$$

At an alpha level of 0.05, on a two-tail test, the value of $z_{critical} = \pm 1.96$. Thus the sample result falls in the rejection region. We can reject the null hypothesis that the proportion of people planning to vote for one of the two major parties is the same as that in the previous election.

Estimating a population proportion

Chapter 8 detailed the procedure for estimating from a sample mean a confidence interval, within which the population mean falls. A similar procedure can be followed to construct a confidence interval from a sample proportion, within which the (unknown) population proportion falls.

Estimating population proportions is common in public opinion surveys. We often read in newspapers that a certain proportion of eligible voters favour one person over another as preferred Prime Minister or President. This percentage figure is not obtained by surveying all eligible voters, but rather through a *sample* of eligible voters. We therefore need to estimate the population value from this sample result. The formula involved in constructing the confidence interval for a proportion is:

$$ci = P_s \pm z \sqrt{\frac{P_s(1 - P_s)}{N}}$$

For example, a company is proposing to set up a landfill site for waste disposal that will increase revenue to the local authority. However, the authority wants to balance this benefit against community concern about such a land-use in the local area. Authority officers take a random sample of 305 residents who are each asked whether she or he opposes the establishment of a landfill site in the local area even though the company would spend some of its profits cleaning up a local river. The proposal is opposed by 275 respondents.

$$N = 305$$

$$P_s = \frac{275}{305} = 0.9$$

At a 95 per cent confidence level, what is the proportion of all local residents that will oppose the landfill?

$$\text{at } \alpha = 0.05, z = 1.96$$

$$ci = P_s \pm z \sqrt{\frac{P_s(1 - P_s)}{N}}$$

$$ci = 0.9 \pm 1.96 \sqrt{\frac{0.9(1 - 0.9)}{305}}$$

$$ci = 0.9 \pm 0.034$$

The upper and lower limits of the confidence interval will be:

$$\text{upper limit} = 0.9 + 0.034 = 0.934$$
$$\text{lower limit} = 0.9 - 0.034 = 0.866$$

Thus the population value lies somewhere between 86.6 per cent and 93.4 per cent.

Example

In a sample of 500 students enrolled in fee-paying postgraduate courses, 55 are from low socioeconomic backgrounds. What is the estimated proportion of all fee-paying postgraduate students that come from low socioeconomic backgrounds?

$$N = 500$$

$$P_s = \frac{55}{600} = 0.11$$

at $\alpha = 0.05$, $z = 1.96$

$$ci = P_s \pm z \sqrt{\frac{P_s(1 - P_s)}{N}}$$

$$ci = 0.11 \pm 1.96 \sqrt{\frac{0.11(1 - 0.11)}{500}}$$

$$ci = 0.11 \pm 0.027$$

In other words, the proportion of students from low socioeconomic backgrounds in the population is, with a 95 per cent confidence level, between 0.083 (8.3%) and 0.137 (13.7%).

Inference using the confidence interval for a proportion

The reason for conducting the above survey is to see if the introduction of fees for postgraduate courses has had an adverse effect on disadvantaged groups. A census of all postgraduate students before the introduction of university fees found that 0.168 (16.8%) of postgrads were from low socioeconomic backgrounds. Can we say that the introduction of fees has affected the recruitment of poorer students? The problem is that we want to compare the population of postgraduate students before the introduction of fees with the population of students afterwards. We have information about the first population (pre-fees), but we only have an estimate of the second proportion from a sample. However, we can see that the proportion for the first population (pre-fees) does not fall into the 95 per cent confidence interval, within which we estimate lies the proportion for post-fee students from low socioeconomic backgrounds. In other words, the two population proportions are different, and the proportion of disadvantaged students in the pre-fees period is higher than that for the post-fees period. Fees do seem to have affected disadvantaged groups (Figure 11.4).

Around the sample proportion of 0.11 we have constructed the 95 per cent confidence interval, which ranges from 0.083 to 0.137. This is the interval that includes the population proportion of fee-paying postgrads from disadvantaged

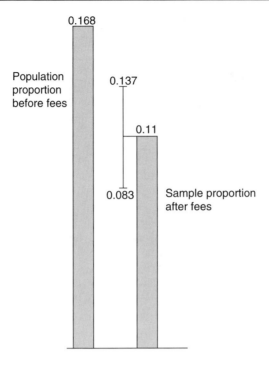

Figure 11.4

backgrounds. Clearly this interval does not include the value of 0.168, which is the proportion of postgraduate students from disadvantaged backgrounds before fees were introduced. Even though we only have exact information about one of the populations in question, the pre-fees postgrads, we can still argue that there is a difference based on the estimate for the unknown population value, derived from the sample.

To drive the point home further, we will in fact conduct an inference test to show that the conclusion is the same:

$$z_{sample} = \frac{(P_s - 0.005) - P_u}{\sqrt{\dfrac{P_u(1 - P_u)}{N}}}$$

$$= \frac{(0.11 - 0.005) - 0.168}{\sqrt{\dfrac{0.168(1 - 0.168)}{500}}}$$

$$= -3.77$$

On a one-tail test the critical value of *z*, at a 0.05 significance level (the equivalent of the 95 % confidence level), will be –1.64 (Figure 11.5). Therefore we reject the null hypothesis of no difference.

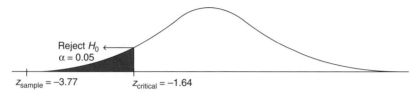

Figure 11.5

On a one-tail test the critical value of z, at a 0.05 significance level (the equivalent of the 95 % confidence level), will be –1.64 (Figure 11.5). Therefore we reject the null hypothesis of no difference.

Exercises

11.1 In order to estimate the proportion of a population giving a certain response to a survey we need to take a larger sample for larger populations. Is this statement true or false? Why?

11.2 For the following sets of statistics, conduct a z-test of proportions using both a one-tail and two-tail test, with alpha of 0.05:

(a)

$P_u = 0.52$
$P_s = 0.61$
$N = 110$

(b)

$P_u = 0.42$
$P_s = 0.39$
$N = 50$

11.3 A random sample of 900 jail prisoners are surveyed to gauge the success of an in-prison resocialization program. Of the total, 350 stated that the program had been effective in reducing the likelihood of repeat offence. The program's target was a 40 per cent success rate in reducing the likelihood of repeat offence. Using a z-test of proportions, can we say that the program was successful? Construct a 95 per cent confidence interval to estimate the population value. How does this confirm the result of the z-test?

11.4 A survey of 120 eligible voters are polled the day before an election and 63 state that they will vote for the opposition candidate. This candidate declares that the election is a waste of time since he will clearly win. Is this argument justified? Explain.

11.5 A physiotherapist is interested in whether ankle taping has reduced the incidence of ankle sprains in basketball players. The incidence of ankle sprains in basketball players has been reported to be 8 per cent. The physiotherapist randomly selects 360 basketball players who tape their ankles and finds that 11 have sprained their ankles. Does this suggest that taping reduces the incidence of ankle sprain?

11.6 A study of 500 people finds that 56 per cent support the decriminalization of marijuana use. What is the 95 per cent confidence interval for the proportion of all people in favor of decriminalization? Can we say that a

12

One sample non-parametric tests

Parametric and non-parametric tests

The previous chapters discussed situations where we made an hypothesis about a population parameter. We hypothesize that the population mean or proportion is a specific value and then determine the likelihood of drawing from this population a sample with a different mean or proportion. We do this by calculating a z-score or a t-score and looking up the corresponding probability in the appropriate table. If the difference between the sample statistic and the hypothesized population parameter is large, the corresponding probability that it is drawn from this population will be low. In short, the question boils down to whether an observed difference between a sample statistic and population value is 'big enough'.

We call such tests **parametric tests** because they test hypotheses about population parameters. However, there are many instances in which the conditions for using parametric tests do not hold, or else we are interested in aspects of the population other than its parameters. In such instances we use **non-parametric tests**. These are tests that are not concerned with the specific values of population parameters. For example, the chi-square goodness-of-fit test (χ^2 — pronounced 'ki-square'), which we will detail in this chapter, is a non-parametric test that looks at the frequency distribution of the population *across a range of values*, rather than trying to infer the particular value of the mean, or the proportion of the population below (or above) a certain point on the scale. The nature of the question addressed by the goodness-of-fit test, as opposed to the parametric tests we have encountered, is shown in Figure 12.1.

The benefits of non-parametric tests are twofold:

- **With interval/ratio data, non-parametric tests do not require the assumption that the distribution of the population is normal**. Even if we have interval/ratio data we might feel uncomfortable assuming that the population is normally distributed, an assumption that underlies the use of t-tests and small sample z-tests.
- **Non-parametric tests can be applied to variables measured at the ordinal and nominal level**. We will see, for example, that the chi-square goodness-of-fit test analyses the frequency distribution of cases, and since

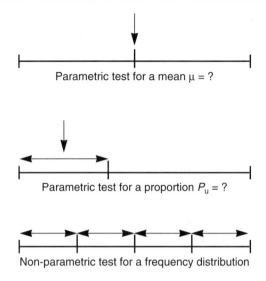

Parametric test for a mean $\mu = ?$

Parametric test for a proportion $P_u = ?$

Non-parametric test for a frequency distribution

Figure 12.1

frequency distributions can be constructed for nominal and ordinal data, as well as interval/ratio, it can be used for all levels of measurement.

These less restrictive assumptions ensure that non-parametric tests of significance have a wide applicability in the social sciences.

The chi-square goodness-of-fit test

The chi-square goodness-of-fit test draws inferences about the frequency distribution of the population across a range of values or categories. This is a question that can be addressed to all levels of measurement, since a frequency distribution, as we saw in Chapter 2, is a way of summarizing data measured at all levels. We will introduce the goodness-of-fit test as applied to nominal and ordinal data, where data are arranged into discrete categories. We will then show how this test can also be useful in analysing the frequency distribution of interval/ratio data.

We have seen that in the special case of nominal or ordinal data with a binomial distribution we can conduct a z-test of proportions to assess whether the sample came from a population with an hypothesized distribution of cases into one category or the other. What about nominal or ordinal data that have more than two categories? What if responses do not fall into simple Yes/No dichotomies, for example, and instead fall into a range of values such as 'strongly agree', 'agree', 'disagree', 'strongly disagree' (and we are not prepared to collapse these categories down to two)?

In such cases, where variables are measured at the nominal or ordinal level and have more than two categories, we use the chi-square goodness-of-fit test. It is called the chi-square test because the sampling distribution we use

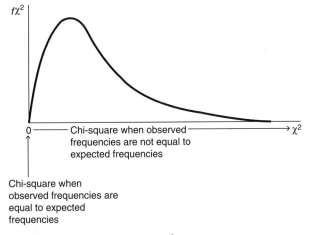

Figure 12.2   Distribution of chi-square (χ^2)

to assess the probability of the null being true is a chi-square distribution,[1] which has the general shape shown in Figure 12.2.

The chi-square distribution is constructed on the same basis as the other sampling distributions we have already encountered: it is the probability distribution we will get from an infinite number of samples drawn from a population with certain features.

To illustrate the goodness-of-fit test we will try to answer the following question: is the crime rate affected by the seasons? We are not interested in the *average* crime rate, but rather the distribution of crime rates across the seasons. We begin by making an hypothesis about the population distribution assuming that there is no relationship between crime rates and seasons. On this hypothesis we will *expect* the number of crimes committed in any year to be evenly distributed across the four seasons.

$$f_e = \frac{total\ number\ of\ crimes}{4}$$

where:

f_e is the expected frequency in each category.

However, in any given year the crime rate might be affected by random events that cause the distribution to be a little bit different from this expected result. In other words, not every sample will conform with this expectation of an exactly equal number of crimes in each season. We can express the

---

[1] A more detailed explanation of the chi-square distribution is reserved for the two or more samples case (Chpater 16), which is the most common use of the chi-square distribution in inference tests. It may be helpful to return to the present chapter after reading Chapter 16. The one-sample case is presented here to maintain the overall logic of this book, which is to present all the one-sample tests first, before moving on to tests for two or more samples.

difference between the *expected* value and the *observed* value by calculating a chi-square statistic:

$$\chi^2_{sample} = \Sigma \frac{(f_o - f_e)^2}{f_e}$$

where:

f_o is the observed frequency in each category.

We can see that if the sample result conformed exactly to the expected result, the value of χ^2_{sample} would be zero. If observed frequencies are the same as expected frequencies then subtracting one from the other will be zero.

What about situations in which the observed distribution is not exactly the same as the expected distribution? Looking at the formula for chi-square we can see that any difference will produce a positive value for χ^2_{sample}. This is because any difference is squared, thereby eliminating negative values. We can also see that the larger the difference between the observed and expected values, called the **residuals**, the higher the (positive) value of χ^2_{sample}. The question then becomes at what point does the value of χ^2_{sample} become so large that it suggests the sample did not come from a population with a uniform spread of crime rates across seasons?

We choose this critical value for chi-square in the same way as with other tests. We choose an alpha level, such as 0.05, and look up the corresponding value from the table for the distribution of chi-square at the back of this book. To find the critical value of chi-square for a given alpha level we need to take into account the number of degrees of freedom. Since the expected frequencies must equal the total number of observed frequencies, we lose 1 degree of freedom. In other words:

$$df = k - 1$$

where:

k is the number of categories.

Thus if a variable has four categories, as in this case, the degrees of freedom will be:

$$df = 4 - 1 = 3$$

From the distribution of chi-square, at an alpha level of 0.05 and with 3 degrees of freedom, we see that the critical region begins with a chi-square value of 7.815 (Table 12.1 and Figure 12.3).

$$\chi^2_{critical} = 7.815$$

We can now calculate the sample value for chi-square to see if it falls within this critical region (region of rejection). For example, if we actually observe the following (hypothetical) distribution of crime shown in Table 12.2 can we conclude that crime is indeed affected by the seasons?

Table 12.1   Distribution of chi-square

df	\.99	\.90	\.70	\.50	\.30	\.20	\.10	\.05	\.01	\.001
				Area under the distribution (α)						
1	.000157	.0158	.148	.455	1.074	1.642	2.706	3.841	6.635	10.827
2	.0201	.211	.713	1.386	2.408	3.219	4.605	5.991	9.210	13.815
3	.115	.584	1.424	2.366	3.665	4.642	6.251	7.815	11.341	16.268
4	.297	1.064	2.195	3.357	4.878	5.989	7.779	9.488	13.277	18.465
5	.554	1.610	3.000	4.351	6.064	7.289	9.236	11.070	15.086	20.517
6	.872	2.204	3.828	5.348	7.231	8.558	10.645	12.592	16.812	22.457

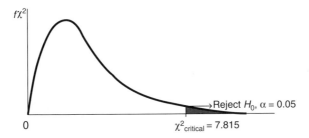

Figure 12.3   Distribution of chi-square ($df = 3$)

Table 12.2   Distribution of crime by season

	Summer	Spring	Winter	Autumn	Total
Observed	300	270	200	250	1020
Expected	255	255	255	255	1020
Residual	45	15	−55	−5	

The expected values are the total divided by the number of seasons:

$$f_e = \frac{1020}{4}$$

$$= 255$$

The row called 'Residual' is simply the difference between the observed and expected values. To get a better picture of the logic behind this test, we have graphed the data (Figure 12.4).

The straight line represents the height that the bars would be if the observed values were equal to the expected values. However, we can see that this is not the case: Summer and Spring have higher than expected values, whereas Winter and Autumn fall short. The gap between the line and each bar is the residual.

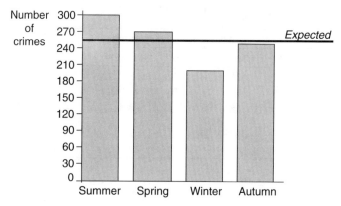

Figure 12.4   Distribution of crime by season

We can now substitute the sample results into the formula for chi-square.

$$\chi^2_{sample} = \Sigma \frac{(f_o - f_e)^2}{f_e}$$

$$= \frac{(300 - 255)^2}{255} + \frac{(270 - 255)^2}{255} + \frac{(200 - 255)^2}{255} + \frac{(250 - 255)^2}{255}$$

$$= 20.78$$

The value of χ^2_{sample} clearly falls into the critical region and therefore will cause us to reject the null hypothesis of an even distribution of crime across seasons.

Chi-square goodness-of-fit test using SPSS

Filename 12–1.sav   The data from this test have been entered into SPSS. This data file comprises a column of 1020 numbers representing the season in which each crime was committed, which is given the variable name **season**. The value labels and values for this variable are:

```
Summer=1
Spring=2
Autumn=3
Winter=4
```

To conduct a one-sample chi-square test on this data we work through the following procedure shown in Table 12.3.

Table 12.3   Chi-square goodness-of-fit test using SPSS

SPSS command/action	Comments
1 From the menu select **Statistics/Nonparametric Tests/ Chi Square...**	This will bring up a window headed **Chi Square Test**
2 Click on the variable name **season**	**season** will now be highlighted
3 Click on ➤	This will paste **season** into the **Test Variable List:**
4 In the area called **Expected Values** the small circle next to **All categories equal** will be selected	This is the default setting: SPSS will automatically calculate the number of expected cases in each category by dividing the total by the number of categories
5 Click on **OK**	

The output from this set of instructions will be:

```
- - - - - Chi-Square Test

    SEASON     Crime By Season

                          Cases
               Category  Observed  Expected  Residual

    Summer         1        300     255.00     45.00
    Spring         2        270     255.00     15.00
    Autumn         3        200     255.00    -55.00
    Winter         4        250     255.00     -5.00
                                   ----
               Total       1020

        Chi-Square          D.F.        Significance
         20.7843              3             .0001
```

We can compare these results with the 'hand' calculations above. As with all inference tests on SPSS the first part of the output is the descriptive statistics that summarize the sample. In this case, the distribution of cases across the four seasons is provided. A column of expected frequencies is also generated, based on the assumption that an equal number of cases is expected in each season. The values in the **Expected** column are subtracted from the **Cases Observed** column to give the **Residual** values. This is simply a replication of the frequency table we used above, but turned 'on its side' so that the seasons are down the left of the table rather than across the top.

Below this frequency table is the chi-square test. The sample chi-square is 20.7843 (as we calculated above), which, with 3 degrees of freedom, has a probability of occurring if crime is evenly spread across seasons one time in every ten thousand samples. Such a low probability leads us to reject the null hypothesis: crime rates do seem to be related to the seasons.

Example

In 1994, 40 per cent of sales by a car dealer were four-cylinder cars, 30 per cent were six-cylinder, and 30 per cent eight-cylinder. A random sample of sales in recent months produced the distribution shown in Table 12.4.

Table 12.4   Sales distribution

Engine type	Observed number of sales
Four-cylinder	42
Six-cylinder	26
Eight-cylinder	12
Total	80

Can we say that this reflects a trend toward smaller cars? First we calculate the expected number of sales, based on the 1994 percentages (Table 12.5).

Table 12.5   Expected sales

Engine type	Expected number of sales
Four-cylinder	$\frac{40}{100} \times 80 = 32$
Six-cylinder	$\frac{30}{100} \times 80 = 24$
Eight-cylinder	$\frac{30}{100} \times 80 = 24$
Total	80

Substituting observed and expected frequencies into the formula for chi-square:

$$\chi^2_{sample} = \Sigma \frac{(f_o - f_e)^2}{f_e}$$

$$= \frac{(42 - 32)^2}{32} + \frac{(26 - 24)^2}{24} + \frac{(12 - 24)^2}{24}$$

$$= 9.29$$

The critical value for chi-square, with 2 degrees of freedom and a 0.05 level of significance, is 5.991 (Figure 12.5).

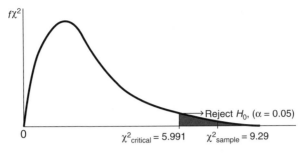

Figure 12.5   Distribution of chi-square ($df = 2$)

We therefore reject the null — the frequency is different from last year. There is a trend towards smaller cars.

The chi-square goodness-of-fit test for normality

We have worked through examples of the chi-square goodness-of-fit test on nominal data, and it is fairly clear that the same procedure can be used to assess ordinal data, since these will also fall into discrete categories. Any test that can be applied to nominal and ordinal data, though, can also be applied to the higher levels of measurement of interval/ratio. Even though the data may not fall into distinct categories, we can create the necessary categories by specifying ranges of values, much like specifying class intervals, and assessing the distribution of cases in these ranges. Thus if we have a set of cases ordered according to age in years, we can select certain ranges for age, such as 0–17, 18–65, and over 65, and compare the distribution of a sample across these categories with some hypothesized population distribution.

This logic makes the goodness-of-fit test particularly useful when analysing interval/ratio data to assess whether they come from a normal population. In this way, this non-parametric test can be a useful preliminary and complement to parametric tests, which require the assumption that a sample comes from a normal population. Remember from Chapter 6 that a normal distribution is defined by the distribution of cases shown in Table 12.6, and Figure 12.6.

Table 12.6   Distribution of the normal curve

Range of values	Percentage of cases
Further than 2 standard deviations below the mean	2
Between 1 and 2 standard deviations below the mean	14
Within 1 standard deviation below the mean	34
Within 1 standard deviation above the mean	34
Between 1 and 2 standard deviations above the mean	14
Further than 2 standard deviations above the mean	2

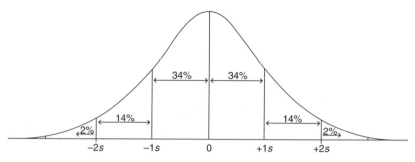

Figure 12.6 Area under the theoretical normal curve

Suppose that we have a sample and we want to assess whether it was drawn from a population with a normal distribution. We can use the percentage values in Table 12.6 to calculate the expected values in the formula for chi-square. Notice that unlike the previous example of crime rates, we are not assuming that cases are evenly distributed across the categories; instead the expected frequency distribution is based on the characteristics of the normal curve.

For example, assume that we have a sample of 110 people whose age is recorded. The mean age for this sample is 45 years, with a standard deviation of 10 years. If this sample is normally distributed we will expect to find the numbers of people within these ranges (using the sample values as population estimates) as shown in Table 12.7. The table includes the calculations for the first three ranges to show the method involved.

Table 12.7 Expected distribution of the sample

Range of values	Percentage of cases (%)	Number of cases
25 years or less (further than 2 standard deviations below the mean)	2	$0.02 \times 110 = 2.2$
26–35 years (between 1 and 2 standard deviations below the mean)	14	$0.14 \times 110 = 15.4$
36–45 years (within 1 standard deviation below the mean)	34	$0.34 \times 110 = 37.4$
46–55 years (within 1 standard deviation above the mean)	34	37.4
56–65 years (between 1 and 2 standard deviations above the mean)	14	15.4
66 years or over (further than 2 standard deviations above the mean)	2	2.2

However, we might actually get the distribution within the sample as shown in Table 12.8.

Table 12.8   Observed distribution of the sample

Range of values	Number of cases
25 years or less	5
26–35 years	17
36–45 years	33
46–55 years	33
56–65 years	17
66 years or over	5

There is obviously some difference between the observed and expected values: should this cause us to reject the hypothesis that the population is normally distributed? To answer this we need to calculate chi-square:

$$\chi^2_{sample} = \Sigma \frac{(f_o - f_e)^2}{f_e}$$

$$= \frac{(5 - 2.2)^2}{2.2} + \frac{(17 - 15.4)^2}{15.4} + \frac{(33 - 37.4)^2}{37.4} +$$

$$\frac{(33 - 37.4)^2}{37.4} + \frac{(17 - 15.4)^2}{15.4} + \frac{(5 - 2.2)^2}{2.2}$$

$$= 8.5$$

We need to compare this with a critical value for chi-square, which depends on the degrees of freedom. Here we have six categories, so that degrees of freedom will be 6 – 1 = 5. At an alpha level of 0.05 the critical value for chi-square is 11.070 (Table 12.9).

Table 12.9   Distribution of chi-square

df	.99	.90	.70	.50	.30	.20	.10	.05	.01	.001
					Area under the distribution (α)					
1	.000157	.0158	.148	.455	1.074	1.642	2.706	3.841	6.635	10.827
2	.0201	.211	.713	1.386	2.408	3.219	4.605	5.991	9.210	13.815
3	.115	.584	1.424	2.366	3.665	4.642	6.251	7.815	11.341	16.268
4	.297	1.064	2.195	3.357	4.878	5.989	7.779	9.488	13.277	18.465
5	.554	1.610	3.000	4.351	6.064	7.289	9.236	11.070	15.086	20.517
6	.872	2.204	3.828	5.348	7.231	8.558	10.645	12.592	16.812	22.457

The sample value for chi-square is smaller than the critical value so we do not reject the hypothesis that the sample comes from a normally distributed population (Figure 12.7).

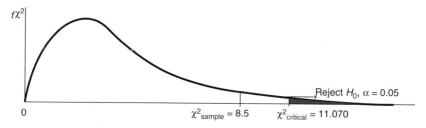

Figure 12.7 Distribution of chi-square ($df = 5$)

Another non-parametric test: The runs test for randomness

With binomial data, the proportion of the sample that falls in one category or the other is not the only descriptive statistic we might be interested in. We might have no interest in the question of what proportion of the *total* sample falls in one category or the other. Instead we might be interested in the *series or sequence of scores*: how each score follows on from the previous. Usually we look at the sequence of cases with a particular question in mind: is a series of events **random**?

> An event is **random** if its outcome in one instance is not affected by the outcome in other instances.

For example, the sex of a child in a family is random if it is not affected by the sex of other children in the family. If a woman has given birth to nine daughters already, and the sex of each child is a random event, we should not expect that the next child is any more likely to be female than it is to be male.

To decide whether the value of a variable in one case is random with respect to the value it takes in other cases, we conduct a z-test on the number of *sample runs* — the 'runs test'.[1]

> A **run** is a sequence of cases that have the same value for a variable.

The idea behind a runs test of randomness is simple. If the outcome of a coin toss is random, and an unbiased coin is tossed and comes up heads, the probability of the *next* toss being either heads or tails should be 50/50. There should be a fairly even spread of heads and tails after each toss. If any of the

---

[1] Where the sample size is less than 20, the distribution of sample runs will not be approximately normal, and therefore an exact probability test should be conducted. Some statistics books, such as P. Newbold, 1988, *Statistics for Business and Economics*, 2nd edn, Prentice-Hall, London, p. 843, present a table of the distribution of sample runs in the small sample case, to which readers are referred if an exact test is required. In our test we will only be working with samples larger than 20 where the normal approximation is applicable.

following three results occurs from tossing a coin 20 times we might get a little suspicious:

Set 1: T T T T T T T T T T T T T T T T T T T T

Set 2: H H H H H H H H H H H H H H H H H H H H

Set 3: H T H T H T H T H T H T H T H T H T H T

In each set, it seems that each case is not random. In the first two sets of tosses each flip generally leads to the same result in the next — tails seem to determine tails, and heads seem to determine heads. In the third set of tosses, tails determine heads and vice versa. Either way, the outcome of a coin toss does not appear to be random. But another interpretation could be that each of these outcomes occurred simply on the basis of chance. Coin tosses might be random, but we just happened by fluke to get these outcomes.

To decide between these explanations, we describe the results of each set of tosses by calculating the number of *runs*: how many *sequences* of like results there are. In the first two sets we have 1 run each:

Set 1
T T T T T T T T T T T T T T T T T T T T
1 run

Set 2
H H H H H H H H H H H H H H H H H H H H
1 run

In the third set of tosses we have 20 runs:

Set 3
H T H T H T H T H T H T H T H T H T H T
1 2 3 4 5 6 7 8 9 10 11 12 13 14 15 16 17 18 19 20
20 runs

It is conceivable that I could toss an unbiased coin and get such results — they could happen just by chance. This is the null hypothesis of randomness. However, such results are very unlikely. The probability of getting either 1 run or 20 runs from 20 coin tosses, *if* the toss of a coin is truly random, is extremely low. On average, we expect to get between 1 and 20 runs. In fact, the value we expect to get if the results are random is given by the formula:

$$\mu_R = \frac{2N_1N_2}{N} + 1$$

where:
N_1 is the number of cases with a given value
N_2 is the number of cases with the other value.

This is the value we use in the null hypothesis. The alternative hypothesis is therefore a statement that this is not the situation:

$$\mu_R \neq \frac{2N_1 N_2}{N} + 1$$

However, even though coin tosses are random, individual samples will not always have this many runs. The spread of possible sample results around the expected value is given by:

$$\sigma_R = \sqrt{\frac{N^2 - 2N}{4(N-1)}}$$

Given this information we can perform a z-test to determine whether the sample value of R is likely to be the result of chance or something systematic:

$$z_{sample} = \frac{(R + 0.5) - \mu_R}{\sigma_R} \text{ where } R < \mu_R$$

or

$$z_{sample} = \frac{(R - 0.5) - \mu_R}{\sigma_R} \text{ where } R > \mu_R$$

where:
  R is the number of runs in the sample
  μ_R is the number of runs expected from repeated sampling
  σ_R is the standard error of the sampling distribution.

We simply follow the hypothesis testing procedure we have learnt and compare the sample z-score and probability with a pre-chosen critical value and decide either to reject or not to reject the null hypothesis. It is important when conducting this test that the data are ordered in the sequence in which they were generated. For example, when looking at time series, as we do below, the data are ordered according to year.

Example
One of the most common uses of the runs test is with time series data. Time series refers to a sequence of cases occurring over successive time periods. For example, we might be interested in people's propensity to save: how much do people set aside from their income instead of consuming? More specifically, is the proportion of saving out of household income in any given year related to the amount saved in the previous year? Do years of relatively high saving tend to follow each other and do years of low saving tend to follow each other?

Table 12.10 provides the raw data for a hypothetical country over a 33 year period.

Table 12.10   Savings, household income and saving rate from 1949–50 to 1981–82 ($ million)

Year	Savings	Household income	Saving rate (%)
1949–50	454	4434	10.2
1950–51	984	6080	16.2
1951–52	272	6307	4.3
1952–53	722	7061	10.2
1953–54	494	7389	6.7
1954–55	540	7906	6.8
1955–56	664	8581	7.7
1956–57	721	9168	7.9
1957–58	275	9169	3.0
1958–59	650	9874	6.6
1959–60	641	10 867	5.9
1960–61	724	11 678	6.2
1961–62	831	12 130	6.9
1962–63	880	12 925	6.8
1963–64	1213	14 359	8.4
1964–65	1300	15 712	8.3
1965–66	1158	16 533	7.0
1966–67	1662	18 329	9.1
1967–68	1013	19 288	5.3
1968–69	1838	21 700	8.5
1969–70	1853	23 974	7.7
1970–71	2410	26 870	9.0
1971–72	2999	30 418	9.9
1972–73	4346	34 992	12.4
1973–74	6033	42 952	14.0
1974–75	7718	53 568	14.4
1975–76	7978	62 703	12.7
1976–77	8552	71 679	11.9
1977–78	9222	79 145	11.7
1978–79	10 418	88 206	11.8
1979–80	10 309	98 404	10.5
1980–81	12 253	112 632	10.9
1981–82	14 315	130 145	11.0

In order to conduct a runs test on such a time series of data we need firstly to categorize each year as exhibiting either a 'high' or a 'low' rate of saving. A number of options are available, but in this instance we will call any year with saving rate above the median a high saving year, and any year with a rate below the 33 year median as a low saving year. The median for these 33 saving rates is 8.5 per cent. To see whether years of low or high saving occur in 'patches' or are distributed randomly across years, we will put a plus or minus sign next to the rate for each year, depending on whether it is above or below the median score of 8.5 (the median score is assigned a plus) (Table 12.11).

Table 12.11

Year	Savings rate (%)	Above or below median	
1949–50	10.2	+	Run 1
1950–51	16.2	+	
1951–52	4.3	−	Run 2
1952–53	10.2	+	Run 3
1953–54	6.7	−	
1954–55	6.8	−	
1955–56	7.7	−	
1956–57	7.9	−	
1957–58	3.0	−	
1958–59	6.6	−	
1959–60	5.9	−	Run 4
1960–61	6.2	−	
1961–62	6.9	−	
1962–63	6.8	−	
1963–64	8.4	−	
1964–65	8.3	−	
1965–66	7.0	−	
1966–67	9.1	+	Run 5
1967–68	5.3	−	Run 6
1968–69	8.5	+	Run 7
1969–70	7.7	−	Run 8
1970–71	9.0	+	
1971–72	9.9	+	
1972–73	12.4	+	
1973–74	14.0	+	
1974–75	14.4	+	
1975–76	12.7	+	Run 9
1976–77	11.9	+	
1977–78	11.7	+	
1978–79	11.8	+	
1979–80	10.5	+	
1980–81	10.9	+	
1981–82	11.0	+	

Thus we are able to describe our sample result by saying that there are 9 runs. How likely is this to occur if the saving rate in any given year is random with respect to the rate in the previous year? To specify the null hypothesis we need to calculate:

$$\mu_R = \frac{2N_1 N_2}{N} + 1$$

$$= \frac{2(16)(17)}{33} + 1$$

$$= 17.5$$

Thus the null and alternative hypotheses will be:

$$H_0: \mu_R = 17.5$$

$$H_a: \mu_R \neq 17.5$$

The probability of getting the actual sample result of 9 runs, on the assumption that the null hypothesis is true, can be calculated:

$$z_{\text{sample}} = \frac{(R + 0.5) - \mu_R}{\sqrt{\dfrac{N^2 - 2N}{4(N - 1)}}}$$

$$z_{\text{sample}} = \frac{9.5 - 17.5}{\sqrt{\dfrac{33^2 - 2(33)}{4(33 - 1)}}}$$

$$z_{\text{sample}} = -2.83$$

From the table for the area under the standard normal curve, this z-score has a probability of occurring (on a two-tail test) by chance less than 5 times in 1000. Therefore we reject the null hypothesis of randomness, and argue that the saving rate does seem to be affected by the rate in the previous year. In other words, there appears to be a cyclical process at work.

The runs test using SPSS

Filename 12–2.sav   The data from this example have been entered into SPSS. The variable indicating the saving rate for each year is called **saverate** (Table 12.12).

Table 12.12   Runs test on SPSS

SPSS command/action	Comments
1 From the menu select **Statistics/Nonparametric Tests/ Runs...**	This will bring up a window headed **Runs Test**
2 Click on the variable name, **saverate**	
3 Click on ➤	This will paste **saverate** into the **Test Variable List:**
4 In the area called **Cut Point** click on the square next to **Median**	This will place × in the box to show that the median of the series will be used to decide whether a particular year is to be assigned as high or low
5 Click on **OK**	

The output from the runs test, for this data, will be:

```
- - - - - Runs Test

SAVERATE  Household Saving Rate

   Runs:  9              Test value = 8.50 (Median)

  Cases: 16   LT Median
         17   GE Median                Z = -2.8271
         --
         33   Total        2-Tailed P =   .0047
```

This indicates that there were 16 years in which the saving rate was below the median, and 17 years that were equal to or above the median. Provided the data were entered in chronological order, so that 1949–50 was on the first row of data and 1981–82 was on the last, SPSS calculates that there are 9 runs. The z-score of –2.8271 has a two-tail probability of 0.0047, if the null hypothesis of randomness is true. (If we want to convert the two-tail probability into a one-tail probability, we halve its value.) This is so improbable that we reject the null hypothesis.

Exercises

12.1 What will be the number of degrees of freedom, and the value of $\chi^2_{critical}$ for both $\alpha = 0.10$ and $\alpha = 0.05$, for a goodness-of-fit test on a variable with:

	df	$\alpha = 0.10$	$\alpha = 0.05$
3 categories			
5 categories			
8 categories			

12.2 Conduct a goodness-of-fit test on the following data to test the hypothesis that the sample comes from a population with a uniform distribution of cases across categories:

(a)

Value	Number of cases
1	45
2	40
3	55
4	54
5	38

(b)

Value	Number of cases
1	120
2	111
3	119
4	125
5	120
6	127
7	118

12.3 According to a 1991 Census of Population and Housing, people between the ages of 25 and 34 years had the following distribution according to marital status:

Marital status of the population aged 25–34 years, 1991

Marital status	Number of persons
Never married	896206
Married	1591010
Separated not divorced	104296
Divorced	117673
Widowed	14216
Total	2723401

A survey of 350 residents aged between 25 and 34 is taken in a local area, which had the following distribution according to marital status:

Marital status of a survey of local residents

Marital status	Percentage of sample (N = 350)
Never married	40
Married	50
Separated not divorced	6
Divorced	2
Widowed	2
Total	100

Using the census information to calculate the expected values, can we say that this area is significantly different from the rest of the population? In which direction are the differences?

12.4 Ninety people are surveyed and the amount of time they each spend reading each day is measured. The researcher wants to test the assumption that this sample comes from a normal population. The mean for the sample is 45 minutes, with a standard deviation of 15 minutes. The distribution of the sample across the following ranges of values is:

Observed distribution of the sample

Range of values	Number of cases
Less than 16 minutes	3
16–30 minutes	15
31–45 minutes	34
46–60 minutes	31
61–75 minutes	5
Over 75 minutes	2

Using an alpha level of 0.05 test the assumption of normality for the population.

12.5 Five American schools are compared in terms of the proportion of students that proceed to university. A sample of 50 students who graduated from each school is taken and the number who entered university from each school are:

School 1   22
School 2   25
School 3   26
School 4   28
School 5   33

Calculate the expected values and then conduct a chi-square goodness of fit test. What do you conclude about the prospects of entering university from each of the schools? Enter your results into the appropriate places in the following SPSS output:

```
- - - - - Chi-Square Test

  SCHOOL

              Cases
  Category  Observed  Expected  Residual

      1        22        ?         ?
      2        25        ?       -1.80
      3        26        ?         ?
      4        28        ?        1.20
      5        33        ?         ?
              ---
   Total      134

       Chi-Square            D.F.       Significance
           ?                  ?            .6460
```

Optional exercises

12.6 A cricket captain has recorded the outcome of 20 coin tosses for the last 20 games. These tosses had the following sequence of results:

heads, tails, heads, heads, tails, tails, tails, heads, heads, heads,
tails, heads, heads, tails, tails, heads, tails, tails, tails, tails,

Why is a runs test applicable to such data? Conduct a runs test to see if the outcome of these tosses is random.

If these data were coded with heads = 1 and tails = 2 and SPSS used to analyse the results, fill in the following output with your calculations:

```
- - - - - Runs Test

   COINTOSS


      Runs:     ?           Test value = 2

      Cases:    9   LT 2
                ?   GE 2                Z =      ?
                --
                20   Total 2-Tailed P =    .8526
```

12.7 A hospital has kept a tally of the years in which a majority of boys were born and those in which a majority of girls were born. The sequence of results is as follows:

boys boys boys girls boys boys girls boys girls boys boys boys
boys boys girls boys boys girls boys boys boys boys girls

How many runs describe this sequence? How many runs would we expect to get if the proportion of boys and girls born was purely random with respect to the previous year's outcome? At a 0.05 level of significance, can we say that the outcome is a non-random event?

Enter these data on SPSS and conduct a runs test to confirm your own calculations.

Part

2

Inferential statistics

B

Hypothesis testing for two or more independent samples

13

The *t*-test for the equality of two means

All the tests covered thus far have been dealing with the one-sample case. That is, they all involve making an inference about one population only: we don't have information about the population, so we infer it from the sample result. We make this inference so that we can compare the result with another population for which we do have information. But what if we don't have information about this other population either? In this situation we have to make an inference about this second population as well. For example, in Chapter 10 we worked through an example where we were interested in the average amount of television watched by Australian and British children between the ages of 5 and 12 years. We would have liked to compare the population parameters, but unfortunately we only had population values for British children. For Australian children we took a sample of 20 and made an inference based on this sample result. However, what if we did not have information on the population of British kids either? The best we could do would be to take a random sample of British children as well, and make another inference from this second sample. In such a situation we would have to conduct a **two-sample test of significance** (Figure 13.1).

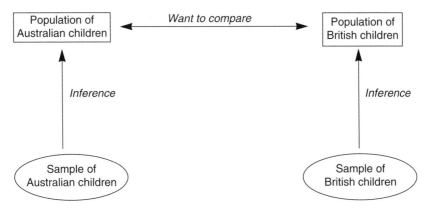

Figure 13.1   Hypothesis testing: The two-sample case

In fact, we could extend this to a situation in which we want to compare more than two populations. For example, we might be interested in comparing children from a number of countries in terms of their average amount of TV viewing. Generally, the choice of inference test is affected by the number of samples from which an inference is being made. In particular, it is common practice to distinguish between one-sample tests, two-sample tests, and tests for more than two samples. When making inferences for more than two samples we speak of tests for k-samples, where k is a number greater than two. Often the change involved in moving from the one-sample to the two-sample, or to the k-sample situation will not be great, but as an organizing principle it is useful to keep in mind whether the number of samples from which an inference is being made is one, two, or more than two.

Dependent and independent variables

Let us look again at the example of comparing Australian and British children in terms of their average amount of television viewing. We conducted a survey of kids from each country. Although in *practice* we may think in terms of one sample, which included both Australian and British children, *conceptually* we say that we were working with two samples: one from each of the populations for which we will make an inference. That is, although in the actual mechanics of data collection we had one big collection of children who had been surveyed as part of the same research process, when analysing the data we treat the two groups of children as separate samples.

This process of sorting cases into distinct samples for the purpose of statistical analysis is, in effect, a way of sorting cases in terms of a variable, which SPSS calls a **Grouping Variable**. This grouping variable defines the number of samples from which inferences will be made. These comparisons are then made on the basis of another variable, which SPSS calls a **Test Variable**. Thus, in the above example, children are first grouped according to the variable 'Country of residence' and the two samples thus formed (Australian and British children) are compared in terms of a test variable, 'Amount of TV watched each night' (Figure 13.2).

In other words, each case is assigned two values. The first 'tags' each case as belonging in a group according to country of residence. The second value is the amount of television each child watches in minutes, which is the variable on which the groups will be compared.

Usually the grouping variable is called the **independent variable** and the variable that we use to compare the samples is the **dependent variable**.

A **dependent variable** is explained or affected by an **independent variable**.

In our example of children, we may suspect that country of residence somehow affects or causes the amount of TV they watch (due possibly to factors such as the weather or the quality of programming in different countries).

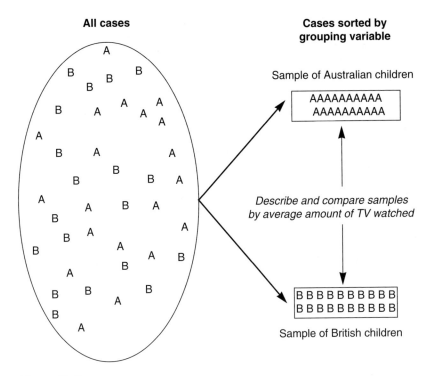

All cases

Cases sorted by grouping variable

Sample of Australian children

AAAAAAAAAA
AAAAAAAAAA

Describe and compare samples by average amount of TV watched

B B B B B B B B B B
B B B B B B B B B B

Sample of British children

Figure 13.2

However, in other instances, it may not be so easy to identify which variable is dependent and which is independent. An example we will use in Chapter 22 illustrates this point. We have a set of local government areas (LGAs), and we calculate the rate of unemployment and the crime rate for each. Of these two variables, which do we say is independent and which is dependent? Do we form groups of LGAs according to crime rates and then compare across these groups using unemployment rates, or do we group the LGAs by unemployment rates and then compare them according to crime rates?

One might argue that unemployment in an area affects the number of crimes, due to the higher number of people who feel alienated from society. Therefore the unemployment rate is the independent variable. Alternatively, one might argue that crime rates depend on factors other than unemployment, and that unemployment is a consequence of crime as businesses move to safer areas. According to this argument we would use crime rate as the independent variable. The choice of dependent and independent variable is, in other words, affected by the theoretical arguments from which research hypotheses are derived. It is not an issue that the statistical tests themselves can prove. Statistical tests cannot explore the complete nature or channels of any causality. All that statistics can do is compare differences *given* the way that the problem has been posed.

All these considerations involved in organizing data are summarized in Table 13.1.

Table 13.1

Type of variable	SPSS name	Function in inference test
Independent	Grouping variable	Sorts cases into a number of samples from which inferences will be made about the populations
Dependent	Test variable	Calculated to describe each sample and used to determine whether the populations are the same

The sampling distribution of the difference between two means

As with all other hypothesis tests, we begin by *assuming* that the null hypothesis of no difference is correct. We then build up a **sampling distribution of the difference between two means**. We then use this sampling distribution to decide whether the probability of getting a difference between two sample means from populations with no difference is so small that it warrants us to reject this hypothesis.

For example, let's begin by assuming that average TV viewing is the same in both Australia and Britain. This null hypothesis of no difference is formally written as:

$$\mu_1 = \mu_2$$

or

$$\mu_1 - \mu_2 = 0$$

If this assumption is true, what will we get if we take repeated samples from each country and calculate the **difference** between each pair of samples? Intuitively, we expect that the most common result will be that the difference is small, if not zero. Since we are assuming no difference between the two populations, we expect the sample means to be equal as well (or have very little difference) (Figure 13.3. The three dot triangle is mathematical shorthand for 'therefore'.)

But obviously this will not always be the result. Occasionally we might draw a sample from Australia that has a lower than average amount of TV viewing coupled with a sample from Britain that has a higher than average amount of TV viewing (Figure 13.4).

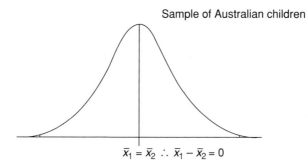

Sample of Australian children

$$\bar{x}_1 = \bar{x}_2 \therefore \bar{x}_1 - \bar{x}_2 = 0$$

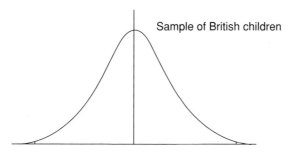

Sample of British children

Figure 13.3

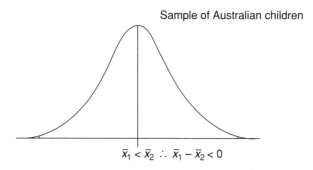

Sample of Australian children

$$\bar{x}_1 < \bar{x}_2 \therefore \bar{x}_1 - \bar{x}_2 < 0$$

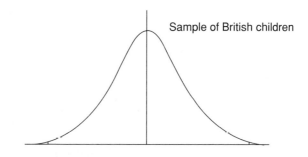

Sample of British children

Figure 13.4

Similarly we might get, through the operation of random chance, the opposite situation:

$$\overline{X}_1 > \overline{X}_2 \therefore X_1 - \overline{X}_2 > 0$$

If we take a large number of these repeated random samples and calculate the difference between the two sample means, we will end up with a **sampling distribution of the difference between two means** that has the following properties:

- It will be a t-distribution:

$$t_{sample} = \frac{\overline{X}_1 - \overline{X}_2}{\sigma_{\overline{X} - \overline{X}}}$$

- The mean of the difference of sample means will be zero:

$$\mu_{\overline{X} - \overline{X}} = 0$$

- The spread of scores around this mean of zero will be defined by the formula:[1]

$$\sigma_{\overline{X} - \overline{X}} = \sqrt{\frac{N_1 s_1^2 + N_2 s_2^2}{N_1 + N_2 - 2}} \sqrt{\frac{N_1 + N_2}{N_1 N_2}}$$

We will use the following hypothetical results to illustrate the t-test for the equality of means. A survey of 20 Australian children and 20 British children is conducted. The research wants to asses whether TV viewing time is affected by country of residence, so that children are grouped into two samples according to country of residence (the independent variable), and the average amount of TV watched (the dependent or test variable) is calculated. (Although it is the situation in this example, the two-sample t-test does not require the same number of cases in each sample.)

$$\overline{X}_1 = 165.85$$
$$s_1 = 29.29$$
$$N_1 = 20$$

$$\overline{X}_2 = 186.75$$
$$s_2 = 29.563$$
$$N_2 = 20$$

[1]This is called the **pooled variance estimate**. This estimate assumes that the populations have equal variance. Sometimes this assumption cannot be sustained, in which case a separate variance estimate is used. As we shall see, SPSS will calculate t using each estimate, plus information that allows us to choose one or the other. But when doing hand calculations this pooled variance estimate is generally used since it is much easier, and will usually lead to the same conclusion as the separate variance estimate.

We will work through this example using the five-step hypothesis testing procedure, so that we can re-acquaint ourselves with it.

Step 1: State the null and alternative hypotheses

H_0: There is no difference in the average amount of TV watched by children in Australia and Britain

$$\mu_1 = \mu_2$$
or
$$\mu_1 - \mu_2 = 0$$

H_a: There is a difference in the average amount of TV watched by children in Australia and Britain

$$\mu_1 \neq \mu_2$$
or
$$\mu_1 - \mu_2 \neq 0$$

Step 2: Choose the test of significance

The following three factors are relevant in choosing the test of significance:

- We are making an inference from two samples: that for Australian children and that for British children. Therefore we need to use a two-sample test.
- The two samples are being compared in terms of a variable measured at the interval/ratio level: amount of TV time measured in minutes. Therefore the relevant descriptive statistic is the mean of each sample.
- The population standard deviations are unknown.

These factors lead us to choose the two-sample *t*-test for the equality of means as the relevant test of significance.

Step 3: Establish the critical score(s) and critical region

Since we have to assume that the sample variances are equal to the (unknown) population variances, we have imposed two restrictions on the data. This means that the number of degrees of freedom is:

$$df = N - 2$$
$$= 40 - 2$$
$$= 38$$

From the table for the *t*-distribution, with 38 degrees of freedom, at an alpha level of 0.05, and using a two-tail test (based on the alternative hypothesis), the critical values for *t* are as shown in Table 13.2.

The table does not have a row of probabilities for 38 degrees of freedom. In such a situation, we refer to the row for the nearest reported number of degrees of freedom *below* the desired number, which in this case is 30 (Figure 13.5):

$$t_{\text{critical}} = \pm 2.042$$

Table 13.2 Distribution of t

Degrees of freedom (df)	Level of significance for one-tail test (α)				
	0.10	0.05	0.025	0.01	0.005
	Level of significance for two-tail test (α)				
	0.20	0.10	0.05	0.02	0.01
1	3.078	6.314	12.706	31.821	63.657
2	1.886	2.920	4.303	6.965	9.925
3	1.638	2.353	2.182	4.541	5.841
4	1.533	2.132	2.776	3.747	4.604
5	1.476	2.015	2.571	3.365	4.032
. . .	. . .	. . .	. . .	. . .	. . .
26	1.315	1.706	2.056	2.479	2.779
27	1.314	1.703	2.052	2.473	2.771
28	1.313	1.701	2.048	2.467	2.763
29	1.311	1.699	2.045	2.462	2.756
30	1.310	1.697	**2.042**	2.457	2.750
40	1.303	1.684	2.021	2.423	2.704
60	1.296	1.671	2.000	2.390	2.660
120	1.289	1.658	1.980	2.358	2.617
∞	1.282	1.645	1.960	2.326	2.576

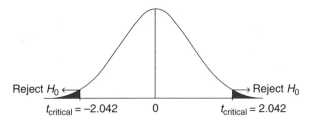

Reject H_0 ←   Reject H_0 →

$t_{\text{critical}} = -2.042$ 0 $t_{\text{critical}} = 2.042$

Figure 13.5 Critical regions for the sampling distribution of the difference of two sample means (df = 30, α = 0.05, two-tail test)

Step 4: Calculate the sample score(s)

The equation for calculating the sample t-score is:

$$t_{\text{sample}} = \frac{\overline{X}_1 - \overline{X}_2}{\sigma_{\overline{X} - \overline{X}}}$$

where:

$$\sigma_{\overline{X} - \overline{X}} = \sqrt{\frac{N_1 s_1^2 + N_2 s_2^2}{N_1 + N_2 - 2}} \sqrt{\frac{N_1 + N_2}{N_1 N_2}}$$

If we substitute the sample data into these equations we get:

$$\sigma_{\bar{x}-\bar{x}} = \sqrt{\frac{(20 \times 29.29^2) + (20 \times 29.563^2)}{20 + 20 - 2}} \sqrt{\frac{20 + 20}{20 \times 20}}$$

$$= 9.5$$

$$t_{sample} = \frac{165.85 - 186.75}{9.5}$$

$$= -2.2$$

Step 5: Make a decision

Since the sample score falls within the critical region we reject the null hypothesis (Figure 13.6).

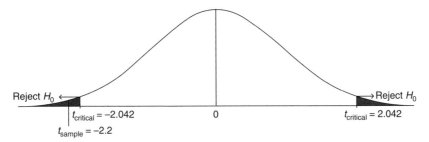

Figure 13.6   Sampling distribution of the difference of 2 sample means ($df = 30$, $\alpha = 0.05$, two-tail test)

Australian and British children do differ in the average amount of TV they watch each night.

The two-sample *t*-test using SPSS

We can now work through this example using SPSS. SPSS calls this test the 'Independent samples *t*-test'. The word 'independent' is very important because it raises conceptual issues for hypothesis testing and practical issues for SPSS coding. We will define independent samples in Chapter 17, when we can compare them with dependent samples, since their basic character is most evident when compared with dependent samples.

Filename 13.sav   In SPSS the data for the children have been coded for the two variables, with **tvtime** the variable name for the amount of television watched per night in minutes, and **country** indicating the country of residence of each child. Each of these variables occupies a separate

File Edit Data Transfoı

	tvtime	country	va
1	250	1	
2	241	1	
3	240	3	
4	238	1	
5	231	1	
6	228	1	
7	225	3	
8	223	3	
9	221	1	
10	218	1	
11	218	3	
12	212	3	
13	210	1	

Figure SPSS.J

column, so that we have a column of numbers for the amount of TV watched and a column of numbers indicating the country in which each child lives (see Figure SPSS. J). All independent samples tests have data entered in the same way: one column for the test variable and one column for the grouping variable.

The data for this example also contain information for hypothetical samples of children from Canada and Singapore that will be used in the next chapter where we consider the *k*-independent samples situation. The value labels for **country** are:

1 = Singapore
2 = Australia
3 = Britain
4 = Canada

Thus in this example we want to compare values 2 (Australia) and 3 (Britain) for the grouping variable, **country** (see Table 13.3.)

Table 13.3   Independent samples *t*-test for the equality of means using SPSS

SPSS command/action	Comments
1 From the menu select **Statistics/Compare Means/ Independent-Samples T-Test...**	This will bring up a window headed **Independent-Samples T-Test**
2 Click on **tvtime**	**tvtime** will be highlighted
3 Click on the ➤ that points to the area headed **Test Variable(s):**	This will paste **tvtime** into the **Test Variable(s):** list
4 Click on **country**	**country** will be highlighted
5 Click on the ➤ that points to the area headed **Grouping Variable**	This will paste **country** into the **Grouping Variable** list. Notice that in this list the variable appears as **country(? ?)**
6 Click on **Define Group...**	This will bring up the **Define Groups** window
7 In the area next to **Group1:** type **2,** and in the area next to **Group 2:** type **3**	This identifies the two groups to be compared, which are Australia and Britain.
8 Click on **Continue**	
9 Click on **OK**	

These instructions will generate the following output:

```
t-tests for Independent Samples of COUNTRY    Country of Residence


                              Number
Variable                     of Cases        Mean        SD    SE of Mean
-----------------------------------------------------------------------
TVTIME   Minutes of TV Watched per Night

austral                          20       165.8500     29.290      6.550
britain                          20       186.7500     29.563      6.611
-----------------------------------------------------------------------

        Mean Difference = -20.9000

        Levene's Test for Equality of Variances: F= .025    P= .876

        t-test for Equality of Means                                    95%
   Variances  t-value      df   2-Tail Sig    SE of Diff        CI for Diff
-----------------------------------------------------------------------
   Equal        -2.25      38       .031        9.306     (-39.738, -2.062)
   Unequal      -2.25   38.00       .031        9.306     (-39.738, -2.062)
-----------------------------------------------------------------------
```

The first part of the output provides the descriptive statistics: the number of cases, the mean, and the standard deviation for each group. Just below this is a line:

`Mean Difference = -20.9000`

This is the difference between the two sample means, which in the equation used to calculate *t*-scores is represented by $\bar{X}_1 - \bar{X}_2$. There is obviously a difference in the amount of TV watched by the two sample groups, but is this difference enough to suggest that the means for the populations are not equal?

The next part of the output answers this question. Skipping for the moment the information for Levene's test, and looking at the first row of information in the table for t-test for Equality of Means, which is the row for Equal variances, we see that the sample *t*-value is −2.25, which, with 38 degrees of freedom, has a two-tail significance of 0.031:

```
        t-test for Equality of Means                                   95%
Variances  t-value      df   2-Tail Sig   SE of Diff       CI for Diff
---------------------------------------------------------------------------
Equal        -2.25      38       .031        9.306     (-39.738, -2.062)
```

These values all correspond to the values we generated by hand (with some slight differences due to rounding in the hand calculations). Since the sample probability of 0.031 is less than the alpha level of 0.05, we reject the null hypothesis of no difference.

You will also notice that SPSS has generated a 95 per cent confidence interval for the difference in sample means, which is printed as (−39.738, −2.062). This allows us to conduct the same inference test, but using the estimation procedures developed in Chapter 8. This confidence interval indicates that at a 95 per cent level of confidence, the difference between the population means lies somewhere between −39.738 minutes and −2.062 minutes. Since this interval does not include the value of 0, we reject the possibility that the population means are equal.

Before concluding this discussion of the SPSS output, we need to explain the information regarding the test for equality of variance, and how this affects the way we read the results:

`Levene's Test for Equality of Variances: F= .025   P= .876`

In calculating the *t*-score in the example above, we assumed that the variances of the two populations being compared are equal. In practical terms this means using the pooled variance estimate in the calculations. However, this may not always be a valid assumption. The validity of this assumption is tested in this section of the output. The value for *F* is the ratio of the two sample variances, and if this ratio is not equal to 1, it may reflect an underlying difference in the population variances. If the probability for this *F* value is less than 0.05 we conclude that the difference in variances observed in the samples reflects a difference in the variances of the populations from which the samples came. In such a situation we refer to the line of information for Unequal variances:

```
Unequal     -2.25    38.00        .031        9.306     (-39.738, -2.062)
```

If the probability is greater than 0.05 we use the pooled variance estimate, as is the case here. Usually the two estimates will agree with each other in terms of whether to reject or not reject the null, but in strict terms, we should use the relevant estimate, either that for Equal or Unequal variances.

One-tail and two-tail tests

In the above example we had no reason to suspect that either population watched more TV than the other, as reflected in the alternative hypothesis, which is simply a statement of difference:

$$\mu_1 \neq \mu_2$$

Given this formulation of the alternative hypothesis, a two-tail test is used. However, we might argue that because of the warmer weather Australian children might be less inclined to watch as much TV as children in Britain. Here we not only suspect a difference, but also a direction of difference. In this situation the alternative hypothesis will be:

$$\mu_1 > \mu_2$$

This would involve a one-tail test. The SPSS output provides the two-tail significance as the default setting. To convert this into a one-tail significance we simply divide the two-tail probability in half. The area under the curve beyond a *t*-score of ± 2.25 is 0.031 of the total area under the *t*-distribution. If two tails take up this amount of area, then one tail will take up half this amount:

$$\text{one-tail probability} = \frac{\text{two-tail probability}}{2}$$

$$= \frac{0.031}{2}$$

$$= 0.0155$$

Example

A study is conducted to investigate whether foreign companies pay attention to local health and safety codes compared with domestic companies. A survey of 50 foreign-owned and 50 domestic companies of similar size and in similar industries are selected. Inspectors record the number of breaches of health and safety regulations they observe when inspecting these establishments. On average, the 50 foreign firms were found to make 4.2 breaches per firm:

$$\text{foreign: } N_1 = 50$$

$$s_1 = 1.3$$

$$\overline{X}_1 = 4.2$$

The domestic firms were found to make 3.5 breaches per firm:

$$\text{domestic: } N_2 = 50$$

$$s_2 = 1.2$$

$$\overline{X}_2 = 3.5$$

We will use an alpha level of 0.05, which on a two-tail test, and with 98 degrees of freedom, gives us a critical score of:

$$t_{\text{critical}} = \pm 2.0$$

To calculate the sample t-score we need to firstly calculate the standard error (using the equal variance estimate):

$$\sigma_{\overline{X} - \overline{X}} = \sqrt{\frac{N_1 s_1^2 + N_2 s_2^2}{N_1 + N_2 - 2}} \sqrt{\frac{N_1 + N_2}{N_1 N_2}}$$

$$= \sqrt{\frac{50(1.3)^2 + 50(1.2)^2}{50 + 50 - 2}} \sqrt{\frac{50 + 50}{50 \times 50}}$$

$$= 0.25$$

The sample t-score will be:

$$t_{\text{sample}} = \frac{\overline{X}_1 - \overline{X}_2}{\sigma_{\overline{X} - \overline{X}}}$$

$$= \frac{4.2 - 3.5}{0.25}$$

$$= 2.8$$

We can see that the sample score is further from zero than the critical score. In other words, it falls in the region of rejection (Figure 13.7).

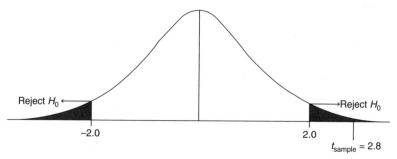

Figure 13.7   Distribution of t, $df = 98$

We reject the null hypothesis of no difference. The results suggest that foreign firms are more inclined to breach local health and safety codes.

Appendix: The *z*-test for two means

This chapter looked at ways of testing the difference between sample means using the *t*-test. We used the *t*-test for both large and small samples. However, with large samples we could also have used a *z*-test instead and got the same result, but since the *t*-test applies in both large and small samples, we (and SPSS) used it in every case. For completeness, though, the formulas involved in a *z*-test of sample differences (when sample size is large), are presented here.

With large samples, the sampling distribution of the difference in sample means, drawn from populations that are not different in terms of the variable of interest, will be:

$$\sigma_{\bar{X} - \bar{X}} = \sqrt{\frac{s_1^2}{N_1 - 1} + \frac{s_2^2}{N_2 - 1}}$$

where:
  s_1 is the standard deviation of sample 1
  s_2 is the standard deviation of sample 2
  N_1 is the size of sample 1
  N_2 is the size of sample 2.

Given this information we can take any sample differences that we *actually* observe and convert this difference into a *z*-score, according to the following formula:

$$z_{\text{sample}} = \frac{\bar{X}_1 - \bar{X}_2}{\sigma_{\bar{X} - \bar{X}}}$$

where:
  $\bar{X}_1$ is the mean of sample 1
  $\bar{X}_2$ is the mean of sample 2.

This allows us to look up the table for the area under the standard normal curve to see the probability of getting the sample results we actually obtained, *if the null hypothesis is true*. If this observed probability is smaller than the critical probability, then we reject the assumption that the null hypothesis is true, and instead accept the alternative hypothesis that the difference is due to something systematic.

Exercises

13.1 What assumptions need to be made about the distribution of the populations before an independent samples *t*-test is conducted?

13.2 For the following sets of results, test for a significant difference using a two-tail test and $\alpha = 0.05$ (assuming equal population variance):

(a)
  Sample 1: $\bar{X}_1 = 72$
       $s_1 = 14.2$
       $N_1 = 35$

Sample 2: $\bar{X}_1 = 76.1$
$$s_1 = 11$$
$$N_1 = 50$$

(b)

Sample 1: $\bar{X}_1 = 2.4$
$$s_1 = 0.9$$
$$N_1 = 140$$

Sample 2: $\bar{X}_2 = 2.8$
$$s_2 = 0.9$$
$$N_2 = 100$$

(c)

Sample 1: $\bar{X}_1 = 72$
$$s_1 = 14.2$$
$$N_1 = 35$$

Sample 2: $\bar{X}_2 = 76.1$
$$s_2 = 11$$
$$N_2 = 50$$

(d)

Sample 1: $\bar{X}_1 = 450$
$$s_1 = 80$$
$$N_1 = 120$$

Sample 2: $\bar{X}_2 = 475$
$$s_2 = 77$$
$$N_2 = 100$$

13.3 A researcher is interested in the effect that place of residency has on the age at which people begin to smoke cigarettes. She divides a random sample of people into 91 rural and 107 urban residents. She finds that rural dwellers started smoking at an average age of 15.75 years, with a standard deviation of 2.3 years, whereas the urban dwellers began to smoke at a mean age of 14.63 years, with a standard deviation of 4.1 years. Is there a significant difference (using the pooled variance estimate)?

13.4 A Water Authority wishes to assess the effectiveness of an advertising campaign to reduce water consumption. Before the campaign the Authority randomly selects 100 households throughout a region and records water usage for a morning shower as averaging 87 litres, with a standard deviation of 15 litres. It then randomly selects another 100 households after the campaign. These households average 74 litres per shower, with a standard deviation of 14 litres. Is there a significant difference? What conclusions can they make about the advertising campaign? Should the test be a one-tail or two-tail test? What factors need to be considered when selecting the appropriate test?

13.5 A new form of organic pest control is developed for crop growing. Fifty plots of grain are sprayed with traditional pesticide, whereas 50 are sprayed with the new pest control. The output, in tonnes, of each set of plots, is recorded as follows:

	Old pesticide	Organic pesticide
Mean:	1.4	2.2
Standard deviation:	0.3	0.35

Since the organic pesticide is much more expensive, farmers want to be convinced that any improvement in yield is not due to chance. They therefore set an alpha level of 0.01. Conduct a *t*-test to assess the effectiveness of the new method. Should the test be a one-tail or two-tail test?

13.6 A study is conducted to investigate the political awareness of children in public (state-funded) and private schools. Twenty-four students from a private school and 20 students from a nearby public school are randomly selected, and asked a series of questions relating to the political system. The scores for each school are recorded. The average score for the public school is 64, and for the private school the average score is 46. Both samples had a standard deviation of 18.5.

(a) Conduct an independent samples *t*-test for the equality of means to assess whether the two school systems are significantly different.

(b) Enter your results in the following output where they would appear if this data was analysed on SPSS:

Variable	Number of Cases	Mean	SD	SE of Mean
SCORE Political Awareness Score				
Public	20	?	?	4.124
Private	?	?	?	3.762

Mean Difference = 18.0750

Levene's Test for Equality of Variances: F= .061   P= .806

t-test for Equality of Means Variances	t-value	df	2-Tail Sig	SE of Diff	95% CI for Diff
Equal	?	?	.002	5.582	(6.810, 29.340)
Unequal	3.24	40.57	.002	5.582	(6.798, 29.352)

(c) How does the 95 per cent confidence interval confirm your decision regarding the null hypothesis?

(d) If you were conducting a one-tail test, what would the significance level be?

(e) What aspect of the output would cause you to use the Unequal Variance test?

14

Analysis of variance

Hypothesis testing with more than two samples: The general idea

In Chapter 13 we considered the t-test for two independent samples, and tested the assumption that the samples came from populations with the same mean:

$$H_0: \mu_1 = \mu_2$$

We worked through an example where we had a sample of 20 children from Australia and 20 from Britain. Each child was asked how much TV they watched on average per night. We compared the samples in order to test the null hypothesis that there was no difference in the average amount of TV watched between children from the two countries (Figure 14.1).

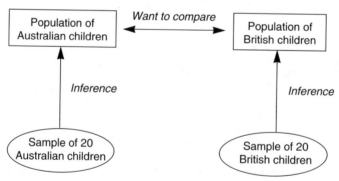

Figure 14.1   Hypothesis testing: the two-sample case

We call this a two-sample problem because we are using two samples to make inferences about each population. However, sometimes the problem we are addressing is slightly wider. Instead of just comparing two countries, we might be interested in comparing the average amount of TV watched by children in a number of countries. For example, we have samples of 20 children from

Australia, Britain, Canada, and Singapore, and want to see if the means for all these four populations are equal:

$$H_0: \mu_1 = \mu_2 = \mu_3 = \mu_4$$

This is called the problem of k-independent samples, where k is any number greater than two. Here k is four, and this example can be illustrated as in Figure 14.2.

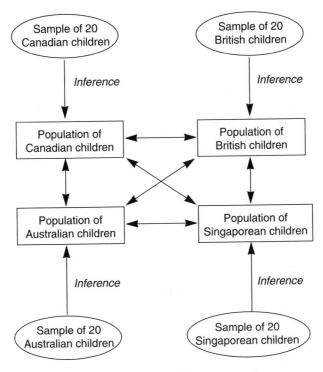

Figure 14.2   Hypothesis testing for more than two samples

One way to do this is simply to test all the possible two-sample combinations. With four samples the maximum number of combinations is six, illustrated in Figure 14.2 by the number of arrows running from each population to the others:

Australia ↔ Singapore
Australia ↔ Canada
Australia ↔ Britain
Singapore ↔ Canada
Singapore ↔ Britain
Canada ↔ Britain

Thus we can undertake six separate t-tests and see if there are any significant differences. However, when we are working with more than two samples we can test for the equality of means *all at once* using the analysis of variance *F*-test (ANOVA).[1] This procedure tests the null hypothesis that the samples come from populations with equal means for a variable measured at the interval/ratio level.

If the null hypothesis is true, samples drawn from such populations will have means roughly equal in value. In the example of children and TV time, the samples will all have roughly similar averages. Of course, we do not expect the sample means to be equal, even if the population means are the same, since random variation will affect the sampling process. The question we are addressing is whether the *differences between the samples* are consistent with the assumption of *equality between the populations*.

Consider the hypothetical sample results for our four groups of children shown in Table 14.1.

Table 14.1 Average amount of television viewed per night, in minutes (hypothetical data)

Country	Average amount of TV watched per night	Standard deviation
Canada	127	27
Australia	166	29
Britain	187	30
Singapore	203	26

We can see that there is a good deal of variation *between* the means of the four samples. In fact if we compare the highest with the lowest values, which are those for Canada and Singapore, we can see a very large difference in average amounts of TV watched. Notice also the column for the standard deviation for each sample. We can see that *within* the sample for each country the results are clustered together, as indicated by the small standard deviations especially when compared with the differences *across* the samples. In other words, there are distinct differences from country to country, but similarity within each country. On the face of these descriptive statistics we might begin to question the hypothesis that the populations from which these samples came are equal.

This logic is exactly the same as that used by ANOVA in testing the hypothesis of no difference. It compares the amount of variation between the samples with the amount of variation within each sample — hence the name 'analysis of variance'. Thus, although we are interested in the difference between the means, ANOVA actually works with the variance, which is the square of the standard deviation.

---

[1] The reason why a single ANOVA is preferable to multiple *t*-tests is that the risk of making a type I error for the series of *t*-tests will be greater than the stated alpha level for each *t*-test. Thus if the alpha level for each individual *t*-test is 0.05, the chance of making a type I error for all the *t*-tests that can be conducted for a given number of samples will be greater than 0.05. The ANOVA test, on the other hand, has a stated alpha level equal to the risk of making a type I error.

Before working through an ANOVA for our hypothetical survey of children from four countries, we will illustrate the logic behind the test. Consider the two hypothetical sets of distributions in Figure 14.3. Four samples are randomly selected and the mean for each is calculated, together with the overall mean when the cases for all four samples are pooled together ($\overline{X}_{1-4}$). In both (a) and (b) we can see that the means are not equal: there is some variance between the sample means and the overall mean for the total number of cases. Although the sample means are the same in the two sets of distributions, there is also an important and obvious difference. In (a) the spread of cases *within* each sample around the sample mean is quite wide, whereas in (b) the variance within each sample is relatively small. Each sample in (b) seems distinct from the others, whereas in (a) there is considerable overlap in the distributions, so that the samples seem to blend into each other. We would be more inclined to consider the second set of samples (b) to come from populations that are different from each other, whereas the first set (a) can be more easily explained as coming from identical populations, with random variation causing the samples to differ slightly from each other.

We can capture this difference by calculating two numbers and expressing one as a ratio of the other. The first number is the amount of variance *between* means and the grand total mean. Consider the two sets of sample means shown in Figure 14.4.

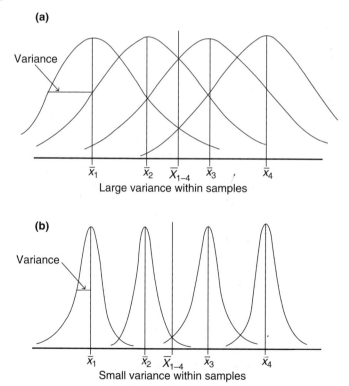

Figure 14.3

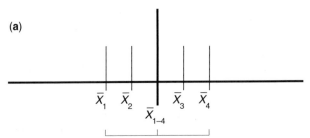

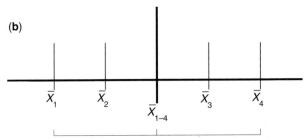

Figure 14.4

We can see that in (a) the variance of the sample means around the overall mean when the samples are pooled together is small relative to the second situation. Thus the samples in (a) are less likely to form distinct clusters of cases that reflect underlying differences between the populations.

However, we cannot jump to this conclusion about the populations just on the basis of the variance between sample means. The variances within each sample in (a) might be very small, so that each sample forms a distinct 'spike' around each sample mean. The variances within each sample in (b), on the other hand, might be very wide so that the samples still blur into each other, despite the differences between the means (Figure 14.5).

Thus we need to calculate a second number, which measures this variance *within* each sample around each sample mean. The extent to which samples will form these distinct spikes around their respective means will be expressed by the ratio of the variance between samples to the variance within samples.

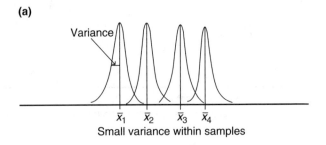

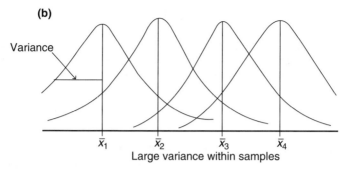

(b)

Variance

$\bar{x}_1$ $\bar{x}_2$ $\bar{x}_3$ $\bar{x}_4$

Large variance within samples

Figure 14.5

The one-way analysis of variance *F*-test

We can now use these general concepts to determine whether there is a significant difference between children in different countries in terms of the average amount of television they watch. To calculate the relevant test-statistic we need to formalize some of these basic concepts. The first is the total amount of variation for all 80 scores of cases sampled. This is measured by a concept called the **total sum of squares (TSS)**. This is calculated using the formula:

$$TSS = \Sigma(X_i - \overline{X})_2$$

This value for the total sum of squares can be divided into two components. The first is the amount of variation within each sample, called the **sum of squares within (SSW)**. The second is the amount of variation between each sample, called the **sum of squares between (SSB)**:

$$TSS = SSB + SSW$$

Each of these components of the total sum of squares can be calculated in the following way:

$$SSW = \Sigma(X_i - \overline{X}_s)^2$$

$$SSB = \Sigma N_s(\overline{X}_s - \overline{X})^2$$

where:
  $\overline{X}_s$ is the mean for a given sample
  N_s is the number of cases in a given sample.

These formulas should remind the reader of the formula for the standard deviation, since they embody the same principle that variance relates to the difference between scores and the average. As with the formula for the standard deviation, these definitional formulas can be difficult to work with. In particular, to calculate the total sum of squares, it is easier to work with the formula:

$$TSS = \sum X_i^2 - N\overline{X}^2$$

Once we have TSS, we only need to calculate either *SSW* or *SSB*, and then use the formula *TSS = SSB + SSW* to calculate the other. In other words, if we calculate *TSS* and *SSB*, we substitute these into the following equation to arrive at *SSW*:

$$SSW = TSS - SSB$$

To see how this is done we will work through our example with the four samples of 20 children. These calculations are best done by constructing a frequency table. The scores for each case are listed, and the samples placed in separate columns (Table 14.2).

Table 14.2   Calculations for ANOVA

Canada		Australia		Britain		Singapore	
X_i	X_i^2	X_i	X_i^2	X_i	X_i^2	X_i	X_i^2
89	7921	102	10404	124	15376	156	24336
92	8464	120	14400	135	18225	165	27225
95	9025	132	17424	156	24336	174	30276
105	11025	134	17956	165	27225	179	32041
106	11236	145	21025	167	27889	180	32400
108	11664	149	22201	172	29584	184	33856
110	12100	156	24336	178	31684	189	35721
113	12769	162	26244	182	33124	189	35721
116	13456	165	27225	184	33856	196	38416
125	15625	165	27225	185	34225	203	41209
128	16384	165	27225	186	34596	204	41616
135	18225	174	30276	187	34969	207	42849
138	19044	179	32041	189	35721	210	44100
139	19321	180	32400	198	39204	218	47524
140	19600	187	34969	209	43681	221	48841
146	21316	189	35721	212	44944	228	51984
146	21316	196	38416	218	47524	231	53361
154	23716	201	40401	223	49729	238	56644
167	27889	206	42436	225	50625	241	58081
194	37636	210	44100	240	57600	250	62500
$\sum X_i = 2546$		$\sum X_i = 3317$		$\sum X_i = 3735$		$\sum X_i = 4063$	
	$\sum X_i^2 = 337732$		$\sum X_i^2 = 566425$		$\sum X_i^2 = 714117$		$\sum X_i^2 = 838701$

From this information we can calculate the mean for each sample, and the mean for all the samples combined:

$$\overline{X}_{canada} = \frac{2546}{20} = 127.3 \text{ min}$$

$$\overline{X}_{\text{australia}} = \frac{3317}{20} = 165.85 \text{ min}$$

$$\overline{X}_{\text{britain}} = \frac{3735}{20} = 186.75 \text{ min}$$

$$\overline{X}_{\text{singapore}} = \frac{4063}{20} = 203.15 \text{ min}$$

$$\overline{X} = \frac{(2546 + 3317 + 3735 + 4063)}{80} = 170.76 \text{ min}$$

Using this information we can calculate the *TSS* and *SSB*:

$$
\begin{aligned}
TSS &= \Sigma X_i^2 - N\overline{X}^2 \\
&= (337\ 732 + 566\ 425 + 714\ 117 + 838\ 701) - 80(170.76) \\
&= 2456\ 975 - 2332\ 786 \\
&= 124\ 189
\end{aligned}
$$

$$
\begin{aligned}
SSB &= \Sigma N_s(\overline{X}_s - \overline{X})^2 \\
&= 20(127.3 - 170.76)^2 + 20(165.85 - 170.76)^2 + \\
&\quad 20(186.75 - 170.76)^2 + 20(203.15 - 170.76)^2 \\
&= 64\ 353
\end{aligned}
$$

$$
\begin{aligned}
SSW &= TSS - SSB \\
&= 124\ 189 - 64\ 353 \\
&= 59\ 836
\end{aligned}
$$

The actual test statistic we use to determine whether the between-samples variance is significantly different from the within-samples estimate is called the *F*-ratio. We have actually encountered this test statistic before when analysing SPSS output for a two-sample *t*-test. Just as in that case, the *F*-ratio tests for a difference between variances. The *F*-ratio is a ratio of the two variances, the *SSB* and *SSW*, each corrected for the appropriate degrees of freedom:

$$F = \frac{\dfrac{SSB}{k-1}}{\dfrac{SSW}{N-k}}$$

where:
   k is the number of samples.

Substituting the relevant numbers into this equation we get:

$$F = \frac{\dfrac{SSB}{k-1}}{\dfrac{SSW}{N-k}}$$

$$= \frac{\dfrac{64\ 353}{4-1}}{\dfrac{59\ 836}{80-4}}$$

$$= \quad 27.25$$

This is the sample value for F. As with the other test statistics we have come across, namely z-scores, t-scores and chi-square, we need to compare this sample value with a critical value in order to decide whether to reject or not reject the null hypothesis. To find the critical value we refer to the table for the distribution of F (Table 14.3).

To determine the critical value for F we have to take into account three factors:

- The degrees of freedom for the estimate of the variance between samples. This is the number of samples minus one, and appears in the numerator of the F-ratio;

$$dfb = k - 1$$

- The degrees of freedom for the estimate of the variance within the samples. This is the total number of cases minus the number of samples, and appears in the denominator of the F-ratio;

$$dfw = N - k$$

- The alpha level.

Since the number of degrees of freedom for both the within and between estimates change from research problem to research problem, whereas usually the alpha level is set at 0.05, Table 14.3 (and that in most textbooks) provides the F-scores for various degrees of freedom at the given probability level of 0.05. We would need a different table if the alpha level was not equal to 0.05.

In this example, we will use an alpha level of 0.05. We have four samples and a total of 80 cases, so that the relevant number of degrees of freedom are:

$$
\begin{array}{llllll}
dfb & = & k-1 & \quad dfw & = & N-k \\
& = & 4-1 & & = & 80-4 \\
& = & 3 & & = & 76
\end{array}
$$

Table 14.3   Distribution of F ($\alpha = 0.05$)

	Degrees of freedom for estimates of variance between samples ($k - 1$)									
$N - k$	1	2	3	4	5	6	7	8	9	∞
1	161.4	199.5	21507	224.6	230.2	234.0	236.8	238.9	240.5	254.3
2	18.51	19.00	19.16	19.25	19.30	19.33	19.35	19.37	19.38	19.50
3	10.13	9.55	9.28	9.12	9.01	8.94	8.89	8.84	8.81	8.53
4	7.71	6.94	6.59	6.39	6.26	6.16	6.09	6.04	6.00	5.63
5	6.61	5.79	5.41	5.19	5.05	4.95	4.88	4.82	4.77	4.36
6	5.99	5.14	4.76	4.53	4.39	4.28	4.21	4.15	4.10	3.67
7	5.59	4.74	4.35	4.12	3.97	3.87	3.79	3.73	3.68	3.23
8	5.32	4.46	4.07	3.84	3.69	3.58	3.50	3.44	3.39	2.93
9	5.12	4.26	3.86	3.63	3.48	3.37	3.29	3.23	3.18	2.71
10	4.96	4.10	3.71	3.48	3.33	3.22	3.14	3.07	3.02	2.54
11	4.84	3.98	3.59	3.36	3.20	3.09	3.01	2.95	2.90	2.40
12	4.75	3.88	3.49	3.26	3.11	3.00	2.91	2.85	2.80	2.30
13	4.67	3.80	3.41	3.18	3.02	2.92	2.83	2.77	2.71	2.21
14	4.60	3.74	3.34	3.11	2.96	2.85	2.76	2.70	2.65	2.13
15	4.54	3.68	3.29	3.06	2.90	2.79	2.71	2.64	2.59	2.07
16	4.49	3.63	3.24	3.01	2.85	2.74	2.66	2.59	2.54	2.01
17	4.45	3.59	3.20	2.96	2.81	2.70	2.61	2.55	2.49	1.96
18	4.41	3.55	3.16	2.93	2.77	2.66	2.58	2.51	2.46	1.92
19	4.38	3.52	3.13	2.90	2.74	2.63	2.54	2.48	2.42	1.88
20	4.35	3.49	3.10	2.87	2.71	2.60	2.51	2.45	2.39	1.84
21	4.32	3.47	3.07	2.84	2.68	2.57	2.49	2.42	2.37	1.81
22	4.30	3.44	3.05	2.82	2.66	2.55	2.46	2.40	2.34	1.78
23	4.28	3.42	3.03	2.80	2.64	2.53	2.44	2.38	2.32	1.76
24	4.26	3.40	3.01	2.78	2.62	2.51	2.42	2.36	2.30	1.73
25	4.24	3.38	2.99	2.76	2.60	2.49	2.40	2.34	2.28	1.71
26	4.22	3.37	2.98	2.74	2.59	2.47	2.39	2.32	2.27	1.69
27	4.21	3.35	2.96	2.73	2.57	2.46	2.37	2.30	2.25	1.67
28	4.20	3.34	2.95	2.71	2.56	2.44	2.36	2.29	2.24	1.65
29	4.18	3.33	2.93	2.70	2.54	2.43	2.35	2.28	2.22	1.64
30	4.17	3.32	2.92	2.69	2.53	2.42	2.33	2.27	2.21	1.62
40	4.08	3.23	2.84	2.61	2.45	2.34	2.25	2.18	2.12	1.51
60	4.00	3.15	2.76	2.52	2.37	2.25	2.17	2.10	2.04	1.39
120	3.92	3.07	2.68	2.45	2.29	2.17	2.09	2.02	1.96	1.25
∞	3.84	2.99	2.60	2.37	2.21	2.09	2.01	1.94	1.88	1.00

Degrees of freedom for estimates of variance within samples

A 'cut-down' version of the table is reproduced in Table 14.4 to show how we use this information to determine critical scores of *F*.

Table 14.4   Distribution of *F* (α = 0.05)

	N – k	1	2	3	4	5	6	7	8	9	∞
	1	161.4	199.5	215.07	224.6	230.2	234.0	236.8	238.9	240.5	254.3
	2	18.51	19.00	19.16	19.25	19.30	19.33	19.35	19.37	19.38	19.50
	3	10.13	9.55	9.28	9.12	9.01	8.94	8.89	8.84	8.81	8.53
	4	7.71	6.94	6.59	6.39	6.26	6.16	6.09	6.04	6.00	5.63
	5	6.61	5.79	5.41	5.19	5.05	4.95	4.88	4.82	4.77	4.36
	6	5.99	5.14	4.76	4.53	4.39	4.28	4.21	4.15	4.10	3.67
	7	5.59	4.74	4.35	4.12	3.97	3.87	3.79	3.73	3.68	3.23
	8	5.32	4.46	4.07	3.84	3.69	3.58	3.50	3.44	3.39	2.93
	9	5.12	4.26	3.86	3.63	3.48	3.37	3.29	3.23	3.18	2.71
	10	4.96	4.10	3.71	3.48	3.33	3.22	3.14	3.07	3.02	2.54
	...	...	...	...	...	...	...	...	...	...	...
	40	4.08	3.23	2.84	2.61	2.45	2.34	2.25	2.18	2.12	1.51
	60	4.00	3.15	2.76	2.52	2.37	2.25	2.17	2.10	2.04	1.39
	120	3.92	3.07	2.68	2.45	2.29	2.17	2.09	2.02	1.96	1.25
	∞	3.84	2.99	2.60	2.37	2.21	2.09	2.01	1.94	1.88	1.00

Notice that Table 14.4 does not have a line for the degrees of freedom within equal to 76. In fact, whole ranges of values are skipped after the first 30. This is because the critical scores do not decrease very much for incremental increases in the degrees of freedom after 30. Where we have degrees of freedom that do not appear in the table we refer to the closest value that appears in the table below the desired number. Here the closest value below 76 that appears in the table is 60. Thus the critical value in this instance for *F* is 2.52. We reject the null hypothesis of no difference if the sample value for *F* is greater than the critical value:

$$\text{Reject null if } F_{sample} > F_{critical}$$

Here $F_{sample} = 27.25$, and $F_{critical} = 2.52$ (Figure 14.6).

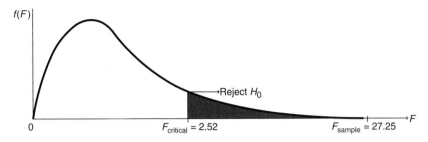

Figure 14.6   Distribution of F ($dfb = 4$, $dfw = 60$, $\alpha = 0.05$)

We therefore reject the null hypothesis. At least one of the populations of children is different from the others.

Notice the particular wording of the conclusion: at least one population differs from the rest. The F-test itself does not tell us which of the populations, and how many, differ. Obviously, if there are differences, then at the very least these must include the groups with the highest and the lowest sample average, in this instance Canada and Singapore. But whether any other possible combinations are significantly different cannot be answered by the F-test.

To determine which samples are significantly different, after having performed an F-test and rejected the null, we turn to a set of techniques called **post-hoc comparisons**. Unfortunately, there is little agreement within the literature as to which comparison to use. When in doubt, the most conservative test should be used, namely, the one that is the least likely to find a significant difference, and this usually is the **Scheffe** post-hoc comparison.

ANOVA using SPSS

Filename 14.sav   The data from the previous example have been entered into SPSS. The number of minutes of TV watched by each child surveyed is coded with the variable name **tvtime**. The country that each child comes from is entered under the variable **country**, with the following values and value labels:

$$1 = \text{Singapore}$$
$$2 = \text{Australia}$$
$$3 = \text{Britain}$$
$$4 = \text{Canada}$$

To conduct an ANOVA using all four samples, we work through the procedures listed in Table 14.5.

Table 14.5   One-way ANOVA on SPSS

SPSS command/action	Comments
1 From the menu select **Statistics/Compare Means/One-way ANOVA...**	This will bring up the **One-way ANOVA** dialogue box
2 Click on **tvtime**	
3 Click on ➤ pointing to the box below **Dependent List:**	This will select **tvtime** as the dependent variable, which is the variable used to compare the samples
4 Click on **country**	
5 Click on ➤ pointing to the box below **Factor:**	This will select **country** as the variable that will form the samples to be compared. Notice that **country** appears in the factor box with (**? ?**). This indicates that we need to determine which of the values for **country** are to be compared
6 Click on **Define Range...**	This will bring up the **One-Way ANOVA: Define Range** dialogue box. The cursor will flash in the box next to **Minimum:**
7 Type **1** into the box next to **Minimum:**	
8 Type **4** into the box next to **Maximum:**	This tells SPSS to compare all cases coded either 1,2,3 or 4 for the variable **country**. If we only wanted to compare children from Singapore, Australia, and Britain we would only type **3** in the **Maximum:** box
9 Click on **Continue**	
10 Click on **OK**	

The results of this set of commands will be:

```
- - - - - O N E W A Y - - - - -


    Variable   TVTIME
 By Variable   COUNTRY

                        Analysis of Variance

                        Sum of        Mean           F       F
    Source      D.F.    Squares       Squares        Ratio   Prob.

Between Groups    3    64353.4375    21451.1458     27.2464  .0000
Within Groups    76    59835.0500      787.3033
Total            79   124188.4875
```

Looking at the SPSS output we can see the results we calculated by hand. The sum of squares between, the sum of squares within, and the total sum of squares are calculated, together with the relevant degrees of freedom. From these, the F-ratio is 27.25, which is the same as that calculated above. The probability is printed as $p = 0.0000$. This does not mean that the probability of obtaining an F-ratio of 27.25 is zero. SPSS rounds off the probability to four decimal places, so that this result is read as 'less than 5-in-100 000'.

We must stop at this point and be clear about what this F-test ANOVA has determined. The null hypothesis is that the samples come from populations with the same mean:

$$\mu_1 = \mu_2 = \mu_3 = \ldots = \mu_k$$

As noted in the earlier discussion, by rejecting the null hypothesis after conducting an F-test, we have decided that *at least one of these populations has a mean that is not equal to the others*. However, the F-test itself does not tell us *which* of these populations is different.

Thus when conducting an F-test we normally ask for some follow-up information to be provided, so that if we do discover a statistically significant difference, we can determine which of the populations differs(s) from the others.

In the **One-Way ANOVA** dialogue box click on **Post Hoc...** This will bring up the **Post Hoc Comparisons** dialogue box, which provides us with a range of options for comparing the samples so that we can determine exactly which ones come from populations different from the others. We will not explore the subtle differences between the choices: in most situations they will all lead to the same conclusions. The most commonly used is the **Scheffe** test, so by clicking on the box next to it, the following output will be generated in conjunction with the basic ANOVA output we got above:

```
- - - - - O N E W A Y - - - - -


        Variable   TVTIME
     By Variable   COUNTRY

Multiple Range Tests:  Scheffe test with significance level .05

The difference between two means is significant if
  MEAN(J)-MEAN(I)   >= 19.8407 * RANGE * SQRT(1/N(I) + 1/N(J))
  with the following value(s) for RANGE: 4.04

    (*) Indicates significant differences which are shown in the lower
triangle
```

```
                          a   s
                          u b i
                          c s r n
                          a t i g
                          n r t a
                          a a a p
                          d l i o
                          a i n r
     Mean        COUNTRY

     127.3000    canada
     165.8500    australi   *
     186.7500    britain    *
     203.1500    singapor   * *
```

Homogeneous Subsets (highest and lowest means are not significantly different)

Subset 1

Group	canada
Mean	127.3000

- - - - - - - - -

Subset 2

Group	australi	britain
Mean	165.8500	186.7500

- - - - - - - - - - - - - - -

Subset 3

Group	britain	singapor
Mean	186.7500	203.1500

- - - - - - - - - - - - - - -

The important part of this output is the small matrix formed by the countries:

```
                          a   s
                          u b i
                          c s r n
                          a t i g
                          n r t a
                          a a a p
                          d l i o
                          a i n r
     Mean        COUNTRY

     127.3000    canada
     165.8500    australi   *
     186.7500    britain    *
     203.1500    singapor   * *
```

This matrix pairs each sample group with all the others, and places a * where a significant difference is discovered between the means. This is similar to conducting all the possible combinations of t-tests that could be performed on these data. There are four * in this matrix indicating four combinations of samples that are significantly different (and by implication two that are not significantly different). Looking at the top-most * first, this is the intersection of the row for Australia and the column for Canada, indicating that there is a statistically significant difference, at the 0.05 level, between children in these two countries in terms of average TV watched per night. In fact, if we look at the sample means printed along the left edge of the matrix it is clear that Canadian children watch less TV (according to this hypothetical example).

The next * is at the intersection of the row for Britain and column for Canada, and the one below that is the intersection of Singapore and Canada, indicating that Canadian children differ significantly from children in these two countries as well. Indeed, this follows logically from the fact that there is a difference between Australia and Canada: if Canadian children differ significantly from those with the nearest sample mean, they will also differ from those whose sample mean was even further away.

The last * is that for the intersection of the row for Singapore and the column for Australia, indicating a significant difference between these populations. Looking at the sample averages, it is clear that difference is due to Australian children watching *less* TV, on average, than those in Singapore, according to this hypothetical example.

There are two aspects to such a matrix that are worth pointing out:

- There will never be a * along the diagonal of such a matrix: the diagonal is each sample paired with itself, so this obviously can never produce a significant difference.
- There will also never be a * in the top triangle of this matrix, since it is the mirror image of the bottom triangle. That is, if the intersection of the row for Australia and the column for Canada has a * then the intersection of the column for Australia and the row for Canada need not also have a * since it is the same combination of samples.

We could look at this matrix to see where a * is not located. This will indicate pairs of samples that do not come from populations with different means. Rather than finding such pairs this way, the last part of the output actually provides a list of such pairs, called homogeneous subsets.

Exercises

14.1 A comparison is made between five welfare agencies in terms of the average number of cases handled by staff during a month. The research is aimed at finding whether the workload is significantly different between agencies. Explain why an ANOVA should be used to explore this issue. State the null hypothesis for this research in words and using mathematical notation. From the following hypothetical results calculate the F-ratio and make a decision about the null ($\alpha = 0.05$):

Variation	Sum of squares	Degrees of freedom
Between agencies	50	4
Within agencies	7210	110
Total	7260	114

14.2 A university instructor uses different teaching methods on three separate classes. She wants to assess the relative effectiveness of these methods by testing for a significant difference between the classes. The data on final grades are:

Method A	Method B	Method C
21	28	19
19	28	17
21	23	20
24	27	23
25	31	20
20	38	17
27	34	20
19	32	21
23	29	22
25	28	21
26	30	23

(a) Calculate the mean and standard deviation for each sample. Can you anticipate from these descriptive statistics the result of an ANOVA conducted on these data?

(b) Conduct the ANOVA to assess your expectations.

14.3 The price ($) of an item was collected from the stores of three separate retail chains. Using a significance level of 0.05, can we say that these stores do not price this good differently?

Chain A	Chain B	Chain C
3.30	3.20	2.99
3.30	3.35	3.00
3.45	3.15	3.30
3.35	3.10	3.45
3.20	2.99	3.40
3.25	3.30	3.25
3.30	3.15	3.25

14.4 The following data were obtained from a hypothetical study of the effects of blood alcohol levels on driving performance. Subjects were randomly assigned into four groups, with each group being assigned a different blood alcohol level. Each group was then measured by time in seconds spent on target when steering a car in a simulated environment.

Level 1	Level 2	Level 3	Level 4
216	178	180	166
187	144	132	145
166	176	172	148
242	132	137	136
229	188	154	126
276	168	154	176
233	204	176	133
166	187	178	184
208	165	169	155
224	193	188	177
213	201	175	189
254	197	186	165
227	183	179	172
203	176	168	172
206	196	188	179
221	182	176	166
219	202	185	180
220	190	195	176
196	202	177	165
230	188	186	193

Using an ANOVA *F*-test, determine whether driving ability is significantly reduced with higher blood alcohol levels.

14.5 Enter your calculations from the previous question where they would appear in an SPSS analysis of the same data.

- - - - - O N E W A Y - - - - -

Variable   MINUTES
By Variable   LEVEL

Analysis of Variance

Source	D.F.	Sum of Squares	Mean Squares	F Ratio	F Prob.
Between Groups	3	?	10395.0833	?	?
Within Groups	?	32144.3000	422.9513		
Total	79	63329.5500			

Enter these data on SPSS and confirm your results for 14.4 and 14.5. Note you will need two columns: one column for minutes for each subject, and one column for the blood-alcohol level of each subject.

14.6 For the analysis in Exercise 14.5, a Scheffe Post-Hoc comparison is conducted to see where the significant difference comes from:

```
- - - - - O N E W A Y - - - - -


        Variable  MINUTES
      By Variable  LEVEL

   Multiple Range Tests:  Scheffe test with significance level .05

   The difference between two means is significant if
     MEAN(J)-MEAN(I)  >= 14.5422 * RANGE * SQRT(1/N(I) + 1/N(J))
     with the following value(s) for RANGE: 4.04

     (*) Indicates significant differences which are shown in the lower
   triangle

                                    G G G G
                                    r r r r
                                    p p p p

                                    4 3 2 1
         Mean        LEVEL

       165.1500     Grp 4
       172.7500     Grp 3
       182.6000     Grp 2
       216.8000     Grp 1      * * *

   Homogeneous Subsets (highest and lowest means are not significantly
   different)

   Subset 1

   Group        Grp 4         Grp 3         Grp 2

   Mean        165.1500      172.7500       182.6000
   - - - - - - - - - - - - - - - - - - - - - - - - -

   Subset 2

   Group        Grp 1

   Mean        216.8000
   - - - - - - - - - -
```

From this comparison, what can you say about the effect of alcohol on driving ability?

14.7 The following data are from a hypothetical sample of 20 children from the USA, representing the number of minutes of television watched per night:

195	184	165	162
168	196	217	190
212	232	204	205
217	210	230	197
180	192	190	198

How will the addition of this sample to the ANOVA of Australian, British, Canadian, and Singaporean children affect the number of degrees of freedom?

Enter these data into the file with the data for the Australian, British, Canadian, and Singaporean children and recalculate the ANOVA and post-hoc analysis on SPSS. What do you conclude about the amount of TV watched between the samples?

15

Ordinal tests for two or more samples

The previous two chapters discussed situations where two or more samples were compared in terms of a variable measured at the interval/ratio level. However, in social science we often do not work with interval/ratio data but ordinal-level data instead. Sometimes this ordinal-level data looks like interval/ratio, especially with attitude scales that have a large number of points. For example, we could construct an 'index of satisfaction', whereby we ask individuals to rate themselves on a scale of 1-to-10, with 1 indicating 'Not at all satisfied' and 10 indicating 'Extremely satisfied':

1——2——3——4——5——6——7——8——9——10

Not at all   *Extremely*
satisfied   *satisfied*

Such an index is ordinal because the numbers assigned to each group are purely arbitrary. We can just as easily, and just as validly, label the grades on the index: 2, 5, 8, 12, 100, 133, 298, 506, 704, 999, rather than 1, 2, 3, 4, 5, 6, 7, 8, 9, 10. All we need to do in constructing an index is preserve the ranking of cases, since we are not measuring satisfaction by some unit, as we do when measuring height by centimetres, or age by years. All we can say is that one case is more satisfied than the other, but we do not have a unit of measurement that allows us to say *by how much* one case is more satisfied than the other (i.e. we cannot say that someone with a score of 6 is three times more satisfied than someone with a score of 2). In fact, instead of using numbers to label the categories, we could have used terms like 'Moderately satisfied' and 'Very satisfied' without losing any information at all. the problem is that when we use a 'continuous' ordinal scale, like 1,2,3, ... 10, there is the *appearance* of interval/ratio data, which might tempt us to calculate a mean. This is, strictly speaking, not a correct procedure.

Unfortunately, calculating a mean on essentially ordinal data is not an infrequent occurrence. Market research companies in fact do this as a standard procedure when tabulating survey data. Indeed, this writer's own academic institution has introduced course evaluation measures, much like the above satisfaction scale, and uses the means of such scales to compare student evaluations of courses and instructors. However, what a score of 5.6, for example, is meant to signify, and whether this is different in any meaningful way from a score of say 5.3 is not very obvious. Clearly, even such an august institution as this is not immune from statistical silliness!

Even if an argument is made that it is legitimate to calculate the mean on such data, to conduct an inference test on this mean requires the additional assumption (when working with small samples) that the population is normally distributed. This assumption is sometimes suspect. For example, we know that income is not normally distributed: it is usually skewed to the right. Therefore, it is inappropriate to conduct a t-test of mean income. Fortunately, just as there are non-parametric tests for ordinal data in the one-sample case, there is a range of non-parametric tests for the two-sample and k-sample situations.

To see the logic of these non-parametric tests, we need to remind ourselves of the relationship between descriptive and inferential statistics. We begin with the raw data from a sample, and then calculate a descriptive statistic that somehow captures the 'essence' of these data. We then use inferential statistics to see if we can generalize from this sample result to the population. With ordinal data the mean is not an appropriate descriptive statistic. We need to generate a different descriptive statistic from a sample, and then apply our inferential statistics to it. The obvious choice is to use the median, which we learnt in Chapter 4 to be the appropriate measure of central tendency for ordinal data (and for interval/ratio data that is skewed). Indeed, many non-parametric tests use the median in some way to describe a sample, before then carrying out inference tests.

The Wilcoxon rank sum test

The Wilcoxon rank sum or W-test is a non-parametric test for ordinal data.[1] With ordinal data, we can order cases from lowest to highest according to the 'score' each case receives on the ordinal scale. Once arranged in this order, each case can be assigned a rank that indicates where in the order they appear: first, second, third, and so on. Think of the way that tennis players are given a ranking, with the best player ranked number one, the second best ranked two, and so on. Just as we can rank order people according to their tennis-playing ability, we can rank order cases according to any variable measured at least at the ordinal level. To see how this information is used in conducting a rank sum test, we will work through the following example.

We want to see if people from rural areas are more or less conservative than people from urban areas. We asked a random sample of 22 people from rural areas and 22 people from urban areas a detailed set of questions, and from

---

[1]The Wilcoxon test is equivalent to the Mann–Whitney U-test (discussed in the Appendix to this chapter). Although each of these tests are based on different descriptive statistics, they are mathematically equivalent and will lead to the same conclusion regarding the null hypothesis. SPSS conducts these two tests simultaneously under the same command.

their responses constructed an 'index of conservatism', which ranges from 1 to 40. A score of 40 indicates someone who is extremely conservative, while a score of 0 indicates someone who is not at all politically conservative. All 44 scores are listed in Table 15.1.

Table 15.1 Score on conservatism index: Sample of rural and urban residents

Urban	Rural
0	2
1	3
4	6
5	7
10	8
11	9
13	12
14	17
15	18
16	19
18	21
18	22
20	24
23	25
26	28
27	29
31	30
32	33
35	33
35	34
37	36
38	39

To illustrate the idea of ranking, imagine that all of these 44 people are arranged in a line, with the person scoring the lowest on the scale of conservatism first in the line, and the person with the highest score last in line (Figure 15.1).

We see that an urban resident scored the lowest with zero, so she appears first in line, while a rural dweller had the highest score of 39, and appears at the end of the line. Ranks are assigned to each person according to his or her position in the line-up. The rank is simply a number telling us where in line each case appears, and this ranking is printed under the scores for each case.

A problem arises in assigning ranks when two or more cases score the same value for the variable. These are called **tied** cases. For example, in the above example, two urban residents each scored 35 on the scale.

To assign ranks to **tied cases** divide the **sum** of the ranks to be filled by the **number** of ranks to be filled.

	U	U	R	R	U	U	R	R	R	U	U	R	U	U	U	U	R	R	R	U	U	R	R	U	U	R	R	R	R	U	U	R	R	U	U	R	R	U	U	R
Score	0	1	2	3	4	5	6	7	8	9	10	11	12	13	14	15	16	17	18	18	18	19	20	21	22	23	24	25	26	27	28	29	30	31	32	33	34	35	36	37	38	39
Rank	1	2	3	4	5	6	7	8	9	10	11	12	13	14	15	16	17	18	**18**	**18**	**18**	19	**20**	**20**	22	23	24	25	26	27	28	29	30	31	32	**33**	**33**	34	**35**	**35**	36.5	**36.5**	38	**39.5**	**39.5**	39.5	41	42	43	44

Urban residents:

	U	U		U	U						U	U		U	U	U	U				U	U			U		U			U	U			U	U			U	U	U		U	U
Rank	1	2		5	6						11	12		14	15	16	17		**20**	**20**		23			26			29	30			34	35					**39.5**	**39.5**		42	43

Sum of ranks for urban residents, $\sum R_1 = 480$

Rural residents:

	R	R		R	R	R	R		R			R		R	R		R	R		R	R		R	R	R			R	R	R		R		R
Rank	3	4		7	8	9	10		13			18		**20**	22		24	25		27	28		31	32	33			**36.5**	**36.5**	38		41		44

Sum of ranks for rural residents, $\sum R_2 = 510$

Figure 15.1

In the example, these two urban residents occupy two ranks, which are 39th and 40th in the line:

$$\frac{39 + 40}{2} = 39.5$$

Similarly, with the two rural residents who each scored 33 — they occupy two ranks, which are 36th and 37th in line:

$$\frac{36 + 37}{2} = 36.5$$

The same logic applies when more than two cases are tied on the same score. For example, one rural and two urban dwellers each scored 18 on the index of conservatism. Together, these three people occupy three spaces, which are 19th, 20th, and 21st in line:

$$\frac{19 + 20 + 21}{3} = 20$$

Therefore they are each assigned a rank of 20. Notice that in assigning this rank of 20 to each of these three cases, we do not use rank 19 or rank 21 for the cases immediately preceding or following them in line.

If we sum the ranks for each group, we get descriptive statistics that indicate the relative spread of the two groups in the combined distribution:

$$\Sigma R_1 = 480$$

$$\Sigma R_2 = 510$$

These sums of ranks, in other words, give a sense as to whether one sample is more or less conservative than the other. Here we see that the sum of ranks for the urban sample is 480, whereas for the rural sample it is 510. This indicates that urban residents tended to have lower scores on the conservatism scale than rural residents, giving them on average smaller ranks.

The extreme situation is if all sample rural residents are more conservative than the sampled urbanites. The urban residents will then occupy the first 22 ranks in the line, and rural residents will occupy ranks 23–44. The two rank sums will then be:

$$\Sigma R_1 = 1 + 2 + 3 + \ldots + 22 = 253$$

$$\Sigma R_2 = 23 + 24 + 25 + \ldots + 44 = 737$$

It is possible to randomly select two samples that produce these extreme rank sums, even though there is no difference between the populations. However, such a result is highly improbable. If the two populations do not differ, the more likely result is that the sample of urban and the sample of rural dwellers are evenly spread through the distribution. The sum of ranks in this situation is defined by the following equation:

$$\mu_w = \frac{1}{2} \ N_1 \ (N_1 + N_2 + 1)$$

Where:
  N_1 is the smallest of the two samples
  N_2 is the largest of the two samples.

In the above example, the value of μ_w is:

$$\mu_w = \frac{1}{2} \ 22(22 + 22 + 1)$$

$$= 495$$

Therefore the null and alternative hypotheses for this example are:

$$H_0: \mu_w = 495$$
$$H_a: \mu_w \neq 495$$

In the example, the rank sums are different from the value assumed in the null hypothesis. Can we conclude from this that the *populations* are different as well? The Wilcoxon rank sum test decides this question. It does this by comparing a sample statistic called **Wilcoxon's W** to the value of μ_w.

Wilcoxon's W is the smallest of the two rank sums.

This rank sum is just another descriptive statistic, like the mean or median, which captures some feature of the sample we are interested in. In this example the smallest of the two rank sums is that for urban dwellers, so that:

$$W = 480$$

The Wilcoxon test analyses whether 480 is 'different enough' from the expected value of 495 to suggest that there is also a difference between the populations. For sample sizes larger than 20, a z-test of the sample W is used:[1]

---

[1]Strictly speaking, the sampling distribution W is only approximately normal, but this a reasonable approximation for sample sizes larger than 20. Some texts produce a table for the exact distribution for W, which should be used to look up probabilities in the smalll-sample case. In the small-sample cases SPSS will automatically conduct an exact test rather than use the normal approximation.

$$z_{sample} = \frac{W - \mu_w}{\sigma_w}$$

where:

$$\sigma_w = \sqrt{\frac{1}{12} N_1 N_2 (N_1 + N_2 + 1)}$$

The standard error of the sampling distribution of rank sums, σ_w, for this example is:

$$\sigma_w = \sqrt{\frac{1}{12} 22 \times 22 (22 + 22 + 1)}$$

$$= 42.6$$

The z-test of W produces the following result:

$$z_{sample} = \frac{W - \mu_w}{\sigma_w}$$

$$= \frac{480 - 495}{42.6}$$

$$= -0.352$$

From the table for the area under the normal curve, a z-score of 0.352, on a two-tail test, has a probability of occurring of 0.7247, if the null hypothesis is true. In other words, the difference between the two samples in their rank sums is not large enough for it to be attributed to a difference between the two popualtions: nearly three times in every four samples drawn from populations with no difference will produce this much variation or more.

The Wilcoxon rank sum test using SPSS

Filename 15.sav   The data for this example have been entered into SPSS. The political conservatism variable has been given the variable name **score**, and area of residence has been given the variable name **area**. A Wilcoxon rank sum test involves the procedures listed in Table 15.2.

Table 15.2 Wilcoxon rank sum test using SPSS

SPSS command/action	Comments
1 From the menu select **Statistics/Nonparametric Tests/ 2 Independent Samples...**	This will bring up a window headed **Two-Independent-Samples Tests**. Notice that in the area for **Test Type** the square next to **Mann Whitney U** has × indicating that this is the default test. This is the same test as the Wilcoxon. In other words, the Wilcoxon test will automatically be generated under this command
2 Click on **score**	**score** will be highlighted
3 Click on the ➤ that points to the area headed **Test Variable(s):**	This will paste **score** into the **Test Variable(s):** list
4 Click on **area**	**area** will be highlighted
5 Click on the ➤ that points to the area headed **Grouping Variable**	This will paste **area** into the **Grouping variable** list. Notice that in this list the variable appears as **area (??)**
6 Click on **Define Groups...**	This will bring up the **Define Groups** window
7 In the area next to **Group 1:** type **1**, and in the area next to **Group 2:** type **2**	This identifies the two groups to be compared, which are urban and rural residents
8 Click on **continue**	
9 Click on **OK**	

The results from this set of instructions will be:

```
- - - - - Mann-Whitney U - Wilcoxon Rank Sum W Test

     SCORE      Score on Conservatism Index
   by AREA      Area of Residence


   Mean Rank    Cases

      21.82        22  AREA = 1  urban
      23.18        22  AREA = 2  rural
                   --
                   44  Total

                              Corrected for ties
        U            W          Z       2-Tailed P
      227.0        480.0      -.3522       .7247
```

The output firstly tells us the mean rank for each group. These are the rank sums we have already calculated (480 and 510) divided by the number of cases in each group. Below this descriptive information is printed the value of W, which is 480 (the smallest of the two rank sums).

The z-score obtained is -0.3522, which has a two-tail probability, if the null hypothesis of no difference is true, of 0.7247. (The one-tail probability is half of the two-tail probability: 0.36235.) Clearly, the difference between the sample of rural and urban residents should not be taken to indicate a difference between the population of rural and the population of urban residents. We do not reject the null hypothesis of no difference.

Other non-parametric tests for two or more samples

This chapter has worked through one of the most common non-parametric tests: the Wilcoxon test for two independent samples. The other common non-parametric test is the chi-square test, which we briefly introduced in Chapter 12, but which will be detailed for the two-or-more samples case in Chapter 16. Social researchers, in fact, can tackle most problems they encounter with a sound knowledge of the Wilcoxon and the chi-square tests. However, there are many other non-parametric tests available, to which some reference should be made. Indeed, the attentive reader will have noticed that SPSS offered a number of choices in the **Test Type** area when conducting a test of two independent samples. This range of choices is further extended when we consider situations in which more than two samples are being compared.

Kruskal–Wallis H-test on more than two samples

The Wilcoxon test compares two samples in terms of a variable measured at least at the ordinal level. In the previous example, we had a sample of rural and a sample of urban residents. But what if we have more than two samples that we want to compare? What if we want to compare urban, rural, and semi-rural residents?

One way of doing this is to simply conduct multiple Wilcoxon tests, using all the possible combinations of samples:

Urban by rural
Urban by semi-rural
Rural by semi-rural

Thus with three samples to compare we will need to undertake three separate two-sample Wilcoxon tests. In practical terms, on SPSS, this will involve specifying one test at a time, under **Define Groups**, and each possible combination of values for the grouping variable, and then re-running the test. This is obviously a cumbersome procedure.

When we have more than two samples, a more direct path is to conduct a Kruskal–Wallis H test. A Kruskal–Wallis test compares all possible combinations of the samples in one go. It has very similar logic to the Wilcoxon test, in that it compares rank sums for each sample being compared. The test statistic, though, is no longer a z-test. The Kruskal–Wallis test uses a chi-square test to assess the null hypothesis that the populations have the same distribution on some ordinal scale.

The difference between the Wilcoxon W and Kruskal–Wallis H-tests is analogous to the difference between a two-sample t-test and ANOVA. These latter tests compare the relevant number of samples in terms of some interval/ratio variable, whereas the W and H-tests compare samples in terms of an ordinal variable.

Wald–Wolfowitz runs test

This test uses the same logic as the one-sample runs test we introduced in Chapter 12. It can be used in similar situations to the Wilcoxon rank test, where the cases in the two samples are pooled and ordered in terms of their scores on an ordinal scale. The number of runs of cases from each sample is counted, and this number of runs is the sample statistic tested. In the extreme case, using the example in Figure 15.1, all 22 rural residents will be at one end of the distribution and all 22 urban residents at the other end, thus forming only two runs. Such a sample result will strongly suggest that the two populations are different in terms of this ordinal scale. On the other hand, if the two samples were scattered throughout the combined distribution, the number of runs would be much higher. The Wald–Wolfowitz runs test conducts a z-test on the difference between the number of runs from the samples and the expected number of runs, if the null hypothesis of no difference in the population distributions is true. One limitation of this test though is that it is seriously affected by tied ranks.

Appendix: The Mann–Whitney U-test

In generating the results of the Wilcoxon test on SPSS, we actually clicked on the box under **Test Type** next to Mann–Whitney U-test. The SPSS output produced, together with the Wilcoxon W, another statistic called a Mann–Whitney U. This is also common in many textbooks, and is based on a slightly different calculation. Since it is a little more complicated than simply looking at the sum of the ranks, and will always result in the same probability value as the Wilcoxon rank sum test, we have detailed the latter in the text. However, for those who are interested, the logic of the Mann–Whitney U is presented here. In the example, the 44 respondents in the sample were lined up from highest to lowest rank on the conservatism scale. We ask the rural resident who scored 39 to step out of the line and count how many urban residents he or she is ranked above. This of course will be all 22 urban residents. We then ask the second highest ranked rural dweller to step out of the line and count how many urbanites he or she is ahead of in the line. If we get each rural resident to do this and add up all the figures, the number obtained is the sample U-statistic. This sample statistic can be calculated for any sample using the following formula:

$$U = N_1N_2 + \frac{N_1(N_1 + 1)}{2} - \Sigma R_1$$

where:
N_1 is the size of sample 1
N_2 is the size of sample 2
ΣR_i is the sum of ranks for sample 1.

If the two samples came from populations that were not different in terms of this variable, then we would on average randomly select samples that produced a U-statistic given by:

$$\mu_u = \frac{N_1 N_2}{2}$$

In this example, the expected value of U would be 22(22)/2, which equals 242. From the SPSS output we see that the sample U is 227. We can conduct a z-test to see if the difference between the sample and expected value of U is large enough to warrant the rejection of the null hypothesis.

$$Z_{sample} = \frac{U - \mu_u}{\sigma_u}$$

where:

$$\sigma_u = \sqrt{\frac{N_1 N_2 (N_1 + N_2 + 1)}{12}}$$

The z-score obtained would be exactly the same as that derived from conducting a Wilcoxon rank sum test on the same data, and therefore, regardless of the test used, the conclusion regarding the null hypothesis will be the same.

Exercises

15.1 When comparing two samples, under what conditions would you use a Wilcoxon rank sum test rather than a t-test?

15.2

(a) Order the following data, assigning ranks to each case:

Group 1	Group 2
1	12
15	25
12	29
16	8
23	15
9	20
11	7

(b) What are the rank sums for each group?

(c) Which rank sum is the sample statistic for conducting the Wilcoxon test?

(d) Calculate the value for μ_w

(e) Conduct a Wilcoxon rank sum test to assess whether there is a significant difference in rankings.

15.3 A trial is used to evaluate the effectiveness of a specific exercise program to improve standing-up performance of individuals who have suffered a stroke. Twenty subjects are randomly assigned to either a treatment or a control group, and their individual scores on a motor assessment scale (MAS), which measures standing-up performance for stroke patients on a scale of 0 to 6, are recorded:

Treatment group		Control group	
Subject	MAS	Subject	MAS
1	0	11	3
2	4	12	1
3	5	13	0
4	6	14	2
5	4	15	3
6	4	16	6
7	6	17	1
8	3	18	2
9	6	19	2
10	2	20	2

Using the Wilcoxon rank sum test assess the effectiveness of the exercise program. Enter this data on SPSS and conduct the test.

15.4 A survey is undertaken to assess the effect that a breakaway football league has had on players' salaries. Players from the traditional league are allocated into group 1, and the 'rebels' into group 2. Players are rank-ordered according to their salaries, and a Wilcoxon rank sum test is conducted using SPSS. Why was a non-parametric test used on these data rather than a two-sample t-test?

The results of the Wilcoxon W test are:

```
- - - - - Mann-Whitney U - Wilcoxon Rank Sum W Test

    SALARIES   Salaries ('000)
  by COMP        Football Competition


  Mean Rank    Cases

     72.68        68  COMP = 1
     69.44        73  COMP = 2
                 ---
                 141  Total

                                Corrected for ties
       U            W             Z       2-Tailed P
     2368.0       4942.0        -.4721       .6369
```

What do the mean ranks tell us about the distribution of the *samples*? Is the difference significant?

16

The chi-square test for independence

The chi-square test and other tests of significance

This chapter will look at the most popular technique for hypothesis testing of categorical data. This is the chi-square test of independence. The earlier chapters emphasized that the choice of inference test is mainly affected by two considerations:

- the number of samples to be compared (i.e. one sample, two samples, or more than two samples);
- the level of measurement of the variable with which the samples are to be compared (i.e. nominal, ordinal, or interval/ratio).

The chi-square test is widely used because it is very flexible with respect to each of these considerations:

- Most other tests have to be modified according to whether we are working with two samples or more than two samples. The Wilcoxon rank sum test for ordinal data, for example, is designed for the two-sample case, whereas with three or more samples the Kruskal–Wallis test is employed on ordinal data. Similarly, for interval/ratio data a t-test of sample means is used with two samples, and ANOVA is used where there are more than two samples. The chi-square test, on the other hand, does not have to be modified: it is exactly the same operation regardless of whether there are only two samples being compared or more than two samples.
- The chi-square test is also flexible with respect to the level of measurement of the test variable. The t-test of means and ANOVA can only be applied to interval/ratio data, and the Wilcoxon W and Kruskal–Wallis tests can be applied to ordinal and interval/ratio data but not nominal. Chi-square, on the other hand, can be applied to nominal data and, by implication, also to variables measured at higher levels. It does not require any kind of ranking of cases. All that is required is categorization of cases in terms of the test variable (see Table 16.1).

Table 16.1   Inference tests for two or more samples

Level of measurement of the test variable	Number of samples	
	Two samples	More than two samples
Interval/ratio only	*t*-test	ANOVA
Interval/ratio and ordinal only	Wilcoxon *W*	Kruskal–Wallis
Interval/ratio (collapsed), ordinal, and nominal	Chi-square	

Before proceeding to explore the chi-square test in detail, we must spend some time discussing the descriptive statistics on which the test is based. The purpose of inferential statistics, you will recall, is to assess whether a sample result tells us something about a wider population, so a suitable description of the sample result in the first place is a necessary preliminary to conducting inference tests. In order to conduct a chi-square test, data from a sample need to be described in the form of a **bivariate table**, which crosstabulates data.

Describing a sample: Crosstabulations

If cases have been measured in terms of two separate variables, the data can be described by using two separate frequency distributions — one for each variable of interest. For example, if we collect data from children by asking each child whether she or he watches the news on TV or not, and also recording the sex of the child, we can generate one frequency table to show how many children watch news on TV, and another frequency table showing how many are boys and how many are girls. However, this will not capture the particular *combination* of values that each case has for the two variables: how many children of a certain sex *also* watch news on TV.

To capture this information for variables measured at either a nominal or ordinal level we use a **bivariate table** or **crosstabulation** (also known as a contingency table or 'crosstab' for short).

> A **bivariate table** displays the joint frequency distribution for two variables.

For example, a survey was conducted to investigate children's TV viewing habits. Each child in the survey was asked: 'Do you ever watch the news on television, even if it is only sometimes?'. The sex of each was also recorded. The joint distribution of responses to these two questions was as shown in Table 16.2.

There are some general rules for the construction of such a bivariate table:

- A crosstab should always have a title with clear labelling of both variables.
- The source of data should also be indicated in the text immediately before or after the table, or as a footnote attached to the table (as in the example shown in Table 16.2).

Table 16.2 Children's TV news-watching by sex

Watch news on TV?	Sex		
	Girl	Boy	Total
Yes	754	726	1480
No	51	71	122
Total	805	797	1602

Source: Australian Broadcasting Authority, *Children and Television*, Part I, 1994.

- If there is reason to believe that one of the variables is dependent on the other, the independent variable should be arranged across the columns and the dependent variable down the rows. In this situation it is easy to specify the independent variable since the sex of a child is clearly determined before the question about watching TV News is asked. The only possible chain of causality must run from the sex of the child to news-watching behavior.

In addition to presenting the raw scores, a crosstab can also provide relative frequencies. This presents the information in terms of percentages of either the column totals or the row totals. In our example, the column percentages (with the calculations for the first column) are as given in Table 16.3.

Table 16.3 Children's TV news-watching by sex

Watch news on TV?	Sex		
	Girl	Boy	Total
Yes	$\frac{754}{805} \times 100 = 93.7\%$	91.1%	92.4%
No	$\frac{51}{805} \times 100 = 6.3\%$	8.9%	7.6%
Total	805 = 100%	797 = 100%	1602 = 100%

$N = 1602$

The value of 93.7 per cent is the number of girls who responded 'Yes' as a percentage of the total number of girls:

$$\frac{754}{805} \times 100 = 93.7\%$$

The value of 6.3 per cent is the number of girls who responded 'No' as a percentage of the total number of girls:

$$\frac{51}{805} \times 100 = 6.3\%$$

Similarly, the crosstab can provide the relative frequencies in terms of the **row totals**. To work out row percentages, on the other hand, we calculate the number of girls who answer 'Yes' as a percentage of all respondents who answer 'Yes':

$$\frac{754}{1480} \times 100 = 50.9\%$$

A complete table of row percentages, with the calculations for the first row, is shown in Table 16.4.

Table 16.4   Children's TV news-watching by sex

Watch news on TV?	Sex		
	Girl	Boy	Total
Yes	$\frac{754}{1480} \times 100 = 50.9\%$	$\frac{726}{1480} \times 100 = 49.1\%$	1480 = 100%
No	41.8%	58.2%	122 = 100%
Total	49.7%	50.3%	1602 = 100%

$N = 1602$

When generating relative frequencies it is important to include the raw sample size so that percentages can be converted back into raw data if required by the reader. Sometimes these tables can be combined to give the raw data *and* the relevant percentages by adding extra columns or rows. The appropriate structure depends on the context in which the data are being used and the intended audience.

Some terminology accompanies the construction of a crosstabulation:

- It is common to talk about the size or **dimensions** of a table. The size of the table is defined as the number of categories for the row variable by the number of categories for the column variable. In this example there are two categories for TV news-watching (Yes or No) and two categories for Sex (Girl or Boy), producing a 2-by-2 table. If TV news-watching is measured on a four-point scale, on the other hand, such as 'Every day', 'Frequently', 'Rarely', and 'Never', the dimensions of the table will be 4-by-2.
- Each square in the table contains the number of cases that have a particular *combination* of values for the two variables. These squares are called **cells**. Thus the top-left 'cell' in Table 16.2 tells us that there were 754 kids in the sample who were girls *and* answered 'Yes' to the question on TV.
- The entries in the **Totals** columns are called **marginals**, and when calculating the total number of cells in a table we *do not* include the row and column marginals. The total number of cells is simply the product of the dimensions: in a 2-by-2 table therefore there are four cells, and in a 3-by-4 table there are 12.

Crosstabulations using SPSS

Filename 16-1.sav   The data from the previous example have been entered in SPSS, so we can see how to generate crosstabs (Table 16.5).

Table 16.5   Crosstabs on SPSS

SPSS command/action	Comments
1 From the menu select **Statistics/Summarize/ Crosstabs...**	This will bring up a window headed **Crosstabs**
2 Click on the variable that will form the rows of the table; in this case **tvnews**	This will highlight **tvnews**
3 Click on the ➤ that points to the area headed **Row(s):**	This will paste **tvnews** into the **Row(s):** list
4 Click on **sex**	**sex** will be highlighted
5 Click on the ➤ that points to the area headed **Column(s):**	This will paste **sex** into the **Column(s):** list
6 Click on **OK**	

The following crosstab will appear in the output window:

```
TVNEWS  by  SEX   sex of child

                    SEX            Page 1 of 1
            Count  |
                   |girl    boy
                   |                   Row
                   |    1  |    2  | Total
TVNEWS      -------|-------|-------|
            1  |   754 |   726 |  1480
yes            |       |       |  92.4
               |-------|-------|
            2  |    51 |    71 |   122
no             |       |       |   7.6
               |-------|-------|
        Column    805     797    1602
        Total    50.2    49.8   100.0
```

Number of Missing Observations: 0

The crosstabs command can be extended to provide the relative frequencies as well. This option is selected by clicking on the **Cells...** button at the bottom of the **Crosstabs** window. This will bring up another window headed **Crosstabs: Cell Display**. This window provides the options for deciding how much information each cell will contain. The default setting, which we just used, is for the cells to contain the raw count only. If we wanted the row percentages in addition to the raw count we click on the small square next to **Row**. This will place a × in the square to show that it is selected. Similarly, if we want column percentages we click on the square next to **Column**. If we select both types of relative frequencies at the same time the output will be:

```
TVNEWS  by  SEX  sex of child

                      SEX            Page 1 of 1
              Count  |
              Row Pct |girl     boy
              Col Pct |                    Row
                      |    1  |     2  | Total
TVNEWS        --------|-------|--------|
                 1 |    754  |   726  | 1480
yes               |   50.9  |  49.1  | 92.4
                  |   93.7  |  91.1  |
                  |--------|--------|
                 2 |     51  |    71  |  122
no                |   41.8  |  58.2  |  7.6
                  |    6.3  |   8.9  |
                  |--------|--------|
              Column    805      797    1602
              Total    50.2     49.8   100.0

Number of Missing Observations:  0
```

Notice in the square to the top-left of the table the words Count, Row Pct, Col Pct appear in descending order. SPSS is providing a key as to what each of the numbers in each of the cells represents: the top number is the actual number of cases with that combination of values, the one immediately below is this number as a percentage of the row total, and the one below that is the count as a percentage of the column total.

Statistical independence and the relationships between variables

In the example of children's news-watching habits we noted that there is some difference between boys and girls in terms of their tendency to watch TV news. However, this is a sample result, and we must therefore be wary that it may be due to random variation when sampling from populations in which there is no relationship between the sex of children and TV news-watching behavior. The chi-square test (χ^2) of independence assesses this possibility.

> Two variables are said to be **statistically independent** if classifying a case in terms of one variable does not affect how that case is classified in terms of the other variable.

This statement of independence forms the null hypothesis for the test, and if the null is rejected, the two variables are connected or related *in some way*. However, the test itself does not tell us what the nature of any relationship is. Some of the possible patterns of dependence are illustrated in the following diagrams. The first, called a **spurious relationship** is where two variables under observation (X, Y) are both affected by changes in an unobserved third variable:

Spurious relationship

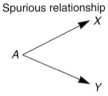

For example, we might observe a dependent relationship between academic performance (X) and satisfaction with life (Y). Yet these might both be caused by income security (A).

Alternatively, the third variable may be **intervening** between the two observed variables.

Intervening relationship

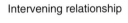

There might be a strong dependence between the position of the sun in the sky (X) and the hands that indicate time on my watch (Y). But this is clearly due to a third intervening variable, namely my own hands setting the time (A).

Another pattern of dependence might be one of **mutual dependence**.

Relationship of mutual dependence

Academic performance (X) and time spent studying (Y) might be dependent, but the causality may run in both directions. Doing better at exams may spur a student on to study harder, which in turn may improve grades, spurring further study, and so on.

Lastly, we may have a strict **one-way causal relationship**:

One-way dependence

For example, studying harder (X) leads to higher future income (Y).

Any of these relationships (and many more complex interactions) will lead us to reject an assumption of independence between two variables. In other words, variables may be connected to each other through many different channels, and any of these connections will affect the chi-square test.

Thus it is important not to confuse the test of independence with the closely related but distinct problem of specifying dependent and independent variables. It is only in the case of one-way dependence that it is appropriate to specify one of the observed variables as independent and the other observed variable as dependent. It is clear, for example, that in assessing the sex of children and TV news-watching behavior that any relationship between the two variables must run from sex to TV watching. However, in other instances it may not be so easy to specify the direction in which any relationship runs. In other words, a chi-square test simply tells us whether two variables are independent of each other; how to characterize any pattern of dependence is up to the researcher.

In this book, we largely deal with simple causal relationships. Thus the test of independence in the examples below is largely equivalent to assessing whether one variable is causally dependent on another, rather than due to one of the more complex forms of relationship illustrated above. To explore more complex forms of relationship would take us into the realm of multivariate analysis — the investigation of relationships between more than two observed variables, which is beyond the scope of this book. However, it is important to keep in mind when interpreting results the fact that any observed relationship between variables may be more complicated than the simple cause-and-effect model we specify.

The chi-square test for independence

Now we will look at the chi-square test in detail. In the particular example we are working with we suspect that TV news-watching somehow depends on a child's sex. In fact, this problem can be stated in the now familiar form of hypothesis testing:

H_0: TV news-watching behavior is independent of a child's sex

H_a: TV news-watching behavior is dependent on a child's sex

If these variables are independent, knowing that a child is a boy or a girl should tell me nothing about whether they have a higher or lower rate of watching TV news than the other group.

To see how the chi-square test helps us to assess whether these two variables are independent of each other in the population, we begin by looking at the row marginals and percentages (Table 16.6).

Table 16.6 TV news-watching: All respondents

Watch news on TV?	Total	Percentage
Yes	1480	92.4
No	122	7.6
Total	1602	100

These row totals and percentages are the basic reference points from which the chi-square test is conducted. The argument is that if 92.4 per cent of *all respondents* answered 'Yes', then 92.4 per cent of each group (boys and girls) should also answer 'Yes'. This is what we should *expect* to find *if* the two variables are independent.

Under the null hypothesis of independence the relative frequencies of responses for each group is expected to be the same as that for the groups combined.

However, even if the two variables are independent of each other in the population, so that exactly the same proportion of *all* boys watches news as for *all* girls, we should not always expect random *samples* of boys and *samples* of girls to reflect this. For example, we might draw samples of boys and girls from populations in which the two variables are independent, and get any of the three separate results shown in Table 16.7.

Table 16.7   Three different samples

Sample 1			
Watch news on TV?	Sex		
	Girl	Boy	Total
Yes	92%	93%	92.4%
No	8%	7%	7.6%

Sample 2			
Watch news on TV?	Sex		
	Girl	Boy	Total
Yes	89%	96%	92.4%
No	11%	4%	7.6%

Sample 3			
Watch news on TV?	Sex		
	Girl	Boy	Total
Yes	80%	98%	92.4%
No	20%	2%	7.6%

Sample 1 is a situation in which the observed frequency very closely reflects the expected percentages, *assuming* that the two variables are independent. However, occasionally we might find the situation shown in sample 2, where there is a difference between the expected and actual outcomes, but it is not too great. Sample 3 shows a freak situation in which the samples just happened to pick up members of the populations from either end of the scale, causing the expected and actual frequencies to diverge a great deal. Although this is a possibility in any random sampling, it is also highly unlikely.

In fact, we can take an infinite number of random samples from a population in which the two variables are independent and observe the spread of results.

Obviously most would be like samples 1 and 2, and very few like sample 3.

> The **chi-square statistic** is calculated from the difference between the observed and expected frequencies in each cell of a bivariate table. The **chi-square distribution** is the probability distribution of the chi-square statistic for an infinite number of random samples of the same size drawn from a population in which the two variables are independent of each other.

The exact formula for calculating chi-square is:

$$\chi^2 = \Sigma \, \frac{(f_o - f_e)^2}{f_e}$$

where:
   f_o is observed cell frequencies
   f_e is expected cell frequencies.

Occasionally we draw samples that are 'true' to the population so that there is no difference between the actual and expected frequencies. In this case the value of chi-square will be zero:

$$f_o = f_e \;\; \rightarrow \;\; (f_o - f_e)^2 = 0 \;\; \rightarrow \;\; \chi^2 = 0$$

But this will not always be the case. We will occasionally take samples that select, through random chance, slightly more cases for one group from one end of the distribution or the other. The result is that chi-square will take on a positive value:

$$f_o \neq f_e \;\; \rightarrow \;\; (f_o - f_e)^2 > 0 \;\; \rightarrow \;\; \chi^2 > 0$$

In the formula for chi-square, notice that differences between observed and expected frequencies are squared. This ensures that the range of all possible chi-square values must start at zero and increase in a positive direction. Regardless of whether the expected frequency is larger than the observed frequencies or vice versa, squaring any difference will produce a positive number.[1] (See Figure 16.1.)

The greater the difference between the actual frequencies and the expected frequencies, the larger the value of chi-square. The chi-square distribution has a long tail, reflecting the fact that it is *possible* to select random samples that yield a very high value for chi-square, even though the variables are independent in the population, but this is highly improbable. It will be a fluke to just

---

[1] Since chi-square is calculated on the basis of the difference between expected and actual scores *squared*, and not on the *direction* of difference, there is no sense in which we have to choose between a one-tail or a two-tail inference test. All differences between observed and expected scores, regardless of whether they are due to the observed scores being above or below the expected scores, will take on a positive value.

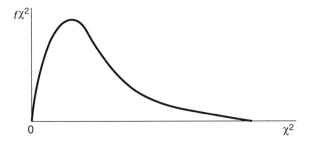

Figure 16.1   The chi-square distribution
Note: This is the general shape of the chi-square distribution. Each specific chi-square distribution will vary with the number of degrees of freedom.

happen to select a sample from one group in which all cases come from one end of the distribution and another sample from the other group that comes from the other end of the distribution, *if* the null hypothesis of independence is true. Therefore the area under the curve for very large chi-square values is small, reflecting the low probability of this happening by chance.

> From the sampling distribution of chi-square we can determine the probability that the difference between actual and expected scores in any given sample is due to random variation when sampling from a population in which the two variables are independent.

For example, we might find that sample 3 above will be drawn one time in one thousand ($p = 0.001$) *if* the two variables are independent of each other. This will be considered so unlikely as to warrant us to argue that there really is a dependence between sex and news-watching — our assumption about independence should be dropped.

We will now use the example of children's TV news-watching behavior to provide a concrete illustration of this procedure. The survey consisted of 805 girls and 797 boys, with the distribution of responses as shown in Table 16.8.

Table 16.8   Children's TV news-watching by sex

Watch news on TV?	Sex		
	Girl	Boy	Total
Yes	754	726	1480
	93.7%	91.1%	92.4%
	(743.7)	(736.3)	
No	51	71	122
	6.3%	8.9%	7.6%
	(61.3)	(60.7)	
Total	805	797	1602

The first number in each cell is the actual count of girls or boys who answered 'Yes' or 'No'. The percentage figure is the number of children in that cell as a proportion of the column total. That is, 93.7 per cent of the total number of girls surveyed watch the news, which is 754. On the other hand, 91.1 per cent of all boys responded 'Yes'. There is obviously a difference, but could this be due to random variation?

The number of respondents we expect to find in each cell, if the variables are independent, is represented in brackets. For example, if 92.4 per cent of all children answered 'Yes', then we expect to find 92.4 per cent of girls to answer 'Yes':

$$\text{Expected number of girls answering 'Yes'} = \frac{92.4}{100} \times 805 = 743.7$$

The same calculations for the other cells are:

$$\text{Expected number of girls answering 'No'} = \frac{7.6}{100} \times 805 = 61.3$$

$$\text{Expected number of boys answering 'Yes'} = \frac{92.4}{100} \times 797 = 736.3$$

$$\text{Expected number of boys answering 'No'} = \frac{7.6}{100} \times 797 = 60.7$$

From the actual and expected values in each cell, the chi-square for this sample is:

$$\chi^2_{\text{sample}} = \Sigma \frac{(f_o - f_e)^2}{f_e}$$

$$= \frac{(754 - 743.7)^2}{743.7} + \frac{(726 - 736.3)^2}{736.3} + \frac{(51 - 61.3)^2}{61.3} + \frac{(71 - 60.7)^2}{60.7}$$

$$= 3.769$$

Degrees of freedom

To work out the probability of obtaining a chi-square of 3.769 just by random chance, we need to take into account the degrees of freedom. Notice that, in calculating the expected frequencies for each cell in the crosstab, as soon as I have worked out that 743.7 girls are expected to answer 'Yes', the number of boys expected to answer 'Yes' *has to be* 736.3. Otherwise the total expected will not equal the actual total of 1480. In other words, 1 degree of freedom is lost when working across the columns, since the total expected value in the cells *has to equal* the observed total.

Similarly when calculating that the expected number of girls who answered 'Yes' is 743.7, the expected number who answered 'No' *has to be* 61.3 for the sum of expected values to equal the total number of girls in the sample. So we have also lost 1 degree of freedom when working down the rows. In fact, for any table the number of degrees of freedom will be:

$$df = (r - 1)(c - 1)$$

where:
  r is the number of rows
  c is the number of columns.

In a 2-by-2 table such as this, therefore, there is 1 degree of freedom.

The distribution of chi-square

Having obtained a value for $\chi^2_{sample} = 3.679$ we refer to the table for the distribution of chi square to obtain a critical value with which to compare the sample score.

A portion of the table is reproduced in Table 16.9 to illustrate its use in this example.

Table 16.9   Distribution of chi-square

df	Area under the distribution (α.)									
	.99	.90	.70	.50	.30	.20	.10	.05	.01	.001
1	.000157	.0158	.148	.455	1.074	1.642	2.706	3.841	6.635	10.827
2	.0201	.211	.713	1.386	2.408	3.219	4.605	5.991	9.210	13.815
3	.115	.584	1.424	2.366	3.665	4.642	6.251	7.815	11.341	16.268
4	.297	1.064	2.195	3.357	4.878	5.989	7.779	9.488	13.277	18.465
5	.554	1.610	3.000	4.351	6.064	7.289	9.236	11.070	15.086	20.517
6	.872	2.204	3.828	5.348	7.231	8.558	10.645	12.592	16.812	22.457

This table is very similar to that for the distribution of t, with the values for chi-square in the body of the table, the number of degrees of freedom down the side, and a select set of significance levels across the top. As Siegel and Castellan state, 'if an observed value of chi-square is equal to or greater than the value given in [the table] ... for a given level of significance, at a particular *df*, then H_0 may be rejected at that level of significance'. (S. Siegel and N.J. Castellan, 1988, *Nonparametric Statistics for the Behavioural Sciences*, 2nd edn, McGraw-Hill, New York.)

In our example, if we choose an alpha level of 0.05, with 1 degree of freedom, the critical value will be $\chi^2_{critical} = 3.841$. The sample chi-square is 3.769 and, as evident in Figure 16.2, this does not lie in the critical region of rejection, so we do not reject the null hypothesis of independence: TV news-watching among children does not seem to be affected by the sex of the children.

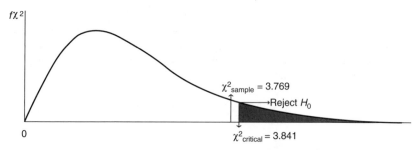

Figure 16.2 The chi-square distribution with $\alpha = 0.05$, $df = 1$

Example

A randomly sampled group of 50 migrants from non-English-speaking backgrounds (NESB) and a group of 50 migrants from English-speaking backgrounds (ESB) are asked whether or not they feel they have ever been discriminated against in seeking employment or promotion. We suspect that perception of discrimination is somehow dependent on language background, so that we will form crosstabs with language background as the independent variable and perception of discrimination as the dependent variable. However, this suspicion may not be correct. These two variables may in fact be independent. *Remember that two variables are said to be independent if classifying cases in terms of one variable does not affect how cases are classified in terms of the other variable*: knowing that a migrant is ESB or NESB should tell us nothing about whether that migrant feels a stronger or weaker sense of discrimination.

The samples resulted in the distribution of *all* respondents shown in Table 16.10.

Table 16.10   Perception of discrimination

Discrimination	Total
Yes	60
No	40
Total	100

If the two variables are independent then we should expect to find the percentage distribution of 'Yes' and 'No' responses *within each group* to be the same as for the two groups combined (Table 16.11).

Table 16.11   Expected distribution of responses

Discrimination	Status		Total
	NESB	ESB	
Yes	$\frac{50 \times 60}{100} = 30$	$\frac{50 \times 60}{100} = 30$	60
No	$\frac{50 \times 40}{100} = 20$	$\frac{50 \times 40}{100} = 20$	40
Total	50	50	100

Table 16.11 illustrates the simplest way to calculate expected frequencies.

> To calculate the expected frequency for each cell multiply the column marginal by the row marginal and divide the product by the total sample size.

However, the actual sample results produced the distribution shown in Table 16.12, instead of these expected values.

Table 16.12   Observed distribution of responses

Discrimination	Status		
	NESB	ESB	Total
Yes	45	15	60
No	5	35	40
Total	50	50	100

We could stop here and let the descriptive statistics contained in these tables speak for themselves. In the samples, NESB migrants do have a relatively higher perception of being discriminated against than ESB migrants. However, we must remember that because we are only working with samples rather than the populations, the result can simply be due to random variation. We might just happen to select in the sample a higher proportion of NESB migrants who feel discriminated against and/or a slightly lower proportion of English-speaking background migrants who feel discriminated against, even though in the population there is no difference. This is where the chi-square test can help. Table 16.13 combines these crosstabs, with each cell containing the count of actual responses, with the expected values in brackets:

Table 16.13   Actual and expected responses

Discrimination	Status		
	NESB	ESB	Total
Yes	45 (30)	15 (30)	60
No	5 (20)	35 (20)	40
Total	50	50	100

$$\chi^2_{sample} = \Sigma \frac{(f_o - f_e)^2}{f_e}$$

$$= \frac{(45-30)^2}{30} + \frac{(5-20)^2}{20} + \frac{(15-30)^2}{30} + \frac{(35-20)^2}{20}$$

$$= \frac{225}{30} + \frac{225}{20} + \frac{225}{30} + \frac{225}{20}$$

$$= 37.5$$

In a 2-by-2 table such as this, there is 1 degree of freedom. Looking at the table for the distribution of chi-square, with 1 degree of freedom, the critical value for chi-square at an alpha level of 0.05 is 3.841 (Table 16.14).

Table 16.14   Distribution of chi-square

df	Area under the distribution (α)									
	.99	.90	.70	.50	.30	.20	.10	.05	.01	.001
1	.000157	.0158	.148	.455	1.074	1.642	2.706	3.841	6.635	10.827
2	.0201	.211	.713	1.386	2.408	3.219	4.605	5.991	9.210	13.815
3	.115	.584	1.424	2.366	3.665	4.642	6.251	7.815	11.341	16.268
4	.297	1.064	2.195	3.357	4.878	5.989	7.779	9.488	13.277	18.465
5	.554	1.610	3.000	4.351	6.064	7.289	9.236	11.070	15.086	20.517
6	.872	2.204	3.828	5.348	7.231	8.558	10.645	12.592	16.812	22.457

This means that, with 1 degree of freedom, the probability of getting this sample result of $\chi^2 = 37.5$, *if* the two variables are independent, is less than 0.05 (Figure 16.3).

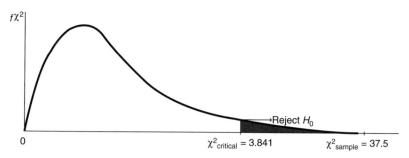

Figure 16.3   The chi-square distribution with $\alpha = 0.05$, $df = 1$

Therefore we reject the null hypothesis of independence, and argue that the perception of discrimination does systematically differ between migrant groups, such that NESB migrants have a systematically higher perception of discrimination than ESB migrants.

The chi-square test using SPSS

Filename 16–2.sav   The data from this hypothetical survey have been entered into SPSS. Perception of discrimination has been given the variable name **discrim**, with the following value labels: **1=yes** and **2=no**. Language background has been given the variable name **language**, with value labels **1=NESB** and **2=ESB**.

In Chapter 12 we generated the one-sample chi-square test under the **Statistics/Nonparametric Tests** command. However, with two or more samples, chi-square tests are calculated under the **Statistics/Summarize/ Crosstabs...** command (Table 16.15).

Table 16.15   Crosstabs with chi-square test on SPSS

SPSS command/action	Comments
1 From the menu select **Statistics/Summarize/ Crosstabs...**	This will bring up a window headed **Crosstabs**
2 Click on the variable that will form the rows of the table; in this case **discrim**	This will highlight **discrim**
3 Click on the ➤ that points to the area headed **Row(s):**	This will paste **discrim** into the **Row(s):** list
4 Click on **language**	**language** will be highlighted
5 Click on the ➤ that points to the area headed **Column(s):**	This will paste **language** into the **Column(s):** list
6 Click on the button **Statistics...**	This will bring up the **Crosstabs: Statistics** window. In the top left corner you will see **Chi-square** with a little box next to it
7 Select **Chi-Square** by clicking on the box next to it	This will place × in the box to show that it has been selected
8 Click on **Continue**	
9 Click on **OK**	

By clicking on the **Cell...** button in the **Crosstabs: Statistics** window a range of options as to the information to be printed in each cell of the table will be provided. For the purpose of comparison with the earlier hand calculation, it will help to go into this window and select **Expected** in the area headed **Counts**. The choice of information to be calculated and printed in each cell is really up to the person conducting the research, and what he or she thinks is needed to make a reasonable assessment. Generally (although we are not generating them in this instance), the column percentages are useful numbers to have, together with the actual distribution. The column percentages allow us to 'eyeball' the data and make a preliminary judgment as to whether we think the two variables are independent or not.

Given this consideration, the output from the preceding commands, together with a request for the expected values, will be:

DISCRIM Perception of Discrimination by LANGUAGE Language Background

```
                    LANGUAGE        Page 1 of 1
             Count  |
             Exp Val |NESB     ESB
                    |                    Row
                    |    1 |     2  | Total
DISCRIM      --------|--------|--------|
             1  |    45 |    15  |   60
yes             |  30.0 |  30.0  | 60.0%
                |--------|--------|
             2  |     5 |    35  |   40
no              |  20.0 |  20.0  | 40.0%
                |--------|--------|
             Column     50      50      100
             Total    50.0%   50.0%   100.0%
```

Chi-Square	Value	DF	Significance
Pearson	37.50000	1	.00000
Continuity Correction	35.04167	1	.00000
Likelihood Ratio	41.00761	1	.00000
Mantel-Haenszel test for linear association	37.12500	1	.00000

Minimum Expected Frequency -   20.000

Number of Missing Observations: 0

A great deal of information is printed beneath the crosstabulation, but the key line is that for Pearson:

Chi-Square	Value	DF	Significance
Pearson	37.50000	1	.00000

Under Value and next to Pearson (the name of the statistician who devised the chi-square test) is the chi-square value of 37.5, which is the same as that calculated above. The subsequent lines are usually not of interest.[1] Under DF is printed the degrees of freedom; in this instance $df = 1$.

The last column, called Significance, gives the probability of obtaining a sample with this chi-square from a population in which the two variables are independent. Although the probability printed here is 0.00000, this does not actually mean a zero probability. SPSS simply rounds off the

---

[1] As will be discussed below, we might refer to the value for Continuity Correction if *one* of the expected values is below 5, given that this is a 2-by-2 table.

significance to five decimal places so that any value less than 0.000005 will be rounded off to 0.00000. Therefore, this significance should be interpreted as less than five in one million.

Problems with small samples

You may have noticed the very last line in the SPSS output:

Minimum Expected Frequency -   20.000

This line is a check to see whether any cells in the crosstab have an expected frequency of less than 1, or if too many cells have an expected frequency of 5 or less. SPSS firstly identifies which of the expected values in the cells of the table is the smallest and prints it: in this case it is 20. If this expected frequency is 5 or less, SPSS will then go back through the table and indicate *how many* cells in total have a value of 5 or less, and the *percentage* of cells that have an expected value of 5 or less.

The reason why SPSS goes through such an elaborate procedure to check whether any of the expected values are 5 or less, and if so, how many, is because a problem can arise with the use of a chi-square test when working with small samples. If the use of small samples leads to either of the following situations, the chi-square statistic becomes difficult to interpret:

- Any cell in the bivariate table has an expected frequency of less than 1.
- The expected frequency of cases in a large percentage of cells is 5 or less. Usually 20 per cent of cells is considered too high, but any cells with expected values of 5 or less can create a problem.

If the last line in the SPSS output indicates that one of these conditions has been violated, the chi-square test cannot be meaningfully interpreted. In such situations, there are some alternatives, depending on the dimensions of the table. With 2-by-2 tables some writers suggest using Yate's correction for continuity, which SPSS automatically calculates for such tables:

$$\chi_c^2 = \Sigma \frac{(|f_o - f_e| - 0.5)^2}{f_e}$$

Other writers suggest that for 2-by-2 tables, Fisher's exact probability test should be used. (See H.T. Reynolds, 1977, *The Analysis of Cross-Classifications*, Free Press, London, pp 9–10, for a discussion of these procedures.)

With tables larger than 2-by-2 the only possible solution is to collapse categories together for either or both variables so as to increase expected frequencies. Before doing this, though, we need to justify the procedure because information is lost when categories are collapsed together. Originally there was enough information to say that one case differed from another case in terms of a variable, but when these cases are combined after collapsing categories we are now saying that such cases are the same. For example, we might need to collapse the four-point scale shown in Figure 16.4 into a two-point scale in order to avoid small expected frequencies.

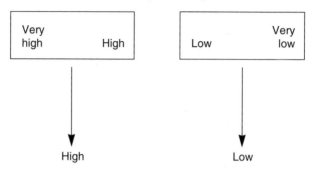

Figure 16.4

Thus cases that were previously classified into separate groups, such as Low and Very low, now are classified in the same group, namely, Low. The scale was originally constructed for supposedly good theoretical reasons, and we should be wary of abandoning that scale simply to allow us to use a statistical procedure.

Problems with large samples

The other main problem with the use of chi-square as a test of independence is that it is especially sensitive to large samples. The chance of finding a sample difference to be significant always increases with sample size, regardless of whether we use z-tests, or t-tests, or F-tests, or chi-square. To illustrate this problem, imagine that you are looking at two people standing far away. With the naked eye they look to have the same height. But with a pair of binoculars it is evident that one person is slightly taller than the other. The more powerful the looking device the more likely slight differences will be detected. However, this example should also highlight the important distinction between *statistical* difference and *meaningful* difference. There may be a statistical difference in height of 1 cm between two people, but for all *practical* purposes they are as tall as each other. Using too powerful a looking device may complicate a picture by exaggerating slight differences that aren't really worth worrying about. When performing inference tests, increasing sample size has the effect of intensifying the 'looking device' we are employing and thereby accentuating slight differences that are not important.

> Increasing the sample size increases the chance of detecting a statistical difference that smaller samples will simply attribute to random variation.

Of all the tests we cover, chi-square is especially sensitive to sample size and might result in a statistically significant difference even though no difference exists or is trivial. To see this, assume that we have respondents grouped according to their respective level of education. Level of education is measured by asking if the respondent has had a university education or not. We are interested in whether this affects enjoyment of work, measured according to whether respondents find their job 'Exciting', 'Pretty Routine', or 'Dull'. The distribution, when expressed as percentages of the total for each group is shown in Table 16.16.

Table 16.16   Enjoyment of work by education level: Percentage distribution

Enjoyment of work	University education		
	No (%)	Yes (%)	Total (%)
Exciting	47.0	45.7	46.8
Pretty routine	48.2	47.9	48.2
Dull	4.8	6.4	5.0
Total	100	100	100

If these percentages are derived from a total sample of 1461, consisting of 1242 people without university education and 219 people with university education, the figures for observed and expected values will be as listed in Table 16.17.

Table 16.17   Enjoyment of work by education level

Enjoyment of work	University education		
	No	Yes	Total
Exciting	584	100	684
	(581.5)	(102.5)	48.8%
Pretty routine	599	105	704
	(598.5)	(105.5)	48.2%
Dull	59	14	73
	(62)	(11)	5%
Total	1242	219	1461

Just by looking at the table it is clear that there is little difference between the observed frequencies and the expected frequencies (shown in brackets). As a matter of common sense we will say that the difference between the distribution of those without a university education and those with a university education in terms of job satisfaction is so slight that it could easily be put down to chance: the null hypothesis of independence is not rejected. In fact, the chi-square for this table is:

$$\chi^2_{sample} = 1.08148$$

The probability of getting this by chance alone, with 2 degrees of freedom, is:

$$p_{sample} = 0.58232$$

However, if we obtained exactly the same *pattern* of responses, but from a sample size 10 times as large (N = 14 610) the conclusion would be different. The bivariate table would be as shown in Table 16.18.

Table 16.18   Enjoyment of work by education level

Enjoyment of work	University education		
	No	Yes	Total
Exciting	5840	1000	6840
	(5815)	(1025)	46.8%
Pretty routine	5990	1050	7040
	(5985)	(1055)	48.2%
Dull	590	140	730
	(620)	(110)	5%
Total	12420	2190	14610

All that has happened is that the value in each cell has been multiplied by 10. The chi-square for this table will also be exactly 10 times the value for that calculated from the previous table:

$$\chi^2_{sample} = 10.8148$$

The probability is:

$$p_{sample} = 0.0048$$

This is now a significant result: the difference between observed and expected frequencies is large enough to allow us to reject the null hypothesis of independence. The pattern of responses is the same, yet the conclusion is reversed. This shows that **any difference in frequency distributions can be significant if it comes from a sufficiently large sample**.

One possible solution is to do the opposite to that when confronted with a small sample: use even finer scales to measure the dependent and/or independent variables. For example, here we could use more than three possible responses for the question: 'How much do you enjoy your work?' Unfortunately, by the time this problem arises — the data analysis stage of research — it is usually too late to change the scale and re-survey the respondents. At best it is a solution to an *anticipated* problem, but it does indicate the value of allowing for a wide range of possible responses when working with nominal/ordinal data on large samples.

If this problem is not anticipated and a significant result is obtained that might be due to sample size, there are two possible solutions:

- Look at the percentage distribution of responses alone and make a judgment based on these percentages, without adding the complication of chi-square (i.e. work with the 'naked eye' rather than the statistical binoculars).
- Calculate and interpret a measure of association, such as Cramer's V (which will be discussed in later chapters), and see if these measures indicate a negligible association between the two variables.

Appendix: Hypothesis testing for two proportions

This chapter discussed a widely used test of significance — the chi-square test of independence. The reason for its popularity is that it is applicable in situations in which both variables are measured at the nominal or ordinal level — a situation that is very common in social research. The chi-square test looks at the distribution of responses in a bivariate table and assesses whether a pattern of dependence exists. In the case of a 2-by-2 bivariate table (i.e. when both variables are binomial) a z-test of proportions can also be carried out on the same data; in fact, the two tests are equivalent ways of analysing the same data. Indeed, the z-test of proportions can be considered a special case of the chi-square test, and since it is commonly used in social science, it is worth knowing the mechanics of its calculation.

This appendix will work through an example of a z-test of sample proportions and then use a chi-square test to show that the results will be the same.

The z-test for two proportions

A (hypothetical) survey is conducted to investigate the level of support for social welfare reform, and whether this varies by age. Respondents are grouped according to whether they are aged 'Under 45' or '45 or over', Each respondent is also asked whether the government should do more to alleviate poverty. This is put to respondents as a simple yes/no question.

The null hypothesis is that the proportion of Under 45s responding 'Yes' (p_1) is the same as the proportion of those 45 or over responding 'Yes' (p_2).

$$H_0: \ p_1 = p_2$$

If this is true, samples taken from such populations will usually reflect the equality. In other words, the *difference* between any two sample proportions, if there is no difference in the underlying populations, should be zero or close to it.

But this will not always be the case. Samples do not always exactly reflect the populations from which they are drawn. Random variation may cause us to pick up a few 'extra' young people who are in favor of welfare reform, and a few 'extra' older people who are opposed, causing the sample proportions to differ considerably. This means that if there is a difference between the two sample proportions, we cannot automatically conclude it reflects an underlying difference in the populations. However, larger differences between the sample proportions are less likely to be due to random chance. The z-test for proportions gives us the precise probability of such unlikely events occurring.

The survey consisted of 600 people under the age of 45 and 400 people aged 45 years or older. The proportion of each group responding 'Yes', the government should do more to alleviate poverty, is:

$$\text{Under 45:} \quad P_1 = \frac{490}{600} = 0.82$$

$$N_1 = 600$$

$$\text{45 or older:} \quad P_2 = \frac{232}{400} = 0.58$$

$$N_2 = 400$$

Does this reflect an underlying difference between the age groups on this issue? To determine this we begin with the following formula:

$$P_u = \frac{N_1 P_1 + N_2 P_2}{N_1 + N_2}$$

This is basically a weighted average of the two sample proportions: a sort of mid-point between the two results. If we substitute the relevant numbers into the equation we get:

$$P_u = \frac{N_1 P_1 + N_2 P_2}{N_1 + N_2}$$

$$= \frac{600(0.82) + 400(0.58)}{600 + 400}$$

$$= 0.722$$

This calculation allows us to determine the standard error of the sampling distribution of all possible sample differences. One standard error is defined by:

$$\sigma_{P_1 - P_2} = \sqrt{P_u(1 - P_u)} \ \sqrt{\frac{N_1 + N_2}{N_2 N_2}}$$

$$= \sqrt{0.722(1 - 0.722)} \ \sqrt{\frac{600 + 400}{600\,(400)}}$$

$$= 0.029$$

The actual difference between our two samples in terms of standard deviation units (z-scores) is:

$$z_{\text{sample}} = \frac{P_1 - P_2}{\sigma_{P_1 - P_2}}$$

$$= \frac{0.82 - 0.58}{0.029}$$

$$= 8.3$$

This z-score is significant at the 0.01 level: we reject the null hypothesis of no difference and argue that support for government assistance to the poor does vary with age.

Chi-square test for independence

The alternative way of analysing this data is to organize it into a 2-by-2 bivariate table (Table 16.19).

Table 16.19 Should the government do more to alleviate poverty?

Agree	Age group		
	Under 45	45 or over	Total
No	110	168	278
	(166.8)	(111.2)	27.8%
Yes	490	232	722
	(433.2)	(288.8)	72.2%
Total	600	400	1000

The figures in brackets are the expected values based on the percentage of total respondents who said 'Yes' or 'No'. Notice that 72.2 per cent of *all* respondents agreed with the need for welfare reform. From this figure we calculate the number of 'Under 45' respondents and '45 or over' respondents who are *expected* to agree. The 72.2 per cent is the same figure that popped up in the z-test for proportions as the reference point for calculating the standard deviation of the sampling distribution. In fact, when we calculate chi-square:

$$\chi^2 = \Sigma \frac{(f_0 - f_e)^2}{f_e}$$

$$= \frac{(110 - 166.8)^2}{166.8} + \frac{(168 - 111.2)^2}{111.2} + \frac{(490 - 433.2)^2}{433.2} + \frac{(232 - 288.8)^2}{288.8}$$

$$= 67$$

From the table for the distribution of chi-square the probability of getting this value (or greater) from identical populations is 0.005 — the same as that for the z-test.

The conclusion to draw from this is that while binomial z-tests are very common, and therefore worth knowing, they are in fact a special case of chi-square. Since the formula for the z-test is more cumbersome, and the logic not as intuitively clear, it is probably best to use chi-square in most situations. Also SPSS cannot conduct two-sample z-tests of proportions, but it can calculate a chi-square on a 2-by-2 table.

Exercises

16.1 How many degrees of freedom are there for tables with each of the following dimensions?
   (a) 2-by-4
   (b) 4-by-2
   (c) 6-by-4
16.2 For each of the table dimensions in Exercise 16.1, what will be the value for $\chi^2_{critical}$ with $\alpha = 0.05$ and $\alpha = 0.10$?

16.3 If a chi-square test, with $N = 500$, produces $\chi^2_{sample} = 24$, what will χ^2_{sample} be with the same relative distribution of responses, but with:
(a) $N = 50$,
(b) $N = 1000$?

16.4 For the following table, calculate the expected frequencies for each cell and identify the ones that violate the rules for using chi-square.

	a	b	c	d	Total
a	1	0	6	48	55
b	2	0	7	40	49
Total	3	0	13	88	104

16.5 Stratified samples of 30 people who voted for the conservative party at the last election and 30 people who voted for the progressive party at the last election are drawn to assess whether political preference is related to father's political preference. The results for each person are:

Case	Voting preference	Father's voting preference	Case	Voting preference	Father's voting preference
1	Progressive	Progressive	31	Conservative	Conservative
2	Progressive	Progressive	32	Conservative	Other
3	Progressive	Progressive	33	Conservative	Conservative
4	Progressive	Conservative	34	Conservative	Conservative
5	Progressive	Progressive	35	Conservative	Conservative
6	Progressive	Progressive	36	Conservative	progressive
7	Progressive	Progressive	37	Conservative	Conservative
8	Progressive	Progressive	38	Conservative	Conservative
9	Progressive	Conservative	39	Conservative	progressive
10	Progressive	Conservative	40	Conservative	Other
11	Progressive	Progressive	41	Conservative	Conservative
12	Progressive	Progressive	42	Conservative	Conservative
13	Progressive	Other	43	Conservative	Conservative
14	Progressive	Progressive	44	Conservative	Conservative
15	Progressive	Progressive	45	Conservative	Conservative
16	Progressive	Progressive	46	Conservative	Other
17	Progressive	Other	47	Conservative	Conservative
18	Progressive	Progressive	48	Conservative	Other
19	Progressive	Progressive	49	Conservative	Progressive
20	Progressive	Progressive	50	Conservative	Conservative
21	Progressive	Progressive	51	Conservative	Conservative
22	Progressive	Progressive	52	Conservative	Conservative
23	Progressive	Other	53	Conservative	Progressive
24	Progressive	Other	54	Conservative	Progressive
25	Progressive	Progressive	55	Conservative	Conservative
26	Progressive	Progressive	56	Conservative	Conservative
27	Progressive	Conservative	57	Conservative	Other
28	Progressive	Progressive	58	Conservative	Conservative
29	Progressive	Progressive	59	Conservative	Conservative
30	Progressive	Progressive	60	Conservative	Other

(a) Which of these variables would you consider to be independent and which dependent? What are their respective levels of measurement?

(b) Construct a bivariate table to describe this sample result, either by hand or on SPSS, or both. Looking at these raw figures, do you suspect a dependence between these variables? If so, how would you describe it in plain English?

(c) Conduct a chi-square test to test your hypotheses about independence.

16.6 In earlier chapters we compared hypothetical samples of children from Australia, Canada, Singapore, and Britain, in terms of the amount of television they watch. Assume that this variable was not measured at the interval/ratio level, but rather on an ordinal scale. The results of this survey are:

Amount of TV	Country				
	Canada	Australia	Britain	Singapore	Total
Low	23	25	28	28	104
Medium	32	34	39	33	138
High	28	30	40	35	133
Total	83	89	107	96	375

Can we say that the amount of TV watched is independent of country of residence?

16.7 A sample of 162 men between the ages of 40 and 65 years was taken and the state of health of each man was recorded. Each man was also asked whether he smoked on a regular basis. The results were crosstabulated using SPSS:

```
HEALTH  Health Level  by  SMOKE  Smoking Habit

                      SMOKE          Page 1 of 1
            Count   |
            Exp Val |Doesn't  Does Smo
            Col Pct |Smoke     ke          Row
                    |   0  |    1  | Total
HEALTH      --------+--------+--------+
                1   |   13  |   34  |   47
  Poor           |   28.1 |   ?   |   ?%
                 |   13.4%|   ?%  |
            +--------+--------+
                2   |   22  |   19  |   41
  Fair           |   ?   |   ?   |   ?%
                 |   ?%  |   ?%  |
            +--------+--------+
                3   |   35  |   9   |   44
  Good           |   ?   |   ?   |   ?%
                 |   ?%  |   ?%  |
            +--------+--------+
                4   |   27  |   3   |   30
  Very Good      |   ?   |   ?   |   ?%
                 |   ?%  |   ?%  |
            +--------+--------+
            Column      97      65      162
            Total     59.9%   40.1%   100.0%
```

(a) What are the variables and what are their respective levels of measurement?

(b) Should we characterize any possible relationship in terms of one variable being dependent and the other independent? Justify your answer.

(c) In the table, only the top-left cell is complete. Fill in the values for the column percentages and the expected values if the null hypothesis of independence is true, for the rest of the cells, and the row totals percentages.

(d) Looking at the column percentages you have calculated, do you think that differences in health level between smokers and non-smokers could be the result of sampling variation rather than a difference in the population?

(e) Conduct a chi-square test of independence on these data? Does it confirm your answer to (d)?

(f) Enter the data into SPSS yourself and conduct a chi-square test. Are any of the conditions for conducting a chi-square test violated?

16.8 The following information was obtained from a survey of 50 'blue-collar' and 50 'white-collar' workers. The survey asked respondents if they could sing the National Anthem from start to finish. The results are:

'Blue collar'
Yes   29
No   21
'White collar'
Yes   22
No   28

Arrange these data into a bivariate table, and conduct a chi-square test of independence. Conduct a two-sample test for proportions on the same data and compare your results (optional).

Part 2

Inferential statistics

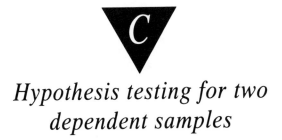

C

*Hypothesis testing for two
dependent samples*

The *t*-test for the mean difference

Dependent and independent samples

In Chapters 13–16 we looked at inference tests for two or more **independent** samples.

> **Independent samples** are those in which the cases that make up one sample do not determine the cases that make-up other samples.

However, there are situations in which the condition of independence needs to be violated. We sometimes want to link cases in one sample with specific cases in another sample, so that if a certain case is included in one sample this necessitates a specific case being included in the other sample. These are called **dependent samples**.

> **Dependent samples** are those in which the criteria of selection in one sample are affected by the criteria of selection in other samples.

There are generally two situations in which such dependence is required:

- **When the same subject is observed under two different conditions**, such as in a before-and-after experiment (sometimes called a pre-test–post-test design). A new drug may be tested on participants in a study. If a person is included in the 'before treatment' sample, then that person will also be included in the 'after treatment' sample. The measurements of each person in the 'before' sample is then matched with their respective measurement after receiving the new drug.
- **When two different subjects are linked for some special reason** An example may be where we want to compare the amount of television watched by a parent with the amount of television watched by his or her particular child. This is called a matched-pairs technique.

It is clear that in either situation the make-up of one of the samples determines the make-up of the other sample. If we choose a certain set of parents, we cannot choose any set of children to compare them with: the sample needs to be comprised of the children of the people making up the parent sample.

The advantage of a dependent sample method is that it controls in a loose fashion for other variables that might affect the dependent variable. For example, we might be interested in whether parents and children differ in the amount of TV they watch. If we take two independent samples of parents and children and compare the means *for the samples as a whole*, we might find that there is a statistically significant difference. But this might not be due to family status. There might be another variable, such as socioeconomic status, that affects TV watching, and because our sample of parents has more cases from one socioeconomic group than the sample of children, a difference has emerged.

It might be safe to assume, however, that any given parent-and-child pair falls into the same socioeconomic group. By taking parent-and-child pairs, therefore, and looking at the difference *for each pair*, the effect of socio-economic status is mitigated. In effect we are saying that all other variables that might determine TV watching are the same for each member of a given pair, and therefore only family relationship differs between them.

The dependent samples *t*-test for the mean difference

To illustrate the use of a paired-sample *t*-test we will work through the following example. A survey of 10 families is conducted and a parent from each house-hold and a child from each household are asked to keep a diary of the amount of TV they watch during a set time period. For each parent–child pair the amount of TV watched in minutes is recorded (Table 17.1).

Table 17.1   Amount of TV watched by household pair

Household	Minutes of TV watched by child	Minutes of TV watched by parent
1	45	23
2	56	25
3	73	43
4	53	26
5	27	21
6	34	29
7	76	32
8	21	23
9	54	25
10	43	21
Mean	$\bar{X} = \dfrac{\Sigma X}{N} = 48.2$	$\bar{X} = \dfrac{\Sigma X}{N} = 26.8$

Since the variable of interest, amount of TV watching, is measured at the interval/ratio level, the mean for each sample has been calculated. If we are comparing *independent* samples of adults and children, we then conduct a *t*-test on the difference between these two sample means. This procedure for the independent sample *t*-test can be summarized as follows:

1   Calculate the mean for *each* sample.
2   Then calculate the difference between the two sample means.

However, here we have selected these two samples so that we can match each member of one sample with a member of the other sample. To conduct a dependent-samples *t*-test, we reverse the order of the two steps:

1   Calculate the difference for each pair of cases (*D*).
2   Then calculate the mean of the differences ($\overline{X}_D$).

To put it even more succinctly, independent-sample *t*-tests look at the *difference between the means*, while dependent-sample *t*-tests look at the *mean of the differences*.

Table 17.2 goes through the first step involved in performing a dependent-samples *t*-test by calculating the difference in the amount of TV watched for each pair:

Table 17.2   Difference in the amount of TV watched by household pair

Household	*Difference in minutes of TV watched (D)*
1	45 – 23 = 22
2	56 – 25 = 31
3	73 – 43 = 30
4	53 – 26 = 27
5	27 – 21 = 6
6	34 – 29 = 5
7	76 – 32 = 44
8	21 – 23 = –2
9	54 – 25 = 29
10	43 – 21 = 22
Mean difference	$\overline{X}_D = \dfrac{\Sigma D}{N} = 21.4$

Let us assume that in the population as a whole there is no difference in the amount of TV watched between parents and their respective children. *If* there is no difference between a parent and her or his child in terms of the amount of TV watched, the average of these differences will also be zero. However, when sampling from such a population, occasionally we might find a parent who watches more TV than their child, and occasionally we might find that a child watches a little more than his or her parent, but *if the null hypothesis of no difference is true*, on average the positive differences will cancel out the negative differences. The null hypothesis is written in the following way:

$$H_0: \mu_D = 0$$

Since we are only working with samples, as we have just noted, it is not unreasonable to expect that random variation might result in a few extra households in which the parent watches less TV than the corresponding child, or vice versa. The bigger the difference between the sample result and the expected result of zero, though, the less likely that this will be due to random variation: the more likely that it reflects an underlying difference between parents and their children.

In this example the average of the differences is 21.4 minutes. Should this difference between the samples cause us to reject the hypothesis that there is no difference between the populations?

The formulas involved in conducting a *t*-test of paired samples are:

$$t = \frac{\overline{X}_D}{s_D \big/ \sqrt{N-1}}$$

where:

$$s_D = \sqrt{\frac{\sum D^2 - (\sum D)^2 \big/ N}{N-1}}$$

Note that in these formulas N refers to the number of pairs, and not the total number of cases. In other words, in this example, $N=10$, even though we have a total of 20 cases made up of 10 parents and 10 children. The sample score will be:

$$s_D = \sqrt{\frac{\sum D^2 - (\sum D)^2 \big/ N}{N-1}}$$

$$= \sqrt{\frac{6400 - 45\,796 \big/ 10}{10-1}}$$

$$= 14.222$$

$$t_{sample} = \frac{\overline{X}_D}{s_D \big/ \sqrt{N-1}}$$

$$= \frac{21.4}{14.222 \big/ \sqrt{10-1}}$$

$$= 4.758$$

Here we have 9 degrees of freedom (the 10 pairs minus 1). At an 0.05 level of significance, the critical score is shown in Table 17.3.

Table 17.3   Distribution of *t*

Degrees	Level of significance for one-tail test				
of freedom	0.10	0.05	0.025	0.01	0.005
(df)	Level of significance for two-tail test				
	0.20	0.10	0.05	0.02	0.01
1	3.078	6.314	12.706	31.821	63.657
2	1.886	2.290	4.303	6.965	9.925
3	1.638	2.353	3.182	4.541	5.841
4	1.533	2.132	2.776	3.747	4.604
5	1.476	2.015	2.571	3.365	4.032
6	1.440	1.943	2.447	3.143	3.707
7	1.415	1.895	2.365	2.998	3.499
8	1.397	1.860	2.306	2.896	3.355
9	1.383	1.833	2.262	2.821	3.250
10	1.372	1.812	2.228	2.764	3.169
. . .	. . .	. . .	. . .	. . .	. . .
∞	1.282	1.645	1.960	2.326	2.576

$$t_{critical} = \pm 2.262$$

If we graph these sample and critical scores for *t* we can see that the null should be rejected (Figure 17.1).

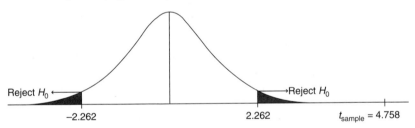

Reject H_0 ←   →Reject H_0

−2.262   2.262 $t_{sample} = 4.758$

Figure 17.1   The distribution of *t*, *df* = 9, with α = 0.05

There is a significant difference in the amount of TV watched between parents and their children.

The dependent samples *t*-test using SPSS

Filename 17.sav   In order for SPSS to do this same calculation, we first need to note the special way in which data are entered in order to conduct a dependent-sample *t*-test. When coding data for paired samples, **each pair has to be treated as one case**. In other words, **the information for each parent-and-child pair has to appear along the same row of data**. The unit of analysis is the pair, *not* the individual people. Thus, in our example, there will only be 10 rows of data (Figure SPSS.K).

File Edit Data Transform

1 :parenttv 23

	parenttv	childtv	var
1	23	45	
2	25	56	
3	43	73	
4	26	53	
5	21	27	
6	29	34	
7	32	76	
8	23	21	
9	25	54	
10	21	43	
11			
12			
13			

Figure SPSS.K

Each row has an entry for the amount of TV the child watches and the amount of TV the parent watches. By placing each pair on the same row of data, we can match their responses during the analysis. This produces a column for the amount of TV the parent watches, which is given the variable name **parenttv**, and a second column for the amount of TV the child watches, which has been given the variable name **childtv**.

If we were treating the two samples, on the other hand, as independent, we enter all 20 scores in the same column, so that there are 20 rows of data. We would then have a second column for the variable indicating the status of each case within a family — either parent or child. Thus an SPSS data file for an independent-samples *t*-test will be as shown in Figure SPSS.L.

Once data have been entered in the appropriate way for a dependent-samples *t*-test, which SPSS calls a paired-samples *t*-test, the following set of instructions is used (Table 17.4).

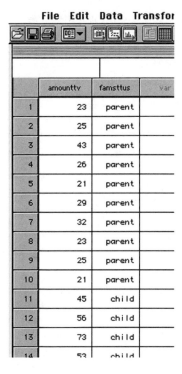

Figure SPSS.L

Table 17.4   Paired-samples *t*-test using SPSS

SPSS command/action	Comments
1 Select from the menu **Statistics/Compare Means/ Paired-Samples T Test...**	This will bring up a window headed **Paired-Samples T Test**. In the top left of the window will be an area with a list of the variables entered in the data page
2 Click on **parenttv** and while holding down the command key click on **childtv**	These two variable names will be highlighted
3 Click on ➤	This will paste the highlighted variables into the area headed **Paired Variables:**
4 Click on **OK**	

If these procedures are followed, these results will appear in the output window:

```
t-tests for Paired Samples
```

Variable	Number of pairs	Corr	2-tail Sig	Mean	SD	SE of Mean
CHILDTV Minutes of TV Watched - Child				48.2000	18.054	5.709
	10	.699	.024			
PARENTTV Minutes of TV Watched - Pare				26.8000	6.647	2.102

Paired Differences					
Mean	SD	SE of Mean	t-value	df	2-tail Sig
21.4000	14.222	4.497	4.76	9	.001
95% CI (11.729, 31.071)					

The output begins by calculating the overall sample means: 48.2 minutes for the 10 children and 26.8 minutes for the 10 parents. The next part of the output goes on to the dependent-samples t-test, and confirms the calculations above. The mean difference is calculated as 21.4 minutes. The t-score for this value is 4.76, which with 9 degrees of freedom will occur, if the null hypothesis of no difference is true, less than one time in every thousand samples (0.001). This is well below any normal alpha level, such as 0.05 or 0.01 so we reject the null hypothesis of no difference.

The output also provides the 95 per cent confidence interval for the estimate of the difference. The lower limit of the estimate is 11.729 while the upper limit is 31.071. We can use this information to conduct the hypothesis test. Since the interval does not include the value of zero, we can conclude that the difference in the population as to the amount of TV watched by parents and their children is not zero.

Exercises

17.1 What is the mean difference for the following 10 pairs of observations? What is the standard error? Conduct a dependent-samples *t*-test on the following data, with a 0.05 level of significance:

Pair	Observation 1	Observation 2
1	12	15
2	10	13
3	8	13
4	14	14
5	12	18
6	15	13
7	14	18
8	9	9
9	18	11
10	13	14

17.2 Test the following hypotheses using the data provided:

(a)

$H_0: \mu_D = 0$
$H_a: \mu_D \neq 0$
$\overline{X}_D = 2.3$
$s_D = 1.4$
$N = 20$
$\alpha = 0.10$

(b)

$H_0: \mu_D = 0$
$H_a: \mu_D < 0$
$\overline{X}_D = -3.2$
$s_D = 20$
$N = 41$
$\alpha = 0.05$

17.3 A company wants to investigate whether changes in work organization can significantly improve productivity levels. It randomly selects 10 workplaces and measures productivity levels in terms of units per hour produced. It then introduces a program in these workplaces giving workers greater discretion over conditions and job structure, and measures productivity levels 6 months later. The results are:

Workplace	Productivity before change	Productivity after change
1	120	165
2	121	154
3	145	120
4	112	155
5	145	164
6	130	132
7	134	154
8	126	162
9	137	130
10	128	142

Has the program significantly improved productivity levels (note the form of the alternative hypothesis)?

17.4 The following data list the asking and selling prices (in dollars) for a random sample of 10 three-bedroom homes sold during a certain period:

Home	Asking price ($)	Selling price ($)
1	140000	144300
2	172500	169800
3	159900	155000
4	148000	150000
5	129900	129900
6	325000	315000
7	149700	146000
8	147900	149200
9	259000	259000
10	223900	219000

Why is a dependent-samples test appropriate in this situation? Using a paired-samples *t*-test, do people receive the price they want when selling their home? Enter these data in SPSS and conduct this test. Compare the results with your hand calculations.

17.5 Consider the following data. A nutritionist is interested in the effect that a particular combination of exercise and diet has on weight loss. She selected a group of people and measured their weight in kilograms before and after a program of diet and exercise. A paired-samples *t*-test was conducted on SPSS with the following results:

t-tests for Paired Samples

Variable	Number of pairs	Corr	2-tail Sig	Mean	SD	SE of Mean
POSTTEST	Weight in Kg Post Test			66.4286	9.641	2.104
	21	.974	.000			
PRETEST	Weight in Kg Pre-Test			70.0952	11.189	2.442

Paired Differences						
Mean	SD	SE of Mean	t-value	df	2-tail Sig
-3.6667	2.817	.615	-5.97	20	.000
95% CI (-4.892, -2.441)					

From this output determine the:
(a) variable name and variable labels assigned to the before and after measurements;
(b) number of pairs in the test;
(c) mean weight for the pre-test sample;
(d) mean weight for the post-test sample;
(e) mean difference between the two samples;
(f) value of t_{sample} and the number of degrees of freedom;
(g) probability of obtaining this mean difference if the null hypothesis of no difference is true;
(h) upper limit of the confidence interval for the estimate of the difference;
(i) lower limit of the confidence interval for the estimate of the difference.
What should the nutritionist conclude about the effect of the program?

17.6 From the previous question if this nutritionist considered an average weight loss of 5 kg or more to be the measure of success of this program, can we say that the program was successful? What does this say about the difference between practical and statistical significance?

Non-parametric tests for dependent samples

The choice of tests for dependent samples, as with tests for independent samples, is affected by the level at which the test variable is measured. For interval/ratio data, in Chapter 17, we used a *t*-test for the mean difference. This chapter will consider non-parametric tests that can be applied to dependent samples compared in terms of nominal or ordinal data:

- **The McNemar test/Sign test**   These are used when the test variable is arranged into a binomial distribution (often after collapsing values).
- **The Wilcoxon signed-ranks test**   This is used when the test variable is measured at least at the ordinal level.

The McNemar test for binomial distributions

Two tests are available to compare paired samples in terms of a binomial variable: the McNemar test and the sign test. These two tests are equivalent, in the sense that they will always produce the same *p*-value for any given difference between the samples. In the text we will detail the McNemar test, since the SPSS output for this test provides slightly more information than with a sign test. After working through the McNemar test we will conduct a sign test on the same data to show the difference in the presentation of the results.

A binomial variable, such as a coin toss, only has two possible outcomes. The McNemar test compares the outcome for each case in one sample with the outcome for the respective pair in the other sample. For example, a political scientist might be interested in whether televised debates between political candidates have an effect on voting intentions. She randomly selects 137 people and asks them whether they plan to vote Progressive or Conservative at the forthcoming election, ignoring all other candidates. She then asks the same question, *after* these same 137 people have watched a televised debate between these two candidates.

In comparing each individual in the 'before' stage with his or her own particular response after the debate, there are four possibilities:

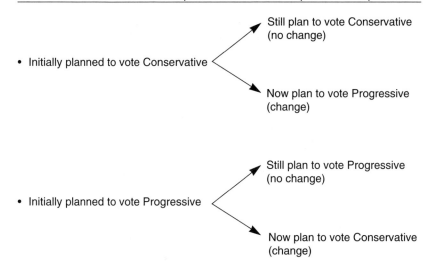

We can draw up a little table to illustrate these possibilities (Table 18.1).

Table 18.1   Joint distribution of survey results

		Before	
		Progressive	*Conservative*
After	*Conservative*	(a) Change	(b) No change
	Progressive	(c) No change	(d) Change

The McNemar test only considers those pairs for which a change has occurred, and analyses whether any changes tend to occur in one direction (e.g. Conservative to Progressive) *or* the other (Progressive to Conservative). The total number of pairs registering a change will be cells (a) and (d) in the table. If the changes induced by watching the TV debate did not favor a shift in one direction or the other, then we should *expect* to find 50 per cent of the total number of changes in cell (a), and 50 per cent in cell (d).

Of course, random variation will cause samples to differ from the expected result, even if the debate did not affect the overall opinion of the population. However, it is very unlikely (although possible) to randomly select a sample where 90 per cent of all pairs registering a change in opinion were in cell (a), even if in the whole population the changes are similar in either direction. The greater the difference between the observed cell frequencies and the expected cell frequencies, the less likely that such an event can be attributed to sampling error.

This discussion of expected and observed cell frequencies should sound similar to the chi-square test. In fact the McNemar test (with large samples) is a chi-square test for the difference between expected and observed cell frequencies. This test statistic is calculated using the following formula:

$$\chi^2_M = \frac{(N_a - N_d - 1)^2}{N_a + N_d}$$

where:

N_a is the observed number of cases in cell a

N_d is the observed number of cases in cell d.

The distribution of responses to this hypothetical study are as shown in Table 18.2.

Table 18.2   Voting intentions before and after TV debate

		Before	
		Progressive	Conservative
After	Conservative	27	28
	Progressive	27	55

We can immediately see the total number of cases that *did not change* their opinion was:

$$27 + 28 = 55$$

whereas the total number of cases that *did* record a change was:

$$55 + 27 = 82$$

Obviously the sample result differs from the expected result, but is the difference big enough to warrant rejecting the null hypothesis? Using the formula for the McNemar statistic we get:

$$\chi^2_M = \frac{(N_a - N_d - 1)^2}{N_a + N_d}$$

$$= \frac{(55 - 27 - 1)^2}{55 + 27}$$

$$= \frac{27^2}{82}$$

$$= 8.89$$

From the table for the distribution of chi-square, with 1 degree of freedom, the critical level of chi-square at the 0.01 level is 6.635 (see Figure 18.1). This leads us to reject the null hypothesis. The TV debate does have an effect on voting intentions. Looking back at the table of raw numbers, it is clear that the direction of change is from Conservative to Progressive.

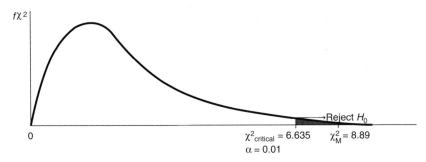

$\chi^2_{critical} = 6.635$ $\chi^2_M = 8.89$
$\alpha = 0.01$

Figure 18.1   The distribution of chi-square, with $df = 1$

The McNemar test using SPSS

Filename 18–1.sav   The data for the previous example have been entered into SPSS. The scores for voting intention before the debate have been given the variable name **before** and those after the debate have been given the variable name **after**. The value labels for both these variables are **1=Progressive** and **2=Conservative**. (See Table 18.3.)

Table 18.3   McNemar test on SPSS

SPSS command/action	Comments
1 From the menu select **Statistics/Nonparametric Tests/2 Related Samples...**	This will bring up a window headed **Two Related Samples Tests**. You will notice that in the area to the bottom-left of the window headed **Test Type** the small square next to **Wilcoxon** is selected. This indicates that the Wilcoxon test for two dependent samples is the default test. Here we want to conduct a McNemar test so we need to 'unselect' Wilcoxon and select McNemar instead
2 Click on the square next to **Wilcoxon**	This will remove × from the square
3 Click on the square next to **McNemar**	This will place × in the square, indicating that it is the selected test
4 Click on **after** and while holding down the command key click on **before**	These two variable names will be highlighted
5 Click on ➤	This will paste the highlighted variables into the area headed **Test Pairs:** This indicates that responses for these two variables will be paired
6 Click on **OK**	

The output from this set of instructions will be:

```
- - - - - McNemar Test

        AFTER       Voting Intention post Debate
    with BEFORE     Voting Intention pre Debate


                       2         1          Cases          137
                  |---------|---------|
               1 |    27   |    28   |     Chi-Square    8.8902
    AFTER         |---------|---------|
               2 |    27   |    55   |     Significance   .0029
                  |---------|---------|
```

The difference between the observed and expected frequencies produces a chi-square value for the sample of 8.8902.[1] With 1 degree of freedom, the exact probability of getting this sample chi-square just by random variation is 0.0029. This is well below any normal alpha level such as 0.05. The researcher concludes that the TV debate is likely to favor a change in opinion, and this change appears to be from Conservative to Progressive.

Before finishing the discussion of the McNemar test, it is worth elaborating on the relationship between this test and the sign test. In Chapter 16 we noted that the chi-square test on a 2-by-2 table is mathematically equivalent to a binomial z-test. The sign test in fact conducts a binomial z-test rather than a chi-square test by comparing the proportion of positive changes (or negative changes) with the test proportion of 0.5. The probability obtained in this way is exactly the same as that from the McNemar test. If we conduct a sign test on the above example the result will be:

```
- - - - - Sign Test

        AFTER       Voting Intention post Debate
    with BEFORE     Voting Intention pre Debate


            Cases

              55   - Diffs (BEFORE LT AFTER)          Z =    2.9817
              27   + Diffs (BEFORE GT AFTER)
              55     Ties                        2-Tailed P =    .0029
             ---
             137     Total
```

The two-tailed probability of 0.0029 on the sample z-score of 2.9817 is the same as that for chi-square in the McNemar test. Therefore the same decision is made regarding the null hypothesis, regardless of which test is used. The advantage of the McNemar test is that the crosstab that is generated as part of the SPSS output provides a more detailed breakdown

---

[1]From Chapter 16 we know that chi-square tests are not appropriate when expected cell frequencies are 5 or less. This rule also applies to the McNemar test, and the same correction is taken. When cell sizes are small, SPSS will automatically conduct the test using the binomial approximation to the normal curve, and print a two-tail probability associated with this approximation.

of the pairs than the output that comes with the sign test. This allows us to see in which direction any changes move.

Example

A study is conducted to investigate attitudes toward computer games. Fifty people are randomly chosen and asked if they believed video games to be of any educational value, with responses restricted to 'Yes' or 'No'. After playing a range of video games each person is asked the same question. The distribution of responses was recorded (Table 18.4).

Table 18.4   Attitude to video games before and after playing

		Before	
		No	Yes
After	Yes	10	7
	No	15	18

Substituting this information into the formula for the McNemar test:

$$\chi^2_M = \frac{(N_a - N_d - 1)^2}{N_a + N_d}$$

$$= \frac{(10 - 18 - 1)^2}{10 + 18}$$

$$= 1.75$$

From the distribution for chi-square table, the critical value with 1 degree of freedom is 3.841. We therefore do not reject the null hypothesis: playing video games does not seem to change people's attitude in one particular way or the other.

The Wilcoxon signed-ranks test for ordinal data

In Chapter 15 we saw that hypothesis tests for ordinal data use the *ranks* of the cases rather than the raw scores. The same principle applies when working with ordinal data and dependent samples. Since we can't calculate a mean on the raw scores, we firstly rank the pairs of cases and use these rank scores in the calculations. For dependent samples compared on an ordinal scale the appropriate test is the Wilcoxon signed-ranks test, and is very similar in logic to the Wilcoxon rank sum test for independent samples (see Table 18.5).

Table 18.5   Ordinal data tests for two samples

Type of samples	Test
Independent	Wilcoxon rank sum (W)
Dependent	Wilcoxon signed-ranks (T)

For example, assume that the researcher who conducted the McNemar test to assess people's attitude to video games (in the example above) is dissatisfied with the results. She suspects that playing video games really does affect a person's attitude to the educational value of such games, and that the simple binomial scale she used in the original study was not sensitive enough to detect this change. She therefore conducts another study involving 15 people who are asked to rate on a 10-point scale whether they believe video games have any educational value, with 1 indicating no educational value and 10 indicating very high educational value. Each of these 15 people is then asked to play a variety of video games and again rate whether he or she believes video games are of educational benefit. What effect does actually playing the game have on opinion?

The scores for each person, before and after playing, are recorded in Table 18.6, together with the difference, for each pair.

Table 18.6   Before and after attitude to video games

Case	Before	After	Difference in score
1	3	5	+2
2	5	5	0
3	2	8	+6
4	3	4	+1
5	8	7	−1
6	6	3	−3
7	4	4	0
8	7	6	−1
9	2	7	+5
10	6	7	+1
11	1	9	+8
12	9	7	−2
13	8	1	−7
14	5	5	0
15	6	2	−4

The first step is to exclude the cases with no change in scores. As with the McNemar test, cases that show no change are not used in the analysis. Here cases 2, 7, and 14 record no change in their scores before and after.

It would be tempting to simply calculate an average change in scores and conduct a *t*-test on the difference. However, we are working with an ordinal scale and such averages are not appropriate. Instead we take a slightly more difficult route. We rank the cases, starting with those registering the smallest change in scores (this will be cases 4, 8, 5 and 10, which each registered a change of 1) to the largest change (case 11 with a change of 8). Pairs, that is, are ordered according to the absolute difference between their 'Before' and 'After' scores (Table 18.7).

Table 18.7   Ordering of all non-tied pairs

Pair number	4	5	8	10	1	12	6	15	9	3	13	11
Difference	+1	−1	−1	+1	+2	−2	−3	−4	+5	+6	−7	+8
Rank	2.5	2.5	2.5	2.5	5.5	5.5	7	8	9	10	11	12

Notice that cases that have the same absolute change in scores have been assigned an average rank. For example, four cases each changed their score by 1 point on the scale. Since collectively these cases occupy ranks 1,2,3, and 4, the average rank for these four cases is:

$$\frac{1 + 2 + 3 + 4}{4} = 2.5$$

If playing video games has no effect on attitudes regarding their educational value, there should not be a tendency for pairs with either positive or negative changes to bunch up at one end of the ranking or the other. Another way of assessing this is to compare the rank sum for pairs registering a positive change in attitude to the rank sum for pairs registering a negative change in attitude. If the positive and negative changes are equally distributed through the ranks, the sum of these ranks will be equal, and can be calculated using the following formula:

$$\mu_T = \frac{N(N + 1)}{4}$$

$$\mu_T = \frac{12(12 + 1)}{4} = 39$$

This is the value we use for stating the null hypothesis:

$$H_0: \ \mu_T = 39$$

The value of μ_T is the rank sum we expect from samples drawn from a population where attitude to video games does not change systematically in one direction or the other. However, even if this is the case, random samples drawn from such a population will not *always* produce a value of 39. We need to compare this hypothesized value with the sample statistic we obtain, and assess whether any difference can be attributed to random variation.

We derive this sample statistic by separating out those cases that have a positive change (increase) in their score after playing the video games from those cases that have a negative change (reduction) in score. We then sum the ranks for each group (Table 18.8).

Table 18.8   Ordering of negative change pairs

Pair number	5	8	12	6	15	13
Difference	−1	−1	−2	−3	−4	−7
Rank	2.5	2.5	5.5	7	8	11

Sum of negative ranks: $\Sigma R_- = 2.5 + 2.5 + 5.5 + 7 + 8 + 11 = 36.5$

Table 18.9   Ordering of negative change pairs

Pair number	4	10	1	9	3	11
Difference	+1	+1	+2	+5	+6	+8
Rank	2.5	2.5	5.5	9	10	12

Sum of positive ranks: $\Sigma R_+ = 2.5 + 2.5 + 5.5 + 9 + 10 + 12 = 41.5$

In this example we have rank sums of 36.5 and 41.5. What is the probability of obtaining such a sample result if the null hypothesis is true? The sample statistic, called Wilcoxon's T, is the smallest rank sum, which in this case is the rank sum for the positives. We conduct a z-test on the difference between the value of μ_T and the sample value, T:

$$z = \frac{T - \mu_T}{\sigma_T}$$

$$\sigma_T = \sqrt{\frac{N(N + 1)(2N + 1)}{24}}$$

If we substitute the data from the example into these equations, we get:

$$\sigma_T = \sqrt{\frac{N(N + 1)(2N + 1)}{24}}$$

$$= \sqrt{\frac{12(12 + 1)(2 \times 12 + 1)}{24}}$$

$$= \sqrt{162.5}$$

$$= 12.75$$

$$z = \frac{T - \mu_T}{\sigma_T}$$

$$= \frac{36.5 - 39}{12.75}$$

$$= -0.1961$$

This value for z, from the table for the area under the standard normal curve, has a two-tail probability of 0.8445. We cannot reject the null hypothesis since differences observed in the pairs could easily come about through sampling error when drawing from a population in which playing video games has no effect on attitude to their educational value.

The Wilcoxon signed-ranks test using SPSS

Filename 18–2.sav   The data from the previous example have been entered into SPSS. The variable names are **before** and **after**. The actions required to conduct this test are listed in Table 18.10.

Table 18.10   Wilcoxon signed-ranks test on SPSS

SPSS command/action	Comments
1 From the menu select **Statistics/Nonparametric Tests/2 Related Samples...**	This will bring up a window headed **Two Related Samples Tests**. You will notice that in the area to the bottom-left of the window headed **Test Type** the small square next to **Wilcoxon** is selected. This indicates that the Wilcoxon test for two dependent samples is the default test
2 Click on **after** and while holding down the command key click on **before**	These two variable names will be highlighted
3 Click on ➤	This will paste the highlighted variables into the area headed **Test Pairs:**
4 Click on **OK**	

These instructions will produce the following output:

```
- - - - - Wilcoxon Matched-Pairs Signed-Ranks Test

      AFTER      Attitude after Videos
with BEFORE      Attitude pre Videos


   Mean Rank     Cases

       6.92          6  - Ranks (BEFORE LT AFTER)
       6.08          6  + Ranks (BEFORE GT AFTER)
                     3    Ties (BEFORE EQ AFTER)
                    --
                    15    Total

      Z =    -.1961             2-Tailed P =  .8445
```

The SPSS output gives us the same results as those we calculated by hand. First, there are six pairs that registered an increase in score: BEFORE LT AFTER (the LT is short for 'Less Than'). There are also six pairs that registered a decrease: BEFORE GT AFTER; and three pairs whose score did not change: BEFORE EQ AFTER.

Second, SPSS calculates the mean rank for the positives and negatives. If we multiply these mean ranks by the number of cases in each group we get the sum of ranks calculated above (although there is some slight difference due to rounding):

$$\Sigma R_+ = 6.92 \times 6 = 41.5$$
$$\Sigma R_- = 6.08 \times 6 = 36.5$$

The z-test conducted on the rank sums indicates that we should not reject the null hypothesis, given that the probability of 0.8445 is greater than the alpha level of 0.05. In other words, even if video-game playing makes no difference in attitude toward their educational value, we will still get sample results such as this more than 8 times out of 10.

Exercises

18.1 Conduct a McNemar test on the following data ($\alpha = 0.05$):

(a)

		Before	
		1	2
After	2	34	28
	1	27	22

(b)

		Before	
		1	2
After	2	50	17
	1	12	55

(c)

		Before	
		1	2
After	2	79	12
	1	32	134

18.2 Brothers and sisters are matched and asked if they play regular sport. The results are:

		Brother	
		Yes	No
Sister	Yes	18	11
	No	16	15

Conduct a McNemar test to assess whether there is a difference between brothers and sisters in terms of sport playing.
These data are entered in SPSS, using value labels:
Yes = 1
No = 2
Replace ? in the SPSS output with your results:

```
- - - - - McNemar Test

      BROTHER     brother plays sport
  with SISTER     sister plays sport


                      SISTER
                    2         1          Cases           60
                +---------+---------+
             1 |    ? |      18 |      Chi-Square       ?
  BROTHER       +---------+---------+
             2 |   15 |       ? |      Significance    .4414
                +---------+---------+
```

18.3 The following are scores of 12 matched pairs in a before-and-after experiment:

Before	After
75	65
63	67
82	51
37	43
46	47
59	61
39	52
33	85

Use the Wilcoxon signed-ranks test to assess whether there is a difference (use $\alpha = 0.05$).

18.4 Ten people are asked to rate the effectiveness of two training programs, with 1 equal to 'Very poor' and 10 equal to 'Very good'. The responses are:

Prog. 1	Prog. 2
3	5
2	6
3	7
2	7
1	4
4	2
5	5
1	8
6	9

Can we say that one program is preferred over another, at a 0.01 level of significance?

Enter your results where they would appear if this test was conducted on SPSS.

```
- - - - - Wilcoxon Matched-Pairs Signed-Ranks Test

     PROG1

with PROG2


    Mean Rank     Cases

        1.50         ?   - Ranks  (PROG2 LT PROG1)
        4.93         ?   + Ranks  (PROG2 GT PROG1)
                     ?     Ties   (PROG2 EQ PROG1)
                     -
                     9     Total

        Z =   ?                2-Tailed P =      ?
```

Enter this data on SPSS and confirm your results.

Part

3

Measures of association

19

Introduction to measures of association

We have previously made the general point that statistical significance and theoretical or practical significance are not the same. We may, for example, find a relationship between age and exam grades. However, the mere fact that there is a difference in exam scores between age groups gives no guidance as to whether the relationship between these variables is very strong or very weak. Should it warrant running separate classes for students in different age groups? Does it justify a change in the current thinking about education and cognitive skills? Tests of significance do not help much in answering such questions. They do not measure the strength of a relationship, but rather indicate whether a relationship between two variables exists in the population. Measures of association, on the other hand, are designed to provide such information.

Measures of association as descriptive statistics

Measures of association comprise a class of descriptive statistics that quantify a relationship between variables.

> **Association** exists if the distribution of one variable is related to the distribution of another variable. **Measures of association** indicate, in quantitative terms, the extent to which a change in the value of one variable is related to a change in the value of another variable.

When age increases does height also increase (or decrease)? Is a change in religious beliefs associated with a change in attitude to capital punishment? Measures of association give us precise numerical answers to such questions. If such a measure is derived from a sample, we then refer to inferential statistics to see whether the association holds in the population. To put it another way, measures of association try to quantify an observed relationship between variables, and tests of significance tell us whether this relationship exists in a population.

Unfortunately, putting the concept of association into practice is a slippery problem. Working with measures of association can be a very frustrating experience because there are a large number to choose from, each with its own peculiarities and limitations, and often they do not lead to the same result.

For example, many measures of association are sensitive to the decision as to which variable is designated as independent and which is dependent. Such measures are called **asymmetric**. We looked at some of the various ways in which two variables may be related in Chapter 16. Asymmetric measures are especially useful where there is strong reason to believe that the relationship is due to one variable being dependent on the other. If, on the other hand, we suspect that the relationship is not that of one-way dependence, we use other measures of association which take on the same value regardless of the variable that is specified to be independent and specified to be dependent. These are called **symmetric** measures.

Table 19.1 provides some guide for choosing between the measures of association detailed in the following chapters. As with inference tests the starting point for selecting a measure of association is the level at which each variable is measured. (Those wanting a more complete treatment of measures of association that covers the full range of measures available should consult either of the two following texts, which provide an excellent, although sometimes very technical, discussion: H.T. Reynolds, 1977, *The Analysis of Cross-Classifications,* The Free Press, New York; A.L. Liebetrau, 1983, *Measures of Association*, Sage Publications, Beverly Hills.)

Table 19.1 Measures of association

Lowest level of Measurement	Measures of association
Nominal	Cramer's *V* Lambda
Ordinal	Gamma Spearman's rank order correlation coefficient
Interval/ratio	Correlation coefficient/coefficient of determination

When two variables are measured at different levels, as a general rule, the choice of a measure of association will depend on the lowest level of measurement of the two. For example, in investigating whether there is an association between sex (nominal) and job satisfaction (ordinal) the lowest level of measurement of these two variables is nominal, and this will determine the measures of association that can be calculated.

It is important to remember that all that these measures do is detect association. They do not necessarily show the stronger relationship where one variable *causes* a change in another. For example, it may be the case that every day when the hands of my watch both point to 12 the sun is directly above me in the sky. There is an association between the two events, and we can calculate measures of this association. However, it is clear from this example that the stronger argument that one event causes the other cannot be sustained. We may suspect theoretically that one variable causes a change in the other, but the statistics we will learn here cannot prove causation.

When we investigate association between two variables we ask ourselves two questions:

- If an association exists, how strong is it?
- What is the pattern and, where appropriate, the direction of association?

If an association exists, how strong is it?

Usually when a test statistic such as chi-square is not equal to zero some pattern of association exists *in the sample*. But because test-statistics like chi-square, *z*-scores and *t*-scores are very sensitive to sample size, they are not always a good guide as to the strength of any association. We cannot say that a *t*-score of 5.6 reflects a stronger association than a *t*-score of 1.4, because the difference may be due to the relative sample sizes. We therefore calculate specific measures of association whose values are not affected by sample size.

These measures of association can be thought of as a numerical index that ranges between two extremes. One extreme is the case of **perfect association**. In the case of perfect association, cases with a particular value for one variable *all* have a certain value for the other variable. Table 19.2, illustrates the case of perfect association between hair color and productivity.

Table 19.2   Example of perfect association

Productivity	Hair color		
	Brown	Blonde	Red
High	0%	0%	100%
Moderate	0%	100%	0%
Low	100%	0%	0%

For this group of cases we can say that all the variation in the dependent variable (productivity) is explained by the variation in the independent variable (hair color): the reason why any two cases differ in terms of productivity can be explained just by referring to the difference in their hair color. In other words, given knowledge of a respondent's hair color we would know exactly where that respondent would fall on the productivity scale. Hair color thereby is, for this group of cases, a perfect predictor of productivity: knowing the color of a person's hair allows us to perfectly predict her or his productivity.

The opposite extreme is the case of no association: knowing the value of a case along one variable gives no indication as to its likely value on the other variable (Table 19.3).

Table 19.3   Example of no association

Productivity	Hair color		
	Brown	Blonde	Red
High	33.3%	33.3%	33.3%
Moderate	33.3%	33.3%	33.3%
Low	33.3%	33.3%	33.3%

In this example it is clear that knowledge of a respondent's hair color gives no guide as to productivity level.

It is ideal for measures of association to take on the value of 1 (or -1 where appropriate) in situations of perfect association, and zero for situations of no association:

Association when at least one variable is measured at the nominal level

Association when both variables are measured at least at the ordinal level

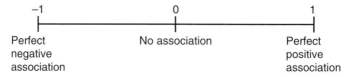

Such standardized scales provide a range of possible values that can be used for comparison. Unfortunately this is not always the case, and the cause of much of the frustration tied up with using measures of association. Some measures can take on values larger than 1, while others can take on the value of 1 where perfect association does not exist. Still other measures can take on a value of 0, even where an association is evident to the naked eye.

The pattern and/or direction of the association

When one of the variables studied is measured at the nominal level, it is only possible to talk about the **pattern** of the relationship. For example, in the previous discussion of perfect association we would conclude that red hair was associated with high productivity, blond hair was associated with moderate productivity, and brown hair with low productivity. But because we were working with a nominal scale (hair color) we couldn't talk about an increase or decrease in hair color being associated with an increase or decrease in productivity. It makes no sense to talk about hair color getting greater or smaller.

However, when both variables are measured at least at the ordinal level we can actually talk about the association having **direction**.

A **positive association** exists where movement along the scale of a variable in one direction is associated with a movement in the same direction along the scale of the other variable. Conversely, a **negative association** is one where movement along the scale of one variable is associated with a movement in the opposite direction along the scale of the other variable.

An example of a positive association is where exam scores increase with students' age: older students tend to have higher grades. A negative association is the opposite situation, where older students tend to get worse grades.

Measures of association and tests of significance

The difference between tests of significance and measures of association has already been touched on above. However, the nature of this difference is a great source of confusion, since the two sets of statistics sometimes *seem* to be doing the same job. The important thing to remember is that measures of association are *descriptive statistics* that capture some quality of the sample only. They tell us, *only for the cases for which we have information*, whether a change in the value of one variable is likely to be associated with a change in the value of another variable.

However, as with any descriptive statistic that has been calculated from a sample result, the particular value may be due to sampling error and not a result of some underlying relationship in the population from which the sample is drawn. For example, a sample might result in a measure of association with a value of 0.9 (indicating a very strong relationship within that set of cases) but what is the likelihood that in the population there is a zero association and the sample just happened to pick up a few odd, non-representative, cases? To answer this question we turn to inferential statistics such as chi-square, t, F, or z.

In practice, these two sets of statistics can be looked at in one of two ways.

- **Begin with the measures of association** We could look at the measure of association first and decide whether there is an association present in the data that is worth worrying about. For example, if a sample produced a measure of association of 0.02, this relationship is extremely weak and almost trivial. The further question of whether such an extremely weak association also holds in the population is pointless — if it did, so what? In this situation we wouldn't even bother referring to the inferential statistics to answer this last issue. It is analogous to finding that two groups have a difference in average height of 1 cm: a statistical difference exists in the sample that may or may not exist in the population, but who cares? On the other hand, where the measure of association indicates a relationship that is strong enough to be worth worrying about, we then undertake the inference test to see if the association observed in the sample holds in the population.
- **Begin with the test of significance** It might be of interest to find *any* significant relationship that holds in the population, regardless of how weak or strong the association proves to be. Only after having discovered a significant difference do we then proceed to the measures of association to give a guide as to the strength and pattern of association (and also possibly to check whether the significance is just the result of sample size).

In practice, with the common use of statistical packages such as SPSS, the two sets of statistics are calculated simultaneously on any given set of data. It is up to the individual researcher whether one deals with the question of significance first and then refers to the measures of association, or refers to measures of association and then tests of significance.

Exercises

19.1 What is the difference between asymmetric and symmetric measures of association? Which is the appropriate measure to use in situations in which two variables are thought to be mutually dependent?

19.2 Why do we not speak of association between two variables as being either positive or negative, when at least one variable is measured at the nominal level.

19.3 If decreases in the value of a variable seem to be associated with increases in the value of another variable, what is the direction of association?

19.4 In what situations is it appropriate to calculate measures of association but not tests of significance?

20

Measures of association for nominal data

This chapter discusses measures of association for two variables when at least one of the variables is measured at the nominal level. It will concentrate on two frequently used measures for such data: Cramer's *V* and lambda.

Cramer's *V*

We will work through an example from Chapter 16 to illustrate a measure of association for nominal data. It will also help us to demonstrate the difference between measures of association and tests of significance. In Chapter 16 we conducted a chi-square test to assess whether there was a relationship between level of education and enjoyment of work. We used this example to illustrate the effect that sample size can have on the value of a test statistic such as chi-square (see Table 20.1).

In Table 20.1A the value of chi-square is not large enough to warrant the rejection of the null hypothesis of independence: the two variables do not seem to be related. Yet by multiplying the sample size by 10, the value of chi-square in Table 20.1B is now very large and significant: the difference between observed and expected frequencies is large enough to allow us to reject the null hypothesis of independence. But if we focus on the column

Table 20.1A   Enjoyment of work by education level

Enjoyment of work	University education		
	No	Yes	Total
Exciting	584	100	684
	(581.5)	(102.5)	
Pretty routine	599	105	704
	(598.5)	(105.5)	
Dull	59	14	73
	(62)	(11)	
Total	1242	219	1461
$\chi^2 = 1.08148$, $p = 0.58232$			

Table 20.1B   Enjoyment of work by education level

Enjoyment of work	University education		
	No	Yes	Total
Exciting	5840	1000	6840
	(5815)	(1025)	
Pretty routine	5990	1050	7040
	(5985)	(1055)	
Dull	590	140	730
	(620)	(110)	
Total	12420	2190	14610

$\chi^2 = 10.8148$, $p = 0.0048$

percentages, and ignore the chi-square test for a moment (Table 20.2), it is clear that the large value of chi-square in Table 20.1B is due to the large sample size, rather than due to any strong pattern of dependence between the two variables.

Table 20.2   Enjoyment of work by education level

Enjoyment of work	University education		
	No	Yes	Total
Exciting	47%	45.7%	46.8%
Pretty routine	48.2%	47.9%	48.2%
Dull	4.8%	6.4%	5%
Total	100%	100%	14610

'Eye-balling' the relative frequency table suggests that the slight variation exhibited in the data can be put down to random variation. This indicates that any given value of a test statistic such as chi-square, t, F, or z, does not by itself indicate a strong, moderate, or weak relationship between variables. These values are too easily influenced by sample size (especially chi-square).

In this example, to confirm our suspicion that the significant result in the second table is due to large sample size, a measure called Cramer's V can be calculated. The formula for Cramer's V is given by:

$$V = \sqrt{\frac{\chi^2}{N(k-1)}}$$

Where:

k is either the number of rows or the number of columns, whichever is smaller.

This formula in effect adjusts the value of chi-square to take account of the sample size. For Table 20.1A (where $N = 1461$):

$$V = \sqrt{\frac{\chi^2}{N(k-1)}}$$

$$V = \sqrt{\frac{1.08148}{1461(2-1)}}$$

$$V = 0.027$$

For Table 20.1B (where $N = 14\,610$):

$$V = \sqrt{\frac{\chi^2}{N(k-1)}}$$

$$V = \sqrt{\frac{10.8148}{14\,610(2-1)}}$$

$$V = 0.027$$

Cramer's V is exactly the same in each case. Cramer's V, as with most measures of association, ranges between 0 (no association) and 1 (perfect association). Although there is no direct interpretation for any particular value of V between 0 and 1, generally anything under 0.1 is considered very weak. Therefore, in this example, even if a relationship does hold in the population, it is so weak as to be trivial. This highlights one of the main uses of Cramer's V: it provides a way of assessing a suspicion that a significant chi-square test is due merely to sample size rather than some underlying relationship between the variables.[1]

Cramer's V using SPSS

File name 20–1.sav   The data for the table comparing enjoyment of work with university attendance has been entered into SPSS, with the following variable information:

---

[1] Another chi-square-based measure of association, called phi, is often discussed together with Cramer's V. The formula for phi is:

$$\phi = \sqrt{\frac{\chi^2}{N}}$$

The problem with phi is that it can have a maximum value greater than 1 for tables larger than 2-by-2. Therefore, for such tables it is difficult to decide whether any particular value of phi is high or low. It is also clear from the formula for phi that it is a special case of Cramer's V: where tables have two rows and/or two columns, the two measures will be the same. And since in larger tables only Cramer's V is useful, there seems to be no reason for bothering with phi at all.

Variable: Work
Variable label: Enjoyment of work
Value labels: 1 = Exciting
                  2 = Routine
                  3 = Dull

Variable: Uni
Variable label: Attendance at university
Value labels: 1 = No
                  2 = Yes

In SPSS, Cramer's *V* is generated as part of a crosstab, in a similar manner to chi-square. In fact, in this example we will generate the two together (Table 20.3).

Table 20.3   Cramer's *V* on SPSS

SPSS command/action	Comments
1 From the menu select **Statistics/ Summarize/crosstabs...**	This will bring up a window **Crosstabs**
2 Click on the variable that will form the rows of the table; in this case **work**	This will highlight **work**
3 Click on the ➤ that points to the area headed **Row(s):**	This will paste **work** into the **Row(s):** list
4 Click on **uni**	**uni** will be highlighted
5 Click on the ➤ that points to the area headed **Column(s):**	This will paste **uni** into the **Column(s):** list
6 Click on the button **Statistics...**	This will bring up the **Crosstabs: Statistics** window. In the top-left corner you will see an area headed **Nominal Data**. These are the measures of association available for this level of measurement
7 Select **Phi and Cramer's V** by clicking on the box next to it	This will place × in the box to show that it has been selected
8 Select **Chi-square** by clicking on the box next to it	This will place × in the box to show that it has been selected
9 Click on **Continue**	
10 Click on **OK**	

The output from these instructions will be:

WORK Enjoyment of Work by UNI Attendance at University

```
                  UNI           Page 1 of 1
           Count |
           Col Pc |No      Yes
                  |                    Row
                  |   1  |     2  |  Total
WORK       -------|--------|--------|
         1 |   584  |   100  |   684
   Exciting  |  47.0  |  45.7  |  46.8
             |--------|--------|
         2 |   599  |   105  |   704
   Routine   |  48.2  |  47.9  |  48.2
             |--------|--------|
         3 |    59  |    14  |    73
   Dull      |   4.8  |   6.4  |   5.0
             |--------|--------|
        Column    1242      219     1461
         Total    85.0     15.0    100.0
```

Chi-Square	Value	DF	Significance
Pearson	1.08148	2	.58232
Likelihood Ratio	1.01450	2	.60215
Mantel-Haenszel test for linear association	.48819	1	.48474

Minimum Expected Frequency - 10.943

Statistic	Value	ASE1	Val/ASE0	Approximate Significance
Phi	.02721			.58232 *1
Cramer's V	.02721			.58232 *1

*1 Pearson chi-square probability

Number of Missing Observations: 0

Notice that the values for Cramer's *V* and phi are the same, since there are only two columns in the table. If both the number of columns and the number of rows were greater than two we would focus solely on Cramer's *V*.

The other thing to notice is that the approximate significance for Cramer's *V* is 0.58232, which is the same as that for the chi-square statistic. This is to be expected since Cramer's *V* is derived from chi-square. Taken together this information tells us that the relationship is so weak as to be trivial, and in any event cannot be attributed to a relationship in the population.

Proportional reduction in error measures of association

The problem with Cramer's V is that apart from very low values (close to zero) or very high values (close to 1), it is very difficult to interpret any particular value as indicating a weak, moderate, or strong association. In other words, if Cramer's V comes out to be 0.5, it is difficult to say in words how strong an association this indicates. Cramer's V can only be interpreted in a relative sense; for example, if all previous research into the association between two variables had resulted in values for V of around 0.3, a value of 0.5 would be considered strong. That is, Cramer's V for any given set of data can only be interpreted in the light of those for other sets.

As a result of these problems of interpretation, in recent times measures of association based on chi-square have become less popular. In their place other measures of association, called proportional reduction in error measures (PRE), are calculated. Cramer's V is still useful in determining whether a significant chi-square result is due to sample size, but if the conditions for the use of PRE measures hold, these are preferred as actual measures of association.

All PRE measures follow a similar logic: we predict the dependent variable while ignoring the information provided by the independent variable, and then we predict the dependent variable using knowledge of the independent, and see if we make fewer mistakes. The PRE measure for nominal data is lambda (λ)

Lambda

The general formula for lambda is given by:

$$\lambda = \frac{E_1 - E_2}{E_1}$$

where:
   E_1 is the number of errors without information on the independent variable
   E_2 is the number of errors with information on the independent variable.

To see how this applies in practice, consider the following example. I suspect that gender and height are associated, such that men are generally taller than women. One hundred people are selected and each person is asked to walk one-by-one into a room. Before each person enters I have to guess whether that person is tall (over 175 cm) or short (175 cm or less). However, I am given no information about each person before she or he enters: I have to make a blind guess about each person's height. The only information I am given is that for the sample as a whole the modal response for the dependent variable (the one with most cases) is the 'Tall' category. Limited to this information, the best strategy is to guess that *all* 100 people are Tall. Since this is the category with the most observations we make the fewest errors by predicting that all cases fall into it (Table 20.4).

Table 20.4   Classifying with no knowledge of the independent variable

Height	Total
Tall	100
Short	0
Total	100

The same 100 people are taken back out, and then asked to randomly re-enter the room one-by-one. This time, though, before each person enters I am told whether they are male or female. Suspecting that there may be an association between height and sex I decide to predict that every female is short and every male is tall (Table 20.5).

Table 20.5   Classifying with knowledge of the independent variable

Height	Sex		
	Male	Female	Total
Tall	50	0	50
Short	0	50	50
Total	50	50	100

The question is whether I have made fewer mistakes when given the extra information. Did my suspicion about a possible association between these two variables reduce the error rate when making these guesses? To calculate whether the error rate has changed I compare the two sets of guesses with the actual sample result (Table 20.6).

Table 20.6   Sample result

Height	Sex		
	Male	Female	Total
Tall	44	8	52
Short	6	42	48
Total	50	50	100

Without any knowledge of the independent variable (i.e. whether a person is male or female), 42 short females are incorrectly classified as being tall, and 6 short males are incorrectly classified as being tall. Therefore total errors made are:

$$E_1 = 42 + 6$$

$$= 48$$

However, with knowledge of a person's sex, 6 short males are incorrectly classified as being tall, and 8 tall females are incorrectly classified as being short. Therefore total errors made in this situation are:

$$E_2 = 6 + 8$$

$$= 14$$

Lambda simply calculates the difference in the two error rates as a proportion of the initial situation where I had no knowledge of the independent variable — hence the term 'proportional reduction in error':

$$\lambda = \frac{E_1 - E_2}{E_1}$$

$$= \frac{48 - 14}{48}$$

$$= 0.71$$

Therefore, by having information about sex we are able to minimize errors when predicting a person's height by 71 per cent.

The great advantage of PRE measures is that they have a direct interpretation since they measure something meaningful: changes in error rates. Regardless of the variables involved, a PRE measure of 0.71 would be considered as reflecting a strong association. Generally, we speak of association between variables as being either weak, moderate, or strong (or some combination of these, such as 'very weak' or 'moderately strong'). There is no sharp dividing line that determines when PRE values are to be called weak and when they are called strong, but to give a guide, one author suggests the terminology shown in Table 20.7. (See T.H. Black, 1993, *Evaluating Social Science Research*, Sage Publications, London, p. 137.)

Table 20.7

Range (+/–)	Relative strength
0.0–0.2	Very weak, negligible relationship
0.2–0.4	Weak, low association
0.4–0.7	Moderate association
0.7–0.9	Strong, high, marked association
0.9–1.0	Very high, very strong relationship

It is clear that the maximum possible value of lambda is 1 and the minimum is 0. If I make no errors with information about the independent variable ($E_2 = 0$) then the equation will simply be:

$$\lambda = \frac{E_1}{E_1} = 1$$

This indicates that in the sample there is perfect association between the two variables.

Where I make the same number of errors, with and without knowledge of the independent variable ($E_1 = E_2$), then the value of lambda will be:

$$\lambda = \frac{0}{E_1} = 0$$

Although lambda will always equal zero where there is no association, the converse is not necessarily true: whenever lambda equals zero there may indeed be association. This limitation to the use of lambda will be explored further after looking at the SPSS procedure.

Lambda using SPSS

Filename 20–2.sav   As with Cramer's *V*, lambda can be generated as part of a crosstab. Using the hypothetical data on sex and height, we follow the procedure given in Table 20.8.

Table 20.8   Lambda on SPSS

SPSS command/action	Comments
1 From the menu select **Statistics/ Summarize/Crosstabs...**	This will bring up a window headed **Crosstabs**
2 Click on the variable that will form the rows of the table; in this case **height**	This will highlight **height**
3 Click on the ➤ that points to the area headed **Row(s):**	This will paste **height** into the **Row(s):** list
4 Click on **sex**	**sex** will be highlighted
5 Click on the ➤ that points to the area headed **Column(s):**	This will paste **sex** into the **Column(s):** list
6 Click on the button **Statistics...**	This will bring up the **Crosstabs: Statistics** window. In the top-left corner you will see an area headed **Nominal Data**. These are the measures of association available for this level of measurement
7 Select **Lambda** by clicking on the box next to it	This will place × in the box to show that it has been selected. We could, in addition, select Cramer's *V* to be calculated in conjunction with lambda
8 Select **Chi-square** by clicking on the box next to it	This will place × in the box to show that it has been selected
9 Click on **Continue**	
10 Click on **OK**	

This will produce the following output:

```
HEIGHT by SEX

                    SEX            Page 1 of 1
            Count  |
                   |male     female
                   |
                   |    1 |     2 | Row
HEIGHT      -------|-------|-------| Total
                1  |   44 |     8 |    52
    tall          |      |       |    52.0
                   |-------|-------|
                2  |    6 |    42 |    48
    short         |      |       |    48.0
                   |-------|-------|
            Column     50      50      100
            Total    50.0    50.0    100.0
```

Chi-Square	Value	DF	Significance
Pearson	51.92308	1	.00000
Continuity Correction	49.07853	1	.00000
Likelihood Ratio	57.80991	1	.00000
Mantel-Haenszel test for linear association	51.40385	1	.00000

Minimum Expected Frequency - 24.000

Statistic	Value	ASE1	Val/ASE0	Approximate Significance
Lambda :				
symmetric	.71429	.07558	6.06977	
with HEIGHT dependent	.70833	.07956	5.48387	
with SEX dependent	.72000	.07332	6.08164	
Goodman & Kruskal Tau :				
with HEIGHT dependent	.51923	.09962		.00000 *2
with SEX dependent	.51923	.09958		.00000 *2

*2 Based on chi-square approximation

Lambda comes in both symmetric and asymmetric versions. The symmetric version is used when there is no reason to suspect that one of the variables is dependent on the other. It is actually calculated as a weighted average of the two asymmetric versions: in this example the symmetric value of 0.71429 falls somewhere in between the two asymmetric values. The asymmetric version will have two possible values, according to which of the two variables is suspected of being dependent. SPSS calculates all three possible values for lambda, from which we choose the one appropriate to the research question. In this example we believe that height is the dependent variable (there is no sense in which we could argue that sex is dependent on height), so we refer to the following portion of the output:

```
with HEIGHT dependent     .70833
```

This is the same value for lambda as that calculated above 'by hand'. When generating lambda as part of the output we could have asked for other statistics to be generated simultaneously, just by clicking on the square next to the desired measure. In particular we could have also generated Cramer's *V*. If we had selected Cramer's *V* the output would have included the following line:

```
Cramer's V                .72058                    .00000 *1
```

This is very close to the value of lambda, indicating that these two alternative measures both indicate association between the two variables.

Given that we have observed a strong association between these two variables, we need to then ask whether the association in the sample is due to an association between the variables in the population. This is why we generated the chi-square test in conjunction with lambda. The chi-square value of 50.92308 has a *p*-value of less than 0.00005. This is clearly significant, and therefore indicates a dependence between these two variables in the population.

SPSS also calculates a great deal of other information which we have not explored, since at the this level we do not want to complicate the discussion unduly.

Limitations on the use of lambda

Despite its intuitive appeal and ease of calculation, a problem is all too frequently encountered when using lambda. The problem manifests itself when lambda is calculated as zero even though an association really is present in the data. The cause of the problem is data that are highly skewed along the dependent variable.

Lambda will equal zero when the modal category for the dependent variable is the same for all values of the independent variable.

To see what this means in practice, we will analyse the data introduced in the appendix to Chapter 16. In this hypothetical example respondents were asked whether the government was doing enough to alleviate poverty (Table 20.9).

Table 20.9 Should the government do more to alleviate poverty?

Agree	Age group		
	Under 45	45 or over	Total
No	110	168	278
Yes	490	232	722
Total	600	400	1000

The modal response for people under 45 is 'Yes'. The modal response for people aged 45 or over is also 'Yes'. This skewed distribution for the dependent variable will produce a value for lambda of zero.

To see why, I need to firstly calculate the number of errors when predicting without knowledge of the independent variable (Age group). I predict that all 1000 cases will fall in the 'Yes' category, since this will minimize my error rate. I therefore make 278 mistakes.

With knowledge of the independent variable, I will still make the same number of mistakes. Considering firstly the respondents aged under 45, I predict that all 600 respond 'Yes' (110 mistakes). Secondly, I predict all 400 people aged 45 or over respond 'Yes' (168 mistakes). This sums to 278 total errors, which is the same as predicting without knowledge of the respondents' sex.

$$\lambda = \frac{E_1 - E_2}{E_1} = \frac{278 - 278}{278} = 0$$

But if we look at these data using column percentages there is clearly a difference (Table 20.10).

Table 20.10 Should the government do more to alleviate poverty?

Agree	Age group	
	Under 45	45 or over
No	18.3%	42%
Yes	81.7%	58%

However, the lambda value of zero has failed to pick up this relationship, which is evident to the naked eye. This highlights one important rule:

Whenever lambda equals zero inspect the relative frequency distribution to decide whether this actually reflects no association or whether it is due to a skewed distribution of the dependent variable.

If an inspection of the column percentages leads you to suspect that a value of zero for lambda is due to a skewed distribution (as in this case), there are three options:

- **Don't bother with measures of association** Stick to the percentage distributions, which require the researcher to make some subjective judgments, but as long as the figures are there for the readers to assess for themselves, there is no problem with structuring an argument using only the percentage distributions as evidence. These percentage distributions sometimes 'speak for themselves': calculating all the technical statistics on top (and all the problems that sometimes come with them) may only serve to bury important information in an avalanche of suspect numbers.
- **Calculate other measures of association** In the previous example, for a chi-square of 7.7, the value of Cramer's V will be:

$$V = \sqrt{\frac{\chi^2}{N(k-1)}} = \sqrt{\frac{7.7}{1215(2-1)}} = 0.08$$

This suggests that the association between these variables is pretty weak anyway.

There are other measures of association for nominal data that can be used if there are problems with the use of lambda. Another PRE measure, which appeared in the SPSS output but which we did not comment on, is the Goodman–Kruskal tau. Like lambda this is an asymmetric measure of association that ranges between 0 and 1. Unlike lambda it does not use the modal response for the independent variable in making predictions, but rather the frequency distribution of cases across all the categories of the independent variable. Since it is less sensitive to skewed marginal distributions than lambda it is a convenient alternative when skewness causes lambda to equal zero.

- **Standardize the table so that the row totals are all equal** This is a slightly more complicated procedure, and one not often suggested by advanced texts on statistics. (For a more complete discussion of standardization procedures and their use with measures of association see Y.M.M. Bishop, S.E. Feinberg, and P.W. Holland, 1975, *Discrete Multivariate Analysis: Theory and Practice*, MIT Press, Cambridge, pp. 392–3, and H.T. Reynolds, 1977, *The Analysis of Cross-Classifications*, Macmillan, London, pp. 31–33.)

Appendix: Standardizing crosstabulations when lambda is zero

The process of standardizing a table involves trying to eliminate the variation in the data brought about by the skewed totals, while still retaining the variation that may exist *between* groups.[1] When working with lambda we standardize the row marginals so that each row sums to 100. This involves the calculation of the row percentages, which are then treated *as if* they are real numbers of cases. That is, we calculate the percentage of the total 'yes' respondents that are under 45 and the percentage that are 45 or over. We do the same for the 'No' responses (Table 20.11).

---

[1] In a report that uses this procedure it should be made clear that lambda is not calculated on the raw data. This can be done by adding a comment (maybe in a footnote) such as the following: 'In calculating the measure of association, row marginals are standardized to sum to 100. This is due to the skewed distribution of the dependent variable.'

Table 20.11   Should the government do more to alleviate poverty?

Agree	Age group		
	Under 45	45 or over	Total
No	$\frac{110}{278} \times 100 = 40\%$	$\frac{168}{278} \times 100 = 60\%$	100%
Yes	$\frac{490}{722} \times 100 = 68\%$	$\frac{232}{722} \times 100 = 32\%$	100%
Total	600	400	1000

We then use these percentage figures as if they were counts of actual cases (Table 20.12).

Table 20.12   Should the government do more to alleviate poverty?

Agree	Age group		
	Under 45	45 or over	Total
No	40	60	100
Yes	68	32	100
Total	108	92	200

Remember that these are percentages: 40 represents 40 per cent of 278 total 'No' responses, and so on. But we treat them as if they are individual cases. This means that the total sample size 'is' 200 rather than 1000: the 100 'Yes' 'respondents' and the 100 'No' 'respondents'.

Using the data from the standardized table (Table 20.12), I recalculate lambda. Without knowledge of the independent variable, I classify all 200 'respondents' in either 'Yes' or 'No', and therefore make 100 errors:

$$E_1 = 100$$

With knowledge of the independent variable I make the following predictions. Starting with the under 45, I predict that all said 'Yes', since this gives me the lowest error rate (40 mistakes). For 45 and over I predict that all said 'No', and therefore make 32 mistakes:

$$E_2 = 40 + 32$$
$$= 72$$

Lambda will therefore equal:

$$\lambda = \frac{E_1 - E_2}{E_1}$$

$$= \frac{100 - 72}{100}$$

$$= 0.28$$

After standardization, there turns out to be a weak association between these variables, which confirms the conclusion reached on the basis of Cramer's V.

Exercises

20.1 A study finds that the association between two variables, using Cramer's *V* as the measure, is 0.34. In the past, studies have measured association between the same variables using *V* as ranging from 0.15 to 0.21. How should the researchers report their result?

20.2 Calculate Cramer's *V* for the following sets of data:

Set 1: $\chi^2 = 3.5$
   $N = 20$
   rows = 4, columns = 2

Set 2: $\chi^2 = 9.8$
   $N = 90$
   rows = 2, columns = 4

Set 3: $\chi^2 = 12$
   $N = 800$
   rows = 3, columns = 3

20.3 Why is it important, when calculating lambda, to decide whether one variable is likely to be dependent on the other, and if so to specify which is dependent and which is independent?

20.4 Calculate lambda for the following tables, and interpret the strength of any relationship:

(a)

Dependent	Independent		
	1	2	Total
1	30	60	90
2	45	50	95
Total	75	110	85

(b)

Dependent	Independent			
	1	2	3	Total
1	56	40	10	106
2	15	30	50	95
Total	71	70	60	201

(c)

Dependent	Independent			
	1	2	3	Total
1	70	90	120	280
2	50	45	38	133
3	43	30	14	87
Total	163	165	172	500

(d) (optional)

If any of these tables produce a lambda equal to zero, standardize the distribution and recalculate lambda.

20.5 A researcher is interested in the relationship between gun ownership and attitude toward capital punishment. She surveyed 3000 people and obtained the following results:

Capital punishment	Gun owners	Non-owners
For	849	367
Against	191	1593

Calculate lambda for these data and interpret the result.

20.6 A survey of 50 'blue-collar' and 50 'white-collar' workers asked respondents if they could sing their National Anthem from start to finish.

'Blue-collar'
    Yes   29
    No   21
'White-collar'
    Yes   22
    No   28

Arrange these data into a crosstabulation. What should be the dependent and independent variables? Calculate lambda for these data.

Measures of association for ordinal data

This chapter concentrates on measures of association for variables measured at the ordinal level. These are PRE measures of association that are similar to lambda. With ordinal data, though, we have more information than with nominal data; in particular we know the ranking of cases. Ordinal measures of association take advantage of this extra information. With lambda, we tried to predict the value an *individual* case takes for the dependent variable. Since ordinal measurement allows us to rank any two cases ordinal measures of association try to predict the order of *pairs* of cases.

Gamma

Gamma is a common PRE measure of association for two variables measured at least at the ordinal level and arranged in a bivariate table. Gamma is a symmetric measure of association so that the value calculated will be the same regardless of which of the variables is specified as independent and which is specified as dependent.

To see the logic behind gamma we will work through the following example. A survey investigated the frequency of TV watching by children. Children were classified into two age groups: 10 years or less, and over 10 years of age. Children were also asked if they watched TV:

'Every day'
'Most days but not always'
'A few days a week'
'Less than a few days a week'

Suppose two children from the sample are selected and we have to predict which one watches more TV than the other. Notice that we are not simply trying to predict the amount of TV watched by *each* child; we are trying to guess the ranking of the *two* children. Is our ability to predict how these two children stand in relation to each other for one variable improved by know-ledge of where they stand in terms of the other? In other words, does the knowledge that one child is older than the other help us to predict whether that child also watches more or less TV than the other? Although gamma is a symmetric measure of association, and therefore does not rely on specification of dependent and independent variables, in this example it is clear that the only pattern of dependence can be of TV watching on age; there is no sense in which a child's age can depend on the amount of TV watched. Thus in this example we will try to predict the ordering of cases in terms of TV watching from knowledge of their ordering in terms of age.

The distribution of response to this survey, together with the column percentages, is presented in Table 21.1.

Table 21.1   Frequency of TV watching by children's age

TV watching	Age	
	10 years or less	Over 10 years
Less than a few days	42	15
	4.1%	2.6%
A few days a week	86	31
	8.5%	5.3%
Most days	316	123
	31.2%	20.9%
Every day	569	419
	56.2%	71.3%
Total	1013	588

It is very important in constructing a bivariate table to calculate ordinal measures of association (as will become evident below) that the values increase when going down the rows and across the columns. That is, the table begins with the lowest value for the row variable (which is normally the dependent variable) and moves down to the greatest value. Similarly the first column should be the smallest value for the column variable (usually the independent variable) and increases across the page.

Looking at the column percentages in this table it is evident that there is a relationship. For example, a higher percentage of older children watched TV every day (71.3%) than younger children (56.2%). For this group of children, TV watching increases in frequency with age, which indicates some level of positive association. By calculating gamma we get an exact quantitative measure of this impression.

Concordant and discordant pairs

Assume that one of the 419 children aged over 10 years who watched TV every day is named Jessie, and one of the 316 children aged 10 years or less who watched TV most days is called Kim. These two can be ranked against each other for each of the two variables:

- In terms of age Jessie is ranked above Kim.
- In terms of TV watching Jessie is also ranked above Kim, since she watches TV every day whereas Kim watches only most days (Figure 21.1).

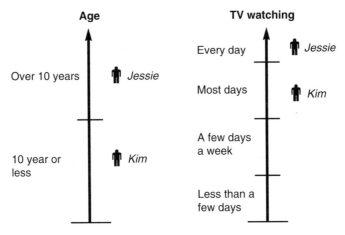

Figure 21.1   Ranking of a pair of children

This relationship is also presented in Table 21.2.

Table 21.2   A concordant pair of cases

Independent variable Age	Dependent variable TV watching
Jessie ranked above Kim (is older)	Jessie ranked above Kim (watches more)

Therefore these two cases have the same relationship to each other for each variable: *they are ranked the same for each variable*. This might sound like a strange use of language: how can they be the sme if they have different values? The point is that they are *ranked* the same: Jessie is ranked above Kim for both variables. Pairs of cases such as Jessie and Kim are called **concordant pairs**.

Concordant pairs are two cases that are ranked the same on both variables.

Now if I take one of the 569 children who are 10 years or less in age and watch TV every day, and compare them with one of the 123 children aged 11 or more who watch TV most days, the ranking will not be the same for both variables. The first child will be ranked below the other in terms of age (since that child is younger), but ranked above the other child in terms of TV watching. Such cases are called **discordant pairs**.

Discordant pairs are two cases that are ranked differently on both variables.

The reason why we look at these concordant and discordant pairs is that they give us information that we can use in prediction:

- **Positive association between variables** The sample will contain a lot of concordant pairs and few discordant pairs. If this is the situation, and I am told that one child ranks above another in terms of age, I will also predict that that child ranks above the other in terms of frequency of TV watching as well.
- **Negative association between variables** The sample will contain a lot of discordant pairs, so I will make the opposite prediction: knowing that a child ranks above another in terms of age will lead me to guess that that child ranked below the other in terms of frequency of TV watching.
- **No association between variables** The sample will contain just as many concordant pairs as discordant pairs, and I will not increase my predictive power.

Gamma formalizes this logic, using the equation:

$$G = \frac{N_c - N_d}{N_c + N_d}$$

where:
N_c is the number of concordant pairs
N_d is the number of discordant pairs.

Calculating the number of concordant pairs

How do we calculate the total number of concordant pairs? Look at the shaded cells in the bivariate table (Table 21.3).

Table 21.3   Frequency of TV watching by children's age

TV watching	Age	
	10 years or less	Over 10 years
Less than a few days	42	15
A few days a week	86	31
Most days	316	123
Every day	569	419

In the discussion above I formed a concordant pair by matching Jessie, who was one of the 419 cases who were over 10 years of age and also watched TV every day, with Kim, who was one of the 316 children who were 10 years of age or less and watched TV most days. In fact I can pair Jessie up with each of the 316 children who were 10 years of age or less and watched TV most days, producing 316 concordant pairs: Jessie plus each of the 316 other children. I can then do the same for any of the other 419 who were over 10 years of age and watched TV every day. This will produce 419 lots of 316 concordant pairs:

$$419 \times 316 = 132\,404$$

Looking at the table again though, we see that there are still more combinations of concordant pairs in this sample (Table 21.4).

Table 21.4   Frequenc of TV watching by children's age

TV watching	Age	
	10 years or less	Over 10 years
Less than a few days	42	15
A few days a week	86	31
Most days	316	123
Every day	569	419

Each of the 419 cases in the bottom-right cell is also ranked above each of the 86 and 42 cases in the two top-left cells: they are both older and watch more TV. So this will add the following number of concordant pairs:

$$419(86 + 42) = 53\ 632$$

In fact, any case will form a concordant pair with any other case in a cell *above and to the left* of it in the table. The total number of concordant pairs, therefore, will be as shown in Table 21.5.

Table 21.5

42	15
86	31
316	123
569	419

$$419(316 + 86 + 42) = 186\ 036$$

+

42	15
86	31
316	123
569	419

$$123(86 + 42) = 15\ 744$$

+

42	15
86	31
316	123
569	419

$$31(42) = 1302$$

$$
\begin{aligned}
N_c &= 186\ 036 + 15\ 744 + 1302 \\
&= 203\ 082
\end{aligned}
$$

Calculating the number of discordant pairs

To calculate the total number of discordant pairs we begin with the bottom-left cell in the table and match it with all cells above and to the right of it (see Table 21.6).

Table 21.6

42	15
86	31
316	123
569	419

$569(123 + 31 + 15) = 96\ 161$

+

42	15
86	31
316	123
569	419

$316(31 + 15) = 14\ 536$

+

42	15
86	31
316	123
569	419

$86(15) = 1290$

$$N_c = 96\ 161 + 14\ 536 + 1290$$
$$= 111\ 987$$

Putting all this into the formula for calculating gamma, we obtain:

$$G = \frac{N_c - N_d}{N_c + N_d} = \frac{203\ 082 - 111\ 987}{203\ 082 + 111\ 987} = 0.29$$

This tells me that there is a mild, positive association between these variables: an increase in age is associated, in this sample, with an increase in the frequency of TV watching.

It is evident that the range of possible values for gamma is between −1 and 1. A gamma of −1 indicates perfect negative association: knowing that a case ranked above another along one variable will always indicate that it ranked below for the other variable. Such a result would be obtained if there were only discordant pairs in the sample. If, on the other hand, there were only concordant pairs the value of gamma would be +1, indicating perfect positive association: knowing a case ranked above another for the independent variable indicates that it also ranked above for the dependent variable. A gamma of zero indicates no association. If there are just as many concordant pairs as there are discordant pairs, then knowing the ranking along one variable gives no guide as to the ranking on the other variable.

Gamma using SPSS

Filename 21-1.sav   We can obtain exactly the same result using SPSS. Gamma is one of the statistics that can be requested when constructing a cross-tab (together with chi-square, lambda, and a range of other statistics).

Table 21.7   Gamma using SPSS

SPSS command/action	Comments
1 From the menu select **Statistics/Summarize/ Crosstabs...**	This will bring up a window headed **Crosstabs**
2 Click on the variable that will form the rows of the table; in this case **tvwatch**	This will highlight **tvwatch**. Remember that if we have reasons for believing that a particular variable is dependent on the other, this should be the row variable
3 Click on the ➤ that points to the area headed **Row(s):**	This will paste **tvwatch** into the **Row(s):**
4 Click on **age**	**age** will be highlighted. Remember that if we have reason to believe that one variable is independent of the other, this should be the column variable
5 Click on the ➤ that points to the area headed **Column(s):**	This will paste **age** into the **Column(s):**
6 Click on the button **Statistics...**	This will bring up the **Crosstabs: Statistics** window. You will see an area headed **Ordinal Data**, which is a list of the measures of association available for this level of measurement
7 Select **Gamma** by clicking on the box next to it	This will place × in the box to show that it has been selected
8 Select **Chi-square** by clicking on the box next to it	This will place × in the box to show that it has been selected
9 Click on **Continue**	
10 Click on **OK**	

The results of this set of instructions will be:

```
TVWATCH  Frequency of TV Watching  by  AGE  Age in Years

                   AGE           Page 1 of 1
          Count  |
                 |10 or le Over 10
                 |ss
                 |    1  |    2  | Row
                 |       |       | Total
TVWATCH   --------|-------|-------|
             1  |   42  |   15  |    57
Less than a few |       |       |   3.6
                |-------|-------|
             2  |   86  |   31  |   117
A few days a wee|       |       |   7.3
                |-------|-------|
             3  |  316  |  123  |   439
Most days       |       |       |  27.4
                |-------|-------|
             4  |  569  |  419  |   988
Every day       |       |       |  61.7
                |-------|-------|
        Column    1013     588     1601
         Total    63.3     36.7    100.0
```

Chi-Square	Value	DF	Significance
Pearson	35.98264	3	.00000
Likelihood Ratio	36.71614	3	.00000
Mantel-Haenszel test for linear association	28.21057	1	.00000

Minimum Expected Frequency -   20.934

Statistic	Value	ASE1	Val/ASE0	Approximate Significance
Gamma	.28913	.04684	6.14370	

Number of Missing Observations: 0

We see that the value for gamma is the same as that calculated above:

Gamma   .28913

This reflects the weak-to-moderate association that exists between these two variables for this group of cases. If there was a negative association, a negative sign would be printed in front of the value, provided that the data were arranged in the table in the correct format: with values increasing across the columns and down the rows.

Given that we have observed an association in the sample, can we attribute this to a non-random relationship in the population? Referring to the chi-square test, which is also generated in this procedure, we see:

```
Chi-Square                  Value         DF        Significance
--------------------        -----------   ----      ------------

Pearson                     35.98264       3           .00000
```

This indicates that there is a significant relationship: age and amount of TV watched are related in the population as a whole.

Example

A survey was conducted to assess whether the presence of union officials in the workplace affected the accident rate for that workplace. One hundred and seventy-seven workplaces were included in the survey and these were classified according to such factors as the number of shop stewards present, as having either a low, moderate, or high level of union presence. These workplaces were also classified as having either a high or low accident rate. Both of these variables are measured on an ordinal scale. The results of the survey are presented in the crosstabulation, Table 21.8.

Table 21.8   Workplaces by union presence and accident rates

Accident rate	Union presence		
	Low	Moderate	High
Low	17	32	35
High	43	27	23

Can we detect an association between these variables?

To calculate gamma we begin with concordant pairs. For a 2-by-3 table such as this the combination of concordant pairs will be as shown in Table 21.9.

Table 21.9

17	32	35
43	27	23

$23(17 + 32) = 1127$

$+$

17	32	35
43	27	23

$27(17) = 459$

$$N_c = 1127 + 459$$
$$= 1586$$

To calculate the number of discordant pairs we work in the opposite direction (Table 21.10).

Table 21.10

17	32	35
43	27	23

$43(32 + 35) = 3311$

+

17	32	35
43	27	23

$27(35) = 945$

$$N_d = 3311 + 945$$
$$= 4256$$

Putting this information into the equation for gamma we get:

$$G = \frac{N_s - N_d}{N_s + N_d}$$

$$= \frac{1586 - 3826}{1586 + 3826}$$

$$= -0.41$$

This indicates that in predicting the order of pairs on the dependent variable, we will make 41 per cent fewer errors if we take into account the way that the pairs are ordered on the independent variable (level of unionization). There is a moderate, negative association between these two variables. Higher unionization is associated with a lower accident rate.

The following SPSS output calculates both gamma and chi-square for these data so that we can assess whether any association detected in the sample is also likely to hold in the population.

```
ACCIDENT  Accident Rate  by  UNION  Union Presence

                   UNION                        Page 1 of 1
            Count  |
                   |Low      Moderate High
                   |
                   |   1  |     2  |    3  | Row
                   |      |       |       | Total
ACCIDENT    -------+--------+--------+--------+
          1 |   17  |    32  |   35  |   84
  Low         |       |       |       |   47.5
            +--------+--------+--------+
          2 |   43  |    27  |   23  |   93
  High        |       |       |       |   52.5
            +--------+--------+--------+
          Column   60        59       58      177
          Total    33.9      33.3     32.8    100.0
```

Chi-Square	Value	DF	Significance
Pearson	13.75108	2	.00103
Likelihood Ratio	14.11597	2	.00086
Mantel-Haenszel test for linear association	12.13681	1	.00049

Minimum Expected Frequency -   27.525

Statistic	Value	ASE1	Val/ASE0	Approximate Significance
Gamma	-.41390	.10495	-3.68052	

We see that within the sample there is a moderate, negative association and, from the significance of chi-square, we see that this is also likely to hold in the population of all workplaces.

Spearman's rank-order correlation coefficient

Gamma is a PRE measure of association when both variables are measured at least at the ordinal level. It is most widely used in situations where the ordinal scales do not have too many categories so that they can be displayed in a crosstabulation. In situations where the ordinal scales have a wide range of possible scores another PRE measure is available. This is Spearman's rank order correlation coefficient, which is also known as Spearman's rho. When working with scales that have many distinct values, we use the word correlation rather than association to describe the relationship between two variables, although for our purposes correlation and association describe the same general concept. The basic logic underlying rho is the same as that for gamma, in so far as it tries to predict the ranking of pairs of cases on the dependent variable given their ranking on the independent variable. However, it makes use of the longer scale.

To illustrate the calculation of rho, we will work through the following hypothetical example. A physiotherapist uses a new treatment on a group of patients and is interested in whether their age affects their ability to respond to the treatment. After taking into account a number of other variables, such as the severity of the injury, each patient is given a mobility score out of 15, according to his or her ability to perform a number of tasks. The results of the study are shown in Table 21.11.

Table 21.11   Age and mobility scores

Patient	Age	Score
A	23	14
B	25	15
C	28	12
D	30	8
E	35	13
F	37	10
G	38	11
H	39	8
I	40	10
J	41	9
K	45	10
L	50	9
M	52	7
N	55	8
O	60	4
P	62	6

To calculate Spearman's rho we give each case a rank for each variable, remembering to give an average rank for tied cases (Table 21.12).

Table 21.12   Ordering of patients by age

Patient	A	B	C	D	E	F	G	H	I	J	K	L	M	N	O	P
Age	23	25	28	30	35	37	39	40	41	45	50	50	52	55	60	62
Rank	1	2	3	4	5	6	7	8	9	10	11	12	13	14	15	16
Score	14	15	12	8	13	10	11	8	10	9	10	9	7	8	4	6
Rank	15	16	13	5	14	10	12	5	10	7.5	10	7.5	3	5	1	2

To calculate the value of rho we calculate the difference in rank for each case, D, and then square these differences (Table 21.13).

Table 21.13   Calculating rank differences

Case	Age rank	Score rank	Rank difference (D)	D^2
A	1	15	$1 - 15 = -14$	196
B	2	16	$2 - 16 = -14$	196
C	3	13	$3 - 13 = -10$	100
D	4	5	$4 - 5 = -1$	1
E	5	14	$5 - 14 = -9$	81
F	6	10	$6 - 10 = -4$	16
G	7	12	$7 - 12 = -5$	25
H	8	5	$8 - 5 = 3$	9
I	9	10	$9 - 10 = -1$	1
J	10	7.5	$10 - 7.5 = 2.5$	6.25
K	11	10	$11 - 10 = 1$	1
L	12	7.5	$12 - 7.5 = 4.5$	20.25
M	13	3	$13 - 3 = 10$	100
N	14	5	$14 - 5 = 9$	81
O	15	1	$15 - 1 = 14$	196
P	16	2	$16 - 2 = 14$	196
				$\Sigma D^2 = 1225.5$

Having made these calculations we can enter the information into the equation for Spearman's rho

$$r_s = 1 - \frac{6\Sigma D^2}{N(N_2 - 1)}$$

$$= 1 - \frac{6 \times 1225.5}{16(16^2 - 1)}$$

$$= -0.8$$

Spearman's rho is a PRE measure, and therefore has a concrete interpretation. A value of 0.8 indicates a strong correlation between these two variables, and the negative sign indicates that this is a negative correlation. In other words, increases in age reduces the effect of the treatment. The older the patient, the less benefit received from the program.

Spearman's rho using SPSS

Filename 21-2.sav   The data used in the previous example have been entered into SPSS. The commands needed to calculate rho for these data are shown in Table 21.14.

Table 21.14   Spearman's correlation coefficient using SPSS

SPSS command/action	Comments
1 From the menu select **Statistics/Correlate/Bivariate...**	This will bring up a window headed **Bivariate Correlations**. You will notice an area called **Correlation Coefficients**, with the box next to **Pearson** selected. This is the default setting. Pearson's coefficient is applicable to interval/ratio data, so is not appropriate here
2 Click on **age**	This will highlight **age**
3 Click on ➤	This will paste **age** into the **Variables:** list
Click on **tvwatch**	This will highlight **tvwatch**
4 Click on ➤	This will paste **tvwatch** into the **Variables:** list
5 Click on the box next to **Pearson**	This will remove × from the box to show that it is no longer selected
6 Click on the box next to **Spearman**	This will place × in the box to show that it has been selected
7 Click on **OK**	

The output from this command will be:

```
- - - SPEARMAN   CORRELATION   COEFFICIENTS ---

SCORE           -.8045
             N(   16)
             Sig .000

                 AGE

(Coefficient / (Cases) / 2-tailed Significance)

" . " is printed if a coefficient cannot be computed
```

What does all this mean? The line below the statistics is the explanation:

(Coefficient / (Cases) / 2-tailed Significance)

This says that the first number in the little grid is the value of the rho coefficient: –0.8045, which is the same figure we calculated above. This indicates a strong, negative relationship between these two variables.

The next line in the grid is the number of cases: 16. And lastly, SPSS calculates the two-tailed significance for this value of rho with this number of cases. Although we have Sig .000 this does not mean a zero significance. The exact probability is less than 1-in-1000 (i.e. $p < 0.001$), which SPSS has rounded off to 0.000. Thus this probability should be read as 'less than 1-in-1000', which is clearly a significant result. The strong relationship we have detected in the sample is due to such a relationship holding in the population, and not just due to sampling error.

Example

An instructor is interested in whether the heavy use of formal exams as a form of assessment is biased against students who might perform better under different exam conditions, such as verbal presentations. A group of 15 students are selected and assessed in terms of their verbal presentation skills and in terms of their formal examination skills. These 15 students are rank-ordered on each of these variables as indicated in Table 21.15.

Table 21.15

Student	Rank on exam	Rank on presentation
1	4	15
2	6	3
3	9	14
4	12	9
5	3	10
6	13	11
7	5	6
8	1	4
9	14	8
10	2	1
11	10	2
12	7	5
13	15	7
14	8	12
15	11	13

To calculate rho we need to calculate the difference in rank for each student, and then the square of the difference (Table 21.16).
Substituting these data into the equation for rho:

$$r_s = 1 - \frac{6\Sigma D^2}{N(N^2 - 1)}$$

$$= 1 - \frac{6 \times 416}{15(15^2 - 1)}$$

$$= -0.257$$

This indicates a weak association between the two types of skills. The instructor might therefore conclude that exams are not a good indicator of other forms of learning skills: students who perform poorly in exams might perform well in verbal presentations. Similarly, students who do well in exams might not relatively do all that well when other skills are required.

Table 21.16

Student	Rank on exam	Rank on presentation	Difference D	D²
1	4	15	−11	121
2	6	3	3	9
3	9	14	−5	25
4	12	9	3	9
5	3	10	−7	49
6	13	11	2	4
7	5	6	−1	1
8	1	4	−3	9
9	14	8	6	36
10	2	1	1	1
11	10	2	8	64
12	7	5	2	4
13	15	7	8	64
14	8	12	−4	16
15	11	13	−2	4
			$\Sigma D^2 = 416$	

Other measures of association for ordinal data

This chapter introduced two measures of association (or correlation) for ordinal data. However, as would have been observed when generating these measures on SPSS, they are certainly not the only measures available. Unfortunately, there is no easy rule for deciding which is the 'best' measure available. Part of the problem lies with the notion of association itself, and the fact that this concept is operationalized in slightly different ways. For example, gamma and rho are both symmetric measures, whereas others are asymmetric; the strength of the relationship will appear to vary depending on which variable is specified as independent and which is specified as dependent. Here we will briefly describe the main alternatives to rho and gamma, and some of their respective properties:

Somer's D

This is an asymmetric PRE measure of association for ordinal data arranged in a bivariate table. As with gamma it compares the number of concordant and discordant pairs, but unlike gamma, it makes use of cases tied on the dependent variable in its calculation:

$$d = \frac{N_s - N_d}{N_s + N_d + T_y}$$

where:

T_y is the number of tied cases on the dependent variable.

Notice that this is almost the identical equation to that for gamma, except for the term in the denominator for the number of dependent variable ties. As a result, whenever there are such tied cases, d will always have a lower value than gamma. In other words, by ignoring tied cases, gamma may overstate the strength of association between two variables when there are many tied cases.

Kendall's tau-*b*

Kendall's tau-*b* is a symmetrical, PRE measure of association for ordinal data arranged in a bivariate table. Its main feature is that it makes use of the information provided by cases tied on the dependent *and* independent variables:

$$tau - b = \frac{N_s - N_d}{\sqrt{(N_s + N_d + T_y)(N_s + N_d + T_x)}}$$

where:

T_y is the number of tied cases on the dependent variable

T_x is the number of tied cases on the independent variable.

Unfortunately, tau-*b* will only range between −1 and +1 where the number of rows in the bivariate table equal the number of columns, and is therefore generally only used in this special case.

Exercises

21.1 For the highlighted cells in each of the following tables, calculate the number of concordant pairs, assuming that the numbers on the edge of each table indicate the values of an ordinal variable:

(a)

	1	*2*	*3*
1	60	24	12
2	32	14	8

(b)

	1	*2*	*3*
1	60	24	12
2	32	14	8

(c)

	1	*2*	*3*	*4*
1	12	17	25	42
2	10	14	19	24
3	6	11	16	20

(d)

	1	*2*	*3*	*4*
1	12	17	25	42
2	10	14	19	24
3	6	11	16	20
4	3	9	14	22

21.2 For the highlighted cells in each of the following tables, calculate the number of discordant pairs, assuming that the numbers on the edge of each table indicate the values of an ordinal variable:

(a)

	1	*2*	*3*
1	60	24	12
2	32	14	8

(b)

	1	*2*	*3*
1	60	24	12
2	32	14	8

(c)

	1	*2*	*3*
1	60	24	12
2	32	14	8

(d)

	1	*2*	*3*	*4*
1	12	17	25	42
2	10	14	19	24
3	6	11	16	20

21.3 Calculate gamma for the following data:

Mother working?	Child achievement level			
	Poor	Good	High	Total
No	20	58	22	100
Part-time	15	62	23	100
Full-time	12	62	26	100
Total	47	182	71	300

Interpret your result.

21.4 A study finds the association between two variables using gamma is 0.35 with a chi-square significance of 0.12. What should we conclude?

21.5 Consider the following crosstabulation generated on SPSS. The table displays the distribution of 162 patients whose health was assessed on a four-point scale, and who were also coded as smokers or non-smokers. This latter variable is considered ordinal for the purposes of this study since it indicates level of smoking. Looking at the raw distribution can you detect an association between these two variables? What is the direction of association? How will this direction manifest when calculating a measure of association?

```
HEALTH  Health Level  by  SMOKE  Smoking Habit

                     SMOKE           Page 1 of 1
          Count   |
                  |Doesn't  Does Smo
                  |Smoke    ke            Row
                  |    0   |    1   | Total
HEALTH      ------|--------|--------|
         1  |    13  |    34  |    47
Poor        |        |        |   29.0
            |--------|--------|
         2  |    22  |    19  |    41
Fair        |        |        |   25.3
            |--------|--------|
         3  |    35  |     9  |    44
Good        |        |        |   27.2
            |--------|--------|
         4  |    27  |     3  |    30
Very Good   |        |        |   18.5
            |--------|--------|
         Column      97       65      162
          Total    59.9     40.1    100.0
```

Calculate gamma and draw a conclusion about the relationship between health and smoking. What does this indicate about the relationship between these variables in the population?

21.6 Eleven countries are rank-ordered in terms of two variables: infant mortality rate and expenditure on the military as a proportion of national income. These ranks are:

Country	Rank on infant mortality	Rank on military spending
A	9	8
B	4	5
C	6	6
D	2	2
E	7	11
F	3	4
G	10	7
H	5	3
I	8	9
J	1	1
K	11	10

Calculate Spearman's rank order correlation coefficient for these data. What can you conclude about the relationship between these variables? Enter the data for these 11 countries on SPSS and calculate rho to confirm your results. Is this a significant relationship?

21.7 Does price reflect quality? When people pay more for something are they actually getting something better? To assess this, a number of expert judges are asked to taste and rank 15 wines whose identity and price are not disclosed to them. The wine rated 15 is considered the highest quality, while the wine scoring 1 is considered the most inferior. The rank of each wine according to the judges and its retail price is listed below:

Quality	Price
1	3.00
2	4.00
3	5.50
4	5.90
5	11.99
6	6.80
7	7.50
8	9.00
9	18.00
10	3.50
11	11.45
12	12.00
13	9.00
14	4.50
15	13.00

Calculate the Spearman's rank order correlation coefficient to assess the nature of any relationship between quality and price. Check your answer by calculating rho through SPSS

21.8 A group of eight runners is interested in whether running ability is associated with age. These eight runners record their ages in years and also their order in finishing a run. The results are:

Name	Age	Place
Kenny	52	4
Schuey	42	3
Ian	40	6
George	32	8
Pat	23	7
Kurt	18	5
Darryl	17	1
Ryan	16	2
Cameron	13	9

Calculate Spearman's correlation coefficient to assess whether there is any relationship between age and running ability. Enter these data on SPSS to assess your answer.

Regression and correlation for interval/ratio data

As with two variables measured on ordinal scales that have many values, when working with two variables measured at the interval/ratio level we no longer talk about association. Instead we talk about *correlation*. For our purposes though, the two concepts are synonymous: we are interested in whether a change in the value of one variable goes hand-in-hand with a change in the other variable.

Scatter plots

In trying to assess whether there is any association between two variables measured at the nominal or ordinal level, the initial step is to organize the data into a crosstabulation. If inspection of the percentage distribution of cases in the table leads us to suspect that these two variables are related, the next step is to calculate measures of association that give a precise numerical value to any such suspicion.

It is difficult to arrange interval/ratio data into crosstabulations. Interval/ratio data do not fall into discrete categories such as large or small, old or young, etc. Such data can of course be collapsed into an ordinal scale, but this is at the cost of information. Since there are usually many values for variables measured at the interval/ratio level, a contingency table will have to have as many rows or columns as there are possible values. If we were looking at the distribution of age in years of a country's population we would need over 100 rows of data to take account of the fact that age spreads out over a wide range. To take account of the greater range of values that interval/ratio scales usually have, a *scatter plot* is the best way to organize such data to get an initial impression as to whether any correlation exists. A scatter plot (just like a crosstab) shows the values each case 'scored' on each variable simultaneously.

A **scatter plot** displays the joint distribution of two variables measured at the interval/ratio level. A **coordinate** on a scatter plot indicates the values any given case takes for each variable.

For example, we might be interested in the relationship between unemployment rates and the level of civil disturbances. From official statistics we obtain the following information about the rate of unemployment (which we think is the independent variable, X) and the number of civil disturbances (which we think is the dependent variable, Y) for five towns (Table 22.1).

Table 22.1   Unemployment rates and civil disturbances by town

City	Unemployment rate (X)	Civil disturbances (Y)
A	22	25
B	20	13
C	15	5
D	10	10
E	9	2

Arranging the information in a scatter plot is usually easier to 'read' (Figure 22.1).

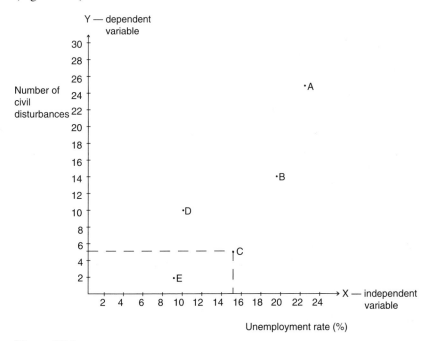

Figure 22.1

It is the convention to put the dependent variable (Y) on the vertical axis and the independent variable (X) on the horizontal axis. If we look at any one of these points (A – E) and draw a straight line down to the horizontal axis, we can find out the unemployment rate in that town. Similarly, by drawing a straight line across to the vertical axis we can 'read off' the number of civil disturbances. Grid lines for city C have been drawn in to illustrate this procedure. For this town the unemployment rate is 15 per cent and there are also five civil disturbances.

Looking at this scatter plot, it can intuitively be seen that a correlation exists, because we can almost imagine a sloping line that runs through these five points. The *direction* of association is indicated by whether this imaginary line slopes up (positive) or down (negative). In this case the slope is positive, indicating that an *increase* in unemployment rate is correlated with an *increase* in the number of civil disturbances.

Linear regression

Regression analysis is simply the task of fitting a line through a scatter plot of cases that 'best fits' the data. Any line can be expressed in a mathematical formula. The general formula for a straight line is:

$$Y = a \pm bX$$

where
 Y is the dependent variable
 X is the independent variable
 a is the Y–intercept (the value of Y when X is zero)
 b is the slope of the line
 + indicates positive correlation
 – indicates negative correlation.

This formula says that a line is defined by two factors. One is its starting point along the vertical axis (a), and the second is the slope of the line from this point ($\pm b$). It is the value of b that we are most interested in since any slope, either positive or negative, indicates some correlation between the variables in the sample (see Figure 22.2.)

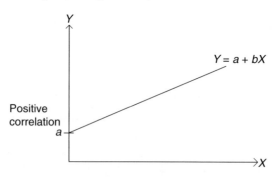

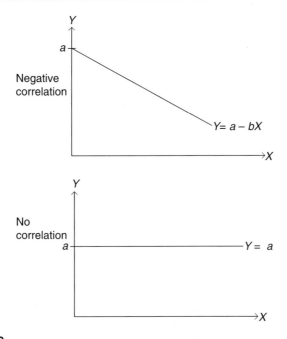

Figure 22.2

Deriving this equation for any particular line is like giving a person a unique combination of first and last names so that this person can be differentiated from everybody else. The general formula for the equation of a line is much like a form that has a space entitled First name and another space entitled Last name.

$$Y = \text{Firstname} \pm \text{Lastname } (X)$$

We write in the specific combination of names that identifies the relevant individual. If I try to identify somebody using just their first name, say Pablo, this will not diffferentiate that person from all the other people with the same first name. Similarly, if I identify someone just by their last name, Picasso, this will not differentiate this person from all other people with the same last name. But writing both names together I identify a unique individual. Similarly with identifying a line. Thousands of straight lines can be drawn through the space marked out by the vertical and horizontal axes of a scatter plot. But to identify the individual line that we think best fits the scatter plot I need to provide it with a unique first and last name. The line's first name is its point of origin along the Y-axis. But obviously this is not enough to distinguish it from the multitude of lines that can start from the same point. This is illustrated in Figure 22.3, which shows only some of the lines that will share the same value for a in their equation.

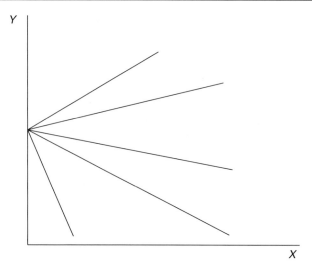

Figure 22.3   Straight lines with the same value for *a*

Specifying the slope of a straight line on its own is also insufficient to distinguish it from all the others that could occupy the space. This is illustrated in Figure 22.4, which presents some lines that will all have the same value for *b*.

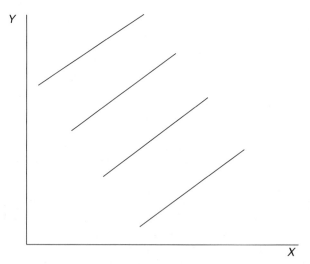

Figure 22.4   Straight lines with the same value for *b*

However, if we specify both the point of origin on the *Y*-axis *and* the slope of the line from that point, then we are able to uniquely identify any line within the space. The trick to linear regression is to come up with the unique combination of values for *a* and *b* that identify the line of best fit.

Looking at the data for the five cities, we could draw many straight lines through this scatter plot, and each of these lines would have their own unique formula. For example, in Figure 22.5 I have drawn a line that seems to fit the data pretty well. I could call this 'line 1' or 'line A' or 'my line'. Instead, I will call it by its mathematical name:

$$Y = -5 + 1.15X$$

Where did this equation come from?

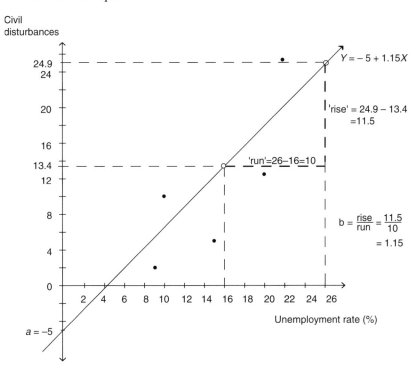

Figure 22.5

- The value for a (−5) is the point on the Y axis where the line 'begins'. This is the number of civil disturbances we would expect to find in a town with an unemployment rate of zero. Obviously it is nonsensical to talk about a negative number of civil disturbances, and we would not extend the Y-axis into negative values. But we do it here to show the logic behind the equation for a line.
- The + sign means that the line has a positive slope, which indicates some positive correlation between these two variables.
- The value of 1.15 for b is the slope, or coefficient, of the regression line: by how much civil disturbances will increase if unemployment increases by 1 per cent.

Since the slope of any straight line is 'rise over run', to actually calculate this value I take any increase in unemployment rate, such as the increase of 10 between 16 and 26. I 'read off' the corresponding values for the number of civil disturbances expected, which are 13.4 and 24.9 respectively, which gives a 'rise' of 11.5. Dividing rise over run, the slope will be:

$$\frac{11.5}{10} = 1.15$$

The line we have just identified gives us a range of expected values for civil disturbance, depending on the value of the unemployment rate. The difference between the expected value and the actual value for civil disturbance at a particular unemployment rate is called the **residual**.

> The **residual** is the difference between the observed value of the dependent variable and the value of the dependent variable predicted by a regression line.

Notice that no straight line will pass through all the points in a scatter plot. In fact, a 'good' line might not touch *any* of the points: there will usually be a gap between each plot and the regression line. Unless a point falls exactly on the line there will be a residual value.

For example, my line predicts that at an unemployment rate of 9 per cent, the number of civil disturbances will be:

$$Y = -5 + 0.77X$$

$$= -5 + 1.15(9)$$

$$= 5.35$$

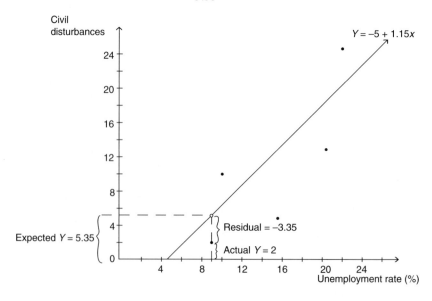

Figure 22.6

Instead, there were 2 civil disturbances for this town with an unemployment rate of 9 per cent. The residual, which is also called the error, at this point is −3.35 (see Figure 22.6):

$$\text{error} = Y_{\text{actual}} - Y_{\text{expected}}$$

$$= 2 - 5.35$$

$$= -3.35$$

I drew this particular line on the basis of what looked to me, with the naked eye, to be the best line that fitted these data. Someone else might think that she could draw a better line through these points, and this new line would have its own equation to define it, and the residuals between the expected values and actual values would be different. It might be hard to determine which of these lines is the 'best' one. Of all the possible lines that could run through these points, it seems plausible to suggest that the best line is the one that makes these residuals as small as possible: the one that *minimizes* the residuals.

Regression analysis uses this idea (although in a slightly more complicated form). The logic is called **ordinary least squares regression** (OLS): we want a line such that the gaps between the estimated values of Y and the actual values of Y (squared) are as small as possible. (We *square* the residuals, rather than just *sum* them, because the sum of residuals for *any* line that passes through the point that is the mean for both the dependent and independent variables will equal zero. To eliminate the effect of the positive and negative signs, the residuals are squared so that we are only dealing with positive numbers.)

> **Ordinary least squares regression** is a rule that tells us to draw a line through a scatter plot that minimizes the sum of the squared residuals.

There are two guides for constructing the OLS regression line:

• The OLS regression line must pass through a point whose coordinates are the averages of the dependent and independent variables ($\overline{Y}$, $\overline{X}$).

The average number of civil disturbances, $\overline{Y}$, is:

$$\overline{Y} = \frac{\Sigma Y_i}{N}$$

$$= \frac{25 + 13 + 5 + 10 + 2}{5}$$

$$= \frac{55}{5}$$

$$= 11$$

The average unemployment rate, $\overline{X}$, is:

$$\overline{X} = \frac{\Sigma X_i}{N}$$

$$= \frac{22 + 20 + 15 + 10 + 9}{5}$$

$$= \frac{76}{5}$$

$$= 15.2$$

Thus the OLS regression line will pass through the point where $Y = 11$ and $X = 15.2$.

• The slope of the OLS regression line, b, is defined by the formula:

$$b = \frac{\Sigma(X_i - \overline{X})(Y_i - \overline{Y})}{\Sigma(X_i - \overline{X})^2}$$

Although this equation captures the essential idea that the line needs to minimize the squared differences between actual and expected values, the value of b is easier to calculate using the following formula:

$$b = \frac{N\Sigma(X_iY_i) - (\Sigma X_i)(\Sigma Y_i)}{N\Sigma X^2_i - (\Sigma X_i)^2}$$

Although this formula still looks scary, if we work through it step-by-step we will see that it is a rather straightforward calculation. The calculations for city A are included in Table 22.2 to show where the numbers come from.

Table 22.2   Calculation of the slope of the regression line (b)

City	Unemployment rate	Civil disturbances			
	X_i	Y_i	X^2_i	Y^2_i	X_iY_i
A	22	25	$22 \times 22 = 484$	$25 \times 25 = 625$	$22 \times 25 = 550$
B	20	13	400	169	260
C	15	5	225	25	75
D	10	10	100	100	100
E	9	2	81	4	18
	$\Sigma X_i = 76$	$\Sigma Y_i = 55$	$\Sigma X^2_i = 1290$	$\Sigma Y^2_i = 923$	$\Sigma(X_iY_i) = 1003$

Putting all this data into the equation for the slope of the regression line, we get:

$$b = \frac{N\Sigma(X_iY_i) - (\Sigma X_i)(\Sigma Y_i)}{N\Sigma X_i^2 - (\Sigma X_i)^2}$$

$$= \frac{5(1003) - (76)(55)}{5(1290) - (76)^2}$$

$$= \frac{5015 - 4180}{6450 - 5776}$$

$$= \frac{835}{671}$$

$$= +1.24$$

The value of b, called the coefficient of the regression line, is very important because it quantifies any correlation between two variables.

> The **slope of the regression** line, b, indicates by how many units the dependent variable will change, given a one unit change in the independent variable.

Now that we have fixed the regression line through a specific point (the averages of X and Y) and also given it a 'last name' by calculating the slope of the line through this point, we can give it a complete label by deriving the value for a. We use the following formula, which uses both of the features of the regression line we have identified (it passess through the average of X and Y, and has a slope equal to b):

$$a = \overline{Y} - b\overline{X}$$

Therefore the value of a will be:

$$a = \overline{Y} - b\overline{X}$$

$$= 11 - 1.24(15.2)$$

$$= -7.85$$

Thus we can define the line of best fit, for this set of cases, with the following equation:

$$Y = -7.85 + 1.24X$$

In Figure 22.7 this regression line is drawn through the scatter plot. What does this tell us about the relationship between unemployment rates and civil disturbances, for this set of cases?

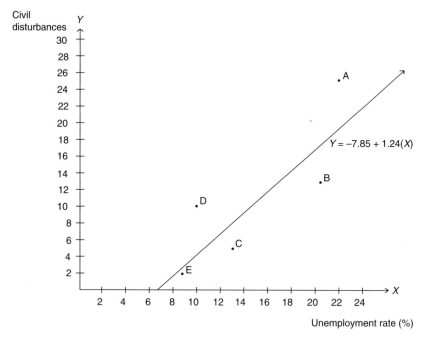

Figure 22.7

- There is a positive relationship between the two variables: an increase (decrease) in the unemployment rate is correlated with an increase (decrease) in the number of civil disturbances.
- We can quantify this positive correlation: an increase in the unemployment rate of 1 per cent is correlated with an increase of 1.24 in the number of civil disturbances.

I can now use this formula for the purpose of prediction: I can predict the number of civil disturbances a town is likely to have, given a certain rate of unemployment. For example, if I was told that another town had an unemployment rate of 18 per cent, my best guess would be to say that it experienced 14.5 civil disturbances:

$$Y = -7.85 + 1.24(18) = 14.5$$

Pearson's correlation coefficient (r)

We have seen that the value of b is an indicator of whether a correlation exists between two variables measured at the interval/ratio level, and also the direction of such correlation. But does it also indicate the *strength* of the correlation? Does a value of $b = 1.24$ indicate a strong, moderate, or weak association? Unfortunately it does not.

The problem is that these units vary from one situation to another. For example, if I use proportions rather than percentage points to measure unemployment rates, so that instead of writing 22, 20, 15, 10, 9, I wrote 0.22, 0.20, 0.15, 0.1, 0.09, the estimated value of *b* will be 124 rather than 1.24. In other words, the value of *b* is not only affected by the strength of the correlation, but also *by the units of measurement*: If I measure some variable in metres, I might get a value of *b* = 0.1, but if I measure the same cases using centimetres the value will be *b* = 10. The actual relationship I am looking at has not changed; only the units of measurement. Therefore there is no way of knowing whether any particular value for *b* indicates a weak, moderate, or strong correlation.

To overcome this, we convert the value of *b* into *a standardized* measure of correlation called the correlation coefficient: **Pearson's r**. Pearson's *r* will always range between −1 and +1, regardless of the actual units in which the variables are measured. The formula for *r* is:

$$r = \frac{\Sigma(X_i - \overline{X})(Y_i - \overline{Y})}{\sqrt{[X_i - \overline{X})^2][(Y_i - \overline{Y})^2]}}$$

or

$$r = \frac{N\Sigma(X_i Y_i) - (\Sigma X_i)(\Sigma Y_i)}{\sqrt{[N\Sigma X_i^2 - (\Sigma X_i)^2][N\Sigma Y_i^2 - (\Sigma Y_i)^2]}}$$

Fortunately, we have already calculated the elements of this equation in the table we used above for calculating *b* (Table 22.2). If we substitute the statistics from this table into this second formula we get:

$$r = \frac{N\Sigma(X_i Y_i) - (\Sigma X_i)(\Sigma Y_i)}{\sqrt{[N\Sigma X_i^2 - (\Sigma X_i)^2][N\Sigma Y_i^2 - (\Sigma Y_i)^2]}}$$

$$= \frac{5(1003) - 76(55)}{\sqrt{[5(1290) - (76)^2][5(923) - (55)^2]}}$$

$$= \frac{5015 - 4180}{\sqrt{[6450 - 5776][4615 - 3025]}}$$

$$= \frac{835}{1035.21}$$

$$= +0.81$$

The value of *r* tells us the strength as well as the direction of association. A value of 0.81 indicates that the correlation between these two variables for this set of cases is a strong positive one.

Explaining variance: The coefficient of determination (r^2)

We have already used the regression line to predict the number of civil disturbances in a city, given a particular rate of unemployment? But we also saw that there would usually be a margin of error in this prediction, depending on how closely clustered around the line were the actual plots. If there was a high variance in the scores we could say that an increase in X would produce so much increase in Y, but our likelihood of being wrong would be greater than in a situation where the scores were tightly packed around the regression line.

We can see in Figure 22.8 that even though the same regression line best fits both sets of plots, we will have a greater confidence in our predictive ability in (**a**) than in (**b**). This is because the regression line in (**a**) explains a greater proportion of the variance of Y than in (**b**). We therefore need some measure of how much variance in the dependent variable is explained by a regression line.

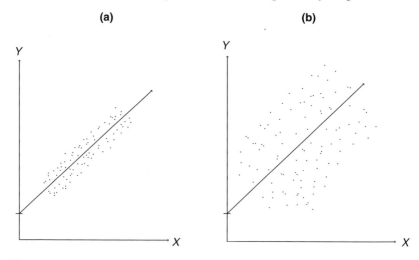

Figure 22.8

Fortunately we can do this by simply squaring r and obtaining the *coefficient of determination*, r^2, the variance explained by the regression line relative to the variance explained in the case of no association:

$$r^2 = (0.81)^2$$
$$r^2 = 0.65$$

The coefficient of determination can be interpreted as a PRE measure of association, much like the PRE measures we encountered in the previous two chapters. We make predictions about the expected value of the dependent variable *without* any information about the independent variable. We then make predictions *with* knowledge of the independent variable and compare the error rates.

For example, if we have to guess the number of civil disturbances in each city, and all we know is that the average number of disturbances for all five cities is 11, the best guess we can make is to say that the number of civil disturbances in *each* city is 11, regardless of the actual unemployment rate. In other words, we draw a straight horizontal line at this value as the regression line through the scatter plot (Figure 22.9).

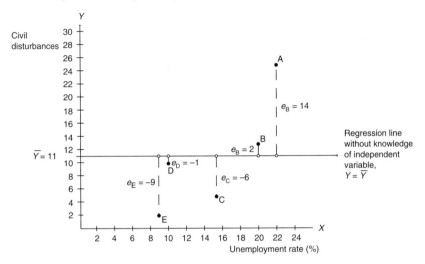

Figure 22.9

This horizontal line is the line we draw if there is no correlation between these two variables; knowing whether the unemployment rate is high or low will not cause me to change my expected number of civil disturbances. Sometimes this line comes very close to the mark. For city D we see that this line predicted, at an unemployment rate of 10 per cent, that there would be 11 civil disturbances. There were in fact 10 civil disturbances producing an error (e) for this city of –1. However, in other instances we make a large error using this line. For city A, at an unemployment rate of 22 per cent we again predict 11 civil disturbances, but in fact there were 25, producing an error of 14.

Now we compare these errors with the errors we make when predicting on the basis of the least squares regression line. Does this line substantially improve our guesswork? (See Figure 22.10.)

We can see that if there is a correlation between these two variables, the least squares regression line that captures this correlation will reduce the error rate. The gaps between the plots and the line will be much smaller when using the least squares regression line than when using the horizontal line based on the assumption of no correlation. It is precisely this aspect of the regression line that the coefficient of determination captures. A value for r^2 of 0.65 indicates that the least squares regression line explains 65 per cent of the variance of the dependent variable relative to the variance explained by the horizontal line. This is a substantial reduction in the error rate.

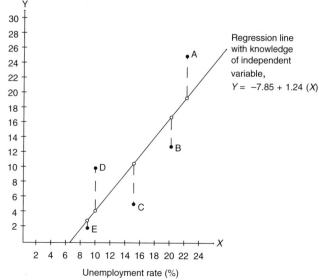

Figure 22.10

It may pay to stop at this point and discuss the difference between *r* and r^2 since they are very closely related. The correlation coefficient is a standardized measure of the relationship between two variables, that is, it indicates the extent to which a change in one variable will be associated with a change in another variable. Thus *r* (like *b*) is primarily a tool for prediction. The coefficient of determination, on the other hand, is a PRE measure of the amount of variation explained by a regression line, and therefore gives a sense of how much *confidence* we should place in the accuracy of our predictions.

> *Example*
> A museum keeps track of the number of visitors on randomly selected days across the year, in order to help it plan for crowds. It suspects that the daily temperature is a good predictor of the number of people who will pass through on any given day. The data on the daily temperature, measured in degrees Celsius, and the number of people attending, together with the calculations needed to construct a regression line, are included in Table 22.3.

Table 22.3 Calculation of the slope of the regression line (b)

Temperature	People			
X_i	Y_i	X_i^2	Y_i^2	X_iY_i
13	501	169	251001	6513
28	175	784	30625	4900
32	390	1024	152100	12480
20	452	400	204304	9040
11	550	121	302500	6050
15	734	225	538756	11010
9	620	81	384400	5580
33	199	1089	39601	6567
16	390	256	152100	6240
29	223	841	49729	6467
12	768	144	589824	9216
15	679	225	461041	10185
18	410	324	168100	7380
26	320	676	102400	8320
18	590	324	348100	10620
17	650	289	422500	11050
27	258	729	66564	6966
32	201	1024	40401	6432
28	458	784	209764	12824
23	534	529	285156	12282
$\bar{X} = 21.1$	$\bar{Y} = 455.1$			
$\Sigma X_i = 422$	$\Sigma Y_i = 9102$	$\Sigma X_i^2 = 10038$	$\Sigma Y_i^2 = 4798966$	$\Sigma(X_iY_i) = 170122$

Putting these figures into the equation for the slope of the regression line, we get:

$$b = \frac{N\Sigma(X_iY_i) - (\Sigma X_i)(\Sigma Y_i)}{N\Sigma X_i^2 - (\Sigma X_i)^2}$$

$$= \frac{20(170\,122) - (422)(9102)}{20(10\,038) - (422)^2}$$

$$= \frac{3402\,440 - 3841\,044}{200\,760 - 178\,084}$$

$$= -19$$

The value of a will be:

$$a = \overline{Y} - b\overline{X}$$
$$= 455.1 - (-19.34)(21.1)$$
$$= 863$$

The OLS regression line will therefore have the following equation:

$$Y = 863 - 19X$$

This indicates that there is a negative correlation between the temperature and the number of people attending the museum. We predict that for every degree that the temperature increases, 19 fewer people will attend the museum. The value for a indicates that when the temperature falls to zero the museum should expect 863 visitors.

To assess the strength of this relationship, and the confidence the museum can place in its predictions, it also calculates the correlation coefficient and the coefficient of determination:

$$r = \frac{N\Sigma(X_iY_i) - (\Sigma X_i)(\Sigma Y_i)}{\sqrt{[N\Sigma X_i^2 (\Sigma X_i)^2][N\Sigma Y_i^2 - (\Sigma Y_i)^2]}}$$

$$r = \frac{20\,170\,122 - (422)(9102)}{\sqrt{[20(10\,038) - (422)^2][20(4798\,966) - (9102)^2]}}$$

$$= -0.8$$
$$r^2 = (-0.8)^2$$
$$= 0.64$$

These indicate that there is a strong negative relationship and that the OLS regression line explains a high proportion of the variance in the data, allowing the museum to make confident predictions.

Plots, correlation, and regression using SPSS

Filename 22.sav   The data from this example have been entered into SPSS, with civil disturbances given the variable name **civildis** and unemployment rate given the variable name **unmplmnt**. The results we obtained above can be generated on SPSS in a number of different ways, each of which provides different amounts of information in slightly different forms. To show the similarities and differences we will work through each method.

Scatter plot only

To obtain a simple scatter plot of the data, we use the following procedures given in Table 22.3.

Table 22.3   Scatter plots using SPSS

SPSS command/action	Comments
1 From the menu select **Graphs/Scatter...**	This will bring up the **Scatterplot** window. You will notice that there is a heavy border around the option **Simple**, which is the default setting. Since we are only after a simple scatter plot here we will not change this setting
2 Click on **Define**	This will bring up the **Simple Scatterplot** window
3 Click on **civildis**	This will highlight **civildis**
4 Click on the ➤ that points to the area headed **Y Axis:**	This will paste **civildis** as the variable to be displayed on the *Y*-axis (dependent)
5 Click on **unmplmnt**	This will highlight **unmplmnt**
6 Click on the ➤ in the area headed **X Axis**	This will paste **unmplmnt** as the variable to be displayed on the *X*-axis (independent)
7 Click on **OK**	

The scatter plot generated will be as shown in Figure SPSS.M.

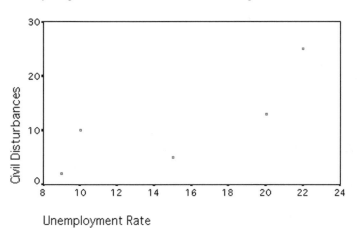

Figure SPSS.M

If we want a regression line to be included with this scatterplot we then proceed with the instructions in Table 22.4.

Table 22.4   Adding a regression line to a scatter plot using SPSS

SPSS command/action	Comments
1 Click on the **Edit** button at the top of the chart	This will redraw the scatterplot, and also provide a new menu at the top of the page
2 From this menu select **Chart/Options...**	This will bring up the **Scatterplot Options** window. You will see an area headed **Fit Line**, which has an option **Total** with a small square next to it
3 Click on the square next to **Total**	This will place × in the square to show that it has been selected
4 Click on **OK**	

This will redraw the scatterplot with the OLS regression line through it (Figure SPSS.N).

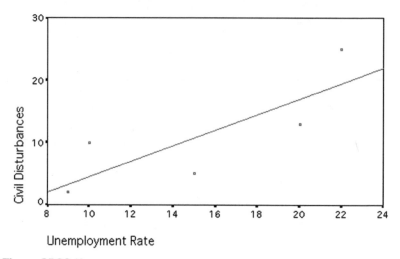

Figure SPSS.N

Scatter plot with equation statistics

Another method that provides a similar plot with a regression line, coupled with statistics for the regression line, is to use the procedure in Table 22.5.

Table 22.5 Regression with curve estimation using SPSS

SPSS command/action	Comments
1 From the menu select **Statistics/Regression/Curve Estimation...**	This will bring up the **Curve Estimation** window
2 Click on **civildis**	This will highlight **civildis**
3 Click on the ➤ that points to the area headed **Dependent(s):**	This will paste **civildis** as the dependent variable
4 Click on **unmplmnt**	This will highlight **unmplmnt**
5 Click on the ➤ in the area headed **Independent**	This will paste **unmplmnt** as the independent variable
6 Click on **OK**	

In the output window will appear the following results:

```
MODEL:  MOD_1.


Independent:  UNMPLMNT


  Dependent Mth   Rsq  d.f.      F  Sigf     b0      b1

   CIVILDIS LIN   .651    3   5.59  .099 -7.8309  1.2389

Hi-Res Chart  # 1:Curvefit for civil disturbances
```

This firstly tells us that **unmplmnt** is the independent variable. It then provides the regression information for the dependent variable **civildis**.

```
Mth

LIN
```

This indicates the estimation method is linear regression.

```
Rsq

.651
```

This indicates that the value for the coefficient of determination, r^2, is 0.651.

```
   b0      b1

-7.8309  1.2389
```

This tells us that the value for the Y-intercept (which we called *a* in the analysis above but SPSS calls b0) is –7.8309, and the slope of the regression line (which SPSS calls b1) is 1.2389. These are the same, apart from slight differences due to rounding, as the values we calculated by hand.

To observe the Hi-resolution chart printed together with this information, from the menu select **Window/Chart Carousel** (Figure SPSS.O).

File	Edit	Data	Transform	Statistics	Graphs	Utilities	**Window**

✓Toolbar
✓Status Bar

21.dat

1 :unmplmnt   22

!untitled output 1
✓21.dat
Chart Carousel

	unmplmnt	civildis	var	var	var	var
1	22	25				
2	20	13				
3	15	5				
4	10	10				
5	9	2				

Figure SPSS.O

The chart that will appear is shown in Figure SPSS.P.

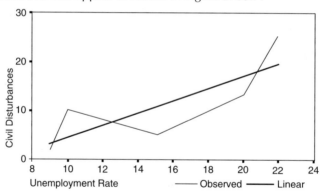

Figure SPSS.P

Regression statistics only

If we did not want to generate a scatter plot, and only want the regression statistics (i.e. the equation for the line, the Pearson's correlation coefficient, and the coefficient of determination) we use the instructions given in Table 22.6. A word of warning though: it is generally a good idea to start with an inspection of the scatter plot to see if the pattern of data is amenable to ordinary least squares regression. As we will discuss shortly, OLS is based on a number of assumptions, and 'eye-balling' the plot may give us a quick indication if these assumptions are not met.

Table 22.6   Regression using SPSS

SPSS command/action	Comments
1 From the menu select **Statistics/Regression/Linear...**	This will bring up the **Linear Regression** window
2 Click on **civildis**	This will highlight **civildis**
3 Click on the ➤ that points to the area headed **Dependent(s):**	This will paste **civildis** as the dependent variable
4 Click on **unmplmnt**	This will highlight **unmplmnt**
5 Click on the ➤ in the area headed **Independent**	This will paste **unmplmnt** as the independent variable
6 Click on **OK**	

The results will be:

```
* * * *   M U L T I P L E   R E G R E S S I O N   * * * *

Listwise Deletion of Missing Data

Equation Number 1   Dependent Variable..  CIVILDIS   Civil Disturbances

Block Number  1. Method: Enter     UNMPLMNT

Variable(s) Entered on Step Number
   1..   UNMPLMNT  Unemployment Rate


Multiple R            .80660
R Square              .65060
Adjusted R Square     .53414
Standard Error       6.08573

Analysis of Variance
                    DF      Sum of Squares       Mean Square
Regression          1          206.89169          206.89169
Residual            3          111.10831           37.03610

F =      5.58622      Signif F =  .0991


------------------ Variables in the Equation ------------------

Variable          B         SE B       Beta         T    Sig T

UNMPLMNT      1.238872     .524165    .806600     2.364   .0991
(Constant)   -7.830861    8.419330               -.930   .4209


End Block Number   1   All requested variables entered.
```

The important information is in the last section of the output, below *Variables in the Equation*

```
Variable               B

UNMPLMNT        1.238872
(Constant)      -7.830861
```

This indicates that the coefficient for unemployment rate in the equation, which is the value of *b*, is 1.238872, and the value of the intercept, *a*, which is called the Constant here, is –7.830861.

The other important information here is:

```
Beta

.806600
```

This is the value for the correlation coefficient, Pearson's *r*. This has already been presented, together with the value for r^2 at the top of the output:

```
Multiple R      .80660
R Square        .65060
```

Testing for significance

So far we have calculated the regression line, and the correlation statistics. These statistics tell us that *in our sample* there is a strong, positive association between civil disturbance and unemployment rates. But this is a result that obtains in the sample, and therefore might not reflect what is happening in *all* cities. It might be sampling error that has caused us to select five cities that are not like the rest. There may be no correlation between these variables in the population of all cities. We therefore need to conduct an inference test on the value of the correlation coefficient we have obtained. The null hypothesis for this test is that there is no correlation, whereas the alternative hypothesis is that there is some correlation:

$$H_0: b = 0$$
$$H_a: b \neq 0$$

Note that the alternative hypothesis does not indicate a direction of association; merely that it is not zero. The test statistic used to decide between these hypotheses is a *t*-test, which is calculated using the following formula:

$$t_{sample} = r\sqrt{\frac{N-2}{1-r^2}}$$

If we substitute the values for r and r^2, from the SPSS output, into this equation, we get:

$$t_{sample} = r\sqrt{\frac{N-2}{1-r^2}}$$

$$= 0.8066\sqrt{\frac{3-2}{1-0.6506}}$$

$$= 2.36$$

In fact, if we look back at the SPSS output, we can see that this t-score has already been calculated. For example, the regression output included the following line:

Variable	B	SE B	Beta	T	Sig T
UNMPLMNT	1.238872	.524165	.806600	2.364	.0991

We see next under T the value of 2.364, the same as we calculated. This has a probability of occurring in a sample drawn from a population with a value of $b = 0$ of 0.0991, or nearly 1-in-10. This is a borderline case where the decision to reject the null hypothesis of no correlation will depend on the choice of alpha levels. At $\alpha = 0.05$ we would not reject the null hypothesis of no correlation, but at $\alpha = 0.10$ we would reject.

It is important to stop and consider what has happened. In the sample we measured a strong positive association, but the inference test tells us that despite this the result might be due to chance. This has probably occurred as a result of the small sample size we were working with ($N = 5$). If we look again at the plots we can see that the regression line has been heavily influenced by the one score for the city with an unemployment rate of 22 per cent and 25 civil disturbances. Because we are working with such a small sample one extreme case can throw out the results for the whole sample. If this one score were different, the regression line would also be very different. Since this is possible, even strong correlations may not turn out to be significant when working with very small samples.

The assumptions behind regression analysis

We have used the concept of least squares regression to derive a measure of correlation between two variables measured at the interval/ratio level. However, implicit in the use of OLS are certain assumptions, which, if violated, will mean that this will not be the best rule for fitting a line through a scatter plot. It is worth noting these assumptions, although a more detailed discussion would take us too far from the needs of this book.

Linear relationships

Least squares regression assumes that the line of best fit is a straight one, or in more technical terms that there is a linear relationship. However, this is not always the case (Figure 22.11).

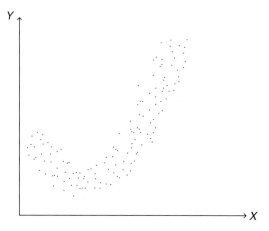

Figure 22.11 A non-linear relationship

It is clear that the line of best fit for this scatter plot will be *curvilinear*. We could ask SPSS to fit a regression line through these data points, and it would give us the best straight line, but clearly the best *straight* line is not the best line!

Stability

Looking back at the example regarding the relationship between unemployment and crime rates, the range of values for the independent variable was 9–22 per cent. It might be tempting to use the regression line fitted for this data to predict the crime rate in a city with an unemployment rate of 30 per cent. In other words, we might try to project the regression line out past the right edge of the scatter plot and use it as a tool for prediction. To do this we have to assume that the relationship is stable: that the correlation coefficient will be the same for the whole range of values over which we want to make predictions.

This can sometimes be a very dangerous assumption. The statistics we have generated apply just to the cases for which we have information, and to extend their domain to cases for which we don't have information requires some justification. It may be, for example, that when unemployment rates hit a certain threshold level, such as 25 per cent, the crime rate jumps up dramatically.

The other aspect of stability relates to time. Unlike the physical sciences, a relationship between two variables in the social sciences is not always the same over time. The relationship between force and mass seems relatively permanent, but the relationship between unemployment and civil disturbance may not be, because history brings about changes to social institutions that may alter the character of the relationship. For example, governments may respond to a strong relationship between unemployment and civil disturbance by creating new social institutions such as income support schemes and community programs that could soften the effect of unemployment. Using the information from one historical period for another historical period may therefore be inaccurate.

Homoscedasticity

The strict definition of homoscedasticity is that the variance of the error terms (residuals) of a regression line is constant. The best way to explain this is through an illustration (Figure 22.12).

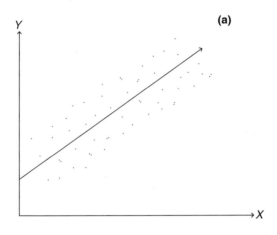

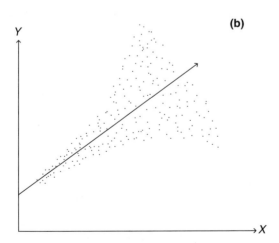

Figure 22.12   Regression where the error terms are *homoscedastic* (**a**); regression where the error terms are *heteroscedastic* (**b**).

In Figure 22.12(a) we can see that the spread of the data points around the regression line is fairly constant over the length of the regression line. The data points form a 'cigar-shape' around the line. In Figure 22.10(b), though, the data points lie far away from the line at one end, and gradually get closer as the value of the independent variable decreases. Graph (**a**) is the case of homoscedasticity, whereas graph (*b*) shows heteroscedasticity. The presence of heteroscedasticity causes any significance test on the value of *r* to be invalid, so that we are not able to generalize from a sample result to the population. Usually a simple inspection of a scatter plot will be sufficient to detect whether this assumption is valid.

Reversibility

This is not so much an assumption regarding the construction of a regression line but rather an assumption in its use. A positive correlation, for example, implies that when the value of an independent variable increases, the value of the dependent variable increases as well, and that when it decreases the dependent variable decreases as well. However, it is not always the case that the same relationship holds for increases as it does for decreases. We all know that there is a positive correlation between income levels and consumption levels: when we have more to spend we spend more! A researcher may look at a period of rising income levels and calculate a value for the regression coefficient (*b*) of 0.8: when income increases by $100, consumption will go up by $80. Can this researcher then argue that if income decreases by the same amount, consumption levels will go back to where they were before the initial increase? The answer is no. Most people adjust their spending patterns to this higher income level, and do not tend to give it up very easily, even if income falls again. People go into debt or sell off assets in order to maintain the higher spending patterns they have become accustomed to, so that the correlation observed in one direction will not be the same as that observed in the other direction.

Summary

This chapter has introduced the concepts of correlation and regression. But in fact we have only just skimmed the surface. We could spend a whole course discussing this topic alone, and still not give it adequate treatment. Moreover, you will have noticed that there were many options within SPSS that we did not explore, sticking only to the bare minimum needed to get the results we were after. It is not within the scope of this book to pursue these issues in more detail — we only want to introduce the key concepts and methods. There are many other books that delve into this and the other topics covered in far more depth. Nevertheless, the key ideas hopefully have emerged by sticking to the basics and not elaborating further on more advanced topics. Having digested this much, the task of absorbing the more advanced material may prove a little easier.

Exercises

22.1 Why should we draw a scatterplot of data before undertaking regression analysis?

22.2 What does the Y-intercept of a regression line indicate?

22.3 What is the principle used for drawing the line of best fit through a scatter plot?

22.4 Explain the difference between the correlation coefficient, r, and the coefficient of the regression line, b.

22.5 Using graph paper draw a scatter plot for the following data:

X:	5	6	9	10	10	13	15	18	22	27
Y:	35	28	30	22	28	28	20	21	15	18

Looking at the data, what do you expect the sign in front of the coefficient to be (i.e. is there a positive or negative correlation)? Draw a regression line through these data using the naked eye. Determine the equation for your line, and predict Y for $X = 12$.

Calculate the least squares regression line through these data and compare it with your freehand line. What is the least squares estimate for Y when $X = 12$?

Enter this data on SPSS and run the regression command to confirm your results.

22.6 A regression line is plotted through data on life expectancy in years and government expenditure on health care per head of population (in $'000) for a group of developing nations. Life expectancy is considered the dependent variable and expenditure the independent variable. The equation for the regression line is:

$$Y = 40 + 0.7X$$

What will life expectancy be if the government spends no money on health care? What will life expectancy be if the government spends $30 000 per head on health care? Does this indicate a strong relationship between the two variables?

22.7 A survey of employed workers found that the correlation coefficient between the number of years of post-secondary education and current annual income measured in dollars is 0.54. The sample size for this survey was 140. The significance of this correlation coefficient was tested using a t-test, which gave a t-value of 7.54. What conclusion should be drawn about the nature of the relationship between these two variables?

22.8 A university lecturer in statistics wants to emphasize to her students the value of study to exam performance. She monitors the amount of time in minutes that *all* 11 students in her class spend in the library per week, and the final grades for each student. The figures are recorded in the following table:

Library time (minutes)	Exam score
41	52
30	44
39	48
48	65
55	62
58	60
65	74
80	79
94	80
100	90
120	86

She analyses these data using the regression command in SPSS, which produces the following output:

```
* * * *   M U L T I P L E   R E G R E S S I O N   * * * *


Listwise Deletion of Missing Data

Equation Number 1    Dependent Variable..   EXAM   exam results

Block Number  1. Method: Enter      MINUTES


Variable(s) Entered on Step Number
   1..    MINUTES    minutes spent in library


Multiple R            .93642
R Square              .87688
Adjusted R Square     .86320
Standard Error       5.78245

Analysis of Variance
                    DF      Sum of Squares       Mean Square
Regression           1         2143.25131        2143.25131
Residual             9          300.93051          33.43672

F =     64.09872       Signif F =  .0000


------------------ Variables in the Equation ------------------

Variable              B        SE B       Beta        T   Sig T

MINUTES          .510917    .063815     .936418    8.006  .0000
(Constant)     33.366402   4.579863                7.285  .0000


End Block Number   1   All requested variables entered.
```

From this information write down the equation for the ordinary least squares regression line for these data. What is the strength and direction of the relationship between these variables? Will a student who spends no time in the library fail? A student wants to use this information so that he can work out the minimum amount of time he needs to spend in the library in order to get a bare pass grade (50). What is the minimum amount of time he needs to spend in the library? Can he be very confident in his prediction? What is the problem with using the regression line for such a purpose? Does the lecturer need to conduct a test of significance on the correlation coefficient?

Draw a scatter plot of these data to check that it was appropriate for the lecturer to use linear regression. Use the raw data to calculate by hand the same values presented in the SPSS output.

Appendix

Table A1 Area under the standard normal curve

z	Area under curve between *points* b	Area under curve beyond *both points* a	Area under curve beyond *one point* a
±0.1	0.080	0.920	0.460
±0.2	0.159	0.841	0.4205
±0.3	0.236	0.764	0.382
±0.4	0.311	0.689	0.3445
±0.5	0.383	0.617	0.3085
±0.6	0.451	0.549	0.2745
±0.7	0.516	0.484	0.242
±0.8	0.576	0.424	0.212
±0.9	0.632	0.368	0.184
±1	0.683	0.317	0.1585
±1.1	0.729	0.271	0.1355
±1.2	0.770	0.230	0.115
±1.3	0.806	0.194	0.097
±1.4	0.838	0.162	0.081
±1.5	0.866	0.134	0.067
±1.6	0.890	0.110	0.055
±1.645	0.900	0.100	0.050
±1.7	0.911	0.089	0.0445
±1.8	0.928	0.072	0.036
±1.9	0.943	0.057	0.029
±1.96	0.950	0.050	0.025
±2	0.954	0.046	0.023
±2.1	0.964	0.036	0.018
±2.2	0.972	0.028	0.014
±2.3	0.979	0.021	0.0105
±2.4	0.984	0.016	0.008
±2.5	0.988	0.012	0.006
±2.6	0.991	0.009	0.0045
±2.7	0.993	0.007	0.0035
±2.8	0.995	0.005	0.0025
±2.9	0.996	0.004	0.002
±3	0.997	0.003	0.0015
±3.1	0.998	0.002	0.0001
±3.2	0.9986	0.0014	0.0007
±3.3	0.9990	0.0010	0.0005
±3.4	0.9993	0.0007	0.0003

Table A1 Cont'd

z	Area under curve between *points* b	Area under curve beyond *both points* a	Area under curve beyond *one point* a
±3.5	0.9995	0.0005	0.00025
±3.6	0.9997	0.0003	0.00015
±3.7	0.9998	0.0002	0.0001
±3.8	0.99986	0.00014	0.00007
±3.9	0.99990	0.00010	0.00005
±4	>0.99990	<0.00010	<0.00005

Table A2 Distribution of *t*

Degrees of freedom (df)	Level of significance for one-tail test (α)				
	0.10	0.05	0.025	0.01	0.005
	Level of significance for two-tail test (α)				
	0.20	0.10	0.05	0.02	0.01
1	3.078	6.314	12.706	31.821	63.657
2	1.886	2.920	4.303	6.965	9.925
3	1.638	2.353	3.182	4.541	5.841
4	1.533	2.132	2.776	3.747	4.604
5	1.476	2.015	2.571	3.365	4.032
6	1.440	1.943	2.447	3.143	3.707
7	1.415	1.895	2.365	2.998	3.499
8	1.397	1.860	2.306	2.896	3.355
9	1.383	1.833	2.262	2.821	3.250
10	1.372	1.812	2.228	2.764	3.169
11	1.363	1.796	2.201	2.718	3.106
12	1.356	1.782	2.179	2.681	3.055
13	1.350	1.771	2.160	2.650	3.012
14	1.345	1.761	2.145	2.624	2.977
15	1.341	1.753	2.131	2.602	2.947
16	1.34	1.746	2.120	2.583	2.921
17	1.333	1.740	2.110	2.567	2.898
18	1.330	1.734	2.101	2.552	2.878
19	1.328	1.729	2.093	2.539	2.861
20	1.325	1.725	2.086	2.528	2.845
21	1.323	1.721	2.080	2.518	2.831
22	1.321	1.717	2.074	2.508	2.819
23	1.319	1.714	2.069	2.500	2.807
24	1.318	1.711	2.064	2.492	2.797
25	1.316	1.708	2.060	2.485	2.787
26	1.315	1.706	2.056	2.479	2.779
27	1.314	1.703	2.052	2.473	2.771
28	1.313	1.701	2.048	2.467	2.763
29	1.311	1.699	2.045	2.462	2.756
30	1.310	1.697	2.042	2.457	2.750
40	1.303	1.684	2.021	2.423	2.704
60	1.296	1.671	2.000	2.390	2.660
120	1.289	1.658	1.980	2.358	2.617
∞	1.282	1.645	1.960	2.326	2.576

Table A3 Distribution of F ($\alpha = 0.05$)

	Degrees of freedom for estimates of variance between samples (k − 1)									
$N - k$	1	2	3	4	5	6	7	8	9	∞
1	161.4	199.5	21507	224.6	230.2	234.0	236.8	238.9	240.5	254.3
2	18.51	19.00	19.16	19.25	19.30	19.33	19.35	19.37	19.38	19.50
3	10.13	9.55	9.28	9.12	9.01	8.94	8.89	8.84	8.81	8.53
4	7.71	6.94	6.59	6.39	6.26	6.16	6.09	6.04	6.00	5.63
5	6.61	5.79	5.41	5.19	5.05	4.95	4.88	4.82	4.77	4.36
6	5.99	5.14	4.76	4.53	4.39	4.28	4.21	4.15	4.10	3.67
7	5.59	4.74	4.35	4.12	3.97	3.87	3.79	3.73	3.68	3.23
8	5.32	4.46	4.07	3.84	3.69	3.58	3.50	3.44	3.39	2.93
9	5.12	4.26	3.86	3.63	3.48	3.37	3.29	3.23	3.18	2.71
10	4.96	4.10	3.71	3.48	3.33	3.22	3.14	3.07	3.02	2.54
11	4.84	3.98	3.59	3.36	3.20	3.09	3.01	2.95	2.90	2.40
12	4.75	3.88	3.49	3.26	3.11	3.00	2.91	2.85	2.80	2.30
13	4.67	3.80	3.41	3.18	3.02	2.92	2.83	2.77	2.71	2.21
14	4.60	3.74	3.34	3.11	2.96	2.85	2.76	2.70	2.65	2.13
15	4.54	3.68	3.29	3.06	2.90	2.79	2.71	2.64	2.59	2.07
16	4.49	3.63	3.24	3.01	2.85	2.74	2.66	2.59	2.54	2.01
17	4.45	3.59	3.20	2.96	2.81	2.70	2.61	2.55	2.49	1.96
18	4.41	3.55	3.16	2.93	2.77	2.66	2.58	2.51	2.46	1.92
19	4.38	3.52	3.13	2.90	2.74	2.63	2.54	2.48	2.42	1.88
20	4.35	3.49	3.10	2.87	2.71	2.60	2.51	2.45	2.39	1.84
21	4.32	3.47	3.07	2.84	2.68	2.57	2.49	2.42	2.37	1.81
22	4.30	3.44	3.05	2.82	2.66	2.55	2.46	2.40	2.34	1.78
23	4.28	3.42	3.03	2.80	2.64	2.53	2.44	2.38	2.32	1.76
24	4.26	3.40	3.01	2.78	2.62	2.51	2.42	2.36	2.30	1.73
25	4.24	3.38	2.99	2.76	2.60	2.49	2.40	2.34	2.28	1.71
26	4.22	3.37	2.98	2.74	2.59	2.47	2.39	2.32	2.27	1.69
27	4.21	3.35	2.96	2.73	2.57	2.46	2.37	2.30	2.25	1.67
28	4.20	3.34	2.95	2.71	2.56	2.44	2.36	2.29	2.24	1.65
29	4.18	3.33	2.93	2.70	2.54	2.43	2.35	2.28	2.22	1.64
30	4.17	3.32	2.92	2.69	2.53	2.42	2.33	2.27	2.21	1.62
40	4.08	3.23	2.84	2.61	2.45	2.34	2.25	2.18	2.12	1.51
60	4.00	3.15	2.76	2.52	2.37	2.25	2.17	2.10	2.04	1.39
120	3.92	3.07	2.68	2.45	2.29	2.17	2.09	2.02	1.96	1.25
∞	3.84	2.99	2.60	2.37	2.21	2.09	2.01	1.94	1.88	1.00

Degrees of freedom for estimates of variance within samples

Table A4   Distribution of chi square

(df)	Area under the distribution (a)									
	.99	.90	.70	.50	.30	.20	.10	.05	.01	.001
1	.000157	.0158	.148	.455	1.074	1.642	2.706	3.841	6.635	10.827
2	.0201	.211	.713	1.386	2.408	3.219	4.605	5.991	9.210	13.815
3	.115	.584	1.424	2.366	3.665	4.642	6.251	7.815	11.341	16.268
4	.297	1.064	2.195	3.357	4.878	5.989	7.779	9.488	13.277	18.465
5	.554	1.610	3.000	4.351	6.064	7.289	9.236	11.070	15.086	20.517
6	.872	2.204	3.828	5.348	7.231	8.558	10.645	12.595	16.812	22.457
7	1.239	2.833	4.671	6.346	8.383	9.803	12.017	14.067	18.475	24.322
8	1.646	3.490	5.527	7.344	9.524	11.030	13.362	15.507	20.090	26.125
9	2.088	4.168	6.393	8.343	10.656	12.242	14.684	16.919	21.666	27.877
10	2.558	4.865	7.267	9.342	11.781	13.442	15.987	18.307	23.209	29.588
11	3.053	5.578	8.148	10.341	12.899	14.631	17.275	19.675	24.725	31.264
12	3.571	6.304	9.034	11.340	14.011	15.812	18.549	21.026	26.217	32.909
13	4.107	7.042	9.926	12.340	15.119	16.985	19.812	22.362	27.688	34.528
14	4.660	7.790	10.821	13.339	16.222	18.151	21.064	23.685	29.141	36.123
15	5.229	8.547	11.721	14.339	17.322	19.311	22.307	24.996	30.578	37.697
16	5.812	9.312	12.624	15.338	18.418	20.465	23.542	26.296	32.000	39.252
17	6.408	10.085	13.531	16.338	19.511	21.615	23.769	27.587	33.409	40.790
18	7.015	10.865	14.440	17.338	20.601	22.760	25.989	28.869	34.805	42.312
19	7.633	11.651	15.352	18.338	21.689	23.900	27.204	30.144	36.191	43.820
20	8.260	12.443	16.266	19.337	22.775	25.038	28.412	31.410	37.566	45.315
21	8.897	13.240	17.182	20.337	23.858	26.171	29.615	32.671	38.932	46.797
22	9.542	14.041	18.101	21.337	24.939	27.301	30.813	33.924	40.289	48.268
23	10.196	14.848	19.021	22.337	26.018	28.429	32.007	35.172	41.638	49.728
24	10.856	15.659	19.943	23.337	27.096	29.553	33.196	36.415	42.980	51.179
25	11.524	16.473	20.867	24.337	28.172	30.675	34.382	37.652	44.314	52.620
26	12.198	17.292	21.792	25.336	29.246	31.795	35.563	38.885	45.642	54.052
27	12.879	18.114	22.719	26.336	30.319	32.912	36.741	40.113	46.963	55.476
28	13.565	18.939	23.647	27.336	31.391	34.027	37.916	41.337	48.278	56.893
29	14.256	19.768	24.577	28.336	32.461	35.139	39.087	42.557	49.588	58.302
30	14.953	20.599	25.508	29.336	33.530	36.250	40.256	42.773	50.892	59.703

Key equations

The mean for a population

$$\mu = \frac{\Sigma X_i}{N}$$

X_i is any score in a distribution
N is all cases from which a measurement is taken

The mean for a sample

$$\overline{X} = \frac{\Sigma X_i}{N}$$

The mean for a frequency distribution

$$\overline{X} = \frac{\Sigma f X_i}{N}$$

f is the frequency of each value in the distribution

The mean for grouped data

$$\overline{X} = \frac{\Sigma fm}{N}$$

m is the class mid-point

The standard deviation for a population

$$\sigma = \sqrt{\frac{\Sigma(X_i - \mu)^2}{N-1}}$$

The standard devation for a sample

$$s = \sqrt{\frac{\Sigma(X_i - \overline{X})^2}{N-1}}$$

$$s = \sqrt{\frac{\Sigma X_i^2 - \frac{(\Sigma X_i)^2}{N}}{N-1}}$$

The standard deviation for a frequency distribution

$$s = \sqrt{\frac{\Sigma f X_i^2 - \frac{(\Sigma f X_i)^2}{N}}{N-1}}$$

Standard deviation (standard error) of the sampling distribution of means

$$\sigma_{\bar{X}} = \frac{\sigma}{\sqrt{N}}$$

σ is the standard deviation of the population
$\sigma_{\bar{X}}$ is the standard deviation of the sampling distribution (standard error)

z-scores for describing a distribution

$$z = \frac{X_i - \bar{X}}{s}$$

One-sample z-test for a mean

$$z = \frac{\bar{X} - \mu}{\sigma_{\bar{X}}} = \frac{\bar{X} - \mu}{\sigma / \sqrt{N}}$$

One-sample t-test for a mean

$$t = \frac{\bar{X} - \mu}{s / \sqrt{N-1}}$$

One-sample z-test for a proportion

$$z = \frac{(P_s - 0.005) - P_u}{\sqrt{\dfrac{P_u(1 - P_u)}{N}}} \quad \text{where } P_s > P_u$$

or

$$z = \frac{(P_s + 0.005) - P_u}{\sqrt{\dfrac{P_u(1 - P_u)}{N}}} \quad \text{where } P_s < P_u$$

P_s is the sample proportion
P_u is the population proportion

Upper and lower limits of a confidence interval

$$\text{Lower limit} = \bar{X} - z\left(\frac{s}{\sqrt{N-1}}\right)$$

$$\text{Upper limit} = \bar{X} + z\left(\frac{s}{\sqrt{N-1}}\right)$$

Chi-square test for independence

$$\chi^2 = \sum \frac{(f_o - f_e)^2}{f_e}$$

f_o is observed cell frequencies
f_e is expected cell frequencies

$df = (r - 1)(c - 1)$

df is number of degrees of freedom
r is number of rows
c is number of columns

Runs test for a single sample

$$z = \frac{(R + 0.5) - \mu_R}{\sigma_R} \quad \text{where } R < \mu_R$$

or

$$z = \frac{(R - 0.5) - \mu_R}{\sigma_R} \quad \text{where } R > \mu_R$$

R is the number of runs in the sample
μ_R is the number of runs expected from repeated sampling
σ_R is the standard deviation of the sampling distribution

$$\mu_R = \frac{2N_1 N_2}{N} + 1$$

$$\sigma_R = \sqrt{\frac{N^2 - 2N}{4(N - 1)}}$$

Two-sample t-test for the equality of means

$$t = \frac{\overline{X}_1 - \overline{X}_2}{\sigma_{\overline{X} - \overline{X}}}$$

$$\sigma_{\overline{X} - \overline{X}} = \sqrt{\frac{N_1 s_1^2 + N_2 s_2^2}{N_1 + N_2 - 2}} \sqrt{\frac{N_1 + N_2}{N_1 N_2}} \quad \text{pooled variance estimate}$$

Wilcoxon rank sum test for two independent samples

$$\mu_W = \frac{1}{2} N_1 (N + 1)$$

N_1 is the smallest of the two samples
N is the total size of the two samples

$$z = \frac{W - \mu_W}{\sigma_W}$$

$$\sigma_W = \sqrt{\frac{1}{12} N_1 N_2 (N + 1)}$$

Mann–Whitney U-test

$$U = N_1 N_2 + \frac{N_1(N_1 + 1)}{2} - \Sigma R_1$$

N_1 is the size of sample 1
N_2 is the size of sample 2
ΣR_1 is the sum of ranks for sample 1

$$\mu_U = \frac{N_1 N_2}{2}$$

$$\sigma_U = \sqrt{\frac{N_1 N_2 (N_1 + N_2 + 1)}{12}}$$

$$z = \frac{U - \mu_u}{\sigma_u}$$

z-test for the difference between proportions

$$P_u = \frac{N_1 P_1 + N_2 P_2}{N_1 + N_2}$$

$$\sigma_{P_1 - P_2} = \sqrt{P_u (1 - P_u)} \sqrt{\frac{N_1 + N_2}{N_1 N_2}}$$

$$z = \frac{P_1 - P_2}{\sigma_{P_1 - P_2}}$$

t-test for two dependent samples

$$t = \frac{\overline{X}_D}{s_D / \sqrt{N - 1}}$$

$$s_D = \sqrt{\frac{\Sigma D^2 - \dfrac{(\Sigma D)^2}{N}}{N - 1}}$$

McNemar test for two dependent samples

$$\chi^2_M = \frac{(N_a - N_d - 1)^2}{N_a + N_d}$$

N_a is the observed number of cases in cell a
N_d is the observed number of cases in cell d

Wilcoxon signed-ranks test for two dependent samples

$$\mu_T = \frac{N(N+1)}{4}$$

$$z = \frac{T - \mu_T}{\sigma_T}$$

T is the smallest of the two rank sums

$$\sigma_T = \sqrt{\frac{N(N+1)(2N+1)}{24}}$$

Cramer's V

$$V = \sqrt{\frac{\chi^2}{N(k-1)}}$$

k is the number of columns or the number of rows, whichever is smaller

Lambda

$$\lambda = \frac{E_1 - E_2}{E_1}$$

E_1 is the number of errors without information on the independent variable
E_2 is the number of errors with information on the independent variable

Gamma

$$G = \frac{N_s - N_d}{N_s + N_d}$$

N_s is the number of pairs of cases ranked the same on both variables (concordant pairs)
N_d is the number of pairs of cases ranked differently on both variables (discordant pairs)

Spearman's rank order correlation coefficient

$$r_s = 1 - \frac{6\Sigma D^2}{N(N^2 - 1)}$$

Equation for a straight line

$$Y = a \pm bX$$

Y is the dependent variable
X is the independent variable
a is the Y intercept (the value of Y when X is zero)
b the slope of the line (+ indicates positive slope; – indicates negative slope)

Slope of the ordinary least squares regression line

$$b = \frac{\Sigma(X_i - \overline{X})(Y_i - \overline{Y})}{\Sigma(X_i - \overline{X})^2}$$

or

$$b = \frac{N\Sigma(X_i Y_i) - (\Sigma X_i)(\Sigma Y_1)}{N\Sigma X_i^2 - (\Sigma X_i)^2}$$

$$a = \overline{Y} - b\,\overline{X}$$

Pearson's correlation coefficient

$$r = \frac{\Sigma(X_i - \overline{X})(Y_i - \overline{Y})}{\sqrt{\left[(X_i - \overline{X})^2\right]\left[(Y_i - \overline{Y})^2\right]}}$$

or

$$r = \frac{N\Sigma(X_i Y_i) - (\Sigma X_i)(\Sigma Y_i)}{\sqrt{\left[N\Sigma X_i^2 - (\Sigma X_i)^2\right]\left[N\Sigma Y_i^2 - (\Sigma Y_i)^2\right]}}$$

Glossary

Association   A relationship between the distribution of one variable and the distribution of another variable.

Binomial variable   A variable that has only two possible values or categories — also known as a **dichotomous variable**.

Bivariate table   A table displaying the joint frequency distribution for two variables; it is also known as a **crosstabulation** or **contingency table**.

Case   An entity that displays or possesses the traits of a given variable.

Census   An investigation that includes every member of the population.

Central tendency   The typical or average value of a distribution.

Class interval   A range of values on a distribution that is used to group cases together for presentation and analysis.

Conceptual definition   The use of literal terms to specify the qualities of a variable; also called a **nominal** definition.

Concordant pairs   Two cases that are ranked the same on two variables.

Confidence interval   The range of values that, it is estimated, includes the population parameter, at a specific level of confidence.

Confidence level   The probability that a confidence interval will contain the population parameter.

Constant   An attribute that does not vary.

Contingency table   See **Bivariate table**.

Continuous variable   A variable measured by units that can be subdivided infinitely; it can take any value in a line interval.

Critical region   The range of scores that will cause the null hypothesis to be rejected. Also called the *region of rejection*.

Crosstabulation   See *Bivariate table*.

Dependent samples   Samples for which the criterion for inclusion in the sample is affected by the composition of other samples.

Dependent variable   A variable that is explained or affected by another variable.

Descriptive statistics   The numerical and graphical techniques for organizing, presenting, and analysing data.

Dichotomous variable   See **Binomial variable**.

Discordant pairs   Two cases that are ranked differently on two variables.

Discrete variable   A variable measured by a unit that cannot be subdivided; it has a countable number of values.

Dispersion   An indication of the spread or variety of scores in a distribution.

Frequency distribution   A distribution that reports for each value or category of a variable the number of cases that have that value or fall into that category.

Hypothesis   A well-defined statement or claim about the characteristics of a population.

Independence   The statistical independence that exists between two variables such that classifying a case in terms of one variable does not affect how that case is classified in terms of the other variable.

Independent samples   Samples for which the criterion for inclusion in one sample is not population is affected by the composition of other samples.

Independent variable   A variable that is not explained or affected by another variable.

Inferential statistics   The numerical techniques used for making conclusions about a population, based on the information obtained from a random sample drawn from that population.

Interquartile range   The difference between the upper limits of the first quartile and third quartile; it is the range for the middle 50 per cent of rank-ordered cases.

Interval scale   A level of measurement that has units measuring intervals of equal distance between values on the scale.

Mean (arithmetic)   The sum of all the scores in a distribution divided by the total number of cases.

Measurement   The process of determining and recording which of the possible categories or values of a variable an individual case exhibits or possesses.

Measures of association   Quantitative measures indicating the extent that a change in the value of one variable is related to a change in the value of another variable.

Median   The value or category of the case in the middle of a rank-ordered distribution.

Mode   The value or category of a distribution with the highest number of cases.

Nominal scale   A level of measurement that only indicates the category that a case falls into with respect to a variable.

Non-parametric test   A test of an hypothesis about features of a population distribution other than its parameters.

Operational definition   The specification of the operations to be used to measure a variable.

Ordinal scale   A level of measurement that, in addition to the function of classification, allows cases to be ordered by degree with respect to a variable.

Ordinary least squares regression   A rule that states that the line of best fit through a scatter plot is one that minimizes the sum of the squared residuals.

Parameter   A numerical value that describes some feature of a population.

Parametric test   A test of an hypothesis about a population parameter.

Percentages   Statistics that standardize a total to a base value of 100.

Population   The set of all cases of interest.

Random selection   A sampling method where each member of the population has the same chance of being selected in the sample.

Range   The difference between the lowest score and the highest score in a distribution.

Rank   A number assigned to a case that indicates its place in an ordered series.

Ratio scale   A level of measurement by which the value of zero indicates cases where no amount of the variable is present.

Region of rejection   See **Critical region**.

Relative frequencies   Frequencies that express the percentage or proportion of cases that have each value, or fall into each category, of a variable.

Run   A sequence of cases that have the same value for a variable.

Sample   A set of cases that does not include every member of the population.

Sampling distribution   The theoretical probability distribution of an infinite number of samples outcomes for a statistic, using samples of equal size.

Standard deviation   A measure of dispersion that is the square root of the variance; the variance is the average distance of scores in a distribution from the mean.

Statistics   Descriptive measures used to summarize a sample.

Type I error   Rejection of the null hypothesis of no difference, even though in fact there is no difference.

A Type II error   A failure to reject the null hypothesis when in fact it is false.

Variable   An attribute that has two or more divisions, characteristics, or categories.

Answers

Chapter 1

1.1 (a) Not exhaustive: no option for people not eligible to vote.

Not mutually exclusive: someone can be either of the first two options and did not vote at the last election.

(b) Not exhaustive: needs an 'other category' at least for students enrolled in other courses.

(c) Not mutually exclusive: someone can have multiple reasons for joining the military

1.2 • Interval/ratio
- Nominal
- Ordinal
- Interval/ratio
- Nominal
- Nominal
- Ordinal
- Interval/ratio
- Ordinal
- Nominal
- Interval/ratio
- Nominal
- Ordinal
- Interval/ratio
- Ordinal
- Nominal

1.5 • Discrete • Continuous • Continuous • Discrete • Continuous

Chapter 2

2.1 A proportion standardizes totals to a base of 1, whereas a percentage standardizes totals to a base of 100.

2.2 A percentage is calculated using the same formula as a proportion **multiplied by 100**, ensuring that the percentage will be a higher number (by a factor of 100) than the corresponding proportion.

2.3 0.01 (1%) • 0.13 (13%) • 1.24 (124%) • 0.0045 (0.45%)

2.4 12% (0.12) • 13.4% (0.134) • 167% (1.67) • 3.5% (0.035)

2.5 21 years 6 months (lower true limit) and 22 years 6 months (upper true limit); 22 years 3.5 months (lower true limit) and 22 years 4.5 months (upper true limit)

2.6

Minutes	Raw frequency	Percentage	Cumulative frequency	Cumulative percentage	Mid-point
1–10	7	17.5	7	17.5	4.5
11–20	5	12.5	12	30	14.5
21–30	7	17.5	19	47.5	24.5
31–40	12	30	31	77.5	34.5
41–50	5	12.5	36	90	44.5
51–60	4	10	40	100	54.5
Total	40	100			

2.7

Attendance at public libraries, 1990–91 ('000)

State	Attendees	Relative frequency (%)
A	1409	31.7
B	1142	25.7
C	713	16.1
D	423	9.5
E	497	11.2
F	130	2.9
G	90	2
H	38	0.9
Total	4442	100

Attendance at popular music concerts, 1990–91 ('000)

State	Attendees	Relative frequency (%)
A	1166	33.7
B	870	25.2
C	604	17.5
D	280	8.1
E	332	9.6
F	99	2.9
G	32	0.9
H	74	2.1
Total	3457	100

This is a nominal scale (State of residence). The ordering of the categories is arbitrary, and therefore the cumulative frequency will be different for each possible ordering of States.

Chapter 3

3.1 A bar graph is constructed for nominal/ordinal data; a histogram is constructed for interval/ratio data. Practically, the bars in a histogram 'touch' each other, whereas in a bar graph the bars have a gap between them.

3.3 This is interval/ratio data so a histogram is appropriate rather than a bar graph. There are six class intervals, which make a pie graph difficult to 'read.'

3.4 (a)

Price ($)	Raw frequency
7000–8499	2
8500–9999	3
10000–11499	6
11500–129999	3
13000–14499	1

Check that your graphs are appropriately labelled.
3.5 Check that all the appropriate labels have been included with your graph.

Chapter 4

4.1 No; the numbers on an ordinal scale are values that have no quantitative significance. They are merely labels that preserve the ordering of cases.

4.2 The advantage of the range is that it is very easy to calculate and everyone understands it. Its disadvantage is that because it only uses two scores it does not use all the information available in a distribution. For the same reason it is very sensitive to extreme values.

4.3 (a) 5,   9,   13,   15,   26,   72
Mean 23.3   Median 14   Range 67   stand. dev. 24.9
(b) 121,   134,   145   212,   289,   306,   367,   380,   453
Mean 267.4   Median 289   Range 332   stand. dev. 120.6
(c) 1.2,   1.4,   1.9,   2.0,   2.4,   3.5,   3.9,   4.3,   5.2
Mean 2.9   Median 2.4   Range 4   stand. dev. 1.4

4.4 This student had a lower than average IQ in the first class, and a higher than average IQ for the class he joined.

4.5 (a) 9, 11, 20, 22, 36, 36, 39, 43, 45, 50, 56, 57, 59, 60, 66, 68, 68, 73, 75, 80, 87
Median 56
(b) 50.5 (rounded to 1 decimal point)
(c) The median is greater than the mean, therefore the distribution is skewed to the **left.**
(d) Mean 57   Median 56.5
The median is a relatively stable measure of central tendency that is not sensitive to extreme outliers, whereas the mean, by including every value in its calculation, is affected by the addition of one extreme score.

4.6 (a) Mean $33 000   Median $32 500   Mode $22 000
(b) Range $60 000   IQR $30 000   stand. dev. $14 183

4.7 Mean (ungrouped) 29.6 minutes
Median (ungrouped) 31.5 minutes
Mean (grouped) 28.25 minutes
Median (grouped) 31.4 minutes
The differences are due to the fact that class intervals do not provide as much information as a listing of the raw scores. Since we use class mid-points rather than the actual data in calculating the mean, the answer will vary. With median and mode we can only report the class, rather than the specific value.

4.8 Degree of enrolment
(a) Nominal
(b) Mode Arts (can't calculate any other on nominal data)
Time spent studying for an exam
(a) Interval/ratio

    (b) Mean 3.275 hours   Median 2 hours   Mode 4 hours

Satisfaction with employment

    (a) Ordinal

    (b) Mode satisfied   Median satisfied

4.9 (a) Mean 8.7 years   Median 9–12 years   Mode 9–12 years

    (b) Distribution is skewed to the right

    (c) Interquartile range

Chapter 5

5.2

TIME   Time to complete (minutes)

Mean	29.550	Median	31.500
Valid cases	40	Missing cases	0

5.3

    MINUTES   Television Watched per Night

Value Label	Value	Frequency	Percent	Valid Percent	Cum Percent
	60	1	10.0	10.0	10.0
	65	1	10.0	10.0	20.0
	120	1	10.0	10.0	30.0
	140	1	10.0	10.0	40.0
	150	1	10.0	10.0	50.0
	160	1	10.0	10.0	60.0
	170	1	10.0	10.0	70.0
	180	1	10.0	10.0	80.0
	200	1	10.0	10.0	90.0
	280	1	10.0	10.0	100.0
	Total	10	100.0	100.0	

Mean	152.500	Median	155.000	Mode	60.000
Std dev	64.172	Range	220.000		

* Multiple modes exist. The smallest value is shown.

Valid cases   10   Missing cases   0

    CHANNEL   Main Channel Watched

Value Label	Value	Frequency	Percent	Valid Percent	Cum Percent
commercial	1	6	60.0	60.0	60.0
public/gov	2	4	40.0	40.0	100.0
	Total	10	100.0	100.0	

Median	1.000	Mode	1.000	Range	1.000

```
Valid cases        10     Missing cases       0




SATSFCIN
```

SATSFCIN

Value Label	Value	Frequency	Percent	Valid Percent	Cum Percent
Not satisfied	1	4	40.0	40.0	40.0
Satisfied	2	4	40.0	40.0	80.0
Very satisfied	3	2	20.0	20.0	100.0
	Total	10	100.0	100.0	

```
Mode           1.000

* Multiple modes exist.  The smallest value is shown.


Valid cases        10     Missing cases       0
```

6.1 (a) 0.097 **(b)** 0.903 **(c)** 0.3082 **(d)** 0.9665 **(e)** 0.0915
(f) 0.110 **(g)** 0.050
6.2 (a) ±1 **(b)** +2.1 **(c)** –1.645 **(d)** ±1.5
6.3 (a) 0 **(b)** –0.8 **(c)** 2.5 **(d)** –1.7 **(e)** 1.3
6.4 The z-score for the poverty line is -0.83. The proportion for $z = -0.8$ is 0.212, and the proportion for $z = -0.9$ is 0.184, therefore the proportion of all families headed by a single mother also living in poverty is between 0.212 and 0.184 or around 1-in-5.
6.5 $z = -1.6$, area under curve is 0.055, therefore 5.5% of light bulbs last 462 hours or less.
6.6 $z = -1.65$, area under curve is 0.05.
$z = \pm1.96$, for $z = -1.96$ the selling price is \$15 292, for $z = 1.96$ the selling price is \$24 308
6.7 $z = 1.4$, probability is 0.081.
$z = 1.645$, distance is 48.225 m
6.8 For 18 years $z = -1.3$, proportion between mean and 18 is 0.403
For 65 years $z = 2.1$, proportion between mean and 65 is 0.486
Proportion between 18 and 65 years is 0.403 + 0.486 = 0.889
Middle 50%: closest probability in table is 0.516 with $z = \pm0.7$
for $z = -0.7$ the age is 26, for $z = 0.7$ the age is 45 (both figures rounded to nearest whole year).
6.9 At \$1.7 million $z = 1$, which has a one-tail probability of 0.1585.
At \$1.2 million $z = -1.5$, which has a one tail probability of 0.067
6.10 At 15 km/h $z = 0.5$, which has a probability of 0.3085. This means that the wind speed will be over 15 km/h 30% of the time, which meets the proposal requirements.

Chapter 7
7.1 A statistic is a numerical measure of a **sample** while a parameter is a measure of some feature of a **population**.
7.2 Descriptive statistics summarize the data from a sample, inferential statistics attempt to generalize from the sample to the population.

7.3 Random variation is the variation in sample outcomes brought about by random selection from a population. It requires us to use probability theory when generalizing to a population.

7.4 In either case the mean of the sampling distribution is 40.

7.5 The standard error is the standard deviation of a sampling distribution. It is always smaller than the standard deviation of the population since extreme individual scores are included in samples along with more representative scores.

7.6 Differences: Where $N = 30$ the distribution has fatter tails than the distribution for $N = 200$, that is the standard error is smaller in the larger sample. They are similar because they both approximate the normal curve and are centred on the population mean.

7.7 It appears to be random because each letter in the hat has an equal chance of being selected; however, since there may not be the same number of students for every letter, it does not mean every student in the class has an equal chance of being selected. For example, if there were a lot of people with a surname beginning with G in the class the sample would over-represent that particular group.

7.8 The sampling method is random because every book in the library has an equal chance of being borrowed and then returned on Thursday and there is nothing about Thursday that will influence the condition of books returned on that day.

7.10 The theorem is important because it allows the use of a normal sampling distribution to carry out statistical analysis, even where samples are drawn from non-normal populations, and such populations are very common in social research.

7.11 There is far greater variation in the sample means from the $N = 20$ samples. The spread of scores still should be centred on the population mean.

Chapter 8

8.1 Interval estimation is the process of inferring the range of values that contain the (unknown) population parameter, together with the probability (confidence level) that this estimate does not include the parameter.

8.2 A confidence level is the probability that a particular range of values will include the population parameter. As the confidence level increases the width of the confidence interval also increases, and vice versa.

8.3 As sample size increases the width of the confidence interval becomes smaller.

8.4 The standard deviation of the population alters the width of the confidence interval by affecting the standard error of the estimate. As the standard deviation increases so does the standard error, meaning the confidence interval will also widen.

8.5 Age   90% confidence level 36.3 [34.3, 38.3]
99% confidence level 36.3 [33.13, 39.47]
Age of Adelaide pre-school children   90% confidence level 3.75 [3.64, 3.86]
99% confidence level 3.75 [3.57, 3.93]
TV watching   90% confidence level 150 [145.24, 154.76]
99% confidence level 150 [142.49, 157.51]

8.6 Economics 6 [5.26, 6.74]   Sociology 4 [3.33, 4.67]
History 4.5 [3.56, 5.44]   Statistics 3 [2.62, 3.38]

8.7 Increase for all workers across the industry at 95% is $1018 [$907.68, $1128.32], and at the 99% confidence level is $1018 [$871.65, $1164.35].

8.8 4.3 days [3.79, 4.82] at 99%. Compared with the hospital it is about the same, although it can't be said which is higher or lower because the confidence interval for the hospital includes the value of 4 days. To improve the accuracy of the estimate it could include more people in the sample.

8.9 8.5 years [8.28, 8.72]

Chapter 9

9.1 The distribution approaches the normal curve as sample size increases towards infinity, as described by the central limit theorem, regardless of the shape of the population distribution.

9.2 Type I error occurs when the null hypothesis is rejected even though it is true; a type II error occurs when the null hypothesis is accepted when a rejection should have been made. As the probability of one happening decreases the possibility of the other occurring increases.

9.3 As the significance level is increased the critical region becomes smaller, that is, the higher the significance level the larger the difference has to be before the null hypothesis is rejected.

9.5

Probability	Test	z-score
0.230	**Two-tail**	±1.2
0.100	Two-tail	**±1.645**
0.018	**One-tail**	±2.1
0.021	Two-tail	±2.3
0.0003	One-tail	±3.4

9.6 $z > 1.645$ $\propto = 0.05$
$z < -1.645$ $\propto = 0.05$
$z > 1.96$ or $z < -1.96$ $\propto = 0.05$

9.7 **(a)** $z = -1.9$ **(b)** $z = -20.9$

9.8 $H_o: \mu = 24$ $H_a: \mu > 24$ Alpha = 0.05
$z_{critical} = 1.645$, we are using a one-tail (right-tail) test because we are interested in whether this judge has an average greater than the rest.
$z_{sample} = 1.73 \; p = 0.0445$
At an alpha of 0.05 the probability of the judge being the same as other judges is less than the alpha level, leading the null hypothesis to be rejected. Note that an alpha level of 0.01, or on a two-tail test, the sample score will not be significantly different from the hypothesized value.

Chapter 10

10.1 **(a)** That the standard deviation of the population is not known.
    (b) The sample is drawn from a normal population.

10.2

t-score	Probability	Test	df
2.015	**0.05**	one-tail	5
2.764	0.02	two-tail	10
1.708	**0.05**	one-tail	**25**
2.000	0.05	two-tail	65
1.282	0.10	one-tail	228

10.3 $t = -3.08$ (reject) — two-tail $t = -3.08$ (reject) — one tail

    $t = -2.18$ (reject) $t = -6.11$ (reject) $t = 1.29$ (not reject) $t = 3.86$ (reject)

10.4 $t_{sample} = -2.35$. At the 0.05 level, $t_{critical} = \pm 1.98$ so the null hypothesis is rejected, the pay rise has not been achieved. However, at the 0.01 level $t_{critical} = \pm 2.617$, so that the null hypothesis is not rejected. Yes, at 95% the pay rise was not achieved, while at the 99% level the interval includes the desired wage increase.

10.5

One Sample t-tests

Variable	Number of Cases	Mean	SD	SE of Mean
VAR00001	25	62.9600	16.629	3.326

Test Value = 70

Mean Difference	95% CI Lower	Upper	t-value	df	2-Tail Sig
-7.04	-13.904	-.176	-2.12	24	.045

10.6 $t_{sample} = -12.96$, $t_{critical} = \pm 2.704$, the null hypothesis is rejected. Hip fractures affect walking speed.

10.7 At an alpha level of 0.05, the following sample-scores and decisions regarding the null apply:

Canada $t_{sample} = 3.85$ (reject)
Singapore $t_{sample} = -6.87$ (reject)
Australia $t_{sample} = 1.02$ (do not reject)

Chapter 11

11.1 The statement is false. The width of an interval estimate is only affected by the sample size, the confidence level, and the sample proportion. No other factor enters into the equation for the confidence interval. Given these factors the interval estimate will be the same regardless of the size of the population from which the sample is drawn.

11.2

	z_{sample}	Two-tail	One-tail
(a)	1.78	Not reject	Reject
(b)	-0.36	Not reject	Not reject

11.3 $z_{sample} = -0.31$, at alpha = 0.05, one-tailed, $z_{critical} = -1.645$, therefore the null hypothesis is not rejected: the sample proportion is not significantly different from the target of 40%, so that the program was successful.
The confidence interval supports this because 40% is inside the 95% confidence interval of 35.6–42.2%.

11.4 At 95%, the confidence interval is 43.6–61.4%. This includes values of less than 50% so that the sample does not confirm that the candidate is a certain winner.

11.5 At an alpha level of 0.05 the z-score of -3.08 will lead us to reject the null hypothesis so that taping does reduce ankle sprain injury.

11.6 The confidence interval is 51.6–60.4%, at a 95% confidence level, meaning that a majority of the population supports decriminalisation.

11.7 Rounded to whole number (a) 14%–36% (b) 16%–34%

Chapter 12

12.1

	df	$\alpha = 0.10$	$\alpha = 0.05$
3 categories	2	4.605	5.991
5 categories	4	7.779	9.488
8 categories	7	12.017	14.067

12.2

    (a) $\chi^2_{sample} = 5.28$, $df = 4$, $p = 0.35$ (approx.): Do not reject null.

    (b) $\chi^2_{sample} = 1.33$, $df = 6$, $p = 0.965$ (approx.): Do not reject null.

12.3 $\chi^2_{sample} = 40$, $df = 4$, $p < 0.01$: Reject null.

12.4 $\chi^2_{sample} = 6.246$, $\chi^2_{critical} = 11.070$ ($df = 5$): Do not reject null.

12.5

```
- - - - - Chi-Square Test

   SCHOOL

               Cases
   Category  Observed  Expected  Residual

       1        22       26.8      -4.8
       2        25       26.8      -1.80
       3        26       26.8      -0.8
       4        28       26.8       1.20
       5        33       26.8       6.2
                ---
   Total       134

       Chi-Square           D.F.      Significance
        2.4925                4           .6460
```

12.6 Runs test is applicable because the results are in sequence and using a binomial distribution.

```
- - - - - Runs Test

   COINTOSS

      Runs:    10                Test value = 2.0 (Median)

      Cases:    9   LT Median
               11   GE Median           Z =  -.1857
               --
               20   Total           2-Tailed P =   .8526
```

12.7 Number of runs expected if null correct: 9.86

```
- - - - - Runs Test

   BORN

      Runs:    12                Test value = 2 (Median)

      Cases:    6   LT Median
               17   GE Median           Z =   .9154
               --
               23   Total           2-Tailed P =   .3600
```

Chapter 13

13.1 The samples come from normal populations, and when using the pooled variance estimate, the populations have the same variance.

13.2

(a) $t_{sample} = -1.464$
$t_{critical} = \pm 2.0$ $(df = 83)$
Do not reject null

(b) $t_{sample} = -13.38$
$t_{critical} = \pm 1.98$ $(df = 238)$
Reject null

(c) $t_{sample} = -14803$
$t_{critical} = \pm 2.0$ $(df = 83)$
Do not reject null

(d) $t_{sample} = -2.4553$
$t_{critical} = \pm 1.98$ $(df = 186)$
Reject null

13.3

$t_{sample} = -2.1983$
$t_{critical} = \pm 1.98$ $(\alpha = 0.05,$ two-tail, $df = 196)$
Reject null hypothesis

13.4 The Authority is interested in whether there is a reduction in water use, therefore a one-tail test is appropriate: $t_{critical} = +1.645$ $(\alpha = 0.05, df = 198)$
Reject null hypothesis of no difference.
Important considerations are the number of samples to be compared, interval/ratio data, population standard deviations are unknown.

13.5 $t_{sample} = -12.158$
Use one-tail test because we are trying to find an improvement between the pesticides.
$t_{critical} = -1.671$ $(\alpha = 0.05, df = 60$ which is the closest reported df in the table)
Reject null hypothesis, the organic pesticide is different and better.

13.6 (a/b)

```
t-tests for Independent Samples of SCHOOL    School System
```

Variable	Number of Cases	Mean	SD	SE of Mean
SCORE Political Awareness Score				
Public	20	64	18.5	4.124
Private	24	46	18.5	3.762

```
Mean Difference = 18.0750

Levene's Test for Equality of Variances: F= .061   P= .806
```

	t-test for Equality of Means				95%
Variances	t-value	df	2-Tail Sig	SE of Diff	CI for Diff
Equal	3.24	42	.002	5.582	(6.810, 29.340)
Unequal	3.24	40.57	.002	5.582	(6.798, 29.352)

Therefore reject null hypothesis.

(c) The confidence interval confirms this because 0 is not included in it.

(d) The one-tail significance will be 0.001.

(e) The Levene test result may make one use the unequal variance test if $p < 0.05$, but it is not in the interval.

Chapter 14

14.1 We are comparing more than two samples in terms of a variable measured at the interval/ratio level.

The F-ratio is 0.245. At $\alpha = 0.05$, and $dfb = 4$ and $dfw = 106$, $F_{critical} = 2.52$

Therefore the null hypothesis is not rejected: all means are equal.

14.2 (a) Method A   mean = 20.27   standard deviation 2.05

Method B   mean = 22.73   standard deviation 2.87

Method C   mean = 29.82   standard deviation 3.95

Looking at the means and the standard deviations it seems that only method C will differ significantly from each of the others.

(b) F-ratio = 29, which is significant at the 0.05 level.

14.4/14.5

```
- - - - - O N E W A Y - - - - -
```

```
Variable  MINUTES
By Variable  LEVEL
```

Analysis of Variance

Source	D.F.	Sum of Squares	Mean Squares	F Ratio	F Prob.
Between Groups	3	31185.2500	10395.0833	24.5775	.0000
Within Groups	76	32144.3000	422.9513		
Total	79	63329.5500			

14.6 The significant difference is between level 1 and all the other levels of blood alcohol, but no other combinations.

14.7 The degrees of freedom between groups will now be 4, and the degree of freedom within groups will now be 95.

```
- - - - - O N E W A Y - - - - -
```

```
Variable  TVTIME    Minutes of TV Watched per Night
By Variable  COUNTRY    Country of Residence
```

Analysis of Variance

Source	D.F.	Sum of Squares	Mean Squares	F Ratio	F Prob.
Between Groups	4	75536.5000	18884.1250	26.7232	.0000
Within Groups	95	67132.2500	706.6553		
Total	99	142668.7500			

- - - - - O N E W A Y - - - - -

Variable   TVTIME   Minutes of TV Watched per Night
By Variable COUNTRY   Country of Residence

Multiple Range Tests: Scheffe test with significance level .05

The difference between two means is significant if
  MEAN(J)-MEAN(I)   >= 18.7970 * RANGE * SQRT(1/N(I) + 1/N(J))
  with the following value(s) for RANGE: 4.44

  (*) Indicates significant differences which are shown in the lower
triangle

```
                         G G G G G
                         r r r r r
                         p p p p p

                         4 2 3 5 1
      Mean      COUNTRY

    127.3000    Grp 4
    165.8500    Grp 2      *
    186.7500    Grp 3      *
    197.2000    Grp 5      * *
    203.1500    Grp 1      * *
```

Homogeneous Subsets (highest and lowest means are not significantly
different)

Subset 1

Group   Grp 4

Mean   127.3000
- - - - - - - - - -

Subset 2

Group   Grp 2   Grp 3

Mean   165.8500   186.7500
- - - - - - - - - - - - - - - - -

Subset 3

Group   Grp 3   Grp 5   Grp 1

Mean   186.7500   197.2000   203.1500
- -

Chapter 15

15.1 A rank sum test is used when (i) the test variable is measured at the ordinal level, or (ii) the test variable is measured at the interval/ratio level but the samples come from populations that are not normally distributed.

15.2 (a) (Ranks in brackets)

Group 1	Group 2
1 (1)	
	7 (2)
	8 (3)
9 (4)	
11 (5)	
12 (6.5)	12 (6.5)
15 (8.5)	15 (8.5)
16 (10)	
	20 (11)
23 (12)	
	25 (13)
	29 (14)

(b) Group 1: 47

Group 2: 58

(c) The smallest rank sum is that for group 1, $W = 47$

(d) $\mu_W = 52.5$

(e) $z_{sample} = -0.7043$, do not reject null hypothesis at alpha of 0.05 (or 0.01).

15.3

```
- - - - - Mann-Whitney U - Wilcoxon Rank Sum W Test

     MAS
  by GROUP


     Mean Rank    Cases

        13.30       10   GROUP = 1
         7.70       10   GROUP = 2
                    --
                    20   Total
```

		Exact		Corrected for ties	
U	W		2-Tailed P	Z	2-Tailed P
22.0	133.0		.0355	-2.1492	.0316

15.4 The distribution of salaries is likely to be non-normal, therefore a t-test is not appropriate. The mean ranks indicate that traditional league players were slightly higher up the pay scale than rebels (higher scores are given higher ranks in SPSS). The difference is not significant at an alpha level of 0.05, which means that the difference between the samples may be due to random variation when sampling from populations with no difference.

Chapter 16

16.1 (a) 3   **(b)** 3   **(c)** 15

16.2 (a)

$\chi^2_{critical} = 7.815 \ (\alpha = 0.05)$

$\chi^2_{critical} = 6.251 \ (\alpha = 0.10)$

(b)

$\chi^2_{critical} = 7.815 \ (\alpha = 0.05)$

$\chi^2_{critical} = 6.251 \ (\alpha = 0.10)$

(c)

$\chi^2_{critical} = 24.996 \ (\alpha = 0.05)$

$\chi^2_{critical} = 22.307 \ (\alpha = 0.10)$

16.3 (a) $\chi^2_{sample} = 2.4$ **(b)** $\chi^2_{sample} = 48$

16.4

	a	b	c	d	Total
a	1.59	0	6.87	46.54	55
b	1.41	0	6.13	41.46	49

The shaded cells violate the rules that expected frequencies should not be less than 5, and should not be equal to 0.

16.5 (a) It is most likely that since a father's voting preference is formed before his own child's, this is the independent variable and the child's voting preference is the dependent variable.

(b)

Own voting preference	Father's voting preference			
	Progressive	Conservative	Other	Total
Progressive	22	4	4	30
Conservative	5	19	6	30
Total	27	23	10	60

Adding column percentage will help to determine by eye whether there is any dependence. The pattern of dependence suggests that children tend to vote in a similar way to their respective fathers.

(c) $\chi^2_{sample} = 20.9$, which is significant at the 0.05 level with 2 degrees of freedom.

16.6 $\chi^2_{sample} = 0.76$ (your answer may differ slightly due to rounding) therefore we cannot reject the null hypothesis of independence, since this is lower than the critical value with 6 degrees of freedom. There appears to be no relationship between country of residence and amount of TV watched.

16.7 (a) The variables are smoking habit and health level. Health level is ordinal. Smoking habit may be considered ordinal since it indicates degree of smoking.

(c/f)

HEALTH   Health Level   by   SMOKE   Smoking Habit

```
                        SMOKE            Page 1 of 1
                Count   |
                Exp Val |Doesn't  Does Smo
                Col Pct |Smoke    ke         Row
                        |    0 |     1 |  Total
HEALTH          --------+--------+--------+
            1   |   13 |    34 |    47
Poor            | 28.1 |  18.9 | 29.0%
                | 13.4%|  52.3%|
                +--------+--------+
            2   |   22 |    19 |    41
Fair            | 24.5 |  16.5 | 25.3%
                | 22.7%|  29.2%|
                +--------+--------+
            3   |   35 |     9 |    44
Good            | 26.3 |  17.7 | 27.2%
                | 36.1%|  13.8%|
                +--------+--------+
            4   |   27 |     3 |    30
Very Good       | 18.0 |  12.0 | 18.5%
                | 27.8%|   4.6%|
                +--------+--------+
            Column     97      65       162
            Total    59.9%   40.1%   100.0%
```

Chi-Square	Value	DF	Significance
Pearson	39.38175	3	.00000
Likelihood Ratio	42.07664	3	.00000
Mantel-Haenszel test for linear association	37.98065	1	.00000

Minimum Expected Frequency -   12.037

16.8

		Job type		
		'Blue collar'	'White collar'	Total
Can sing anthem?	Yes	29	22	51
	No	21	28	49
	Total	50	50	100

$\chi^2_{sample} = 1.96$. With 1 degree of freedom, with $\alpha = 0.05$, the critical score for chi-square is 3.841, therefore do not reject the null hypothesis.

Chapter 17

17.1 $\bar{X}_D = -1.3$

$s_D = 1.212$

$t_{sample} = -1.07$

$t_{critical} = \pm 1.833$ (two-tail test); therefore do not reject null

17.2 (a) $t_{sample} = 7.16$

$t_{critical} = \pm 2.093$

Reject null hypothesis

(b) $t_{sample} = -1.012$

$t_{critical} = -1.684$

Do not reject null hypothesis

17.3 $H_0: \bar{X}_D = 0$

$H_a: \bar{X}_D > 0$

$t_{sample} = 2.5$

$t_{critical} = 1.833$ ($\alpha = 0.05$, one-tail)

Reject the null, the changes in workplace have improved productivity.

17.4

```
t-tests for Paired Samples
```

Variable	Number of pairs	Corr	2-tail Sig	Mean	SD	SE of Mean
ASKING				185580.0000	63617.447	20117.603
	10	.999	.000			
SELLING				183720.0000	60888.601	19254.666

Paired Differences			t-value	df	2-tail Sig
Mean	SD	SE of Mean			
1860.000	4197.671	1327.420	1.40	9	.195
95% CI (-1142.83, 4862.833)					

The two-tail significance is greater than $\alpha = 0.05$, therefore accept the null hypothesis: people do seem, on average, to get the price they offer.

17.5 (a) Variable: Pretest

Variable label: weight in kg pre-test

Variable: post-test

Variable label: weight in kg post-test

(b) 21

(c) 70.0952 kg

(d) 66.4286 kg

(e) –3.6667 kg (note that SPSS is subtracting pre-test scores from post-test scores)

(f) $t_{sample} = -5.97$, $df = 20$

(g) less than 0.0005 (note that SPSS rounds off to three decimal places, so that the probability is not equal to zero)

(h) upper limit = -2.441 kg

(i) lower limit = -4.892 kg

Using the t-test, the sample value is lower than any critical value, therefore reject null — the program is effective in reducing weight. She could also refer to the confidence interval, which does not include the value of 0.

17.6 The 95% confidence interval does not include the value of –5. The range of estimated values for weight loss is below the target value, therefore the program is not successful.

Chapter 18
18.1 For all tables $\chi^2_{critical} = 3.841$
    (a) $\chi^2_M = 2.16$; do not reject null.
    (b) $\chi^2_M = 0.343$; do not reject null.
    (c) $\chi^2_M = 14.723$; reject null.
18.2

```
- - - - - McNemar Test

      BROTHER    brother plays sport
   with SISTER   sister plays sport


                      SISTER
                     2       1          Cases           60
                 +--------+--------+
             1 |   16  |   18  |      Chi-Square      .5926
   BROTHER       +--------+--------+
             2 |   15  |   11  |      Significance    .4414
                 +--------+--------+
```

18.3 $z_{sample} = 0.84$, which has a two-tail probability of 0.4; therefore do not reject the null.
18.4

```
- - - - - Wilcoxon Matched-Pairs Signed-Ranks Test

      PROG1
   with PROG2


   Mean Rank    Cases

      1.50        1   - Ranks  (PROG2 LT PROG1)
      4.93        7   + Ranks  (PROG2 GT PROG1)
                  1     Ties   (PROG2 EQ PROG1)
                  -
                  9    Total

      Z =   -2.3105        2-Tailed P =  .0209
```

Chapter 19
19.1 A symmetric measure of association will produce the same numerical value regardless of the variable that is specified as dependent and as independent. Asymmetric measures will produce different numerical values. If two variables are thought to be mutually dependent, then symmetric measures of association are appropriate.
19.2 Since the nominal level of measurement only classifies cases into categories without giving a sense of increase or decrease , it is not possible to talk about positive or negative association.
19.3 Negative.
19.4 (a) When non-random samples are taken — the measure of association will indicate any relationship that exists between two variables for the cases from which measurements are taken, but we cannot then generalize from this to the population.
    (b) When we have data for the whole population — it is appropriate to calculate descriptive measures, but there is no need to generalize since we already have information for the population.

Chapter 20

20.1 The study indicates that the strength of the association has increased in recent times. In a *relative* sense we might say that the association is strong, but this is only in relation to the past studies, rather than in some absolute sense.

20.2 Set 1: $V = 0.42$ Set 2: $V = 0.33$ Set 3: $V = 0.09$

20.3 It is important to specify the dependent and independent variables since lambda is an asymmetric measure of association, whose value is therefore affected by this choice. If the pattern of dependence is not thought to be that of one-way dependence, the symmetric version of lambda should be used.

20.4 **(a)** Lambda = 0.11 (very weak association).

(b) Lambda = 0.42 (moderate association).

(c) Lambda = 0 (This does not necessarily indicate no association. Looking at the table it is clear that there is some variation between columns, but the modal response for all values of the independent variable are 1, causing lambda to equal 0).

20.5 Lambda = 0.54. Looking at the table the moderate association is due to the higher proportion of gun owners in favor of capital punishment.

20.6

		Job Classification		
		'Blue collar'	*'White collar'*	*Total*
Can sing anthem?	Yes	29	22	51
	No	21	28	49
	Total	50	50	100

Lambda = 0.12

Chapter 21

21.1 (a)

	1	*2*	*3*
1	60	24	12
2	32	14	8

$14(60) = 840$

(b)

	1	*2*	*3*
1	60	24	12
2	32	14	8

No cells above and to the left, therefore no concordant pairs.

(c)

	1	*2*	*3*	*4*
1	12	17	25	42
2	10	14	19	24
3	6	11	16	20

$19(12 + 17) = 551$

(d)

	1	2	3	4
1	12	17	25	42
2	10	14	19	24
3	6	11	16	20
4	3	9	14	22

$16(12 + 17 + 10 + 14) = 848$

21.2 (a)

	1	2	3
1	60	24	12
2	32	14	8

$14(12) = 168$

(b)

	1	2	3
1	60	24	12
2	32	14	8

$32(24 + 12) = 1152$

(c)

	1	2	3
1	60	24	12
2	32	14	8

No cells above and to the right, therefore no discordant pairs.

(d)

	1	2	3	4
1	12	17	25	42
2	10	14	19	24
3	6	11	16	20

$11(25 + 42 + 19 + 24) = 1210$

21.3 • Concordant pairs: $26(20 + 58 + 15 + 62) + 23(20 + 58) + 62(20 + 15) + 62(20) = 9234$
  • Discordant pairs: $12(58 + 22 + 62 + 23) + 15(58 + 22) + 62(22 + 23) + 62(22) = 7334$
  • Gamma: -0.11, therefore a very weak negative relationship between these variables.

21.4 Although there is a moderate positive association between the cases in the sample, the test of significance indicates that this could be due to random variation when sampling from a population with no association between these variables.

21.5 The inspection of the table by eye reveals a negative association, since health level seems to decrease as smoking level increases. This will appear as a negative sign in front of any measure of association calculated on this data. The value for gamma is -0.69, indicating a moderate to strong negative association. Without also conducting a significance test, such as chi-square, we cannot directly generalize from this sample result to the population.

21.6 There is a strong positive association between these variable.

```
-- S P E A R M A N C O R R E L A T I O N   C O E F F I C I E N T S  --


SPEDING          .8455
              N(   11)
              Sig .001

              MORTALITY

(Coefficient / (Cases) / 2-tailed Significance)

" . " is printed if a coefficient cannot be computed
```

The two-tail significance of 0.01 indicates that we can reject the null hypothesis that the sample result is due to random variation when sampling from countries with a zero correlation.

21.7

```
-- S P E A R M A N C O R R E L A T I O N   C O E F F I C I E N T S  --


TASTERNK         .5058
              N(   15)
              Sig .054

              PRICE

(Coefficient / (Cases) / 2-tailed Significance)

" . " is printed if a coefficient cannot be computed
```

21.8 $r_s = 0.07$, therefore there is very weak association between age and running ability.

Chapter 22

22.1 The purpose of drawing a scatter plot is to make a judgment whether the conditions for using a linear regression hold. In particular, we can assess visually whether there is a linear relationship, rather than a curvilinear relationship.

22.2 The Y-intercept indicates the expected value for the dependent variable when the independent variable is zero. It is equal to a in the regression equation.

22.3 The principle, often called the 'ordinary least squares' regression line, is to draw a line that minimizes the sum of the squared residuals between each point in a scatter plot and the regression line.

22.4 The correlation coefficient is a standardized measure of correlation that ranges from -1 to 1, regardless of the units in which the variables are measured. The coefficient of the regression line indicates the amount of change in the dependent variable expected from a one unit change in the independent variable. It is therefore sensitive to the units of measurements.

22.5 We expect a negative sign in front of b, since as the values of X increase the values of Y decrease.

$Y = 34.6 - 0.75(X)$

$Y = 34.6 - 0.75(12) = 25.6$

```
* * * *   M U L T I P L E   R E G R E S S I O N   * * * *
```

Listwise Deletion of Missing Data

Equation Number 1   Dependent Variable..   Y

Block Number 1. Method: Enter   X

Variable(s) Entered on Step Number
     1..   X


```
Multiple R           .84925
R Square             .72123
Adjusted R Square    .68638
Standard Error      3.48483
```

Analysis of Variance

	DF	Sum of Squares	Mean Square
Regression	1	251.34795	251.34795
Residual	8	97.15205	12.14401

F =   20.69728   Signif F = .0019


```
----------------- Variables in the Equation -----------------
```

Variable	B	SE B	Beta	T	Sig T
X	-.746948	.164185	-.849251	-4.549	.0019
(Constant)	34.583796	2.475331		13.971	.0000

End Block Number   1   All requested variables entered.

22.6 $Y = 40$ years, when $X = 0$
$Y = 40 + 0.7(30) = 61$ years; note that we use 30 in the equation not 30 000, since the units of measurement are \$'000.
We cannot use the regression coefficient of +0.7 to assess the strength of the correlation. To do this we need to calculate the correlation coefficient.

22.7 The correlation coefficient indicates a moderate positive correlation between these two variables. The t-test is significant at the 0.05 level with 138 degrees of freedom, which indicates that this correlation can be generalized to the population.

22.8 $Y = 33.366\ 402 + 0.510\ 917(X)$
There is positive relationship that is, from the value for r, very strong.
$50 = 33/366402 + 0.510917(X)$, $X = 32.6$ hours. The high value of r^2 indicates that he can be very confident in his prediction. It is wrong to use the regression line in this way because it is not a deterministic relationship: there is an element of error. The student may not actually work when in the library, thinking that just spending the time will be sufficient.

Index